PROTECTING CIVILIANS DURING
VIOLENT CONFLICT

Military and Defence Ethics

Series Editors

Don Carrick – Project Director of the Military Ethics Education Network based in the Institute of Applied Ethics at the University of Hull, UK.

James Connelly – Professor of Politics and International Studies, Director of the Institute of Applied Ethics, and Project Leader of the Military Ethics Education Network at the University of Hull, UK.

Paul Robinson – Professor in Public and International Affairs at the University of Ottawa, Canada.

George Lucas – Professor of Philosophy and Director of Navy and National Programs in the Stockdale Center for Ethical Leadership at the U.S. Naval Academy, Annapolis MD, USA.

There is an urgent and growing need for all those involved in matters of national defence – from policy makers to armaments manufacturers to members of the armed forces – to behave, and to be seen to behave, ethically. The ethical dimensions of making decisions and taking action in the defence arena are the subject of intense and ongoing media interest and public scrutiny. It is vital that all those involved be given the benefit of the finest possible advice and support. Such advice is best sought from those who have great practical experience or theoretical wisdom (or both) in their particular field and publication of their work in this series will ensure that it is readily accessible to all who need it.

Also in the series

Empowering Our Military Conscience
Roger Wertheimer
ISBN: 978-0-7546-7894-6

Kantian Thinking about Military Ethics
J. Carl Ficarrotta
ISBN: 978-0-7546-7992-9

New Wars and New Soldiers
Edited by Paolo Tripodi and Jessica Wolfendale
ISBN: 978-1-4094-0105-6

Protecting Civilians During Violent Conflict

Theoretical and Practical Issues for the 21st Century

Edited by

DAVID W. LOVELL
*University of New South Wales at The Australian
Defence Force Academy, Australia*

IGOR PRIMORATZ
Charles Sturt University, Australia

ASHGATE

Published by
Ashgate Publishing Limited
Wey Court East
Union Road
Farnham
Surrey, GU9 7PT
England

Ashgate Publishing Company
Suite 420
101 Cherry Street
Burlington
VT 05401-4405
USA

www.ashgate.com

British Library Cataloguing in Publication Data
Protecting civilians during violent conflict : theoretical and practical issues
 for the 21st century. — (Military and defence ethics)
 1. War—Protection of civilians. 2. War—Moral and ethical aspects. 3. Combatants and
 noncombatants (International law) 4. Humanitarian law. 5. War victims—
 Legal status, laws, etc.
 I. Series II. Lovell, David W., 1956– III. Primoratz, Igor.
 172.4'2–dc23

Library of Congress Cataloging-in-Publication Data
Protecting civilians during violent conflict : theoretical and practical issues
for the 21st century / edited by David W. Lovell and Igor Primoratz.
 p. cm. — (Military and defence ethics)
 Includes index.
 ISBN 978-1-4094-3125-1 (hardback : alk. paper) — ISBN 978-1-4094-3126-8 (ebook)
 1. War—Protection of civilians. 2. War—Moral and ethical aspects. 3. War victims—
Legal status, laws, etc. I. Lovell, David W., 1956– II. Primoratz, Igor.
 KZ6515.P758 2012
 172'.42—dc23

2011046423

ISBN 9781409431251 (hbk)
ISBN 9781409431268 (ebk)

MIX
Paper from
responsible sources
FSC
www.fsc.org   FSC® C018575

Printed and bound in Great Britain by the
MPG Books Group, UK.

Contents

List of Tables

Acknowledgements

The idea for this volume originated in discussions between the editors late in 2009. We invited a number of scholars and practitioners to submit papers on the central theme which have been robustly discussed on a number of occasions among the contributors, with revised versions now appearing as the chapters herein. The opportunities for these discussions were provided by the School of Humanities and Social Sciences at the University of New South Wales at the Australian Defence Force Academy, the Centre for Applied Philosophy and Public Ethics, and the Centre of Military Law and Justice of the College of Law at The Australian National University; we thank them for their support. The organizational details of this volume were handled professionally by the College Outreach and Support Team of the ANU College of Law. And lastly, we thank the production team at Ashgate Publishing, particularly Margaret Younger and Kirstin Howgate, who have been characteristically efficient and helpful.

David W. Lovell
Igor Primoratz

List of Contributors

Andrew Alexandra

University of Melbourne

After graduate study at Oxford University, Andrew Alexandra taught at Swinburne, Deakin, Melbourne, Queensland and Charles Sturt universities. Since 2000, he has worked in the Centre for Applied Philosophy and Public Ethics at the University of Melbourne. Andrew has research interests in the areas of the ethics of war and peace, professional and applied ethics, political philosophy, the history of philosophy and issues in intellectual property. He has undertaken collaborative research and consultancies for a range of organizations, including Victoria Police, the Professional Standards Council, the Australian Association of Social Workers, the Australian Anthropological Society, the International Baccalaureate Organization (UK) and the Safety Institute of Australia. Two of his most recent books are: co-authored with Seumas Miller, *Integrity Systems for Occupational Groups* (Aldershot: Ashgate, 2010); and co-authored with Seumas Miller, *Ethics in Practice: Moral Theory and the Professions* (Sydney: University of New South Wales Press, 2009).

Susan Breau

Flinders University of South Australia, Adelaide

Susan Breau joined the law school in 2010 as Professor of International Law. Her immediate past appointment was as Reader in International Law and Assistant Associate Dean for Research at the School of Law, University of Surrey. Prior to that post, she was the Dorset Fellow in International Law at the British Institute of International and Comparative Law. Her first academic post was as a lecturer in International Law at Queen's University, Belfast. Prior to attending the London School of Economics in 1999, where she obtained her Masters in Law and PhD, Susan was a Barrister and Solicitor in Kingston, Canada, where she practised family, criminal and child law for 18 years. Her most recent book is (with Kerim Yildiz) *The Kurdish Conflict: Political Context, the Law of Armed Conflict, and Post-Conflict Mechanisms* (London: Routledge, 2010).

Dean Cocking

Centre for Ethics, Community Engagement and Communication, Victoria Police Academy

Dean Cocking has taught and written extensively in theoretical and applied ethics. He is the author (with Justin Oakley) of *Virtue Ethics and Professional Roles* (Cambridge: Cambridge University Press, 2001), (with Jeroen van den Hoven) *Evil Online* (Oxford: Blackwells, forthcoming [2011]); and *Ethics and the Workplace*

(Cambridge: Cambridge University Press, forthcoming [2012]). He was the lead author of the industry report *Professionalisation, Ethics and Integrity Systems: The Promotion of Professional Ethical Standards and the Protection of Clients and Consumers* (2007), undertaken for the Professional Standards Council (NSW) as part of an Australian Research Council Linkage Grant. He has published in journals such as *Ethics* and *The Journal of Philosophy*. Before commencing with Victoria Police, Dean taught subjects related to military ethics at the University of New South Wales at the Australian Defence Force Academy and many subjects in professional and applied ethics at Charles Sturt University. Before that he taught a range of philosophy subjects at Melbourne, LaTrobe and Monash universities. His area of research and teaching expertise spans most areas within theoretical, applied and professional ethics.

Stephen Coleman

University of New South Wales at the Australian Defence Force Academy, Canberra

Stephen Coleman is Senior Lecturer in Ethics and Leadership and Vincent Fairfax Foundation Fellow in the School of Humanities and Social Sciences. He teaches courses in military ethics at both undergraduate and postgraduate levels. He has written one book (*The Ethics of Artificial Uteruses: Implications for Reproduction and Abortion*, Aldershot: Ashgate, 2004) and more than 20 papers in academic journals and edited collections on a diverse range of topics in applied ethics, including military ethics, police ethics, medical ethics and the practical applications of human rights. In addition to these published papers, he has presented at conferences in Australia, New Zealand, Hong Kong, the United Kingdom and the United States. For the 2009–10 academic year, while on study leave from his permanent position in Australia, he served as Resident Fellow in Ethics at the Vice Admiral James B. Stockdale Center for Ethical Leadership at the US Naval Academy. His latest book, *Introduction to Military Ethics: An Issues-Based Approach*, is nearing publication.

Helen Durham

Australian Red Cross

Helen Durham is the Strategic Adviser, International Law, for the Australian Red Cross and a Senior Fellow at Melbourne Law School. Helen has worked for many years with the International Red Cross and Red Crescent Movement and has been Head of Office for the International Committee of the Red Cross (ICRC) in Australia and regional legal adviser (a position involving working with regional governments to implement their obligations in the area of international humanitarian law). Helen has a doctorate in international criminal and humanitarian law and is admitted as a Barrister and Solicitor of the Supreme Court of Victoria and the High Court of Australia. Helen has been involved in international legal negotiations in New York, Rome and Geneva and has also undertaken short operational missions with the ICRC in Burma, Aceh and the

Philippines. She teaches in the Masters of Law Program at Melbourne Law School and is widely published in the area of the laws of war.

David W. Lovell
University of New South Wales at the Australian Defence Force Academy, Canberra
David W. Lovell is a Professor of Politics and Head of the School of Humanities and Social Sciences. During 2004, he was Acting Rector of the University of New South Wales at the Australian Defence Force Academy, and in 2008 he was Deputy Rector (Special Projects). He is the co-editor of *The European Legacy* and is a member of the Australian Committee of the Council for Security Cooperation in the Asia-Pacific. He has written or edited more than a dozen books on topics including Australian politics, communist and post-communist systems and the history of ideas. David has taught military cadets in a tertiary education environment since 1983, first at the Royal Military College, Duntroon, and now at the Australian Defence Force Academy. He has presided over the introduction of tertiary courses in professional ethics in recent years and cooperated with the Vincent Fairfax Ethics in Leadership Foundation to deploy more teaching resources into this area.

Rob McLaughlin
The Australian National University, Canberra
Rob McLaughlin is an Associate Professor in the College of Law at The Australian National University. He is a Captain in the Royal Australian Navy, and his immediate past posting was as the Director of Operations and International Law in Defence Legal Division and the Director of the Naval Legal Service. His operational service has included Iraq and East Timor and maritime law enforcement off the coast of northern Australia. Previous postings have included appointments as Strategic Legal Adviser, Fleet Legal Officer, Staff Officer Legal in the Deployable Joint Force HQ – Maritime and XO HMAS Wollongong; PhD (Cantab), MPhil (Cantab), LLM (ANU), MA (Brown), LLB (Hons) (UQ), BA (Hons) (UQ).

William Maley
The Australian National University, Canberra
William Maley is the Foundation Director of the Asia-Pacific College of Diplomacy (since 2003). He taught for many years in the School of Politics, University College, University of New South Wales, Australian Defence Force Academy, and has served as a Visiting Professor at the Russian Diplomatic Academy, a Visiting Fellow at the Centre for the Study of Public Policy at the University of Strathclyde and a Visiting Research Fellow in the Refugee Studies Programme at Oxford University. He is also a Barrister of the High Court of Australia, a member of the Executive Committee of the Refugee Council of Australia and a member of the Australian Committee of the Council for Security Cooperation in the Asia-Pacific (CSCAP). In 2002, he was appointed a Member

of the Order of Australia (AM). His recent publications include: 'Australia's Strategic Interests in the Middle East: Lessons from Iraq', in *Australia and the Arab World* (Abu Dhabi: Emirates Center for Strategic Studies and Research, 2009); 'Governance in Australian Discourse', in W.T. Tow and Chin Kin Wah (eds), *ASEAN–India–Australia: Towards Closer Engagement in a New Asia* (Singapore: Institute of Southeast Asian Studies, 2009); and *The Afghanistan Wars*, 2nd edn (Basingstoke: Palgrave Macmillan, 2009).

Eve Massingham
Australian Red Cross
Eve Massingham is an International Humanitarian Law Officer with the Australian Red Cross. Eve has a Master of Laws in Public International Law, a Master of International Development and is admitted as a Solicitor of the Supreme Court of Queensland and the High Court of Australia. Her experience includes working in private legal practice and as an associate to a Federal Court Judge. Eve also spent some time as an army reserve officer and as an intern with the Office of the Prosecutor of the International Criminal Court. Eve's Master of Laws dissertation was published in the *International Review of the Red Cross*.

Penelope Mathew
The Australian National University, Canberra
Penelope Mathew is the Freilich Foundation Professor at The Australian National University. Her main area of expertise is refugee law and she has worked with and for refugees in many capacities. She has published widely in the areas of refugee law, human rights and international law and she is past editor-in-chief of the Australian Yearbook of International Law. She has taught at the law schools of the University of Melbourne, The Australian National University and the University of Michigan.

Hitoshi Nasu
The Australian National University, Canberra
Hitoshi Nasu joined the ANU College of Law in December 2006. Prior to his appointment to The Australian National University, he was a part-time lecturer at the University of Sydney, teaching international law. He completed a PhD in 2006 by submitting a doctoral thesis on *Precautionary Approach to International Security Law: A Study of Article 40 of the UN Charter*. His research interests are in public international law, migration law, international peace and security law, international humanitarian law and UN law. Among his recent publications are 'The Role of the "Responsibility to Protect" in the Law on the Prevention of Armed Conflict', in Takashi Tsugeyama (ed.), *The Essence of Collective Security* (Tokyo: Toshindo, 2010) (written in Japanese) and 'Operationalizing the "Responsibility to Protect" and Conflict Prevention: Dilemmas of Civilian Protection in Armed Conflict', *Journal of Conflict & Security Law*, 14 (2009): 209–41.

Stephen Nathanson
Northeastern University, Boston
Stephen Nathanson teaches courses in ethics and political philosophy. His main research areas are ethics, political philosophy and epistemology; topics of current interest include issues in the ethics of war, economic justice and patriotism. He is the author of *The Ideal of Rationality* (Atlantic Highlands, NJ: Humanities Press International, 1985, 1994); *An Eye for an Eye? The Immorality of Punishing by Death* (Lanham, MD: Rowman & Littlefield, 1987, 2001); *Should We Consent to be Governed?* (Belmont, Calif.: Wadsworth, 1992, 2000); *Patriotism, Morality, and Peace* (Lanham, MD: Rowman & Littlefield, 1993); *Economic Justice* (Upper Saddle River, NJ: Prentice-Hall, 1998); and *Terrorism and the Ethics of War* (Cambridge: Cambridge University Press, 2010).

Igor Primoratz
Charles Sturt University, Canberra
Igor Primoratz is Professorial Fellow at the Centre for Applied Philosophy and Public Ethics (CAPPE) and Emeritus Professor of Philosophy at the Hebrew University of Jerusalem. His main areas of research are ethics, theoretical and applied, political philosophy, philosophy of law and philosophy of human sexuality. Topics of current research interest are the ethics of violence, war and terrorism, and moral issues to do with patriotism and nationalism. His recent publications include edited collections *Terror From the Sky: The Bombing of German Cities in World War II* (Oxford: Berghahn Books, 2010); *Civilian Immunity in War* (Oxford: Oxford University Press, 2007, 2010); and (with C.A.J. Coady) *Military Ethics* (Aldershot: Ashgate, 2008); and papers on the bombing of German cities in World War II (*Deutsche Zeitschrift für Philosophie*, 2008), contemporary terrorism (*Cardozo Law Review*, 2007), patriotism and the value of citizenship (*Acta Analytica*, 2009) and patriotism and morality (*Journal of Moral Philosophy*, 2008). He is currently at work on a book titled *Terrorism: A Philosophical Investigation* (under contract with Polity Press).

Richard D. Rosen
Texas Tech University, Lubbock
Richard D. Rosen is Vice Dean and Professor of Law at Texas Tech University School of Law, Director of the Texas Tech Center for Military Law and Policy and Colonel (retired), US Army. Military assignments include Commandant, Judge Advocate General's School, US Army, Charlottesville, Virginia; Staff Judge Advocate, III Armored Corps at Fort Hood, Texas; Special Counsel to the Assistant Attorney-General for the Civil Division, Department of Justice, Washington, DC; Deputy Legal Counsel to the Chairman of the Joint Chiefs of Staff, The Pentagon, Washington, DC; and Staff Judge Advocate of the 1st Cavalry Division, Fort Hood, Texas. Richard's recent publications include 'Targeting Enemy Forces in a War on Terror: Preserving Civilian Immunity', *Vanderbilt Journal of Transnational Law*, 42 (2009): 683. Richard's educational background includes: BA, The Ohio

State University (1970); Juris Doctor, University of Miami School of Law (1973); Masters of Law, University of Virginia School of Law (1987). Military Education: US Army Judge Advocate Officers' Basic Course (1977); US Army Judge Advocate Officers' Graduate Course, The Judge Advocate General's School, US Army (1977); US Army Command and General Staff College (1989); US Army War College Fellowship (1997).

Michael N. Schmitt
Durham University
Michael N. Schmitt is Chair of Public International Law at Durham University. He was previously Dean of the Marshall Center for Security Studies in Germany. He is a Senior Fellow at the TMC Asser Institute in the Hague, served as the 2007–08 Stockton Visiting Professor of International Law at the US Naval War College and was the 2006 Sir Ninian Stephen Visiting Scholar at Melbourne University. Professor Schmitt served 20 years in the US Air Force, specializing in operational and international law. He is presently the General Editor of the *Yearbook of International Humanitarian Law* and serves on the editorial boards of the *International Review of the Red Cross*, *International Peacekeeping*, *Journal of Military Ethics*, *Connections*, *Journal of International Humanitarian Legal Studies* and the *International Humanitarian Law Series* (Martinus Nijhoff). Professor Schmitt's works on law and military affairs have been published in Australia, Belgium, Chile, Germany, Israel, Italy, Norway, Peru, Sweden, Switzerland, the Netherlands, the United Kingdom and the United States.

David Whetham
King's College London
David Whetham is a Senior Lecturer in the Defence Studies Department of King's College London, based at the Joint Services Command and Staff College at the UK Defence Academy. David initially took a degree in philosophy at the London School of Economics and went on to take a Masters Degree and PhD in War Studies at King's College London. Before joining King's as a permanent member of staff in 2003, David worked as a BBC researcher and with the OSCE in Kosovo, supporting the 2001 and 2002 elections. David's main research interests are focused on the ethical dimensions of warfare and the development of the laws of war. In 2009, David was a Visiting Fellow with the Centre for Defence Leadership and Ethics at the Australian Defence College in Canberra. David's most recent publication is *Just Wars and Moral Victories: Surprise, Deception and the Normative Framework of European War in the Later Middle Ages* (Leiden: Brill, 2009). Other publications include: (as editor), *Ethics, Law and Military Operations* (Basingstoke: Palgrave, 2010) and 'Ethics and the Enduring Relevance of Just War Theory in the 21st Century', in John Buckley and George Kassimeris (eds), *The Ashgate Research Companion to Modern Warfare* (Aldershot: Ashgate, 2010).

Chapter 1

Protecting Civilians During Violent Conflict: An Issue in Context

David W. Lovell

War is a very special human activity. It is both absolutely terrible and relatively commonplace. We devote enormous resources to its preparation, prosecution and commemoration, while we pray that it will never happen again. In modern times, it has helped to define national stories in rarefied terms of sacrifice and courage, while the reality of battlefield slaughter is brought into our living rooms by the nightly television news. Because humans recognize its special nature, they have since at least the time of Augustine in the fourth century CE constructed the conditions for just warfare, especially so as to distinguish the killing in war from murder. One of the key components of these conditions is civilian immunity. The classic theoretical exposition of the general rules of warfare was developed by Hugo Grotius in the seventeenth century; the classic treaties regulating conduct towards non-combatants in warfare are embodied in the Geneva Convention of 1949. The procedures and limitations in these and subsequent treaties are not always observed – otherwise a volume such as this would be happily redundant. In a fight to the death, where crucial matters such as national survival or religious identity are often at stake, the notion of playing by 'Marquess of Queensberry rules' often gets short shrift.

There seems to be an almost unanimous popular presumption that civilians should be protected from the direct effects of violent conflict and that the distinction between combatant and non-combatant should be respected. But in the face of this longstanding ethical principle, and more recently norm of international law, we must acknowledge that the deliberate killing of civilians in conflicts during the twentieth century, and thus far into the twenty-first century, is widespread. (This is not to mention the related issue of collateral damage – the accidental or incidental killing of civilians.) The chapters in this book begin from the straightforward presumption in favour of civilian immunity, but proceed to explore many of the philosophical and practical complexities that soldiers, strategists and political leaders must face when they join a conflict. Is civilian immunity an absolute ethical injunction? How much responsibility should we take for collateral damage? How can we prevent, or minimize, harm to civilians, both in the battle space – in distinguishing between combatants and non-combatants, in devising robust rules of engagement, in preparing soldiers for the ethical challenges they will face and in equipping them with more discriminating technologies of death – and when civilians become displaced by conflict? And have we responded to the investigation of civilian deaths in conflicts by becoming mired in political and legal stalemates? There is nothing particularly straightforward about the answers to any of these questions, and some produce frustratingly counterintuitive outcomes. Nevertheless, the multidisciplinary nature and broad scope of these explorations invite the reader to engage with the many facets of a critically important issue in contemporary warfare.

The Balance of Casualties and the Shift in International Opinion

The issue of civilian immunity is pressing both because civilians now consistently constitute a larger number of casualties than combatants and because contemporary conflicts are less likely to be state-on-state affairs than states against non-state actors: guerrillas, insurgents and terrorists. The shift in the balance of wartime casualties in the twentieth century from primarily soldiers to primarily civilians took perhaps its most decisive step with World War II. During that war, civilians became caught up in the conflicts between states as battles between armies moved quickly from set-piece affairs onto different terrains and especially into cities, as civilians were deliberately targeted by aerial bombing where they worked (in support of the war effort or not) and where they lived, and where the actions of partisans, guerrillas and resistance fighters blurred the lines between combatant and non-combatant, fuelling military revenge against civilian populations. The end of the war brought with it prosecutions at Nuremberg and Tokyo against 'war crimes' – an old notion allied with a new determination by the victors, but often justifying the accusations of 'victors' justice' in that the latter's own crimes went untried and unpunished.[1]

As a consequence of World War II, the international community adopted in 1949 the Fourth Geneva Convention on the protection of civilians in conflict. That protection was then strengthened in 1977 by adopting the Convention's Additional Protocol. In recent times this norm has been repeatedly reinforced by the international community. For the past decade, for example, the UN Security Council has held a biennial debate on the protection of civilians in armed conflict, the International Criminal Court (ICC) was established in 2002 *inter alia* to prosecute war crimes and the International Committee of the Red Cross (ICRC) continues its long and valiant efforts to protect citizens in times of war.

Since 1999, the protection of civilians has also been explicitly mandated in 10 UN peacekeeping missions – a trend that shows every sign of continuing. In recent years, the UN Security Council has increasingly given greater attention to the requirements for the protection of civilians (especially because of the United Nation's egregious failures in the East African nation of Rwanda in 1994 and in

---

1   See Hugo Slim, *Killing Civilians: Method, Madness, and Morality in War* (New York: Columbia University Press, 2008); Igor Primoratz (ed.), *Civilian Immunity in War* (Oxford: Oxford University Press, 2007).

the Bosnian city of Srebrenica in 1995), and a flurry of reports and international conferences has addressed the challenges confronted by peacekeeping missions in implementing effective protection. Recently, the UN Security Council endorsed 'all necessary measures', including military action, to protect civilians in the civil war under way in Libya as this book goes to press.[2] The UN Secretariat, as well as regional bodies such as the African Union, has developed protection guidelines and operational directives, and multinational military operations (such as those in Afghanistan) are giving more attention to 'population protection'. To such examples of the valuing of the lives of non-combatants should be added the doctrine of the 'responsibility to protect',[3] developed by the United Nations in response to the civilian disasters of the 1990s, previously mentioned. This doctrine takes the debate in rather different directions from those pursued in this book, especially because its implementation can challenge the sovereignty of states where such states cannot or do not protect their own civilians. But it confirms the trend in favour of international action to defend civilian immunity.

Civilian Casualties and the Legitimacy of Conflict

The issue of civilian immunity is an issue of particular contemporary concern not simply because its prioritization might be philosophically cogent or because graphic evidence of civilian victims is beamed rapidly around the world by the new communication technologies, but rather because it has a vital connection with the legitimacy of recent conflicts in which Western powers have participated. The ability of such powers to sustain their contribution to a conflict depends to a considerable extent on popular 'home' support, which depends in turn on the extent of casualties to one's own forces and concerns about the justice of the conflict itself, in which civilian immunity forms a large part of the proper conduct of operations.

Following the rules has become important to the 'legitimacy' of war in modern times. Many conflicts in which the Western powers have been involved since World War II – Vietnam, the Gulf War, the war in Afghanistan and the Iraq War – have been contentious (and, on the whole, poorly supported) among the populations of countries that contributed to the cause, especially amongst Americans. In an important sense, these wars have been discretionary. The direct existence of the United States, for example, has not been at risk, even if it is arguably true that US interests are affected. World War II, in contrast, was precipitated by the aggression of Germany, and US involvement in it was a result of the surprise attack by Japan on the US naval base in Hawai'i. If more recent wars by Western powers are

2   UN Security Council, *The Situation in Libya*, Resolution 1973 (2011), http://www.un.org/News/Press/docs/2011/sc10200.doc.htm#Resolution

3   International Commission on Intervention and State Sovereignty, *The Responsibility to Protect: Report of the International Commission on Intervention and State Sovereignty* (Ottawa: International Development Research Centre, 2001).

indeed discretionary they require good reasons for such countries to enter them: good reasons for lives to be put at risk for uncertain outcomes. Those reasons have been argued chiefly in terms of the elements of *jus ad bellum*: fundamentally, is it just to enter a war? Once war is joined those reasons have been argued in terms of *jus in bello*: are the actions taken in war – with regard to combatants, non-combatants and prisoners – appropriate?[4] Whatever 'interests' such countries might have in engaging in a war, they are constrained by very public arguments about the justice of the undertaking.

At first glance, there is something fundamentally wrong with harming 'the innocent', as non-combatants are generally dubbed. This view has become so ingrained in the West, for example, that the very legitimacy of certain conflicts are called into question when Western forces are found to have killed or wounded non-combatants, deliberately or not. No event in recent wars by Western powers has achieved the notoriety of the 1968 massacre of the inhabitants of the village of My Lai by US forces during the second Vietnamese War, though the 2005 Haditha massacre in Iraq might ultimately rival it. The argument over a conflict's legitimacy tends to be played out in the world's media, sometimes to contest the reasons for going to war and sometimes to charge that one side or the other has deliberately targeted civilians. This is such an important argument (especially where the forces are substantially mismatched in military capability, in the so-called 'asymmetric warfare' that is such a common feature of conflicts in which Western forces have been engaged over at least the past two decades) that claim and counter-claim rage over whether civilian deaths are the result of targeting or are accidental or incidental. Keenly aware of the power of this argument, some civilians deliberately place themselves in harm's way, as 'human shields', either to protect some military asset (as we have seen in the recent civil war in Libya, when pro-Gaddafi civilians rushed to place themselves near potential targets of the UN-endorsed, NATO-led air strikes designed to protect civilians from Gaddafi's army) or to ensure their deaths strike at the resolve of their opponents (undermining the domestic political support that Western governments ultimately need to sustain a foreign military campaign).

The targeting of civilians was brought out in its full horror in the 1990s in two genocidal acts in Rwanda and Srebrenica. Both were made more horrific by the presence – and inaction – of UN peacekeepers; in neither case, and despite denials, could there be genuine doubt about the deliberate murder of large numbers of civilians. In Rwanda, over 100 days in 1994, soldiers of the Hutu ethnic majority slaughtered perhaps 800,000 of the Tutsi minority.[5] The second act took place as a consequence of the collapse of communism in Europe, when the Socialist Federal

---

4   The literature on just-war theory is extensive. For a useful introduction, along with a substantive contribution to this literature, see: Michael Walzer, *Just and Unjust Wars: A Moral Argument with Historical Illustrations*, 3rd edn (New York: Basic Books, 2000).

5   Philip Gourevitch, *We Wish to Inform You That Tomorrow We Will Be Killed with Our Families: Stories From Rwanda* (New York: Farrar, Straus and Giroux, 1998).

Republic of Yugoslavia began to break apart in 1991. The accompanying wars saw former neighbours now confront each other as enemies depending on their ethnicity or religion; in particular, 'ethnic cleansing' of parts of the country took place (including attacks by Serbs against Muslims in Kosovo and the expulsion of Muslim Bosnians from the Republika Srpska, which was being carved out of Bosnia). In July 1995, the Army of the Republika Srpska, under the command of General Ratko Mladić, undertook what was the largest mass murder in Europe since World War II: approximately 8,000 Muslim boys and men were massacred in Srebrenica.[6] Radovan Karadžić, then President of Republika Srpska, was finally arrested in Belgrade in 2008 and extradited to the Hague to stand trial before the International Criminal Tribunal for the Former Yugoslavia on charges of genocide, war crimes and crimes against humanity.

Similar allegations of mass murder have recently been raised against the army of Sri Lanka, which, in the final stages of a 30-year civil war against the separatist Tamil Tigers, attacked a small enclave of remaining Tigers in January 2009 in the hopes of ending the war. The Tamil Tigers held hostage hundreds of thousands of civilians, but the army continued its attack. It seems that tens of thousands of civilians were killed. A recent UN report declared that it had

> found credible allegations, which if proven, indicate that a wide range of serious violations of international humanitarian law and international human rights law was committed by the Government of Sri Lanka and the LTTE [Liberation Tigers of Tamil Eelam], some of which would amount to war crimes and crimes against humanity. Indeed, the conduct of the war represented a grave assault on the entire regime of international law designed to protect individual dignity during both war and peace.[7]

Whatever the truth of these allegations, and whatever the outcome of the prosecutions that might ensue, the sad fact is that civilians continue to be seen by some combatants as either a legitimate target in the conflict or pawns of little intrinsic worth.

Developing the Rules of Warfare

Views about the merely instrumental value of non-combatants or about the relatively insignificant value of innocent human life are not now held by the Western powers. Though they might differ on how, and to what degree, to protect

---

6 Jan Willem Honig and Norbert Both, *Srebrenica: Record of a War Crime* (Harmondsworth: Penguin Books, 1996).

7 United Nations, *Report of the Secretary-General's Panel of Experts on Accountability in Sri Lanka*, Publicly released on 25 April 2011, http://www.un.org/News/dh/infocus/Sri_Lanka/POE_Report_Full.pdf

civilians from deliberate attack during violent conflict, they are all committed to such protection, and all have elaborate philosophical, legal, diplomatic and – importantly – operational conventions in place to give effect to it. Just as 'human rights' are now an established benchmark for claims around the world and have been enshrined in the Universal Declaration of Human Rights since 1948, so 'civilian immunity' has reached an almost similar status in the popular mind. In some senses, it is a historically particular view, related to the evolution of warfare, and particularly to the horror of World War II, with its almost indiscriminate carnage. We might like to think that there were more genteel times, when codes of honour meant a respect for damsels and protection of the innocent, while the warrior classes fought it out among themselves in rule-bound splendour; but this is not an accurate picture of the past. Armies have ever fought each other with zeal (perhaps diminished only when fighting was done by mercenaries). And while the coming of democracy and citizen armies seems to have increased the viciousness with which military campaigns are fought, we should not forget the account of the *Iliad*, when Troy was ultimately, but utterly, destroyed by the besieging Greek forces, nor the destruction of Carthage and the salting of its soil at the end of the Third Punic War with Rome in the second century BCE.

The attempt to introduce rules into warfare has been as common a story as war itself. And there have been various warrior codes across different cultures, including the knightly code of chivalry in the Middle Ages in Europe and Bushido, the Japanese Way of the Warrior. But their success should not be gauged by the literature of gallantry, with its emphasis on mercy and fairness and the protection of the weak. Such codes have not extended much beyond the warrior class. Indeed, the earliest Geneva Convention of 1864, for the 'Amelioration of the Wounded' in war, and the 1929 convention relating to the 'Treatment of Prisoners of War' were designed to regulate relations between combatants themselves.

The key problems with attempting to regulate conduct in war – whether between combatants or as their conduct impacts on non-combatants – are, first, that there is no universally accepted neutral arbiter with the strength to apply and enforce the rules; second, there are substantial advantages to one side breaking the rules; and lastly, there is little battlefield advantage to observing the rules when one's opponent does not. Observing the rules assumes that we place our interests at the same level as those of others with whom we are dealing, as distinct from being partial in our own interest. But war is not a contest between philosophers; it is a fight, sometimes to the death, between people who tend to put their lives or other interests above fairness. After all, the stakes in war are high. Death is one of the costs (though the modern desperation to avoid death is rather different from the classical Greek welcome of an honourable death), but for many – especially when fighting an invader – the stakes are the loss of 'nation' or 'freedom'.

It is evident that some combatants might not know of, and some might not care to support, the rules of warfare – a situation that encapsulates the views of numerous insurgents and terrorists.[8] In the West, there is a general acceptance of the rules: armies' rules of engagement are developed to conform with them and punishments are meted out if soldiers do not adhere to them. But it is less clear, for example, whether *jihad* (or at least the militant versions of it) recognizes the difference between combatant and non-combatant. Just as in the Middle Ages Christendom saw all Muslims as enemies, so now many Muslims see all non-Muslims (and even some of their co-religionists) as legitimate targets. (In the current wave of Islamist terrorism, it seems likely that more Muslims have been killed by Islamists than Christians or atheists.) The internecine struggles of Christendom eventually led to a view that using violence to enforce belief, or destroying those who believed differently, was more harmful than useful. As early as the fourteenth century, Marsilius of Padua developed a theory of the separation of church and state; in the seventeenth century, John Locke put the now-mainstream view that the church is a community of believers and the state is a community of citizens, and that the state has no business in saving souls (or enforcing the observance of faith). By contrast, the separation between 'church' and 'state' is not a major theme of Islamic thought.

The 'war on terror' has seen the rise of attacks that are either indiscriminate in targeting enemy armed forces and civilians or deliberate in targeting civilians. The attack on the World Trade Center on 11 September 2001 was entirely indiscriminate in this sense (though quite deliberately aimed at one of the symbols of US power), leading to the deaths of nearly 3,000 people of diverse nationalities and religions. The popular terrorist tactic of improvised explosive devices (IEDs) in Iraq and Afghanistan is likewise indiscriminate, inflicting casualties on Coalition forces, but killing more civilians (and Muslims) than armed opponents. The effect of this mode of attack has a significant military effect on Coalition forces by heightening the uncertainty and stress of those on operations, but it also means that the ultimate political task of settling the conflict is likely to be more difficult. Improvised explosive devices are a variant of the traditional landmine; because of the indiscriminate nature of landmine casualties, and because they remain a considerable threat to civilians long after hostilities have ceased, they became subject to the 1997 Anti-Personnel Mine Ban Convention (another of the major international attempts to protect civilians from indiscriminate weaponry).

The champions of international humanitarian law, including the ICRC and the ICC, have little possibility of prosecuting a case against irregulars and terrorists. Yet we should play by the rules, even if the only ones who can be held

---

8   On 29 April 2011, at the start of the 'fighting season' in Afghanistan, the Taliban issued an alert to civilians, warning them to 'keep away from gatherings, convoys and centres of the enemy so that they will not become harmed during attacks of Mujahideen against the enemy' (http://www.abc.net.au/news/stories/2011/04/30/3204403.htm). Yet on 1 May, a twelve-year-old suicide bomber reportedly killed a number of civilians in a busy marketplace in the south-eastern province of Paktika (http://www.abc.net.au/news/stories/2011/05/01/3204737.htm).

accountable are organized armed forces. And we should play by the rules even if our opponents do not. There are good reasons not just at the philosophical level why the rules should be adhered to in all circumstances. Precisely because of an army's technological superiority and its enormous capacity to inflict harm, it must aim to kill and capture only combatants and to minimize the harm to non-combatants. Restraint is the right policy on consequentialist grounds. Excessive or indiscriminate use of deadly force does harm both to its victims and its perpetrators. Restraint allows soldiers to maintain a sense of perspective and self-esteem about their mission that benefits the achievement of the mission, especially but not solely when the mission has an important 'hearts-and-minds' component; it also eases their ultimate return to normal civilian life, with its reliance on civility and respect for others. Restraint also helps to ensure that the conflict's eventual settlement is not filled with bitterness or the seeds of future conflict. But despite such pragmatic arguments in favour of protecting civilians, there are many ethical issues surrounding the nature and extent of civilian immunity.

The Ethical Case for Protecting Civilians

How compelling are the philosophical arguments in favour of the protection of civilians? The first chapters in this volume examine the philosophical bases for the requirement that civilians should be protected in conflict. They particularly centre on the question of whether protecting civilians is an absolute value, as Stephen Nathanson argues, or an *almost* absolute value, as Igor Primoratz seeks to show. Are there compelling philosophical reasons for overriding a presumption in favour of citizen protection? Nathanson argues that there are not; he defends an absolute prohibition of intentional killing of civilians in war. His argument is based on a rule-utilitarian position that seeks to limit overall human damage and to diminish the ill effects of warfare. But there is another dimension to his position – to wit, the very idea that permissions may be granted to kill civilians intentionally (even under highly restrictive criteria) is problematic; only the strongest possible prohibition could ever stand a chance of preventing civilian deaths, because any loophole in the prohibition is bound to be exploited.

Primoratz points out that the requirement to protect civilians against lethal violence is particularly prominent, and particularly strong, in just-war theory. Some adherents of the theory see civilian immunity as absolute, not to be overridden in any circumstances whatsoever. Others allow that it may be overridden, but only in extreme situations (where, for example, the very survival or freedom of a political community is at stake). Michael Walzer, for example, considers that a 'supreme emergency' might provide the conditions to override the requirement to protect civilians. Primoratz examines some of the issues of interpretation and application of Walzer's 'supreme emergency' view and some of the criticisms that have been levelled against it, and argues that the view is too permissive. He proceeds to construct a position that is structurally similar to Walzer's, but much less permissive, which he terms the 'moral disaster' view. According to this view, deliberate killing of civilians is *almost* absolutely wrong.

Nathanson and Primoratz are concerned to examine arguments about the intentional killing of citizens, and leave to one side the question of collateral damage. Dean Cocking looks carefully at the notion of collateral damage itself, through a discussion about the notion of 'intention', arguing that we should be prepared to take responsibility for inflicting collateral damage where we pursue a plan we know will cause such damage. We do not diminish our responsibility for killing innocents because it is not our direct intention to kill them or because it is not useful to our purposes to kill them. So when is collateral damage acceptable and what is the nature of our choice and responsibility for it? Two central defining conditions have been that the damage we do must be unavoidable if we are to achieve our good and righteous ends and that the disvalue of this damage is not disproportionately greater than the value of the goods and rights we pursue. If these conditions are met, how should we understand our choice and responsibility for collateral damage? Cocking's chapter highlights some of the key problems of choice and responsibility in such cases, and argues that we should have a better understanding of the contexts within which we make our choices.

International Humanitarian Law

Though philosophers continue to differ, there is a substantial body of law – international humanitarian law (IHL) – dedicated to protecting civilians during violent conflict. International humanitarian law has a long history but only in recent times has it a consistent champion in the ICRC and a permanent tribunal before which cases may be tried: the International Criminal Court. There are three groups of such laws: a) rules for the protection of civilians in the conduct of military operations; b) rules for the protection of civilians under the control of the adversary against violence or arbitrary acts; and c) rules for the protection of civilians from the effects of military operations. Michael Schmitt explores the first of these groups in this volume, and Hitoshi Nasu the last two.

Nasu first provides a useful overview of the different types of armed conflict – international armed conflict, military occupation and non-international armed conflict – and the rules of IHL that apply to each. Where, in an international armed conflict, civilians come under the control of an adverse party (or occupying power), the obligations under the Fourth Geneva Convention apply – in particular, the adverse party must not harm civilians, coerce them to provide information or force them to work; but it must also protect civilians against insults, public curiosity and ill treatment. Where part of the territory of a state is occupied militarily by an adversary (and, arguably, in UN peacekeeping operations), all the obligations previously outlined apply to the occupying power with additional injunctions against the removal of the local population or the transfer of its own settlers into the occupied territory. As for non-international armed conflict, the obligations of customary international law seem to have the greater purchase, in that parties to such conflict are prohibited from engaging in acts of violence against civilians, torture and degrading or inhumane treatment, discriminatory treatment, collective punishment, medical or scientific experiments, sexual violence, ethnic cleansing, hostage taking, pillage and enslavement. The Fourth Geneva Convention, and its additional protocols, also prescribes that warring parties not simply refrain from doing violence against civilians, but that they also protect civilians from the effects of attacks. Yet Nasu observes that there are uncertainties about the scope of this precautionary obligation: does it require long-term planning or is it relevant only in times of armed conflict; and can a state be held to this obligation if it disputes the feasibility of taking precautions?

Schmitt is concerned with issues surrounding the protection of civilians when military operations are under way. He argues that no principle is more central to the content and understanding of IHL than military necessity; it has informed the law since its modern inception in the nineteenth century. Yet the principle has also been the subject of misinterpretation and abuse. For instance, the notion of military necessity was offered to justify many of the horrendous abuses suffered by the populations of occupied nations during World War II. Although rejected by war crimes tribunals following the conflict, it continues to be used as a justification for deviation from the tenets of the law governing armed conflict. On the other hand, it is being increasingly suggested that military necessity is a principle that restricts how armies may conduct hostilities, even beyond the specific rules of international humanitarian law. Schmitt's contribution examines the relation of the principle of military necessity to the countervailing principle of humanity. Both represent foundational principles that are meant to permeate all humanitarian law, whether found in treaties or existing as customary international law. Their coexistence serves to balance humanitarian law in a way that best protects individuals and property while allowing states sufficient leeway to conduct military operations effectively. He further examines how the principles are being applied by courts, non-governmental organizations and others involved in the legal assessment of armed conflict, and offers thoughts on whether the trend is positive or negative.

Helen Durham and Eve Massingham, of the Australian Red Cross, explain that the current complex global conflict waged against those engaged in acts of terrorism has led certain commentators to question the relevance and use of some of the principles found in international humanitarian law. But they argue that a deeper examination of the issues in both the practical and the academic discourse indicates that problems do not lie with the actual principles themselves – such as distinction and proportionality – but rather in the capacity to implement these requirements on a battlefield that is no longer neatly divided between civilian and combatant. The ICRC's *Interpretive Guidance on the Notion of Direct Participation in Hostilities* is an attempt to stimulate debates on the practical application of the requirement of distinction in situations where fighters do not adequately differentiate themselves from the civilian population and where civilians directly engage in fighting. Durham and Massingham outline the guidelines and reflect on the major criticisms of them. They go on to examine other useful principles found within IHL, such as the requirement of precautions in attack, which might enhance attempts to protect civilians during times of armed conflict.

Giving Soldiers the Right Tools for the Job

The presumption of protecting civilians is basic to the rules of engagement (ROE) under which regular armed forces operate. Specific ROE are drawn up for each conflict and, while their detail is not made public, they are transmitted to soldiers in every deployment. They aim to ensure that positive identification is made of an enemy before lethal force is used. In any coalition operation (as, for example, we see in current and recent conflicts in Afghanistan and Iraq), ROE between the different coalition forces may differ: different forces have different views, for example, about the level of certainty of identification that must exist before they may engage an enemy. But we should also appreciate the limitations of ROE themselves. Redrafting or otherwise strengthening ROE is not the answer to the challenge of improving the protection of civilians. Rob McLaughlin, formerly a senior Australian military officer charged with oversight of the ROE, demonstrates that there are some inherent limitations and that ROE need to be understood in the round to appreciate what they can and cannot achieve. Rules of engagement are not law: they are a means by which law, but not only law, can be distilled into context-sensitive permissions, prohibitions and guidance. Using the International Institute of Humanitarian Law's *Rules of Engagement Handbook* as a framework, McLaughlin examines the means by which protection of civilians in armed conflict – through the application of both the applicable law and the policy aims of the state or coalition of states engaged in a particular operation – can be built into rules of engagement.

At a fundamental level, ROE must be applied and – just as crucially – understood by soldiers. David Lovell examines the ways in which we educate officers for the challenges of ethical combat. Focused courses on applied ethics are proliferating at officer education academies. The issue is both how that is done and whether that alone is enough to produce a leader with good ethical bearings, who can lead their soldiers through the challenging conditions of combat. Because Lovell believes that a philosophical approach to ethics alone is insufficient, he advocates a broad education in history and literature in order that officers might have some sense of what it is like on the battlefield; and because the battlefield itself, as others report it, is chaotic, frightening, exhilarating and exhausting, the intellectual appreciation of it alone might not be enough. And finally, standing as a barrier to the increased emphasis on ethical development is the question of the ability of people to make cool ethical judgments, an ability related by developmental psychologists to people's levels of emotional and intellectual development. Lovell argues that combatants making ethically appropriate decisions in the theatre of war is important both for their own sense of proper purpose and for the ultimate resolution of a war, which is more than simply military, especially where the conflict is an insurgency. Drawing on the experience of recent conflicts, his chapter examines the preparedness of Australian officers for the ethical dilemmas of combat.

Technology is also a very important part of the modern battlefield, particularly the increased reliance on surveillance technology and precision weapons. And while casualties might, as a consequence, be reduced, the ability to distinguish combatant from non-combatant remains a problem, especially where combatants use the protective cloak of mixing with non-combatants, as seems to be a feature of the 'war against terrorism'. The ability of drones or remotely piloted aerial vehicles to loiter, often unnoticed, in places where enemy combatants are meeting or otherwise preparing their campaign has been a major innovation in warfare in the past decade. The ability of some of these vehicles to launch guided missiles or to direct guided missiles from planes or ships onto targets is also becoming a commonplace. But technology cannot make the calculation – often necessary – about whether the killing of an enemy leader is worth the collateral damage that will be inflicted on the tens or more of non-combatants who might surround them at the time of the explosion.

David Whetham argues that many of the advantages of precision stand-off weaponry are obvious: more precision means fewer weapons are required to achieve the same result; fewer warheads means a reduction in 'collateral damage'; greater accuracy means smaller warheads to achieve the desired effect, resulting in fewer civilian deaths and less damage to infrastructure. Because the threat to ordinary civilians is supposedly minimized through this ever-improving precision technology – increasingly available to Western governments – it is easier for them to maintain the moral high ground in conflicts. Whetham, however, cautions that stand-off weapon systems (and the responses prompted by them) might well also have some worrying implications for civilians in contemporary conflict. The lower political cost associated with using such weapons suggests that force can be easier to justify, leading to the phenomenon of 'drive-by wars' where there is no real moral commitment to the struggle. As World War II bomber crews demonstrated, it is also easier to kill when one is distant from the suffering caused. Dislocated decision makers, detached from the effects of their actions, might well be able to inflict significant collateral damage without heavy emotional and psychological cost. The fact that new technology does not in fact equate to less civilian suffering is borne out by 50 civilians killed for every successful strike against a militant in the Afghanistan/Pakistan border region. There is a 'paradox of precision' that undermines success: if the weapons are as good as advertised, obviously the things (including civilian lives) destroyed by them are assumed to have been the intended target. An over-reliance on stand-off weaponry also risks creating a perception that conventional responses by an opponent are simply futile; if you have a 'just cause' but cannot hurt an enemy directly, terrorist attacks on civilians instead become easier to sell to a sympathetic audience as the weapon of the weak against the strong. Whetham's view is that the sophisticated development of weaponry creates a greater potential for relaxing moral standards and might have the paradoxical effect of more civilian casualties.

Continuing these considerations about the value of advanced technology in reducing civilian casualties, Stephen Coleman observes that there are many situations where it would be extremely useful for military personnel to have access to non-lethal weapons (NLWs), especially in humanitarian, peacekeeping and counterinsurgency operations, and in other situations where the distinction between combatants and non-combatants tends to be blurred. There are, however, also some obvious problems with the use of such weapons, including the fact that some NLWs might violate existing conventions on chemical or biological weapons and that there might be a temptation for personnel equipped with such weapons to use them inappropriately. Perhaps the most serious problem is the fact that many advocates for the military use of NLWs suggest that such weapons might be able to be used without regard for the principle of discrimination. The claim is that since such weapons do not kill they do not cause harm, and thus discrimination might be applied after the use of force rather than before – that is, in decisions about how to deal with persons incapacitated by the use of NLWs rather than in decisions about who to target with such weapons.

Cases

The issue of protecting civilians cannot be fully appreciated without an examination of those who flee the scene of battle, becoming either 'internally displaced' or 'refugees' to foreign countries. The problem of refugees has become an extremely important one in recent times, especially as conflicts increase the numbers fleeing for their safety and as places that might be considered safe havens – Australia and Europe, for example – suffer an internal political backlash against the arrival of large numbers of refugees. Against this background, Penelope Mathew argues that the cardinal principle of *non refoulement* or non-return is arguably the first line of defence for people fleeing armed conflict. In contrast with military intervention, the principle of *non-refoulement* respects the idea encapsulated in the medical ethical principle 'first do no harm'. As many internal armed conflicts reflect racial, ethnic and religious cleavages, the definition of a refugee contained in the 1951 Convention Relating to the Status of Refugees is capable of responding to the needs of many persons displaced by armed conflict. Some persons, however, will be determined not to be refugees as they have fled 'generalized violence'. It is possible to meet the compelling protection needs of such war refugees through expanded refugee definitions (as in the African and American regions) or the notion of 'complementary protection' (as in Europe). Using examples from recent and ongoing conflicts, Mathew explores the argument in favour of surrogate protection for these war refugees, the relevance of international humanitarian law to the allocation of protection responsibilities and the uncomfortable division of labour in human rights protection that is imposed by the state system in which all remain formally sovereign despite huge substantive inequalities.

Andrew Alexandra's chapter begins from the observation that Private Military and Security Companies (PMSCs) have come to play an increasingly important role in the military activities of states, especially of the United States. The functions of PMSCs cover the range of combat operations, training programs and logistical support, but while in the latter two roles they might formally be considered non-combatants (given their separation from the military chain of command) their activities in recent conflicts have created problems for the viability of the distinction between combatant and non-combatant. Alexandra explores the issues surrounding this 'civilianization' of warfare, focusing on the congruence (or otherwise) of interests between PMSCs and the states that employ them, a relationship in which the interests of the states are sometimes put at risk. Such companies might have short-term commercial interests that do not align with the strategic interests of their employer; likewise, states employing PMSCs might have to act in support of the latter's belligerent actions in order to protect their reputation: cases of both are documented. Alexandra urges that, given the unlikelihood of the role of PMSCs being curtailed, their position in conflict zones should be regularized by falling under the military chain of command, and becoming unequivocally lawful combatants.

William Maley, an analyst of the conflicts in Afghanistan since the invasion of the Soviet Union thrust that country into unceasing turmoil, points out that Afghans have spent more than 30 years trying to survive in an unpromising environment. Recent discussions of appropriate counterinsurgency strategies in Afghanistan have focused on the need to shift away from hunting the enemy in favour of a strategy that gives central place to the protection of civilians. While this is a positive development that resonates with the protections for civilians accorded by IHL, it leaves a number of questions unanswered. These include what specific kinds of threat Afghan civilians might face; which particular Afghans might be at risk, and why; what measures Afghans themselves might take to protect their own positions; and how security sector actors can contribute to shaping the security environment. Maley addresses these questions through attention to both Afghan history and contemporary challenges. His broad conclusion is that life in the Afghan war zone is more complex than often realized, with multiple approaches being used to ensure day-to-day survival – the ability to realign politically for prudential reasons being one of the most salient.

This book concludes with chapters by Richard Rosen and Susan Breau, who argue the merits and weaknesses of the 'Goldstone Report' as a contribution both to understanding the particular dynamics of the armed conflict between Israel and Hamas fought in the Gaza Strip in December 2008 and January 2009 and to the clarification of international humanitarian law. Arising from the UN Fact-Finding Mission on the Gaza conflict, the report examined allegations of human rights and IHL violations during the conflict. Justice Richard Goldstone concluded that the Israeli Defence Force and the Palestinian militants had charges of war crimes to face; but in April 2011, he withdrew his earlier claim that it was Israeli Government policy to target civilians.[9] Subsequently, the Goldstone Report's other three co-authors criticized his retraction.

Rosen, as a critic of the report, sees it as a missed opportunity to reflect on the IHL implications for the dynamic of contemporary asymmetrical warfare in which some combatants – particularly members of insurgent and terrorist organizations – discard any attempt to distinguish themselves from civilians and conduct combat operations from civilian population centres. For him, the Gaza conflict is emblematic of this dynamic, with Hamas using live civilians to shield or screen military operations and dead civilians as props in an information war to portray adversaries as indiscriminate and 'heavy-handed' in their use of force. Thus the report delivers an anti-Israeli polemic without dealing with the issues central to the Hamas strategy of placing civilians in danger. Breau, in contrast, examines the criticisms of the UN Fact-Finding Mission and subsequent report that have dogged it since its inception, and finds that there is much to commend in the report. Considering the charges of bias against the mission, and despite the criticisms of Israel made by one of its members, she argues that the report was not biased against Israel. She concedes that improvements might have been made to the mission's methodology, particularly in allowing closed-session interviews of Palestinian witnesses, but argues that this does not introduce a fatal flaw into the report; rather, the mission's ability to produce findings was made far more difficult by Israel's refusal to cooperate. But, above all, and particularly in respect of humanitarian law regarding blockades, targeting and weaponry, Breau argues that the report helps to advance and clarify the laws applicable to armed conflict.

* * * *

The authors of the chapters herein begin with a presumption in favour of civilian immunity in violent conflict and, where they do not absolutely prohibit the killing of civilians, their view is that the conditions under which such killing is ethically justified are highly restrictive. This presumption finds expression in IHL, championed by the ICRC and recently given teeth with the advent of the International Criminal Court. While we might debate the philosophical issues around civilian immunity, and the details of the development of IHL in particular cases, we must nevertheless continue to defend that presumption as the foundation of a humane approach to waging and resolving conflict. For it is a presumption that is constantly and fundamentally under challenge from ideological and religious zealots, to whom opponents appear as an undifferentiated collection of filth and evil no matter whether they have formally joined combat or not. This

---

9 Richard Goldstone, 'Reconsidering the Goldstone Report on Israel and War Crimes', *The Washington Post*, 2 April 2011, http://www.washingtonpost.com/opinions/reconsidering-the-goldstone-report-on-israel-and-war-crimes/2011/04/01/AFg111JC_story.html

indiscriminate approach – encapsulated by opponents being dubbed as 'kulaks', 'Jews', 'Gooks', 'infidels' or any of the hundreds of labels that have been used to dehumanize others – is the foundation for war crimes. It is also, alas, an approach that resonates with the fears, ignorance, desperation and anger of many people around the world. At a time when civilian deaths in violent conflict continue to increase, this book adds to the voices for humanity.

Chapter 2
Are Attacks on Civilians Always Wrong?

Stephen Nathanson

My aim in this chapter is to defend an absolute prohibition against the killing of civilians in war. Some people might wonder why such a defence is necessary. Isn't it obvious that attacking civilians – children, the elderly and other non-participants in war – is a moral outrage, an indefensible act that can never be justified?

While I believe that such attacks are never morally justified, it is important to see that this view has to be defended and that the issues surrounding it are more complicated than they might seem. I believe that unless these difficulties are recognized and confronted, civilian immunity will actually be weakened. My aim here is to face the many challenges to the principle of civilian immunity so that we better understand why the alternatives to it are not justified and why civilian immunity is a central part of a morally sound ethic of war fighting.

Civilian Immunity as a Fundamental Moral Intuition

Some philosophers have affirmed civilian immunity – sometimes described as the prohibition of attacks on innocent people – as a fundamental moral belief. Angelo Corlett writes that 'targeting of the innocent violates the fundamental moral intuition that innocent persons ought not to be targets or victims of violent physical attack'. Similarly, C.A.J. Coady emphasizes the 'depth and centrality of the prohibition on intentionally killing the innocent', describing it as a 'touchstone of moral and intellectual health' whose rejection would amount to 'an upheaval' in our moral perspective.[1]

These claims are echoed in the farewell address given by US President George W. Bush before leaving office. Reflecting on the threat of terrorism, Bush urged Americans to 'maintain our moral clarity' and to recognize that 'good and evil are present in this world, and between the two there can be no compromise. Murdering the innocent to advance an ideology is wrong every time, everywhere.' In this address, Bush both condemns attacks on civilians and appeals to the obvious wrongness of such attacks to suggest that there are two kinds of people in the world: evil people, who are willing to kill the innocent for

---

1   Angelo Corlett, *Terrorism: A Philosophical Analysis* (Dordrecht: Kluwer, 2003), p. 115; C.A.J. Coady, *Morality and Political Violence* (Cambridge: Cambridge University Press, 2008), p. 297.

political reasons, and good people, who condemn these actions and would never do such things themselves.

While I believe that President Bush spoke the truth when he categorically condemned '[m]urdering the innocent to advance an ideology', I doubt that he and many of his listeners actually believe this. My sense is that there is a good deal of moral confusion about acts that kill innocent people and that many people who think that they support an absolute ban on killing civilians might actually believe that such attacks are sometimes justified.

In fact, beliefs about what is permissible in war are quite unstable. The ideals that people affirm in times of peace often change in times of war. Alexander Downes describes such a shift after the start of World War II. 'Most Americans', he writes, 'abhorred bombing civilians before the war', but after Germany invaded Western Europe, there was 'a dramatic reversal in opinion on the subject'. Similarly, public opinion polls taken after the Japanese attack on Pearl Harbor showed that '67 percent [of Americans] favored aerial bombardment of Japanese cities'.[2] Whatever they might have believed before, many people came to believe that 'murdering the innocent' could be the right thing to do. Downes' perceptive conclusion is that 'the norm against inflicting widespread and systematic harm on non-combatants in warfare is a frail one'.[3]

It is not surprising that such shifts in beliefs occur. When we focus on the deaths and injuries of innocent people, we might feel horrified and think that actions that cause these harms must be wrong. But when we focus on the people who carry out these actions, we might think that such people must be thoroughly evil and that any actions that thwart them are justified, even if these actions kill innocent people. Our feelings about these things also depend on who the victims and perpetrators are. We have less sympathy for some victims than for others as well as varying positive and negative attitudes towards perpetrators. If our belief in the ban on attacking civilians is dependent on these emotions then any general commitment to civilian immunity will indeed by frail.

Indeed, even a frail commitment to civilian immunity might be less common than we think. In *Killing Civilians*, Hugo Slim describes civilian immunity as an idea that 'has remained resilient in human consciousness and … continues to play on a universal conscience'. Nonetheless, he says, civilian immunity has been rejected by most 'political and military leaders and many of their spearing, hacking, shooting, bombing and burning subordinates'.[4] His book provides ample testimony to widespread practices of attacking civilians and to the gruesome results of these practices.

---

2 Alexander Downes, *Targeting Civilians in War* (Ithaca, NY: Cornell University Press, 2008), p. 136.

3 Ibid., p. 257. For further evidence of this, see Hugo Slim, *Killing Civilians: Method, Madness, and Morality in War* (New York: Columbia University Press, 2008).

4 Slim, p. 2.

Given not only the frequent violations of civilian immunity but its widespread explicit rejection as well, we need to take seriously the task of determining whether an absolute ban on attacking civilians is morally correct. I will attempt to do this first by describing an array of possible rules of war that compete with civilian immunity. I will then evaluate these rules and try to show why a rule that absolutely forbids attacks on civilians is superior to all other options. My discussion of these issues will focus only on the moral status of attacks that are intended to kill and injure civilians; I will not consider the important subject of attacks on military targets that result in 'collateral damage' harms to civilians.[5]

The Ethics of War Fighting: A Spectrum of Options

The idea that the civilian-immunity rule is obviously correct is weakened when we call to mind the many alternative rules with which it competes. Table 2.1 contains several such possible rules.

Table 2.1   A spectrum of possible rules of war

Degree of permissiveness/ restrictiveness	Type of theory or principle	Possible *jus in bello* rules
Most permissive	Extreme realism	Anything goes.
	Moderate realism	Any attack that has military value is permissible.
	Proportionality	Any militarily valuable attack whose negative effects are proportional to its positive military value is permissible.
	Limited civilian immunity	Combatants may be attacked, but non-combatants may not be intentionally killed or injured unless doing so has significant military value.
	Civilian immunity with a supreme emergency exception	Combatants may be attacked, but non-combatants may not be intentionally killed or injured except in supreme emergencies.
	Strong civilian immunity	Combatants may be attacked, but non-combatants may not be intentionally killed or injured.
Most restrictive	Pacifism	Neither combatants nor non-combatants may be intentionally killed or injured.

---

5   Collateral damage is considered in other essays in this volume. I discuss these issues in *Terrorism and the Ethics of War* (Cambridge: Cambridge University Press, 2010), Chs 7, 17 and 18.

This chart makes clear that there is a range of views about how people are permitted to fight, and brief reflection indicates why people might find the alternatives to civilian immunity plausible. I will briefly describe each view and indicate why none of them can be rejected as obviously stupid or wrong. My purpose is not to support these views but rather to make clear the challenge they pose to civilian immunity.[6]

Extreme Realism

The extreme-realist 'anything goes' rule places no constraints on war fighting and provides no basis for condemning even the most barbaric acts of war. While morally repugnant, this view might not seem obviously wrong. After all, warfare is a special circumstance in which much is at stake and in which the basic moral rules that structure normal life are suspended. In normal life, we are morally prohibited from seriously harming others unless they directly threaten us. In war, however, there is a general permission for soldiers to attack people who pose no immediate threat. Attacks on sleeping soldiers, for example, are permissible, as are attacks from a distance or from the air, even though the targeted soldiers are incapable of threatening the attackers. In war, then, killing is permissible even when it is not in self-defence against an attacker.

Once we accept that many basic moral norms are not operative in war, it is easy to move to the idea that the concept of an ethic of war is naïve if not absurd. But if there is no morality in warfare then there is no reason why people at war should refrain from doing whatever is required for them to win.

Moderate Realism

Moderate realists accept the realist picture of warfare but distinguish between acts of killing, injuring and destroying that have military value and those that make no contribution to achieving victory but are motivated by cruelty and hatred. Such gratuitous violence can be avoided without limiting the efforts of a country or group to win a war. So the moderate realist will accept a rule against gratuitous violence while defending as morally permissible any action that has military value. The moderate-realist rule is more plausible than extreme realism because it makes war less hellish without constraining a belligerent's efforts to achieve victory.

Proportionality

The moderate-realist view is still very permissive. It allows large-scale violence and destruction even if it makes only the smallest contribution to the quest for victory. Someone who recognizes that the enemy group consists of human beings who have

---

6   My aim here is to describe a logical spectrum of possible rules of war and not to attribute these views to particular thinkers. For further discussion of these views and some discussion of their advocates, see ibid., Chs 8–11.

some claim to be treated morally could accept the idea that the amount of morally permissible harm must be proportionate to the value of what is achieved by inflicting it. This is the proportionality principle, which allows large-scale harm only when it is likely to produce large military gains. If an attack will achieve only small military gains then the attack is permissible only if the anticipated harms are also relatively small. Proportionality might seem like a reasonable principle that balances the rights and interests of the enemy with the rights and needs of those fighting against them.

Nonetheless, we should not lose sight of two things about proportionality. First, it is still a very permissive rule that places no absolute limits on the amount of harms inflicted so long as the expected military benefits are proportionate to them. Second, proportionality provides no special protection to civilians and thus does not forbid what President Bush called 'murdering the innocent'. If attacks on innocent civilians will bring proportionate benefits, they are permissible.

Limited Civilian Immunity

Some people might think that any acceptable ethic of war must recognize some special protections for civilians. If civilians are taking no part in a military effort, it seems appalling that they should be attacked. How, one might ask, can it be morally justified to attack children, for example, or very elderly people? From this perspective, it seems morally obligatory to establish some form of immunity for civilians unless they are playing an active role in the war effort. The *limited civilian immunity* view creates a special status for civilians and establishes a rule against attacking them. At the same time, it maintains that because of the importance of winning in war, moral qualms must not interfere with doing what is necessary to achieve victory. With this in mind, the rule that affirms civilian immunity is understood to establish a presumption that may be overridden if circumstances arise in which attacks on civilians are likely to achieve substantial military gains. This view, then, recognizes that civilians have a right to immunity; it permits overriding that right when respecting it comes at too great a cost. The right to fight effectively, according to this view, trumps the rights of civilians not to be attacked.

Civilian Immunity with a Supreme Emergency Exception

This view is structurally similar to 'limited civilian immunity', but it sets the bar for morally justified attacks on civilians much higher. Achieving valuable military goals is not enough. Attacks on civilians are permissible only to prevent horrific evils. Michael Walzer's 'supreme emergency' exception and Igor Primoratz's 'moral disaster' exception are attempts to defend this type of view.[7] Both want to defend civilian immunity, but find an absolute prohibition implausible because

---

7   For these views, see Michael Walzer, *Just and Unjust Wars* (New York: Basic Books, 1977), Ch. 16; and Igor Primoratz, 'Civilian Immunity as an *Almost* Absolute Moral Rule', Chapter 3 in this volume.

they think that there are some threats to people so immense that killing the innocent becomes permissible if it is the only option that stands a chance of preventing this great evil (Walzer) or if there are very strong reasons for believing that it will do so (Primoratz).

Walzer's paradigm case is the situation of the British in 1940. According to Walzer, the British faced the possibility of imminent defeat by Nazi Germany – an extraordinarily evil enemy – and their only means of defence appeared to be bombing attacks on German civilians. Only in such an extreme case would attacks on civilians be justified.

Defenders of this view emphasize the importance of civilian immunity, but they deny that any absolute prohibition can be correct because there is always the possibility that it should be overridden in extraordinary circumstances. This is an attractive view that seems to combine a very strong form of civilian immunity with the recognition that events sometimes put people into impossibly difficult situations.

Strong Civilian Immunity

The strong civilian immunity rule prohibits all attacks on civilians – everywhere, anytime, by anyone. This is the view of international humanitarian law. The 1977 Protocol I additions to the Fourth Geneva Convention affirm the immunity of civilians in forceful, absolute terms.

> Chapter 1. Article 48 ... the Parties to the conflict shall at all times ... direct their operations only against military objectives ...
>
> Chapter 11. Article 51. 2. The civilian population as such ... shall not be the object of attack.

In fact, the Geneva Protocols go beyond strong civilian immunity, which is limited to prohibiting direct attacks on civilians. Article 53.2 forbids actions that 'destroy, remove, or render useless objects indispensable to the survival of the civilian population', and Article 57.1 requires that '[i]n the conduct of military operations, constant care shall be taken to spare the civilian population, civilians, and civilian objects'.

Pacifism

Pacifists reject the view that war can be fought in a morally permissible way. They deny that civilians have a special status and grant the same immunity to soldiers that strong combatant immunity grants to civilians. Pacifists see war as immoral, even if only soldiers are injured and killed. Pacifists share with realists the view that the very nature of warfare is incompatible with moral constraints on how to fight. If it is almost inevitable that people will reject moral principles when they are actually at war then the idea that moral constraints on how to fight can have any influence is an illusion.[8]

How Do We Tell Which Rule is Morally Correct?

I have described these different views to make clear that there are many possible rules and that we cannot reasonably settle on one without considering the others. One reason people's views are unstable is that changing circumstances highlight different factors that a particular rule seems to handle well. In other circumstances, other needs and concerns are highlighted, and different rules appear to be more reasonable. To make a reasonable judgment, we need to hold in view the varying circumstances of war and conflict and assess possible rules in the light of this broad view. In addition, we need a method that helps us to determine which of these possible rules provides the correct standard for judging acts of war fighting.

Suppose that each of us considers the ethics of war from the perspective of our own country's or group's interests.[9] From that perspective, we would want a rule that maximizes our own group's chances of winning in any war or violent conflict. Such a desire is understandable because people generally feel a strong partiality towards their own country or group. We care more about it than we do about others and, during a war, we generally support our group and hope for its victory.

This kind of partiality, however, cannot determine what the correct moral rules of warfare are. Consider the rule that 'Country X may do whatever is necessary to win a war, but all others must never attack civilians'. This would not be a plausible candidate for a moral rule to govern the conduct of war. Indeed, it does not seem to be a moral rule at all. A moral rule must apply generally to everyone, imposing the same constraints and granting the same permissions to all. It must not be partial towards any particular country by allowing it to act in ways that are forbidden to others.

Thus, any plausible rule must be impartial. In saying this, I do not mean that it must require everyone to act impartially. In general, moral rules allow us to act in response to our partialist concerns, but they impose constraints on how we promote those concerns. In business and in sports, for example, competitors may try to do better than their opponents. Nonetheless, they must do this within the limits imposed on how one may compete. A business firm may not compete by destroying the facilities of its competitors or killing its workers. These constraints are built into the rules that apply impartially to everyone and they limit the means

---

8 The pacifist thinker John Howard Yoder questions the power of just-war theory to constrain actual behaviour in war in *When War is Unjust: Being Honest in Just-War Thinking*, 2nd edn (Eugene, Ore.: Wipf and Stock Publishers, 2001).

9 I discuss both countries (that is, states) and 'groups' because I believe that the rules apply to both states and non-state groups. A state or country is one type of group, but there are other types of groups that might also find themselves engaged in violent conflicts.

that people may use in the course of pursuing their own success. The ethics of war has the same function. Its impartial rules allow all to strive for victory but specify constraints that define how one may legitimately fight.

Kantian Ideas Applied to the Ethics of War

Something like this idea of impartiality is implicit in Kant's categorical imperative and its requirement that we should act only on maxims or rules that are universalizable – that is, that could be acted on by everyone.[10]

While this idea provides a basis for rejecting rules that explicitly distribute permissions and constraints in unequal ways, it provides no further guidance. To see why, consider what it would say about the rule 'anything goes'. The Kantian idea tells us only that if 'anything goes' permits any individual country to fight without constraints when it is at war then it must permit all countries to do the same when they are at war. In fact, all of the possible rules of war that I have described would be permitted by this requirement because each of them is applicable to all parties in a consistent, impartial way, and no contradictions are generated by having everyone follow them. For this reason, the universalizability test cannot tell us which of these rules is correct. In particular, it cannot tell us whether attacking civilians is or is not morally permissible.

If we are concerned to defend civilian immunity, Kant's second form of the categorical imperative seems more promising. It tells us always to treat persons as ends in themselves and never as means only.[11] This inspiring ideal emphasizes the idea that every person has intrinsic value and should never be treated merely as an instrument for promoting the interests of others. Applying it to questions about war, it implies that because every civilian is a person and no person may be treated solely as a means, attacking civilians is always wrong.

The trouble with this derivation of civilian immunity, however, is that it forbids not only the killing of civilians but also the killing of soldiers. In war, however, it is accepted that attacking enemy soldiers is a permissible means to achieving victory. The intrinsic value of each soldier appears to be ignored in warfare. One might conclude that war itself is immoral and that pacifists are right in thinking that all the killing that goes on in war is wrong. If we believe that war can sometimes be morally permissible, however, we must accept that using others as means only can sometimes be permissible. If that is so then Kant's second version of the categorical imperative must be rejected as a moral absolute.

Kant's third version of the categorical imperative might be helpful. It tells us that we must test possible moral rules by seeing whether they could be laws in a kingdom of ends – that is, a kingdom in which each person is both the lawmaker

---

10   Immanuel Kant, *Grounding for the Metaphysics of Morals*, 3rd edn (Indianapolis, Ind.: Hackett Publishing, 1993), p. 30.

11   Ibid., p. 36.

and the subject to whom the laws apply.[12] Suppose that all people in a kingdom of ends would endorse laws that sometimes permit people to use others as means only in times of war.

Why would they do this? Because they would realize that individual persons sometimes have deeply conflicting interests. While it is in everyone's interests not to be attacked by others, it is also in everyone's interests that they be allowed to attack those who are attacking them. Rules that grant both a right not to be attacked and a right to attack others who are attacking them would recognize the interests of all while granting people the right to treat others as means when those others have attacked them.

If I defend myself by killing someone who is attacking me, I am killing that person as a means to save myself.[13] Similarly, if war is morally permissible as a means of defending important human interests then legislators for a kingdom of ends might support laws that permit soldiers to kill and injure members of the enemy military as a means of defending their country and its interests.

While this reasoning might help us understand how rules that permit killing in war can be impartially justified and how even the terrible instrumental use of people in war can be permitted, it does not tell us how far the permission to kill and injure in war goes. It does not tell us whether people legislating for a kingdom of ends would embrace or reject rules that permit the killing of civilians.

Utilitarianism and the Ethics of War

The rules that make up an ethic of war must do justice to two important rights: the right to use violence in defence of fundamental interests and the right to immunity from attack. These rights, however, are in tension with one another. The stronger and more permissive the right to defend our life and other vital interests is, the weaker is the right to immunity from attack; and the more stringent the right to immunity to attack is, the more limited is the right of people to defend vital interests. Simply recognizing these rights does not tell us about their relative strength.[14]

One strategy for discovering the correct balance appeals to the understanding of moral impartiality that lies at the heart of utilitarian moral theory. Jeremy Bentham described the essentials of utilitarian morality by emphasizing two things: first, that the goal of morality is to achieve the 'greatest happiness for the greatest number', and second, that when we calculate the likely amounts of happiness and

---

12   Ibid., p. 40.

13   People who use the principle of double effect to defend self-defensive killing deny that the death of the attacker is intended and deny that the attacker who is killed is being used as a means only. Suzanne Uniacke discusses this view in *Permissible Killing: The Self-Defense Justification of Homicide* (Cambridge: Cambridge University Press, 1994), Ch. 4.

14   On the problem of conflicts between rights, see my *Terrorism and the Ethics of War*, pp. 169–74.

suffering caused by different possible actions, every individual's wellbeing must be counted equally.[15]

Utilitarian reasoning is supposed to provide a way to think about how we should act in circumstances in which all the actions available to us will benefit some people and harm others. Bentham's answer is that we should do whatever will result in the greatest overall wellbeing. That is, we should discover what is right to do by considering different possible actions, and we should calculate its net value by adding the benefits and then subtracting the harms. Whichever is most beneficial is the right act. While each person will not benefit equally, each person's interests will be counted equally. Bentham's view is attractive for two reasons. First, it provides a means for deciding how to act when all available options involve both positive and negative effects. Second, it highlights the pursuit of the greatest overall well-being as an appealing overall goal for action and as providing a criterion for making moral and practical judgments.

While act utilitarians use this method to evaluate individual actions, rule utilitarians use it to determine what rules should be part of a moral code. Once these rules are accepted, the morality of individual actions is determined by consulting the rules. If an act is permitted by the rules, it is morally right, and if it is forbidden by them, it is morally wrong. Since I am investigating what rules should be included in an ethics of warfare, I will focus on the rule-utilitarian method.[16]

This is the approach taken by Richard Brandt in 'Utilitarianism and the Laws of War'. Brandt suggests that the question 'what are the correct rules for the conduct of war?' can usefully be reformulated as the question: 'What rules would rational impartial people, who expected their country at some time to be at war, want to have as authoritative rules of war?' Here Brandt echoes Kant's emphasis on impartiality, but unlike Kant, Brandt claims that rational, impartial people would have a goal: the promotion of overall human wellbeing. For this reason, they would adopt those rules whose 'acceptance and enforcement will make an important contribution to long range utility'.[17] Given that long-range utility is the goal of 'rational, impartial people', we can understand that their aim is the wellbeing of human beings in general, not the wellbeing of a particular nation or group. While the rules they choose will allow people to strive for the success of their own groups, the rules will also set the limits on permissible partiality, and those limits will be determined by discovering which rules will best promote the greatest overall wellbeing for all people.

---

15   For the basics of Bentham's method, see Jeremy Bentham, *An Introduction to the Principles of Morals and Legislation* (1781), Ch. 1.

16   For defences of rule utilitarianism, see Richard Brandt, *Morality, Utility, and Rights* (Cambridge: Cambridge University Press, 1992); and Brad Hooker, *Ideal Code, Real World* (Oxford: Oxford University Press, 2000).

17   Richard Brandt, 'Utilitarianism and the Laws of War', in M. Cohen, T. Nagel and T. Scanlon (eds), *War and Moral Responsibility* (Princeton, NJ: Princeton University Press, 1974), p. 30.

Rule utilitarians will approach the question of whether war itself is morally permissible by asking whether people will be better off in a world in which war is sometimes permissible rather than absolutely forbidden. Although war has disastrous effects on many people, one might think that a moral code that permits war will have better overall effects than one that forbids it. If war is forbidden, it is likely that some nations and groups will still use organized violence to achieve their ends and will probably subject defeated people to harsh treatment. A rough utilitarian argument for permitting warfare will claim a permissive rule will lessen damage to humanity as a whole. It will do this by preventing harms to defeated people and diminishing the recourse to war. Recourse to war will be diminished because some potential invaders will be deterred by the knowledge that their potential victims will resist them. As a result, the costs to the invaders will rise and the probability of their success will diminish. If this reasoning is correct then a rule permitting war is in the interests of humanity as a whole.

Rule utilitarians will develop further rules to help differentiate when recourse to war is legitimate and when it is not. The result might well be a view such as the traditional just-war theory – that is, a view with multiple criteria that must be met, including just cause, last resort, probability of success, and so on. Because the just-war rules and criteria might be justifiable from a rule-utilitarian perspective, we can see that it is a mistake to think that these two views are necessarily in conflict with one another. Just-war theory is a set of specific rules about how wars may be permissibly fought. Rule utilitarianism is a method or theory about how to determine which rules are correct. It is plausible to think that a rule-utilitarian method would support just-war theory's criteria for when going to war is legitimate.[18]

Rule utilitarians, then, will want to permit war as a sometimes necessary means for protecting vital values and interests, but they will also seek to minimize the damage caused by warfare. Like just-war theorists, they will introduce *jus in bello* rules that set the bounds on permissible means of fighting. They will seek the rules that allow countries to act partially in defence of their own important interests while setting up impartial constraints on the means of war fighting so as to minimize war's damage to human beings.

Evaluating the Array of Possible Rules of War

Now that we have a method for evaluating proposed rules of war, we can test the possible rules of war that I described earlier. We will reject rules that fail to limit overall human damage and accept rules whose acceptance promises to diminish the ill effects of warfare.

---

18   I use a rule-utilitarian approach to support just-war theory's *jus ad bellum* criteria in 'Are Preventive Wars Always Wrong?', in Deen Chatterjee (ed.), *Gathering Threats: The Ethics of Preventive War* (Cambridge, Cambridge University Press, forthcoming).

Extreme Realism

Although 'anything goes' is an impartial, universalizable principle, utilitarians will oppose its acceptance because it places absolutely no constraints on the harm done in the conduct of war. War, like other activities, must be conducted not only with the idea of achieving its goals but also with a view to avoiding unnecessary harm. 'Anything goes' permits the infliction of harms that have no military value. It would be rejected by rational, impartial people who sought rules of war that advanced the overall wellbeing of human beings.

Moderate Realism

The rule that *any act of war is permissible as long as it has some military value* is also flawed. A rule that permits inflicting huge harms for trivial gains might be in the interests of one country or group, but it does not protect the interests of humanity. From the human perspective, this type of excessive violence would not be permitted.

Proportionality

What about the proportionality principle? Because it considers both gains and losses and requires that the gains produced by an attack be sufficiently large to justify the amount of harms created, this sounds like a rule that utilitarians might embrace. Indeed, proportionality is often equated with a utilitarian view and, if this were correct, it would settle the question of whether utilitarians will accept it.[19]

It is a mistake, however, to equate proportionality with utilitarianism. A utilitarian analysis requires that we compare various possible actions or rules, but proportionality does not. So, for example, if we use a proportionality criterion, we might decide that a certain objective is sufficiently important to justify an attack that will cause a certain level of harms. Suppose, however, that there is another attack that would achieve the same objective but would cause a lesser degree of harm. In that case, a utilitarian method would require choosing the attack that generates less 'disutility' while the proportionality test would not require this because both attacks satisfy the proportionality requirement. If this is correct then the two are not identical.

This argument suggests that even if we choose proportionality, we will need to supplement it with a 'harm minimization' principle. The distinction between minimization and proportionality appears in the Geneva Convention, which require that persons planning an attack should attempt both a) to 'minimize' death and injury to civilians, and b) to refrain from attacks whose negative effects would

19   Michael Walzer equates utilitarianism and proportionality in *Just and Unjust Wars*, Ch. 8.

be 'excessive' (that is, disproportionate) in relation to the military gains.[20] This suggests that there are two senses of 'excessive'. The harms caused by attacks might be excessive because they are disproportionate – that is, the military gains are not great enough to justify the harms caused; or they might be excessive because they are unnecessary – that is, there are less damaging ways of achieving the same gains.

Although it might need to be supplemented, the proportionality principle appears to set real limits to the violence of war. It prohibits both gratuitous violence that makes no contribution to victory and excessive violence that is not justified by the value of the military gain. The fact that the proportionality principle gives no special protection to civilians, however, shows that if it is sufficient then a rule prohibiting attacks on civilians is not required for morally justifiable war fighting.

The Problem with Proportionality

The proportionality principle is open to a version of the familiar complaint that an idea is fine in theory but defective in practice. Michael Walzer raises this criticism, claiming that 'proportionality turns out to be a hard criterion to apply, for there is no ready way to establish an independent or stable view of the values against which the destruction of war is to be measured'.[21] In practice, Walzer thinks, using the proportionality requirement will result in very weak constraints on violence because '[a]ny act of force that contributes in a significant way to winning the war is likely to be called permissible'.[22]

This criticism does not claim that the proportionality principle is inherently flawed. Rather, it rests on a prediction that under conditions of warfare, people applying the proportionality principle will call actions permissible when those actions actually violate proportionality. They will do this because the value of achieving victory is so great that almost any means will be seen as proportionate. In practice, then, a principle that is meant to establish limits on violence will fail to achieve this end.

A defender of proportionality might say that its truth is independent of whether it is likely to be applied properly. But if one can predict that misapplications are very likely and that including the principle in an ethics of war is unlikely to have the desired impact then that is a flaw that needs to be taken seriously. It is a virtue of the rule-utilitarian approach that it takes this factor into account. If the goal is to diminish the destructiveness of war and if one can predict that a particular principle is very hard to apply then that is a strike against it. If a principle is likely to be more effective in limiting the damage of warfare, that is a good reason for seeing it as superior to others that might be 'good in theory but not good in practice'.

---

20 *Geneva Convention Relative to the Protection of Civilian Persons in Time of War of August 12, 1949*, 75 UNTS 287 (entered into force 21 October 1950), Art. 57, 2aii, 2aiii.

21 Walzer, p. 129.

22 Ibid., p. 129.

Walzer – though he is a strong critic of utilitarianism – describes the kind of principle that is needed in order to be effective. Rules of war, he says, must be clearer and less dependent on individual assessments if they are to have an effect on people's behavior. Proportionality leaves too much room for judgment and interpretation, and its use is bound to be skewed under conditions of fear and uncertainty. What we need, Walzer says, are 'clearcut rules – moral fortifications … that can be stormed only at great moral cost'. A clear, exceptionless rule such as 'Do not attack civilians' will be more effective than the vaguer, more permissive rule 'Do not engage in attacks unless the harms that they cause are proportionate to the value of the military gains they achieve'.[23]

Limited Civilian Immunity

This rule prohibits attacks against civilians but includes a permission to override the prohibition if the gains of doing so are large enough.

One could argue that this rule retains some of the benefits of proportionality while avoiding its weaknesses. Following Walzer, we might say that limited civilian immunity avoids both vagueness and the dependence on judgments made under stress that characterize proportionality. It does this by adopting a specific prohibition on attacking civilians. This prohibition provides a clearer guideline while still achieving the aims of proportionality. It is plausible to argue that attacks on civilians are generally disproportionate because the harms done to civilians, unlike those done to combatants, are unlikely to weaken the enemy's ability to fight and thus do little to contribute towards the achievement of victory.

The problem with this rule is that it does not avoid the flaw of the original proportionality principle. 'Don't kill civilians unless doing so achieves enough good' introduces the idea that the prohibition may be swept aside whenever the situation seems to call for it. In circumstances of war, where so much hangs on victory and where individuals constantly face life and death situations, this revised proportionality principle is likely to be as subject to subjective judgment as the original.

One reason for this has to do with the weighting of harms. Judgments about proportionality are likely to be strongly influenced by the partiality of the persons making the judgment. The deaths of enemy civilians will be seen as less terrible than the deaths of one's own troops or the loss of an opportunity for possible military gain. As a result, attacks that seem to promote victory or to spare one's own troops are likely to be seen as proportionate and, as Walzer puts it, are likely to be 'called permissible'. For this reason, the 'limited civilian immunity' rule does not escape the force of Walzer's objection to proportionality.[24]

---

23 For further discussion of proportionality, see my *Terrorism and the Ethics of War*, pp. 271–87.

24 A.P.V. Rogers describes the multiple, inconsistent perspectives from which proportionality judgments are made in 'The Principle of Proportionality', in Howard Hensel (ed.), *The Legitimate Use of Military Force* (Aldershot: Ashgate, 2008), p. 209.

Civilian Immunity with a Supreme Emergency Exception

This view begins with a very strong commitment to civilian immunity. Walzer, its best-known defender, argues that people possess a right to life and that it is wrong to attack them unless they themselves do something to forfeit that right. Soldiers forfeit their immunity by virtue of their membership in the military. As long as civilians do not engage in combat or otherwise play a direct role in carrying out a war, they retain their right to life, and others have a duty not to attack them.

Although Walzer's language strongly suggests an absolute ban on attacking civilians, he explicitly rejects this absolutist view later in his discussion. Although he criticizes proportionality and utilitarianism because they permit attacks on civilians, he believes that the prohibition on attacking civilians ceases to apply when groups are faced with extraordinary and imminent threats. In these 'supreme emergency' circumstances, the right of defence makes it permissible to attack civilians directly. Igor Primoratz (in this volume) criticizes many aspects of Walzer's view but defends a variation on this theme, arguing that civilian immunity may be overridden by 'moral disasters'.

I believe that both of these views are defective for the same reason that Walzer stressed in his argument against proportionality. In the context of war, permitting attacks on civilians in supreme emergencies or moral disasters is too permissive. The circumstances of war and violent political conflict frequently ratchet up the stakes so that persons fighting and their leaders will see their circumstances as exceptional. They will feel quite justified in calling the situation they are in a 'supreme emergency' or 'moral disaster'.[25]

It is instructive to consider the response of the US Government to the 11 September attacks. High officials saw these attacks as a supreme emergency that rendered obsolete various constraints that had been honoured (or at least paid lip-service to) in the past. The Geneva Conventions were dismissed as quaint; the taboo on torture was dismissed as an impediment to defending the United States from terrorist attacks, and the US Constitution was pushed aside to allow widespread wire-tapping, holding citizens without trial and even targeting citizens to be killed without due process of law. Yet, terrible as the events of 11 September were, they come nowhere near satisfying either Walzer's or Primoratz's criteria for circumstances that permit direct attacks on civilians.[26]

Walzer's own words, which he directed against the proportionality criterion, apply to his own view. The supreme emergency exception 'turns out to be a hard criterion to apply, for there is no ready way to establish an independent or stable

25　For detailed criticisms of Walzer's 'supreme emergency' view, see my *Terrorism and the Ethics of War*, Ch. 11 and pp. 204–8.

26　For an insightful discussion of the psychology of such judgments, see Aleksandar Pavković, 'Towards Liberation: Terrorism from a Liberation Ideology Perspective', in Tony Coady and Michael O'Keefe (eds), *Terrorism and Justice* (Melbourne: Melbourne University Press, 2002), Ch. 6.

view of the values against which the destruction of war is to be measured'.[27] In difficult circumstances, 'any act of force that contributes in a significant way to winning the war is likely to be called permissible'.[28] For these reasons, I agree with Walzer's claim that 'clearcut rules – moral fortifications' are needed, but I reject his view that these fortifications 'can be stormed' – that is, can justifiably be violated. In my view, civilian immunity is a principle that may not be overridden, even in the direst of circumstances.

The Case for Strong Civilian Immunity

Having shown that the competing candidates for rules of war all have serious difficulties, I now want to argue more directly for the view that rational, impartial people, whose aim is to promote overall human wellbeing, would support an absolute prohibition of attacks on civilians.

One immediate question about this view is 'who are civilians?' The answer is that civilians are people who are not members of the military and who play no direct role in carrying out a war or other campaign of violence. Thus, government officials who plan and carry out a war are not officially members of the military, but they are directly involved in the war and do not have civilian immunity. Examples of such non-immune civilians include, for example, people engaged in gathering intelligence that is used in planning attacks as well as 'civilian contractors' who are hired to carry out activities that in the past were carried out by soldiers. Anyone who lacks military status or direct involvement in a war effort is a civilian in the sense that supports immunity. This includes the majority of people in any country, even if they pay taxes that support a war, vote for candidates who initiate a war or give their emotional support to it.[29]

The basic justification for civilian immunity as an absolute rule is that it is the best rule for minimizing the overall amount of harm caused by warfare. An ethics of war includes both permissions and constraints. There is a permission to go to war as a means of protecting vital human interests, but the means of fighting must be constrained to prevent war from escalating so that it causes unlimited damage. While groups are permitted to engage in war to promote or defend their rights and interests, the conduct of war must be limited in order to do justice both to the partial interests of groups and to the impartial interests of human beings.[30]

---

27   Walzer, p. 129.

28   Walzer, p. 129.

29   For a defence of the innocence of ordinary citizens, see Robert Sparrow, '"Hands Up Who Wants to Die": Primoratz on Responsibility and Civilian Immunity in Wartime', *Ethical Theory and Practice*, 8 (2005): 299–319.

30   I discuss the conflict between partiality and impartiality and the way to reconcile them in 'Patriotism, War, and the Limits of Permissible Partiality', *Journal of Ethics*, 13/4 (2009): 401–22.

At the beginning of his book *Targeting Civilians in War*, Alexander Downes notes that between 43 million and 54 million civilians are estimated to have been killed in the wars of the twentieth century. Civilian deaths accounted for between 50 and 62 per cent of all twentieth-century wartime deaths.[31] More than half, then, of the century's wartime fatalities were people who were not directly involved in fighting. If we think of the traditional aim of war fighting to be the weakening of the enemy's ability to fight, we can say that millions of civilian deaths did not contribute directly to the achievement of victory.

Two facts are basic to the argument for civilian immunity. First, the total damage done to human beings when civilians are seen as legitimate targets of attack is huge. Second, this damage – unlike the damage to military forces – is unlikely to contribute to the achievement of militarily valuable objectives. For these reasons, there appears to be a utilitarian basis for the view that the ethics of war should contain two provisions: a) a prohibition that forbids deliberate attacks on civilians; and b) a rule that requires unintended, 'collateral damage' harms to civilians to be avoided when possible and minimized when they cannot be avoided. It is no accident that these are precisely the prohibitions that are found in international humanitarian law.

A second set of relevant facts concerns the fallibility of leaders, who are generally the people who decide when to go to war and how to fight. The track record of leaders is not good. In the post–World War II period, the Cold War brought with it the development of nuclear-weapons arsenals whose use would have been genuinely insane. The Cuban Missile Crisis showed how close leaders could come to nuclear conflict. Numerous wars by powers large and small have occurred and campaigns of political violence by non-state groups have added to the tally of civilians who have been killed, injured, raped and displaced. After studying how decisions about warfare are made, Fred Ikle concluded that '[i]f a statesman decides to go to war, or to reject opportunities for ending an ongoing war, he must somehow assume that fighting – or fighting on – will improve the outcome. Far too often, this assumption receives no analysis.'[32]

Many people, such as President Bush, condemn contemporary 'terrorists' for doing the unthinkable: murdering civilians. Yet, according to Alexander Downes, in wars between 1816 and 2003, almost one-third of the countries (52 in total) that were able to attack civilians did so. Often they did this out of desperation because a war was going badly. Often these were democratic rather than autocratic regimes. According to Downes, 'when liberal democratic states were involved in wars of attrition, they adopted civilian victimization strategies 81 per cent of the time'.[33] We tend to think of democratic countries as especially humane and reasonable in their policies, but Hans Morgenthau noted the increased dangers of democracy, noting that 'under conditions of democratic control, the need to marshal public

---

31   Downes, p. 1.
32   Fred Ikle, *Every War Must End* (New York: Columbia University Press, 1991), p. 2.
33   Downes, pp. 79–80.

emotions to the support of foreign policy cannot fail to impair the rationality of foreign policy itself'.[34] Downes backs this up, noting that 'statistical data tend to support the contention that democracies are more likely than non-democracies to target civilians'.[35] Only the strongest possible prohibition of such actions could ever stand a chance of preventing them.

Can an Absolute Prohibition be Justified?

Any proposal in favour of an absolute prohibition faces the challenge that reality is so complex and unpredictable that we simply cannot foresee what future dangers might emerge that would justify people in believing that virtually anything was permissible in order to prevent the greatest and most grotesque of evils. From this perspective, even if a strong prohibition of killing civilians makes sense, there remains a need to leave an opening for extraordinary responses to extraordinary threats.

This response might seem to be especially effective against the utilitarian argument I have given. An objector might say that utilitarians are the last people to deny this possibility since they see utilitarianism as especially powerful because it is responsive to facts and contingencies. Both friends and foes of utilitarianism might think that the theory is incapable of generating absolute prohibitions. This, as Richard Brandt showed, is a mistake. Although Brandt himself did not support an absolute ban on attacking civilians, he showed that a rule utilitarian will ask about any proposed rule both what its content should be and what level of stringency should be attached to it. Should it be a rule of thumb that can easily be overridden, a more stringent rule that requires compelling reasons to override it or an absolute rule that should never be overridden? In deciding on the level of stringency, a rule utilitarian will try to predict whether the non-absolute version of a rule is likely to accomplish its goal – in this case, the goal of greatly limiting the human damages caused by war. If an absolute rule is more promising than a rule that permits exceptions then the rule-utilitarian view will support the absolute rule and oppose the inclusion of justifiable exceptions.[36]

It is for this reason that a rule utilitarian will oppose rules that contain provisions such as the 'supreme emergency' and 'moral disaster' exceptions advocated by Walzer and Primoratz. These 'almost absolute' rules will succumb to the pressures of war too easily. The pressures on leaders to win wars, the strength of people's partiality for their own country or group, the active hostility that people often feel for enemy groups, the sense of desperation that frequently develops when a

34   Hans Morgenthau, *Politics Among Nations: The Struggle for Power and Peace*, 2nd edn (New York: Alfred Knopf, 1954), p. 7.

35   Downes, p. 247.

36   Brandt, pp. 26–7. I discuss Brandt's argument in *Terrorism and the Ethics of War*, pp. 195–7.

war is going badly – all of these will push national leaders towards taking a more destructive path of action. They will opt for attacking enemy civilians even if they themselves have characterized such actions – when done by others – as barbaric.

The historical record testifies to all these effects. If we are going to predict the outcome of different kinds of rules, the most plausible prediction is that only the most stringent rules stand a chance of preventing attacks on civilians in wartime. Anything less stringent will be overridden. Moreover, the people who override them will not see themselves as violating the rule against attacking civilians. Instead, they will see themselves as satisfying the criteria for being in the kind of extraordinary circumstances that justify those attacks. For these reasons, almost absolute is not good enough.

Chapter 3

Civilian Immunity as an *Almost* Absolute Moral Rule[1]

Igor Primoratz

Philosophers agree that the immunity of civilians against deadly violence in war must be the centrepiece of the *jus in bello* part of any plausible ethics of war. Unsurprisingly, they disagree about everything else concerning this immunity: about its ground, scope and stringency.

The division in ethics into consequentialist and non-consequentialist theories is replicated in the ethics of war in the division into consequentialist and non-consequentialist accounts of the morality of war. Consequentialist accounts treat civilian immunity as a rule justified by the good consequences of its adoption. It prohibits targeting a large group of humans by lethal violence and thereby helps reduce the killing, mayhem and destruction wrought by war. Non-consequentialist accounts treat it as a matter of rights and justice. Human beings have a right not to be killed or maimed; unlike soldiers, civilians have done nothing to waive or forfeit this right, and justice demands that it be respected.

Both accounts are exposed to serious queries. The consequentialist interpretation of civilian immunity – just like such interpretation of any other moral rule – seems to make it much too tenuous. Whenever the best consequences attainable under the circumstances will be attained by disregarding civilian immunity, that will be the right thing to do; civilians are made hostage to the vagaries of war, rather than provided strong protection against them. Non-consequentialist accounts of civilian immunity invite the question: is this immunity absolute? Must we always abide by it, whatever the consequences of doing so? If the answer is 'yes' then these accounts might be said to err in the opposite direction and to be just as unacceptable as the consequentialist view – albeit for a very different reason. Surely Hegel was right to warn that '*fiat justitia* should not be followed by *pereat mundus*'.[2] If the answer

---

1   This is an abridged version of a paper first published as 'Civilian Immunity, Supreme Emergency, and Moral Disaster', *The Journal of Ethics*, 15 (2011), pp. 371–86. Copyright Springer Science+Business Media B.V. 2011. Reprinted by permission.

2   G.W.F. Hegel, *Philosophy of Right*, trans. T.M. Knox (Oxford: Oxford University Press, 1965), p. 87.

is 'no', the next question for the non-consequentialist is: just what amounts to a reason weighty enough to override civilian immunity?[3]

The answer to the latter question offered by Michael Walzer in his book *Just and Unjust Wars* reads: supreme emergency. Walzer's supreme emergency argument has received considerable discussion, much of it highly critical. This chapter is a contribution to that discussion.[4] I will look into some recent critiques of Walzer's position, and go on to offer an alternative and, I hope, more convincing view.

Supreme Emergency

Walzer introduces the argument of supreme emergency in the context of presenting and elaborating his account of *jus in bello* and against the background of his analysis of 'the problem of dirty hands'; he understands the former predicament as a special, and extreme, case of the latter.

---

3   Stephen Nathanson's contribution to this volume (Chapter 2) might seem not to fit in this delineation of positions, as he seeks to establish an *absolute* prohibition of deliberate attacks on civilians by a *consequentialist* argument. My main worry about his position is this: assume, for the sake of argument, that the *rule* concerning deliberate attacks on civilians should state that such attacks are always wrong and that this rule should be announced, publicized and taught as an absolute one, because doing so will have the best consequences overall. What of exceptional *particular cases*? In a case where, atypically, refraining from deliberate attacks on civilians will *not* have the best consequences overall, there can be no *consequentialist* reason to refrain. (To be sure, this is not only a problem for Nathanson's rule-consequentialist account of civilian immunity, but one plaguing rule-consequentialism generally. See, for example, J.J.C. Smart, 'Extreme and Restricted Utilitarianism', in *Essays Metaphysical and Moral* [Oxford: Basil Blackwell, 1987], pp. 264–6.)

4   Apart from the writings discussed in this chapter, the literature includes: Alex J. Bellamy, 'Supreme Emergencies and the Protection of Non-Combatants in War', *International Affairs*, 80 (2004); Kenneth L. Brown, '"Supreme Emergency": A Critique of Michael Walzer's Moral Justification for Allied Obliteration Bombing in World War II', *Manchester College Bulletin of the Peace Studies Institute*, 13 (1983); Darrell Cole, 'Death Before Dishonor or Dishonor Before Death? Christian Just War, Terrorism, and Supreme Emergency', *Notre Dame Journal of Law, Ethics and PublicPolicy*, 16 (2002); Martin L. Cook, 'Michael Walzer's Concept of "Supreme Emergency"', *Journal of Military Ethics*, 6 (2007); Frederik Kaufman, 'Just War Theory and Killing the Innocent', in Michael W. Bough, John W. Lango and Harry van der Linden (eds), *Rethinking the Just War Tradition* (New York: State University of New York Press, 2007); Stephen E. Lammers, 'Area Bombing in World War II: The Argument of Michael Walzer', *Journal of Religious Ethics*, 11 (1983); Henry Shue, 'Liberalism: The Impossibility of Justifying Weapons of Mass Destruction', in Sohail Hashmi and Steven Lee (eds), *Ethics and Weapons of Mass Destruction* (Cambridge: Cambridge University Press, 2004); Daniel Statman, 'Moral Tragedies, Supreme Emergencies and National-Defense', *Journal of Applied Philosophy*, 23 (2006); Daniel Statman, 'Supreme Emergencies Revisited', *Ethics*, 117 (2006–07); Christopher Toner, 'Just War and the Supreme Emergency Exemption', *Philosophical Quarterly*, 55 (2005).

We sometimes face a situation where different moral requirements pull us in opposite directions and we can act as required by one only at the price of going against the other. This is sometimes not very difficult to resolve, as one moral requirement can have more weight than the other, whether in general or at least in the particular case. When we decide accordingly, we are not left with a sense of great unease or even guilt. But sometimes the conflict is deep and vexing: it presents us with a moral dilemma, defined by Walzer as 'a situation where [one] must choose between two courses of action both of which it would be wrong for [one] to undertake'.[5] We face such a dilemma whenever we can prevent something extremely bad from happening only by breaking a stringent moral rule. People in all walks of life might have to deal with such a predicament, but those in politics are particularly likely to have to do so. As thinkers such as Machiavelli, Weber and Sartre have pointed out, one cannot govern 'innocently' – at least not successfully and for long. Walzer concurs, and adds that we would not want to be governed by those whose primary concern was to keep their hands 'clean' by strict adherence to moral rules, rather than to safeguard and promote the common good. In politics

> sometimes it is right to try to succeed, and then it must also be right to get one's hands dirty. But one's hands get dirty from doing what it is wrong to do. And how can it be wrong to do what is right? Or, how can we get our hands dirty by doing what we ought to do?[6]

This looks paradoxical, but Walzer embraces the apparent paradox: a political leader facing such a quandary should indeed break the moral rule in order to prevent a development that would be extremely detrimental to the community. Their action will be wrong, in that it will be a breach of a stringent moral rule, and it will also be right, in that it will stave off the threat to the community. It will leave them with dirty hands and a sense of guilt, yet they ought to do it; if they do not, they will fail to live up to the duties of their office.

Quandaries of this sort are particularly dramatic in wartime. Such was the predicament Britain seemed to be facing in early 1942. The Government feared an impending defeat; it also feared that there was nothing its military could do about it, at least as long as they were fighting 'clean'. Moreover, Britain's defeat was not going to be yet another defeat of one country by another, entailing such things as loss of some territory, war reparations, political concessions, and the like. Britain was perceived as the only remaining obstacle to the subjugation of most of Europe by the Nazis. Now the rule of the Nazis over most of Europe would have meant, as Churchill put it, 'an age of barbaric violence'.[7] It would have involved

---

5   Michael Walzer, 'Political Action: The Problem of Dirty Hands', *Philosophy and Public Affairs*, 2 (1972–73): 160.

6   Ibid., p. 164.

7   Quoted in Michael Walzer, *Just and Unjust Wars: A Moral Argument with Historical Illustrations*, 3rd edn (New York: Basic Books, 2000), p. 245.

extermination of some peoples and something very much like enslavement of others. In Walzer's words, 'Nazism was an ultimate threat to everything decent in our lives, an ideology and a practice of domination so murderous, so degrading even to those who might survive, that the consequences of its final victory were literally beyond calculation, immeasurably awful'. It was 'evil objectified in the world ... in a form so potent and apparent that there could never have been anything to do but fight against it'.[8]

Thus Britain was thought to be facing what Walzer (borrowing the term from Churchill) calls a 'supreme emergency': an a) imminent threat of b) something utterly unthinkable from a moral point of view – a moral catastrophe. In such an emergency, and in such an emergency only, we may act in breach of such a basic and weighty moral rule as that of civilian immunity, if that is the only way we can hope to prevent the catastrophe. Accordingly, Churchill's government decided that Britain would no longer fight 'clean' and unleashed its air force on the civilian population of Germany. The onslaught continued almost to the last days of the war. Most of that killing and destruction cannot be defended by this line of argument, since it soon became obvious that Germany was not going to win the war. But in its first stage, in Walzer's judgment, the terror bombing of Germany was morally justified (albeit a crime too). It was morally justified as the only possible response to the supreme emergency Britain was facing.

What if it is only one country, rather than many, that is facing a threat of enslavement or extermination? Walzer holds that the argument of supreme emergency would still apply. He writes:

> Can soldiers and statesmen override the rights of innocent people for the sake of their own political community? I am inclined to answer the question affirmatively, though not without hesitation and worry ... It is possible to live in a world where individuals are sometimes murdered, but a world where entire peoples are sometimes massacred is literally unbearable. For the survival and freedom of political communities – whose members share a way of life, developed by their ancestors, to be passed on to their children – are the highest values of international society. Nazism challenged these values on a grand scale, but challenges more narrowly conceived, *if they are of the same kind*, have similar moral consequences.[9]

Walzer ends his chapter on supreme emergency by emphasizing that the rules of war in general, and the principle of civilian immunity in particular, may not be breached in the face of defeat *simpliciter*, but only in the face of defeat 'likely to bring disaster to a political community'.[10]

---

8   Ibid., p. 253.
9   Ibid., p. 254.
10 Ibid., p. 268.

Some Recent Criticisms of the Supreme Emergency View

Walzer's statement of just war theory has generated much critical discussion, which shows no signs of abating. The issue of supreme emergency looms large in this discussion. In this section, I review and comment on some recent criticisms of Walzer's position on the matter. This should prepare the ground for presenting an alternative view of the limits of civilian immunity in the next section.

Walzer portrays supreme emergency as paradoxical; Brian Orend seeks to remove the paradox. In such an emergency we have two options, each involving a 'serious moral violation', and we must choose one. In Orend's view, this predicament is best described as a 'moral blind alley' or 'moral tragedy'. Whatever we do will be wrong. Therefore we are beyond morality; morality can offer no guidance and no justification. Yet we must choose. Moreover, the options we face in supreme emergencies are matters of life and death; therefore our choice will inevitably be determined by the irresistible pull of survival and we will be forced to use deadly violence against innocent people as the way to survival. Accordingly, 'while wrong, [our] actions may nevertheless be excused on grounds of the most extreme duress'.[11]

Orend deploys an interpersonal analogy. A attacks B in an attempt to murder him and B seeks to save his life by using C, an innocent bystander, as a human shield. Our first response to this would be to say that B acted as 'a selfish and despicable coward'. Yet, upon reflection, we might come to understand that B made a 'desperate choice' in the face of an extremely terrifying threat. Thus our more considered moral judgment of B and B's action might be more discerning and less harsh:

> We might be willing to excuse B's actions, on grounds that the terrible duress and mortal fear operative on him in the situation drove him to make the terrible choice he did. Like any animal filled with mortal terror, he desperately reached out for any means necessary to stave off death. This doesn't make his choice *right* or morally justifiable; it makes it *understandable* and, depending on the exact circumstances, *excusable* from criticism or punishment. It will be excusable if we determine that the pressure … was so extreme that B acted more out of animal instinct than out of a morally culpable decision-making capacity. We would say … that *he was forced to do something terribly wrong.*[12]

The same applies to those who act on behalf of a polity that is facing a supreme emergency. In such a plight, Orend writes, 'as a matter of fact any country … will do whatever it can to prevail. The animal instincts are going to kick in, just

---

11   Brian Orend, *Michael Walzer on War and Justice* (Montreal: McGill–Queen's University Press, 2001), p. 133.

12   Brian Orend, 'Is there a Supreme Emergency Exemption?', in Mark Evans (ed.), *Just War Theory: A Reappraisal* (Edinburgh: Edinburgh University Press, 2005), p. 144.

as in our inter-personal analogy.'[13] Like Walzer, Orend too has a single historical example – that of terror bombing of German cities by the Royal Air Force.

The view of supreme emergency as a moral tragedy that takes us beyond the realm of morality, into a Hobbesian struggle for survival in which we resort to *any* means whatsoever, eliminates all appearance of paradox.

> Walzer suggests that, in a supreme emergency, you have a right to do wrong, and/or a duty to violate duty, whereas no such claims are here made, resulting in a more coherent understanding. You don't have the right to do wrong, or a duty to violate duty; if you do wrong, you do wrong, even under the pressure of supreme emergency conditions.[14]

Some of Walzer's wordings seem deliberately paradoxical, and the sense of paradox is reinforced when he portrays supreme emergency as a case of a 'dirty hands' conundrum.[15] But, as I will argue in the next section, supreme emergency can be sufficiently described without any reference to the contentious issue of dirty hands, a right to do wrong or a duty to violate duty.

The main question, though, is whether Orend's understanding of supreme emergency is superior to that of Walzer's. Walzer speaks of a difficult *moral* conflict, in which extremely weighty consequential considerations lead the agent to decide against extremely weighty deontological considerations. The right decision in such a case makes one's action morally *justified*, all things considered. Orend sees the same predicament as a conflict *beyond morality*, in which an irresistible survival instinct prevents the agent from settling the issue by rational moral thinking and makes them decide under duress. Once they do, their action cannot be justified – it is morally wrong – but they can be *excused* for having performed it.

Some situations in war fit this description. A soldier on the battlefield might fall into the grip of the survival instinct to the extent that they can no longer think rationally or act in a significantly voluntary way and, say, kill some civilians in order to save their own life. But supreme emergency is not something that faces a single soldier on the battlefield. It is rather a problem facing a nation at war or, more accurately, those who lead the nation and decide on its behalf whether to go to war and how to fight it. Again, we can imagine a case where a nation's leaders find themselves under duress in some Dr Strangelove-type situation. But that sort of thing hardly ever happens. What *is* likely to happen is that the option to resort to intentional large-scale killing of enemy civilians is discussed in high political and military committees, in conditions reasonably conducive to rational thinking, on the assumption that such thinking will be engaged in in appropriate detail and without undue haste, and that the pros and cons of that option will be carefully

---

13   Ibid., p. 149.
14   Ibid.
15   Walzer, *Just and Unjust Wars*, pp. 323–5.

assessed and weighed against alternatives. Should a political or military leader involved show signs of thinking, feeling or acting 'like [an] animal filled with mortal terror', they would be excused from the deliberations, rather than allowed to help determine their outcome. Both Walzer and Orend offer the same historical example of deliberate killing of a large number of enemy civilians justified, or excused, by a supreme emergency: that of the bombing of German cities in World War II. The decision-making process that led to that campaign is well documented, not least in the voluminous writings of the person who bears the greatest part of the overall responsibility for it: Prime Minister Winston Churchill. We know that its participants were not 'filled with mortal terror' and did not 'act out of animal instinct', but rather exercised their 'morally culpable decision-making capacity'.

There is one important point of concurrence between Orend and Walzer: both – albeit for different reasons – refuse to condemn morally those who in a supreme emergency resort to large-scale killing of civilians. Other critics of Walzer reach a different conclusion: that civilian immunity must be respected even in such an emergency and that those who fail to do so are to be morally condemned.

One such critic is C.A.J. Coady, who takes Walzer to task for his bias in favour of the state. Several critics have highlighted a certain degree of statism in Walzer's ethics of war in both its prongs. In Walzer's account of *jus ad bellum*, it comes to the fore in particular in his restrictive view of the legitimacy of military intervention, based on an argument about the 'fit' between the state and the political community's traditions and way of life. In his account of *jus in bello*, it is apparent in his restrictive view of the availability of the supreme emergency argument to various agents, which is the question Coady focuses on. Walzer presents this argument in his *Just and Unjust Wars*, which for the most part deals with war between states; and he discusses it solely in that context, as an option the political and military leaders of a state might have to consider. In his discussion of non-state terrorism in that book and in a later essay, titled 'Terrorism: A Critique of Excuses', supreme emergency is never mentioned. Walzer argues that non-state terrorism can never be justified or excused. If it is engaged in in a liberal and democratic state, it is not justified because it is not necessary: there are ample opportunities and venues for voicing and addressing grievances without recourse to violence. If employed in the struggle against a totalitarian state, it is not justified because it is bound to fail; totalitarian states are 'immune' to resistance of any kind, including terrorism.[16] And yet the sole historical instance of wholesale deliberate killing of civilians Walzer considers justified as a response to supreme emergency – the bombing of

---

16   When reprinting the essay in a recent book, Walzer inserted a bracketed remark on this. His amended view is that non-state terrorism might be justified in a supreme emergency, but only in the face of threat of genocide. As a matter of fact, though, 'this kind of a threat has not been present in any of the recent cases of terrorist activity. Terrorism has not been a means of avoiding disaster but of reaching for political success.' Michael Walzer, 'Terrorism: A Critique of Excuses', in *Arguing About War* (New Haven, Conn., and London: Yale University Press, 2004), p. 54.

German cities in World War II – is a case of (state) terrorism employed against a totalitarian state. 'Why', asks Coady, 'should states enjoy the supreme emergency license when other groups do not?'[17] To reply, as Walzer does, that the 'survival and freedom of political communities' are 'the highest values of international society' will not do, if this society is understood – as it is in Walzer's account – as comprising established and internationally recognized political communities.

Some insurgent organizations, too, can reasonably claim to be acting on behalf of political communities. In certain extreme circumstances, such an organization might mount a supreme emergency argument in favour of resort to terrorism. Then again, 'why not allow that the [supreme emergency] exemption can apply to huge corporations, the existence of which is central to the lives and livelihoods of so many? Or ... to individuals when they are really against the wall?'[18] So long as he has produced no good argument for restricting the exemption to states, Walzer seems bound in consistency to make it available to non-state agents as well. But if he did, that would compromise the 'rarity value' of the exemption:

> As the name suggests, the supreme emergency story ... gets its persuasiveness from the idea that its disruptive power to override profound moral prohibitions is available only in the rarest of circumstances. Any broadening of the reach of these circumstances tends to reduce the rarity value of the exemption and hence increase the oddity of the idea that it can be right to do what is morally wrong... The more we move in this direction, the more the currency of supreme emergency is devalued.[19]

Thus we are facing a choice: we can either concede that the supreme emergency exemption applies more generally than Walzer allows – to states, but also to a range of non-state agents – or decide that it applies to no-one and that civilian immunity is an absolute moral rule. Coady opts for the latter choice: 'My own conviction is that we surely do better to condemn the resort to terrorism outright with no leeway for exemptions, be they for states, revolutionaries, or religious and ideological zealots of any persuasion.'[20]

Now Coady is clearly right as far as Walzer's bias in favour of the state is concerned. A stateless people and an organization fighting on its behalf should in principle be as entitled as an established and recognized state to consider resorting to deliberate attacks on civilians when facing a supreme emergency. Corporations and individuals, on the other hand, seem to be in a different position in this respect. It might yet be possible to argue for restricting the exemption to the former and denying it to the latter without inconsistency and while preserving its rarity value.

---

17   C.A.J. Coady, 'Terrorism, Morality, and Supreme Emergency', *Ethics*, 114 (2003–04), p. 784.

18   Ibid., p. 787.

19   Ibid.

20   Ibid., p. 789.

Stephen Nathanson, too, takes a critical look at Walzer's position and reaches the conclusion that the supreme emergency argument should not be allowed to undermine our absolute commitment to civilian immunity and consequent rejection of all terrorism. Nathanson first takes a close look at the ways in which Walzer describes such an emergency. This brings to the fore two different conceptions of supreme emergency: a broad and, to a significant degree, subjective conception, and a specific and objective one. When focusing on the Nazi threat, Walzer uses a broad brush and lays on highly emotional colours: Nazism posed a threat to civilized values, to civilization itself, to 'everything decent in our lives', and this threat properly evoked responses such as abhorrence and horror. When looking beyond that particular case, Walzer portrays supreme emergency as 'a threat of enslavement or extermination directed at a single nation'.

The first, broad and subjective version of supreme emergency is much too flexible and open-ended to provide the kind of ethical guidance we expect of such a criterion. Walzer focuses on World War II and highlights Nazi atrocities, while placing the atrocities committed by the Japanese armed forces in the same war at a lower point on the atrocity scale, where they fall short of supreme emergency. Yet the latter atrocities, too, were systematic and large scale and, when portrayed vividly and in detail, tend to evoke the same emotional response as those committed by the Nazis. They, too, strike us as incompatible with civilized values and a threat to 'everything decent' in our lives. Vivid and detailed accounts by survivors of the terror bombing of German and Japanese cities in that war will also evoke a response of horror and abhorrence in a decent person. Moreover,

> if people are subjected to brutal rule over many years and cannot live normal, secure lives, they are likely to see their own situation as a supreme emergency for them ... It is not clear that Walzer could show why these people are mistaken since any form of extended oppression is a threat to civilized values.[21]

Should we, then, discard the first, broad and subjective approach to supreme emergency and adopt the second, specific and objective conception, according to which only the prospect of extermination or enslavement of a nation amounts to such an emergency? Nathanson finds this version of the supreme emergency criterion clear enough, but faults it for two reasons. First, it does not support Walzer's account of the British predicament at the early stage of war, since Britain was not facing such a threat. Second, it is likely to be rejected as too demanding by people facing the threat of lesser, but still huge disasters. Generally, Nathanson submits, people are likely to perceive any urgent, threatening situation as a supreme emergency:

---

21 Stephen Nathanson, 'Terrorism, Supreme Emergency, and Noncombatant Immunity: A Critique of Michael Walzer's Ethics of War', *Iyyun: The Jerusalem Philosophical Quarterly*, 55 (2006): 22.

Consider the American reaction to the September 11 attacks. Though serious and frightening, these come nowhere near satisfying Walzer's criterion, and yet many people would find the expression 'supreme emergency' quite apt to describe the post–September 11 situation. They feel that their way of life is threatened, that their civilization is threatened, that any means of combating future acts of terrorism are justified. Likewise, supporters of Bin Laden and the September 11 attackers probably see both the United States and Western culture generally as 'an ultimate threat to everything decent' in *their* lives.[22]

The supreme emergency criterion, then, does not provide clear and reliable ethical guidance. Those who adopt it are stepping on a very slippery slope and are liable to end up violating civilian immunity in many cases in which Walzer himself would not condone doing so. Therefore we should rather endorse this immunity as an absolute rule of morality.

Now the first, broad understanding of supreme emergency is indeed unacceptably subjective. If it were all we had to go by, such emergency would be in the eye of the beholder. On the other hand, Nathanson's objections to the narrow conception are not very damaging. That conception might not apply to the historical illustration of supreme emergency Walzer offers – the terror bombing of German cities in World War II – but then so much the worse for that particular illustration.[23] People facing a major crisis that falls short of extermination or enslavement are indeed liable to feel, and claim, that theirs is a supreme emergency too. But any moral rule can be misunderstood, misinterpreted and misapplied. I will come back later to the slippery slope argument Nathanson grounds on his second point.

I am thus in agreement with some of Coady's and Nathanson's objections to Walzer's supreme emergency view, but cannot endorse others, and want to resist their conclusion that civilian immunity must be upheld as an absolute moral rule. I will now propose a position that is structurally similar to Walzer's view, but is not exposed to the objections of bias in favour of the state, loss of the rarity value of the exemption, its vagueness and the slippery slope. I propose to term this position the moral disaster view.

---

22   Ibid., pp. 23–4.

23   Elsewhere I have argued that the bombing campaign cannot be morally justified by a supreme emergency or, indeed, by any other argument –that it was an utterly indefensible and unmitigated atrocity that deeply compromised the just cause for which the Allies were fighting. See 'Can the Bombing Be Morally Justified?', in Igor Primoratz (ed.), *Terror From the Sky: The Bombing of German Cities in World War II* (Oxford and New York: Berghahn Books, 2010).

Moral Disaster

Let me retrace some of my steps. Just what kind of choice is at issue?

Put in the most general terms, it is a choice between two *prima facie* moral requirements, both applying to the circumstances we find ourselves in, but pulling us in opposite directions. We cannot act in accordance with one without at the same time going against the other, and thereby, in that respect, doing something wrong. Yet that is exactly what we must do; there is no third option. This is a case of moral conflict. Walzer, however, calls this a moral dilemma; but his definition of 'moral dilemma', quoted in the first section above, although perhaps in tune with everyday usage, is much too wide for the purposes of philosophical discussion. Not every moral conflict is a moral dilemma; the latter term is better reserved for a certain type of such conflict. In any case of moral conflict, whatever we do, we do something that is in a certain respect wrong. But in some such cases the two courses of action are not equally wrong – one is more so than the other, whether in general or only in that particular case. Accordingly, there is a solution to the conflict: we ought to choose the other course of action. When we do that, we do what, all things considered, we ought to do. But this does not wipe out the *prima facie* wrongness of our action as a violation of the moral requirement that has been overridden; that accounts for the conceptual room and the moral call for awareness of the moral price paid and regret that it had to be paid. This is moral conflict *simpliciter*.[24]

Sometimes, however, the conflicting moral requirements are equally weighty, the two possible courses of action equally wrong. There is no solution to the conflict, nothing that, in the end, we ought to choose. This is a moral dilemma, as the term is usually used in philosophy.[25] In this sense, cases that Walzer presents and discusses as instances of dirty hands, including that of supreme emergency, are not moral dilemmas, but rather instances of moral conflict *simpliciter*.

Moreover, it is not clear just what is gained by portraying a case of supreme emergency as one of dirty hands. Walzer's discussion of the dirty-hands problem, seminal though it is, fails to tell us what is *distinctive* about the problem: what distinguishes it from any case of very serious moral conflict – that is, moral conflict in which the conflicting moral requirements are very weighty indeed. None of the possibilities suggested by Walzer's discussion   conflict between public and private morality or between role morality and universal moral requirements or between deontological and consequential considerations – seems to capture that. Some progress has been made in an essay by Stephen de Wijze, who argues that cases of dirty hands are those of very serious moral conflict in which our choice is forced by the circumstances created by an immoral person or persons, so that

---

24   See W.D. Ross, *The Right and the Good*, ed. Philip Stratton-Lake (Oxford: Oxford University Press, 2002), Ch. II.

25   See Walter Sinnott-Armstrong, *Moral Dilemmas* (Oxford: Basil Blackwell, 1988), Ch. 1.

we end up collaborating with them, furthering their evil project.[26] In this sense, however, a supreme emergency is *not* an instance of dirty hands.

What is it, then? Rather than wade any further into ethical theory and try for a general account of supreme emergency, I will stay within the bounds of the ethics of war and focus on the rule of civilian immunity. Just what would it take for us to be justified in overriding this immunity and engaging in deliberate large-scale onslaught on civilians?

A careful reading of Walzer's book and his more recent essay 'Emergency Ethics' shows that, although he promises a 'touchstone against which arguments about extremity might be judged',[27] what he offers under the heading of supreme emergency is actually a range of answers to this question. First, at one end, we find Walzer speaking of a crisis in which morality itself seems to be at stake. How, he asks, 'can we, with our principles and prohibitions, stand by and watch the destruction of the moral world in which those principles and prohibitions have their hold?' In such a crisis, 'our deepest values are radically at risk' and the prospect we are facing 'devalues morality itself and leaves us free to do whatever is militarily necessary to avoid [it]'.[28] Second, there is the prospect that was facing Great Britain and much of Europe in the early stages of World War II: that of entering an age of barbaric violence, in which entire peoples are exterminated or enslaved. The third point on this scale of enormity is the prospect of extermination or enslavement facing a single nation. Finally, there is a threat to 'the survival and freedom of a political community'.

We should put both the first and the last understanding of supreme emergency to one side. I find the idea of a threat to 'morality itself' unintelligible, because I cannot envisage human existence, however damaged and constrained, bereft of all morality. An essential part of being human is being capable of, and given to, moral deliberation and action. Human beings demonstrate this even in the most trying circumstances; there is, for example, ample evidence that even in Nazi and Soviet camps, both inmates and guards engaged in moral thinking and acted accordingly.

The notion of a threat to 'survival and freedom' of a political community, on the other hand, is unhelpful, because it is ambiguous. In one sense, it is a threat of extermination or enslavement of its people. This takes us back to the third understanding of supreme emergency to be found in Walzer. In another sense, it is a threat to political independence of a state. This kind of threat, however, can hardly have the moral weight required by Walzer's supreme emergency argument. A state might or might not have moral legitimacy. If it does not, its demise might well be morally preferable to its continued existence. But even if it does, its loss of political independence, however deplorable, surely does not amount to the loss of

---

26   See Stephen de Wijze, 'Dirty Hands: Doing Wrong to do Right', in Igor Primoratz (ed.), *Politics and Morality* (Basingstoke and New York: Palgrave Macmillan, 2007).

27   Walzer, *Just and Unjust Wars*, p. 253.

28   Walzer, 'Emergency Ethics', in *Arguing About War*, pp. 37, 40.

'everything decent in our lives' – something that must be staved off by means of the wholesale killing and maiming of civilians.

We are left, then, with extermination or enslavement of entire peoples. If such a prospect facing a single people is enough to put onslaught on enemy civilians on the agenda, the same prospect facing a number of peoples will provide an even more compelling reason to do so. The expression 'extermination or enslavement' needs to be unpacked, however, for the two differ in important respects. First, it is clear what 'extermination' of a people amounts to, whereas 'enslavement' can refer to different things: the status of slaves in the ancient world, the fate the Nazis had in store for the 'racially inferior' peoples of Eastern Europe or a less extreme type of totalitarian oppression (as in the Cold War phrase 'the enslaved nations of Eastern Europe'). Any such fate – appalling as it is – would still be seen as preferable to extermination. Second, extermination, once perpetrated, cannot be reversed, while those enslaved (in any sense of the word) can always hope to be set free. Enslavement of a people, then, is not quite in the same class of moral enormity as extermination; nor does it have the finality that defines the latter.

I believe that extermination of a people amounts to a moral disaster and that its prospect may put deliberate killing of civilians on the agenda. But if so, why not the same prospect facing a smaller group? Why not extend the same moral exemption to a single individual who is about to be murdered and could save their life by using an innocent bystander as a human shield? Part of the answer is: both individual and mass murder is *murder*, but the difference in scale between the two surely has considerable moral significance. Part of the answer is the moral import of the continued existence of a large and comprehensive community such as a people – that is, the community that provides the framework and resources for human life in all its aspects, and relates the life of the individual to a collective past remembered and a collective future hoped for. Walzer puts this point well. He cites Burke's famous portrayal of the political community as a partnership between the living, the dead and those yet to be born and goes on to say:

> This commitment to continuity across generations is a very powerful feature of human life, and it is embodied in the community. When our community is threatened, not just in its present territorial extension or governmental structure or prestige or honor, but in what we might think of as its *ongoingness*, then we face a loss that is greater than any we can imagine, except for the destruction of humanity itself. We face moral as well as physical extinction, the end of a way of life as well as of a set of particular lives, the disappearance of people like us. And it is then that we may be driven to break through the moral limits that people like us normally attend to and respect.[29]

However, a people can be threatened in its 'ongoingness' in a way that falls short of extermination, but might be no less effective: by being ethnically cleansed

---

29   Ibid., p. 43.

from its land. Strangely enough, Walzer never adverts to this. A people needs a homeland, in which it can evolve and maintain its way of life, its traditions and cultural and political institutions. Uprooting a people from its land puts an end to its 'ongoingness' almost as effectively as does its extermination. Indeed, the two are closely related: more often than not, those seeking to annex another people's land, but not its inhabitants, carry out massacres with a view of terrorizing those who survive into fleeing. But while ethnic cleansing is by definition carried out by means of violence, this violence need not reach wholesale extermination of a people. Therefore ethnic cleansing cannot be subsumed under extermination, but constitutes a moral disaster in its own right.

The moral disaster position, then, is structurally similar to that of supreme emergency. Both uphold civilian immunity as an extremely weighty moral rule, which expresses the demands of justice, as it applies in wartime, and determines the rights of civilians. Both also concede that this immunity may be overridden *in extremis* – that is, when extremely weighty consequential considerations enjoin that it give way. But the idea of moral disaster differs from that of supreme emergency in its contents and scope. While supreme emergency ranges from 'threats to morality itself' to threats to political independence of a state, moral disaster includes only extermination and ethnic cleansing of an entire people from its land.

The moral disaster view refers to peoples, rather than states or political communities; therefore it cannot be charged with pro-state bias. Nor is it exposed to the charge of being vague and overly inclusive, for its crucial terms are, I believe, sufficiently clear. While 'genocide' is a legal term whose definition is a matter of some disagreement, 'extermination' is an ordinary language word, but nonetheless quite unequivocal. So is the phrase 'extermination of a people'. 'Ethnic cleansing' is by now a legal term. It is also used in ordinary discourse – much too often in loose and sometimes outright irresponsible ways. But that is not to say that it cannot be properly defined. I find the following definition, offered by Bosnian legal scholar Dražen Petrović, quite helpful: 'Ethnic cleansing is a well-defined policy of a particular group of persons to systematically eliminate another group from a given territory on the basis of religious, ethnic or national origin. Such a policy involves violence and is very often connected with military operations.'[30]

By restricting the notion of moral disaster to extermination or ethnic cleansing of entire peoples – two wrongs that, in view of their enormity *and* finality, constitute a category apart – the present view goes a long way in preserving the rarity value of the exemption it proffers.

Its rarity value is further ensured by attending to an issue that Walzer deals with only very briefly and which has been completely neglected by his critics. The *meaning* of 'supreme emergency' is defined by two criteria: the nature of the danger and its imminence. But for such an emergency to amount to a *justification* of deliberate large-scale attacks on civilians, a third condition must be met: such

---

30   Dražen Petrović, 'Ethnic Cleansing – An Attempt at Methodology', *European Journal of International Law*, 5 (1994): 351.

attacks must be the way, and the only way, of staving off the danger. Just how certain must we be of that? One might argue that when *in extremis*, we cannot apply stringent epistemic standards in deciding how to cope; indeed, if we cannot really know what will work, we must take our chances with what might. This is Walzer's view. In such a predicament, he argues, there can be no certainty. Nor is it a matter of calculating probabilities, for there is no method of quantifying them. What we can, and must, do is study the situation closely, take the best available advice and then 'wager' the 'determinate crime' of large-scale killing and maiming of civilians against the 'immeasurable evil' that is otherwise in store for us. 'There is no option; the risk otherwise is too great.'[31]

I do not accept this position. It highlights the enormity of the threat, while failing to give due weight to the enormity of the means proposed for fending off the threat – the enormity of deliberately killing and maiming innocent people. When that is taken into account, the conclusion should rather be that even *in extremis*, if deliberate onslaught on civilians is to be justified, the reasons for believing that it will work and that nothing else will must be very strong indeed. If we lack such reasons, we must desist. Even in a desperate plight, we should not 'wager' with the lives of people who are enemy civilians, but *innocent* civilians nonetheless.

In a recent reassessment of civilian immunity in just war theory, Frederik Kaufman writes: 'Just shy of absolutism, the supreme emergency is a threshold view; it requires that we refrain from intentionally killing innocent people until the costs of doing so become too high plausibly to do anything else.'[32] I have sought to show that, as a characterization of the supreme emergency view, this is only half true. That view is, indeed, a threshold view; but because the threshold it sets is neither clear enough nor high enough, it is not *just* shy, but rather *well* shy of absolutism. The moral disaster view *is* just shy of absolutism: it maintains that deliberate killing and maiming of civilians in war are *almost* absolutely wrong.

Is the moral disaster view vulnerable to the slippery slope objection? If we allow *any* departure from civilian immunity, do we not make a dent in the prohibition that is likely to become ever wider? Once the rule is no longer absolute, even if some departures from it are justified, there are likely to be others, which are not. The exemption will lend itself to misapplications – both those made in good faith, as a result of mistaken beliefs, and those not so made.

I do not think this type of argument can be assessed in the abstract. Its force rather varies with the circumstances in which it is deployed. In general, it seems that, other things being equal, slippery slope arguments become less convincing as the cost of abiding by the rule at issue becomes higher. Thus in some cases a slippery slope argument might carry great weight, while in others its force might be doubtful. Indeed, in truly extreme cases, such an argument might no longer seem to the point.

---

31 Walzer, *Just and Unjust Wars*, p. 260.
32 Frederik Kaufman, 'Just War Theory and Killing the Innocent', p. 105.

Now, think of a people facing the prospect of extermination, or of being ethnically cleansed from its land, and unable to defend itself against an overwhelmingly stronger enemy while fighting in accordance with *jus in bello*. Suppose we said to them: 'Granted, what you are facing is an imminent threat of a true moral disaster. Granted, the only way of preventing the disaster is by breaching the rule of civilian immunity and attacking enemy civilians. But you must not do that. For if you do, that will make a dent in the rule, and that, in turn, will make possible, and indeed likely, other, unjustified breaches.' Would that be a good moral reason for them to acquiesce in their fate?

There is one more concern I need to address. In seeking to construct a position structurally similar to Walzer's supreme emergency, but much more restrictive, I have argued that only an imminent threat of extermination or ethnic cleansing of an entire people from its land amounts to a moral disaster that may justify us in considering deliberate attacks on civilians as a way of coping with the threat. It might be objected that this position is indeed tighter than Walzer's, but is still dangerously vague. The source of its vagueness is largely the word 'entire'; does it mean, literally, every single member of the threatened people, or does it allow for something short of that and, in that case, where is the line to be drawn? Moreover, a degree of vagueness lurks in the term 'people'; just what is a people and which large human groups qualify?

Part of my reply is the general point made by Aristotle and echoed by many others since:

> Our discussion will be adequate if it has as much clearness as the subject-matter admits of, for precision is not to be sought for alike in all discussions, any more than in all the products of the crafts … It is the mark of an educated man to look for precision in each class of things just so far as the nature of the subject admits.[33]

Now ethics does not always admit of drawing hard and fast lines. My position will not be readily applicable in each and every instance; there will be borderline cases. Furthermore, when facing such cases, we are not left without a clue. The course of action we are considering is one of the worst atrocities human beings can perpetrate: deliberate killing and maiming of innocent civilians. Therefore our approach must be one of restraint. In view of the enormity of what we are considering doing, we may decide to do it only if our predicament is clearly that of moral disaster, rather than a borderline case of such disaster. When in doubt, we must desist.

---

33   Aristotle, *The Nicomachean Ethics*, trans. David Ross (London: Oxford University Press, 1963), 1094b, pp. 2–3.

Chapter 4
Collateral Damage:
Intending Evil and Doing Evil

Dean Cocking

Introduction

Recently a terrible case of child sexual abuse was widely reported in the media. The parents of an eight-year-old boy – both mother and father – had been performing sexual acts on their son. Each had sexual intercourse with him and performed sex acts in front of him and they had taken pictures of their abuse for dissemination online. When caught, these people defended their behaviour as providing sexual education to their son. They claimed not to have *intended* any abuse. Rather, they intended only to educate the boy.

So what do we make of these claims? Might the abuse to their son be altogether unintended? Could these parents have intended sexual relations with their son as their means to the goal of his sexual education and been blind altogether to the harm and abuse involved? Might the abuse, while not directly intended, nevertheless be foreseen and so indirectly intended – that is, collateral damage? Perhaps they saw some harm and abuse to their son but nevertheless were motivated to provide him with sexual education by having sex with him and thought their goal justified the levels of harm and abuse they foresaw.

What a person intends, of course, is not simply 'up to them'. They might, for example, be lying or deluded about their intentions. The content of what a person, say, directly intends, either as a means or an end, is given by those beliefs they have about means and ends that motivate their action. However we make judgments about what to believe is true concerning the content of a person's intentions – that is, about what they believe and are motivated by. And these judgments are guided by what we think is plausible to believe about the person themselves and about the circumstances in which they act.

So, for instance, absent any compelling evidence about these 'parents' themselves thinking this way or being led to do so by their surrounding milieu, say, because of their involvement in some bizarre cult, we will judge that they are not true believers of their claim about how to provide sexual education for one's children. We will judge that they are spinning an especially absurd and self-serving fabrication to provide cover for their pursuit of their own sexual pleasure by having sex with their son. And even if they are, say, longstanding members of some bizarre cult that preaches a positive spin on child abuse and we do believe these people might well be in the grip of some such beliefs, we might nevertheless still judge that an absurd self-serving fabrication is going on in order to provide much needed cover for the pursuit of their own sexual pleasure.

But even if these things are right, these people still need not and plausibly did not intend abuse to their son. First, they need not and very likely did not *directly* intend the abuse – that is, as their means, since it was the having of sexual relations with their son they intended as their means.[1] The abuse resulting on account of, or that is a constitutive part of, their having sex with their son need not play any means role in securing their goal of their own sexual pleasure. If abuse to their son was not a result or part of their having sex with him, this, most likely, would not have rendered their having sex with him any less a means to their goal of securing their own sexual pleasure.

Second, these parents also might well not have even *indirectly* intended their abuse – that is, foreseen that abuse to their child was a result or part of what they were doing. Even if they recognized some pain and distress, they might nevertheless have not seen it as abuse. They might have been motivated by their beliefs about having sex with their son bringing them pleasure, but they might have understood the effects for their son of their doing so in more neutral, even positive, terms than that it was abuse. Perhaps they thought he mostly liked their sexual relations or that it was mostly doing him good and so did not identify the pain and distress as abuse. And third, even if they did identify some of the pain and distress under descriptions involving recognition of the abuse, they might still have thought the abuse was proportional either to the benefit for their son or to their own sexual pleasure.

In short, these evildoers almost certainly did not directly intend their abuse, might well have not even indirectly intended their abuse and even if they did indirectly intend their abuse might well have minimized it and thought it an acceptable cost within their overall plan.

At this point, I suspect most of us focused on the terrible nature of the abuse and the parents' responsibility for it will say: 'So what!' The fact that they might not have intended their abuse, even indirectly, or that they might have minimized their abuse hardly does minimize the abuse or their responsibility for it. It is appalling that they could do such evil and be guided – indeed enabled – to do so by relatively neutral or even positive descriptions of what they were up to. And even if their inclusion in and guidance from some shocking cult perverted and obscured the moral realities of their conduct, they need not 'get off the hook'. One can be both the agent and the victim of one's moral corruption.

If, however, evildoers invariably do not intend evil directly, might commonly not intend evil indirectly and even if they do intend evil indirectly might commonly intend only a minimized view of the evil they bring about then we might want to also focus our attention on the ways in which they are led to do so. That is, in addition to our traditional focus on direct and indirect evil, we might want to

---

1   They also, of course, were most likely aiming at their own sexual pleasure as their goal and so did not intend the abuse directly as an end.

focus on the ways in which evildoers commonly do not act from either directly or indirectly evil intentions.

Intending Evil and Doing Evil

The key principles of *jus in bello* or our rules of engagement in violent conflict are that we must not directly intend civilian casualties as a means to our goal and that we may bring about such casualties indirectly only where this is proportional to our goal. The value of civilian immunity is given by the disvalue we attach to the harming and killing of innocents. It is widely agreed that the killing of the innocent is a monumental evil. And so the prospect that we will commit this evil must figure prominently in guiding the assessment of the acceptability of any of our intentional plans – including what we both directly and indirectly intend.

But if, all too commonly, people who commit evil do not intend to do so – either directly or indirectly – then the injunction against the direct intentional killing of innocents and the restricted permissions of proportionality governing the indirect killing of innocents will have little application. Too often people will not be considering, for example, that their plans do involve the killing of innocents. Perhaps they think those they harm are guilty or close companions of those who are. Perhaps they do not see the innocence of their victims clearly since they are focused on the importance of achieving their own goals or the goals of their superiors in, say, matters of defending their national or religious identity.

I am not suggesting that this applies generally against the idea that we can be morally serious, accurate and responsible concerning times of violent conflict in identifying the evils and good of our plans, in balancing them and in understanding the what and why of that to which we are committing ourselves. Many modern military organizations, of course, operate within, say, relatively functional democracies and so have as an institutional purpose that they are able to make morally justifiable decisions concerning times of violent conflict and their efforts in doing so will be accountable to the community.

The institutional, accountable role played by many modern militaries might then rightly be claimed as hardly analogous in character or circumstance, say, to our evil parents. This, of course, is true. Aside from the fact that many modern militaries have committed terrible atrocities, militaries, like organizations and communities of individuals generally, can be dysfunctional in various ways and degrees that undermine their fulfilling their role. There is now widespread interest in ethical and professional development aimed at promoting morally serious, accurate and responsible military organizations and actors and widespread agreement that this is important. As one part of this picture, military organizations throughout the world now commonly have teaching and research units in military and professional ethics and/or arrangements with universities that provide them. My suggestion is that one focus for this teaching and research aimed at promoting morally serious, accurate and responsible military organizations and actors ought also be the problem of how evildoers commonly do not act from either directly or indirectly evil intentions.

The possibility that evildoers typically do not intend evil, even indirectly, or that even if they do they typically discount the evil they foresee is not just a philosophical hypothetical. It is currently the most widely held and plausible view about evildoers and their intentions.[2] Evildoers commonly act from attitudes, including the content of their intentions, that involve morally neutral or even positive descriptions of what they are up to. Often such attitudes are given 'credibility' by the agent's surrounding milieu and the demands and permissions to which it gives legitimacy. An important focus therefore, for better understanding how evildoers are typically guided by morally neutral or even positive descriptions of their agency, will be to consider more closely issues of culture or milieu and how these enable evildoers and their misguided understandings.

The Traditional Focus on the Intentional Contrast

Indirectly intended or collateral damage to civilians has long been understood and discussed in relation to its counterpart of *directly* intended damage. Our principles of *jus in bello* reflect this by telling us that while we must not target civilians directly as a means to achieving our military goal, we may nevertheless act on a plan where we foresee that we will harm or kill them indirectly, say, as a result of our direct attack on our enemy's munitions factory, where this indirect civilian damage is not disproportionate to the significant good our goal represents. Thus, while the direct targeting of civilians is claimed to be impermissible, indirect collateral damage may be permissible.

An enormous amount of ink has been spilt debating whether there really is this claimed asymmetry in permissibility between direct and collateral damage undertaken in pursuit of a commensurate good. In this section, I set out some problems for the distinction and defend the distinction against one influential problem – namely, that our intentional structures can be relative to motivating beliefs in an at-will and quite *ad-hoc* way. This will be useful for my discussion in the next section, where I argue that while our intentions are not so *ad hoc* or up to us in an at-will way, they are nevertheless relative to our beliefs and in turn our milieu in ways that can undermine the relevance of the intentional contrast – both for assessing the permissibility of action and for protecting civilian immunity.

Many have become disillusioned with thinking about civilian immunity and about our choices and responsibility where we violate this immunity primarily through looking at possible asymmetries between direct and indirect evil. First,

---

2   Hannah Arendt, *Eichmann in Jerusalem: A Report on the Banality of Evil* (New York: Viking Press, 1963) is the landmark and most famous view about the unthinking ordinariness of evildoers' attitudes and intentions. For an excellent discussion of evil agency, see also, Adam Morton, *On Evil* (London: Routledge, 2004).

as mentioned in the introduction to this volume, civilians have often been directly targeted in wars and violent conflict undertaken in the twentieth and twenty-first centuries and civilian casualties have often outnumbered combatant casualties. So not only is the prohibition upon direct killing of civilians widely violated, the relative permissibility of indirect killing might also be thought to be fuelling the proportional rise in civilian casualties.

There are also at least two fundamental theoretical reasons against focusing too much on possible asymmetries between directly and indirectly intended evil as a way to promote the value of civilian immunity. First, it seems hard to deny that one intends what one chooses to do and that one is responsible for what one intends whether directly or indirectly. Second, the value of civilian immunity should have significant primacy in assessing the acceptability of our military plans involving indirectly intended civilian deaths.

The first view about responsibility for what we indirectly intend has been a widely influential and shared view about our choice situations – and our responsibility for what we do as a result of our deliberations about them – that unites many consequentialists and many non-consequentialists in their rejection of normative contrasts between intended and collateral damage. If you choose to go ahead with a plan that you foresee will involve certain effects, such as civilian casualties of a certain order and probability, you are responsible for these effects.

So, whether, say, you intend evil or use people as a means or whether you merely foresee the evil you bring about as a side effect of your good and righteous ends, you are nevertheless responsible for the evil you have chosen to bring about as part of your plan. And, if the damage is symmetrical then many have also been led to think that so too must be your responsibility for it – irrespective of *how*, within your overall plan, you have chosen to cause it.

It seems clear that we cannot deny responsibility for the effects we knowingly choose to bring about. And so it is clear that we cannot avoid responsibility for foreseen collateral damage, such as civilian deaths. And perhaps we also must say, since we choose to bring about this collateral damage, that this is also something we intend. If you accept the overall pros and cons of your plan and choose to go ahead with it then you *intend* to go ahead with all of this – that is, you intend the overall plan including the various considerations you foresee will result from doing so. And so, for example, since a strategic bomber chooses to go ahead with a plan they see will bring collateral damage, this is something they intend, albeit indirectly.

The advocate of normative contrasts between intended/direct evil and merely foreseen/indirect evil need not deny any of this. The burden of their case is to show why directly intending evil is worse than indirectly intending evil. They need not deny that choice, responsibility or intentions apply to what we indirectly intend, such as to the standard cases of collateral damage. It is just that they think we are responsible for something additionally bad in intending evil as a means.

Many problems have been raised against the intentional contrast between directly and indirectly intending evil and against the claim that it is morally significant. One line of objection claims that the contrast makes evil permissible so long as it is only indirectly intended – as if merely foreseen effects are not one's responsibility. The considerations directly above connecting responsibility, choice and intention make plain both why this view is implausible and why advocates of the intentional contrast need not be saddled with it.[3]

On the other hand, another line of objection claims the contrast implausibly makes evil impermissible in all cases where it is directly intended. Key examples of the implausibility of this view have been mercy killing and self-sacrifice cases where while the killing of an innocent seems directly intended it also nevertheless seems permissible. And while this absolutist reading of the injunction against intending evil directly has had some recent revival,[4] absolutists about intending evil have not been thick on the ground for some time. Rather, advocates of the intentional contrast have commonly claimed that intending evil as a means to a commensurate good end is worse than indirectly doing so, and in some cases this can make the difference in the permissibility of the actions.[5] But, for example, where consequences are monumental or one's own life is at stake, there are cases where, all things considered, it is permissible to intend evil directly.

I said in the introduction that what a person intends is not simply 'up to them', that we make judgments about what to believe is true concerning the content of a person's intentions and that these judgments are guided by what we think is plausible to believe about the person themselves and about the circumstances in which they act. And so, for example, absent some such account concerning the parents who sexually abused their son, we would not believe their description of their intentions in terms of providing sexual education.

The idea that our intentions or the structure of our intentions might be relative to our motivating beliefs in this *ad-hoc*, at-will way has, however, been influential in the thinking of many detractors and defenders of the intentional contrast and its moral significance. So, for instance, it clearly informed what Peter Singer had in mind when he objected that '[w]e cannot avoid responsibility *simply by* directing our intention to one effect rather than another' (emphasis added).[6]

Elizabeth Anscombe was also concerned to deny this kind of worry in discussing the idea that rulers may rightfully kill so long as they do not intend the deaths of those they attack. Anscombe flatly rejected the suggestion that we might say that rulers do not intend to kill: '[this idea] has been put forward and, when suitably expressed, may seem high-minded. But someone who can fool himself into this

---

3   Alison McIntyre claims this view is a common misconception about the 'doctrine of double effect'. See Alison McIntyre, 'Doing Away With Double Effect', *Ethics*, 111/2 (2001): 219–55.

4   See T.M. Scanlon, *Moral Dimensions: Permissibility, Meaning, Blame* (Cambridge, MA: Harvard University Press, 2008).

5   For one recent statement of this view, see Ralph Wedgwood, 'Scanlon on Double Effect', *Philosophy and Phenomenological Research* (forthcoming, 2011).

6   Peter Singer, *Practical Ethics* (Cambridge: Cambridge University Press, 1979), p. 210.

twist of thought will fool himself into justifying anything, however atrocious, by means of it.'[7]

Similarly, she attacks the idea that the devout Catholic bomber might escape the negative moral claim against intending evil 'by a "direction of intention" that any shedding of innocent blood that occurs is "accidental"'.[8]

The worry also seems to lie behind Thomas Nagel's claim that the reasons that inform deontic constraints do not 'come from an *aim or project of the individual agent,* for it is not conditional on what the agent *wants*. Deontological restrictions, if they exist, *apply to everyone*' (emphasis added).[9]

And Warren Quinn put the worry this way: 'since more than one thing may be strictly intended in a given choice, the pronouncements of the doctrine may depend on how the choice happens to be described. This relativity is embarrassing. We would like the doctrine to speak with one voice in any given case.'[10]

In an amusing blast, Anscombe laid the blame for much of this on Descartes, or at least the view associated with Cartesian psychology that

> intention was an interior act of the mind which could be produced at will …
> on this theory of what intention is, a marvellous way offered itself of making
> any action lawful. You only had to 'direct your intention' in a suitable way. In
> practice, this means making a little speech to yourself: 'What I mean to be doing
> is …'.[11]

While influential in discussions of the distinction, the idea that the structure of our intentions is solely 'up to us' in *ad-hoc*, at-will ways has been a significant misconception. As I have suggested, an important guiding framework in determining intentional content is given by the judgments *we* make about what is plausible to believe about the person themselves and about the circumstances in which they act. So the structure of our intentions is not something we can simply help ourselves to in *ad-hoc*, at-will ways.[12]

Nevertheless, many concerned with protecting civilians and with our responsibility to respect civilian immunity have tended to shift away from the debate over the direct/indirect intentional distinction. The focus has shifted towards

---

7   Elizabeth Anscombe, 'War and Murder', in Walter Stein (ed.), *Nuclear Weapons: A Catholic Response* (London: Merlin, 1961), pp. 43–62, at p. 45.

8   Ibid., p. 51. Here Anscombe also rejects the idea that one might defend one's practise of *coitus reservatus* by claiming that one does not intend to ejaculate; one merely foresees that one will.

9   Thomas Nagel, *The View From Nowhere* (Oxford: Oxford University Press, 1986), p. 178.

10   Warren Quinn, 'Actions, Intentions, and Consequences: The Doctrine of Double Effect', *Philosophy and Public Affairs*, 18/4 (1989): 334–51, at p. 339.

11   Anscombe, p. 51.

12   And so, for example, the sexually abusive parents cannot easily claim that they only intended sexual education for their son.

looking at our responsibility for what we have chosen and intended to do *across* the direct/indirect intentional contrast. The concern to highlight the importance of civilian immunity and our responsibility to respect it irrespective that the civilian damage might be indirectly intended gives civilian immunity significant primacy in our deliberations.

The focus also perhaps helps guide us in the future from those cases where we bring about *unforeseen* collateral damage, say, where our intelligence about the presence of civilians was wrong. The more primacy we give to civilian immunity, the more we might be concerned to focus our resources on how this sort of intelligence gathering might be improved. Moreover, in the modern era of so-called 'irregular wars' where we have increased difficulties discriminating civilian from military foe yet we are most concerned to win the hearts and minds of the people, the primacy of our concern to protect civilians in guiding our choice of plans and how to improve them is widely and plausibly thought strategically paramount.

The primacy of civilian immunity in guiding our choices of military actions and future directions – such as, for instance, through technological developments improving targeting and non-lethal military responses – is therefore rightly at centre stage for these reasons.[13] And even if there was a compelling account of why directly intended evil was worse than indirectly intended evil, the primacy of civilian immunity for guiding us in these areas would remain in place.

As I have sketched, however, there is a quite different, much broader threat to giving civilian immunity its due by focusing only on intending evil, whether directly or indirectly. The shift away from the paradigm of understanding collateral damage as the poorer cousin to directly intended evil rightly gives primacy to civilian immunity in assessing the acceptability of our intentional, chosen plans. The problem that those who commit evil commonly do not *intend* evil cuts across and undermines the focus solely on our intentional, chosen plans as the way to assess their acceptability and, if necessary, take responsibility for the evil that we do.

Ordinary Evil

As indicated above, not only is evil rarely the object of *direct* intention, it is not commonly the object of *indirect* intention either. Almost no-one apart from sadists chooses evil directly – that is, for its own sake. Quite generally, however – albeit in various different ways – people distance themselves psychologically from their evil deeds and from their moral accountability for them.

Often evildoers do not see themselves as committing evil at all. So, for example, they think that their victims deserved the treatment dished out. And, short of this 'clarity', there is often something of a 'fog' about what is going on. Here the moral character of one's acts is clouded by other powerful reasons for thinking one's

---

13   There is, of course, debate, as reflected in this volume, about whether these moves achieve their aim in practice.

conduct justified or excusable, such as might be given by one's own desperate circumstances or by the authority of the figures and their institutions that order, support or otherwise legitimize one's evil conduct.

I have claimed that we cannot in any at-will or *ad-hoc* way help ourselves to more acceptable morally neutral or positive descriptions of the content of our intentions. So while this sort of view has been quite influential in rejecting the claimed asymmetry between direct and indirect evil, we can reject it. On the other hand, it seems plain that we can develop more 'morally acceptable' understandings of what we are up to over time – in particular, with the contrivance of our surrounding circumstances and milieu. To flesh this out, I give the following two cases describing how such moral fog and inversion of moral realities can come about. In both, evil is significant. In the second case of Rwanda it is, of course, utterly extraordinary. In both, however, evil is also ordinary in terms of motives and intentional content and is not undertaken because of the evil involved or with a clear view of evil as a foreseen effect.

Hitchcock's Sabotage

Adapted from Joseph Conrad's novel *The Secret Agent*, Alfred Hitchcock's film *Sabotage* vividly details how good, ordinary family-minded people can be led to commit acts of unspeakable evil and destruction. The film exhibits in sequential detail not only the ease with which we can be drawn to evil agency, but also how we rationalize and abstract our involvement in evildoing.

Karl Verloc, the protagonist in Hitchcock's cautionary tale, is a quiet, loving family man, who struggles to financially support his wife, stepson and brother-in-law. As a way to make ends meet, Verloc has secretly been engaged by agents from a foreign country to stage destabilizing events in London. After a failed attempt to sabotage a key electricity generator, Verloc is denied payment and informed that if he wants to receive payment he must instead plant a bomb in the crowded Piccadilly section of London during a civic holiday.

At first, Verloc refuses, protesting that he cannot be involved in an act that will result in the loss of innocent life. He is soon persuaded, however, by means of appeal to his capacity for moral abstraction. Informed that he, Verloc, need not deliver the bomb – only find someone who can – Verloc begins to rationalize that the moral responsibility for the loss of life attaches to the person who plants the bomb, not to himself as the mere procurer.

Under constant surveillance by the police, Verloc finds he is unable to offload the preset bomb. In desperation, he deploys his stepson, Stevie, to deliver the bomb on the prearranged day. Despite being warned to deliver the 'package' before 1.30 pm in order to give Stevie time to move away from the area, Stevie is held up in transit. The bomb explodes and Stevie is killed along with his fellow bus passengers.

By rationalizing violence through the process of abstraction – putting the evil deed at 'arm's length' – the bite of the tragic consequences appears removed from those complicit in the events. Even when confronted by his wife, Verloc refuses to assume responsibility for his actions and justifies himself through the standard stratagem of abstraction: 'He didn't intend for Stevie to be killed, he would have taken the bomb himself had he not been under surveillance, he was forced to do it', and so on.[14]

The Rwanda Killers

In a chilling series of interviews with 10 farmers who had become mass murderers in the daily killing sprees of Rwanda, Jean Hatzfeld, in his book *Machete Season: The Killers of Rwanda Speak*,[15] brings out a rather different cohabitation between the ordinary, the good and the evil. These farmers, who seemingly so easily and quickly became mass murderers, did not need deception or a double life to provide cover for their evil.

Instead, their turn to evil flourished under instructions from local authorities, with much support from their community and those close to them and alongside the continuation of their otherwise very ordinary, domestic and even good lives. As one of the farmers-turned-mass-murderer put it:

> Some offenders claim that we changed into wild animals ... that we were blinded by ferocity ... That is a trick to sidetrack the truth. I can say this: outside the marshes, our lives seemed quite ordinary. We sang on the paths ... we had our choice amid abundance. We chatted about our good fortune, we soaped off our bloodstains in the basin, our noses enjoyed the aromas of full cooking pots. We rejoiced in the new life about to begin by feasting on [a] leg of veal. We were hot at night atop our wives, and we scolded our rowdy children ... We put on our field clothes. We swapped gossip at the cabaret, we made bets on our victim, spoke mockingly of cut girls, squabbled foolishly over looted grain. We sharpened our tools on whetting stones. We traded stories about desperate Tutsi tricks, we made fun of every 'Mercy!' cried by someone who'd been hunted down, we counted up and stashed away our goods.[16]

---

14   W.A. Drumin, 'Sabotage: Chaos Unleashed and the Impossibility of Utopia', in D. Baggett and W.A. Drumin, *Hitchcock and Philosophy: Dial M for Metaphysics* (Chicago: Open Court, 2007), pp. 3–16.

15   Jean Hatzfeld, *Machete Season: The Killers in Rwanda Speak* (New York: Farrar, Straus & Giroux, 2005/Picador, 2006).

16   I was led to Hatzfeld's book (where I first found this quote) on reading an excellent essay by Michael Massing, 'Trial and Error', [Sunday Book Review], *The New York Times*, 17 October 2004. Many of the tales in Hatzfeld's book are not for the faint-hearted. The killing of mothers with babies, children and old friends and how these killings were undertaken are horrific. There are stories, for instance, of fathers teaching their young boys how to use the machete – sometimes on the bodies of those already killed, sometimes on live people who had been captured – and of how the boys would mostly 'practise' on other young children because of their relatively similar size. And they are horrific in their ordinariness – for example, often involving uncritically doing as one is told and as one feels

In this, and many other cases like it, our ordinary, otherwise morally and socially functional lives seem to provide normalizing and legitimizing ways to understand our conduct and what is going on around us. And in so doing they seem able to provide much needed cover for evil.

Thus, for example, the Rwandan farmers – who acted under orders from local authorities (with assurances of impunity) and who acted with the support of their thriving family and social lives – commonly reported how easily they were able to trade their daily routine of using machetes to fell crops for the daily routine of using machetes to fell Tutsi.

Similar phenomena where evil has flourished under the cover of the legitimizing and normalizing influences of one's surrounding milieu have, for example, also been widely identified to be at play for many Nazi doctors whose 'euphemistic and scientific language' sanitized horrific 'medical experiments' and in countless social psychology experiments – the most famous being Stanley Milgram's 'electro-shock learning experiments' in 1961 and Phillip Zimbardo's 'mock prison' experiment in 1970.[17] More generally, and usually less extremely, most of us will be familiar with those whose bad conduct flourishes under the cover of descriptions such as 'it is my job' or it is 'just business'.

Conclusion

My suggestion is that these kinds of influences from our surrounding milieu that affect how we understand our choice situations, what we are up to and why should also significantly be the focus of attention if we are to pay collateral damage and civilian immunity their due. Since often when we commit evil we tend to understand what we are doing in ways that minimize or remove altogether our choosing or intending evil as part of our overall plan, we need also to focus attention on the structures and conditions that enable such perversions and obfuscation of our intentional plans – including on our military institutions, their culture and their future direction.

In doing so, we also need to look beyond not only the direct/indirect paradigm but also beyond the more recent shift of focus on the primacy of civilian immunity *across* the intentional structure of our chosen plans. Whilst true, this focus also will have limited application in so far as violations of civilian immunity are *not* what we choose or intend – either directly or indirectly.

---

obliged to do by local authorities and community elders. And, as the quote in the text above illustrates, they are horrific on account of the flourishing of such monstrous evil alongside – indeed, with the support of – otherwise functional, vibrant family and social lives.

17   On this, see Phillip G. Zimbardo, *The Lucifer Effect: Understanding How Good People Turn Evil* (New York: Random House, 2007).

Chapter 5

The Protection of Civilians from Violence and the Effects of Attacks in International Humanitarian Law

Hitoshi Nasu

Introduction

The protection of civilians in time of armed conflict is the bedrock of modern international humanitarian law.[1] In this context, the development of 'Geneva Law' has particularly cardinal significance,[2] as opposed to 'Hague Law', which primarily focuses on the regulation of the conduct and means of warfare.[3] The international rules on the protection of civilians during armed conflict can be divided into three groups: a) rules for protection of civilians in the conduct of military operations; b) rules for protection of civilians under the control of the adversary against violence or arbitrary acts; and c) rules for protection of civilians from the effects of military operations. The first group of rules relates to the

---

1   *Prosecutor v Kupreškić* (ICTY), Case No. IT-95-16-T, Judgment of 14 January 2000, para. 521.

2   *Geneva Convention for the Amelioration of the Condition of the Wounded and Sick in Armed Forces in the Field of August 12, 1949*, 75 UNTS 31 (entered into force 21 October 1950) (hereinafter GCI); *Geneva Convention for the Amelioration of the Condition of Wounded, Sick and Shipwrecked Members of Armed Forces at Sea of August 12, 1949*, 75 UNTS 85 (entered into force 21 October 1950) (hereinafter GCII); *Geneva Convention Relative to the Treatment of Prisoners of War of August 12, 1949*, 75 UNTS 135 (entered into force 21 October 1950) (hereinafter GCIII); *Geneva Convention Relative to the Protection of Civilian Persons in Time of War of August 12, 1949*, 75 UNTS 287 (entered into force 21 October 1950) (hereinafter GCIV); *Protocol Additional to the Geneva Conventions of 12 August, 1949, and Relating to the Protection of Victims of International Armed Conflict (Protocol I)*, 1125 UNTS 3 (entered into force 7 December 1978) (hereinafter API); *Protocol Additional to the Geneva Conventions of 12 August 1949, and Relating to the Protection of Victims of Non-International Armed Conflicts (Protocol II)*, 1125 UNTS 609 (entered into force 7 December 1978) (hereinafter APII).

3   The 'Hague Law' is primarily composed of the Hague Conventions of 1899 and 1907. The text of those conventions is reproduced in Adam Roberts and Richard Guelff, *Documents on the Laws of War*, 3rd edn (Oxford: Oxford University Press, 2000), pp. 59–137.

regulation of the conduct of warfare, which forms the subject of Chapter 6.[4] The present chapter therefore focuses on the second and third groups of rules, which not only prevent states parties from treating civilians in contravention of those rules (negative obligations), but also require them to take positive steps to ensure that civilians are protected from acts of violence and the effects of attacks.

Who is protected as a civilian and to what extent civilian protection measures are required depend, first and foremost, on the classification of the armed conflict in which parties are involved – whether they are engaged in an international armed conflict, military occupation or a non-international armed conflict.[5] Under the law of international armed conflict including military occupation, civilians are defined as any person who is not a member of the armed forces.[6] This negative formulation of the definition of civilians is meant to leave no undistributed middle between the status of combatants and civilians.[7] In case of any doubt, a person is presumed to be a civilian.[8] In non-international armed conflicts, on the other hand, civilians are not explicitly defined in international legal instruments. While persons who are not members of state armed forces or organized armed groups will be seen as civilians,[9] the status of members of organized armed groups remains unclear.[10] As will be explained in this chapter, applicable rules of international humanitarian law differ in each type of armed conflict.

Increasingly, the protection of civilians has become the focus of peacekeeping operations. When peacekeepers are mandated to protect civilians, they are required

---

4   Michael Schmitt, 'The Principle of Military Necessity in International Humanitarian Law', in this volume.

5   See generally, Sylvain Vité, 'Typology of Armed Conflicts in International Humanitarian Law: Legal Concepts and Actual Situations', *International Review of the Red Cross*, 91 (2009): 69; Christopher Greenwood, 'Scope of Application of Humanitarian Law', in Dieter Fleck (ed.), *The Handbook of International Humanitarian Law*, 2nd edn (New York: Oxford University Press, 2008), p. 45.

6   Article 50(1) of the API defines civilians as any person who does not belong to one of the categories of persons referred to in Article 4A(1), (2), (3) and (6) of the GCIII and in Article 43 of the API. For a historical account of the emergence of the civilian status, see, Adam Roberts, 'The Civilian in Modern War', *Yearbook of International Humanitarian Law*, 12 (2009): 13, 34–9.

7   See especially, Marco Sassòli, 'The Status of Persons Held in Guantánamo Under International Humanitarian Law', *Journal of International Criminal Justice*, 2 (2004): 96.

8   API, Art. 50(1).

9   *San Remo Manual on the Law of Non-International Armed Conflict with Commentary* (2006), para. 1.1.3; Michael Bothe, Karl Joseph Partsch and Waldemar A. Solf (eds), *New Rules for Victims of Armed Conflicts* (The Hague: Martinus Nijhoff, 1982), p. 672.

10   The controversy is illustrated by the notion of 'continuous combat function' introduced into this debate by the International Committee of the Red Cross (ICRC) in its *Interpretive Guidance on Direct Participation in Hostilities*. See, Helen Durham, in this volume.

to operate in compliance with that mandate. Even in the absence of such a mandate, however, or in parallel with it, peacekeepers might well have to assume certain obligations relating to the protection of civilians under international humanitarian law. Whether peacekeepers are bound by the rules of international humanitarian law has been a subject of controversy, except when peacekeepers themselves are engaged in armed conflict.[11] References will be made at relevant points to the application or effects of international humanitarian law to civilian protection by peacekeepers.

Civilian Protection from Violence and Arbitrary Treatment

International Armed Conflict

Any armed conflict that arises between two or more sovereign states constitutes an international armed conflict, regardless of any formal declaration of war or any formal recognition of the enemy entity as a state.[12] In contrast, a conflict between a state and an organized armed group operating within or outside the state territory is categorized as a non-international armed conflict, which will be explained further below. Such non-international armed conflicts might become international armed conflicts through military intervention of a foreign power against the central government of the state or where there is overall control of the organized armed group by foreign authorities. This 'overall control' test, for the purpose of the classification of an armed conflict, can be satisfied by showing that foreign authorities have '*a role in organising, coordinating or planning the military actions* of the military group, in addition to financing, training and equipping or providing operational support to that group' (emphasis in original).[13]

In international armed conflicts, Geneva Convention IV provides the scheme for protection of civilians who find themselves under the control of the adverse

---

11　See generally, Daphna Shraga, 'The Secretary-General's Bulletin on the Observance by United Nations Forces of International Humanitarian Law – A Decade Later', *Israel Yearbook on Human Rights*, 39 (2009): 357; Hitoshi Nasu, *International Law on Peacekeeping: A Study of Article 40 of the UN Charter* (The Hague: Martinus Nijhoff, 2009), pp. 195–7, and literature cited therein.

12　GCI–IV, Common Art. 2. See also, Yoram Dinstein, *The Conduct of Hostilities under the Law of International Armed Conflict*, 2nd edn (Cambridge: Cambridge University Press, 2010), pp. 28–9; Greenwood, pp. 46–51.

13　*Prosecutor v Tadić* (ICTY) (Appeals Chamber), Case No. IT-94-1-A, Judgment of 15 July 1999, para. 137. See also, *Prosecutor v Blaškić* (ICTY) (Trial Chamber), Case No. IT-95-14-T, Judgment of 3 March 2000, paras 100–101. The International Court of Justice did not dispute the appropriateness of the 'overall control' test for the purpose of the classification of armed conflicts in *Case Concerning the Application of the Convention on the Prevention and Punishment of the Crime of Genocide (Bosnia and Herzegovina v Serbia and Montenegro)* [2007] ICJ Rep 43, 210 para. 404.

party or the occupying power of which they are not nationals.[14] The scheme is not restricted to civilians physically captured by the adverse party but covers, broadly, anyone who is under the control of the adverse party.[15] The protection does not extend to nationals of a neutral state or of a co-belligerent state who can seek diplomatic protection through their own governments,[16] but does extend to stateless persons and refugees who no longer owe allegiance to the adverse party or its co-belligerent state or a neutral state. Thus, the crucial test for determining protected status is no longer nationality, but which party a person owes allegiance to and benefits diplomatic protection from.[17]

Those protected civilians, once captured, are protected from all acts of violence and threats. This requires the adverse party to comply with various obligations under Geneva Convention IV, which includes, but is not limited to:

- humane treatment (GCIV, Articles 27–34)
- no acts of violence (GCIV, Articles 13 and 27)
- prohibition of coercive interrogation (GCIV, Articles 31–2)
- no discrimination for reasons of race, nationality, language, religious convictions and practices, political opinion, social origin or position or similar consideration (GCIV, Articles 3, 27)
- prohibition of collective penalties, measures of intimidation or terrorism, reprisals and pillage (GCIV, Article 33)
- prohibition of taking of hostages (GCIV, Article 34)
- freedom of repatriation (GCIV, Articles 35–7)
- prohibition of forced labour (GCIV, Articles 40, 51, 95).

These measures of protection provide negative obligations for the adverse party – for example, not to harm civilians, not to coerce them to provide information and not to force them to work. Some of the protection measures, however, also entail positive obligations.

The protection of civilians from inhuman treatment under Article 27 of Geneva Convention IV constitutes one of the fundamental principles of humanity under international humanitarian law, which develops over time under the influence of

---

14   GCIV, Art. 4.

15   Jean Pictet, *The Geneva Conventions of 12 August 1949: Commentary IV* (Geneva: ICRC, 1958), p. 47.

16   GCIV, Art. 4(2); Pictet, pp. 48–9. Whether a state is a co-belligerent state is determined on the basis of the existence of normal diplomatic relations through which the normal diplomatic protection may be claimed. See, *Prosecutor v Blaškić*, paras 126–46. In any event they are still entitled to minimum protection under Article 75 of Additional Protocol I.

17   *Prosecutor v Tadić*, para. 166. For discussion, see Kim Rubenstein, 'Rethinking Nationality in International Humanitarian Law', in Ustinia Dolgopol and Judith Gardam (eds), *The Challenge of Conflict: International Law Responds* (Leiden: Martinus Nijhoff, 2006), pp. 98–102.

changes in society.[18] It requires military troops not only to refrain from operations that might cause harm to civilians, but also to take all precautionary measures in their power to ensure the safety of civilians, which calls for positive action.[19] Thus, as the International Committee of the Red Cross (ICRC) commentary observes, humane treatment requires civilians to be protected even against insults and public curiosity.[20] As a basic norm of international humanitarian law, this obligation applies to peacekeeping troops, even though they are not directly engaging in an armed conflict.[21]

Another positive obligation relevant to the protection of civilians during an armed conflict can be found in Article 16 of Geneva Convention IV. This requires states parties, '[a]s far as military considerations allow … to assist the shipwrecked and *other persons exposed to grave danger*, and to protect them against pillage and ill-treatment' (emphasis added).[22] Given this part covers all of the population of the countries in conflict, without any adverse distinction,[23] the contextual interpretation might allow an expansive reading to prescribe the general obligation to protect civilians under threats during an armed conflict.[24]

Under limited circumstances, states are allowed under Article 5 of Geneva Convention IV to derogate from some of those convention rights if a civilian detainee poses a threat to the security of the detaining power. The derogation is permitted in the territory of the detaining power or in an occupied territory. Hence, when read in conjunction with Article 4 of Geneva Convention IV, no derogation is authorized in non-occupied enemy territory.[25] In occupied territories, only the right of communication may be suspended.

There are three requirements for lawfully derogating from convention rights given to civilian detainees under the control of the adverse party. First, the detaining power must know or have good reason to suspect that a particular individual has engaged in hostile acts. Second, the convention rights may be derogated from to the extent necessary to preserve the security of the detaining power. The necessity of specific derogations needs to be assessed in each individual case. Third, derogations

---

18   Jean-Marie Henckaerts and Louise Doswald-Beck, *Customary International Humanitarian Law* (Cambridge: Cambridge University Press, 2005), Rule 87. For a detailed analysis, see *Prosecutor v Delalić* (ICTY) (Trial Chamber), Case No. IT-96-21-T, Judgment of 16 November 1998, paras 512–44.

19   *Physicians for Human Rights v Commander of the Israeli Defense Forces in the Gaza Strip*, HCJ 4764/04 (2004) (Supreme Court of Israel), para. 21.

20   Pictet, p. 204.

21   Cf. *R v Brocklebank* (1996) 134 DLR (4th) 377 (Court Martial Appeal Court of Canada), paras 63–5.

22   GCIV, Art. 16.

23   Ibid., Art. 13.

24   See Pictet, p. 134.

25   Cf. Richard R. Baxter, 'So-Called "Unprivileged Belligerency": Spies, Guerrillas, and Saboteurs', *British Year Book of International Law*, 28 (1951): 323, 328 (interpreting Article 5 as indicating that GCIV protections do not apply in the zones of active combat).

are permitted only with respect to certain rights and privileges, and under no circumstances may the right to humane treatment and a fair trial be suspended.

More specifically, the internment of protected civilians is permitted as a protective measure if such a measure is absolutely necessary for security reasons, both in the territory of the adverse party and in occupied territories.[26] Yet it may be undertaken only when a) security concerns require it, b) less restrictive measures could not accomplish the objective sought, and c) it is undertaken pursuant to regular procedures that ensure the detainee can be heard and appeal the decision.[27] The regular procedures may be accomplished 'through the establishment of an expeditious judicial or board (quasi-judicial) review process'.[28] The treatment of civilian internees must comply with detailed requirements. For example, civilian internees are not to be transferred to a country where they might have reason to fear persecution for their political opinions or religious beliefs,[29] and must be immediately returned upon the close of hostilities or occupation.[30]

The Special Case of Military Occupation

When a state occupies the territory of an adverse party without its consent, the international law of military occupation comes into effect, regulating the relationship between the occupying power and the residents of the occupied territory. The law of belligerent occupation, strictly speaking, is codified in the 1907 Hague Regulations (Articles 42–56)[31] and 1949 Geneva Convention IV (especially Articles 27–34 and 47–78),[32] and applies to international armed conflicts only. The set of rules relevant to belligerent occupation under Geneva Convention IV will cease to apply after one year from the commencement of occupation, except for the fundamental rules listed in Article 6(3) of the convention. Many of the rules may, however, be considered customary international law, applicable

---

26   GCVI, Arts 41–3, 78–135; Henckaerts and Doswald-Beck, Rule 99.

27   See Hans-Peter Gasser, 'Protection of the Civilian Population', in Dieter Fleck (ed.), *The Handbook of International Humanitarian Law*, 2nd edn (New York: Oxford University Press, 2008), pp. 319–20.

28   *Coard et al. v United States*, Inter-American Commission on Human Rights, Report No. 109/99, Case 10.951 (1999), paras 52–8.

29   GCIV, Art. 45.

30   GCIV, Art. 134.

31   *Regulations Respecting the Laws and Customs of War on Land, Annex to the 1907 Convention (IV) Respecting the Laws and Customs of War on Land*, (1910) 9 UKTS Cd 5030 (entered into force 26 January 1910) (hereinafter Hague Regulations).

32   See generally, Yoram Dinstein, *The International Law of Belligerent Occupation* (Cambridge: Cambridge University Press, 2009); Eyal Benvenisti, *The International Law of Occupation* (Princeton, NJ: Princeton University Press, 1993); Myres S. McDougal and Florentino P. Feliciano, *Law and Minimum World Public Order* (New Haven, Conn.: Yale University Press, 1961), Ch. 7; Morris Greenspan, *The Modern Law of Land Warfare* (Berkeley and Los Angeles: University of California Press, 1959), pp. 209–77.

for the entire duration of military occupation. Also, suggestions have been made that the law of belligerent occupation be applied to UN peacekeeping operations, particularly when the operation involves transitional administration of territory without consent of the host state.[33] The term 'military occupation' is therefore used here to accommodate the potential application of those rules in a wider context.

The law governing military occupation applies whenever a territory comes under the control of a foreign force, even if it does not encounter armed resistance.[34] Exactly when a territory is considered occupied has, however, been a subject of controversy. Article 42 of the Hague Regulations provides:

1. territory is considered occupied when it is actually placed under the authority of the hostile army; and
2. the occupation extends only to the territory where such authority has been established and can be exercised.

These provisions indicate that the law of military occupation applies only once the invading force is in a position to actually exercise the level of authority over enemy territory necessary to enable it to discharge all the obligations imposed by the law of occupation.[35] On the other hand, Article 6 of Geneva Convention IV states that the convention applies 'from the outset' of any conflict or occupation, which might indicate a wider application of the law of military occupation under Geneva Convention IV than Article 42 of the Hague Regulations.[36] Thus, the ICRC observes that:

> Even a patrol which penetrates into enemy territory without any intention of staying there must respect the Conventions in its dealings with the civilians it meets. When it withdraws, for example, it cannot take civilians with it, for that would be contrary to Article 49 which prohibits the deportation or forcible transfer of persons from occupied territory.[37]

One way of reconciling these two conflicting views is to consider that the law of military occupation, under Geneva Convention IV, applies from the 'invasion phase', whilst the law under the Hague Regulations will not come into effect

---

33   See, for example, Michael J. Kelly, *Restoring and Maintaining Order in Complex Peace Operations: The Search for a Legal Framework* (The Hague: Kluwer Law International, 1999), pp. 67–90; Marco Sassòli, 'Legislation and Maintenance of Public Order and Civil Life by Occupying Powers', *European Journal of International Law*, 16 (2005): 661, 686–93.

34   GCIV, Art. 2(2).

35   See, for example, UK Ministry of Defence, *The Joint Service Manual of the Law of Armed Conflict* (London, 2004), para. 11.3; Gasser, p. 274.

36   Pictet, p. 60.

37   Ibid.

until requisite authority is established over the enemy territory. The alternative view was expressed by the Eritrea/Ethiopia Claims Commission, which adopted a functional approach obliging the invading state to undertake the duties in so far as it is possible to do so, according to the extent and length of time the adverse party has been exercising authority in the area.[38]

Where military occupation is established, all the obligations for protecting civilians under Geneva Convention IV, as referred to above, apply to the occupying power. An important additional obligation – relevant to the protection of civilians in the situation of military occupation – concerns the movement of populations. The following obligations are imposed on the occupying power in this respect:

1. not to prohibit the inhabitants of the occupied territory to seek safety from the effects of military operations, except where the safety of the inhabitants is at risk or for compelling military considerations;[39]
2. not to transfer the local population from the occupied territory to other territories (however, should the security of the population or imperative military reasons so demand, the occupying power may temporarily evacuate them within the occupied territory or, if there is no alternative way to guarantee the safety of the evacuees, to the territory of the occupying power or a third state);[40] and
3. not to transfer or resettle its own population into the occupied territory.[41]

In addition, there is increasingly recognition that obligations under international human rights law apply in the situation of military occupation, which is of particular relevance to the protection of civilians. The International Court of Justice has made a general observation that 'the protection offered by human rights conventions does not cease in case of armed conflict save through the effect of provisions for derogation'.[42] In case of military occupation, there are two different ways to explain the applicability of international human rights law in occupied territories.

First, Article 43 of the Hague Regulations might be read in a way that it requires the occupying power to apply international human rights treaties to which it is a

---

38   Eritrea/Ethiopia Claims Commission, *Partial Award – Central Front* (28 April 2004), para. 57; *Partial Award – Western Front* (19 December 2005), para. 27.

39   GCIV, Art. 49(5).

40   Ibid., Art. 49(2). See also, *Cases Concerning Deportation Orders*, Israeli Supreme Court Judgment of 10 April 1988, (1990) 29(1) ILM 139, 177–79 (Bach J at para. 5).

41   GCIV, Art. 49(6); *Rome Statute of the International Criminal Court, July 17, 1998*, 2187 UNTS 3, Art. 8(2)(b)(viii); Henckaerts and Doswald-Beck, Rule 130. See also, *Legality of the Construction of a Wall in the Palestinian Occupied Territory (Advisory Opinion)* [2004] ICJ Rep 136, 192, para. 135 (hereinafter *Palestinian Wall Advisory Opinion*).

42   *Palestinian Wall Advisory Opinion*, 178 para. 106. See also *Legality of the Threat or Use of Nuclear Weapons (Advisory Opinion)* [1996(I)] ICJ Rep 226, 240 para. 25.

party. This provision requires occupying powers 'to restore, and ensure, as far as possible, public order and safety, while respecting, unless absolutely prevented, the laws in force in the country'. This approach was adopted by the International Court of Justice in the *Case Concerning Armed Activities on the Territory of the Congo*,[43] in which it observed: 'This obligation comprised the duty to secure respect for the applicable rules of international human rights law and international humanitarian law, to protect the inhabitants of the occupied territory against acts of violence, and not to tolerate such violence by any third party.'[44]

Thus applicable rules of international human rights law can be relied upon as aids to interpret the obligations under the law of military occupation, such as humane treatment, non-discrimination and no act of violence.[45] Yet it remains unclear which rules of international human rights law (for example, the right to privacy and social, economic and cultural rights) are considered applicable in the situation of military occupation and to what extent those human rights need to be woven into the law of military occupation. Moreover, the application and enforcement of human rights by the occupying power based on its own interpretation might risk violation of Article 43 itself, which requires the occupying power to respect the laws in force in the occupied territory.[46]

Second, it can be argued that human rights obligations apply extraterritorially, independently from the legal regime of military occupation. Irrespective of the application of international humanitarian law, states must assume obligations under human rights treaties they are party to in respect of acts done in the exercise of their jurisdiction, even outside their own territory, when they are exercising 'effective control' over a territory.[47] In *Loizidou*, the European Court of Human Rights considered that the Turkish Army exercised 'effective overall control' in northern Cyprus for the purpose of an extraterritorial application of human rights obligations, merely by reference to the large number of troops engaged in active

---

43   *Case Concerning Armed Activities on the Territory of the Congo (Democratic Republic of the Congo v Uganda)* [2005] ICJ Rep 116 (hereinafter *Armed Activities in the Congo*).

44   Ibid., para. 178.

45   See Henckaerts and Doswald-Beck, Rule 87 (humane treatment), Rule 88 (non-discrimination), Rule 89 (violence to life).

46   For discussion, see for example, Adam Roberts, 'Transformative Military Occupation: Applying the Laws of War and Human Rights', *American Journal of International Law*, 100 (2006): 580; Sassòli, 'Legislation and Maintenance', pp. 662–82.

47   *Palestinian Wall Advisory Opinion*, 180 para. 111; *General Comment No. 31 on Article 2 of the Covenant: The Nature of the General Legal Obligation Imposed on States Parties to the Covenant*, UN Doc. CCPR/C/74/CRP.4/Rev.6 (21 April 2004), para. 10. For details, see for example, Ralph Wilde, 'Triggering State Obligations Extraterritorially: The Spatial Test in Certain Human Rights Treaties', *Israel Law Review*, 40 (2007): 503; Michael J. Dennis, 'Application of Human Rights Treaties Extraterritorially in Times of Armed Conflict and Military Occupation', *American Journal of International Law*, 99 (2005): 119.

duties in the area.[48] In contrast, the same court in *Banković*,[49] and UK courts in *Al-Skeini*,[50] required a higher degree of control, denying an extraterritorial application of human rights obligations unless a state has the power to provide the full package of rights and freedoms guaranteed by international human rights instruments.[51] However, the European Court of Human Rights in *Al-Skeini* rejected this approach and observed that the factual question as to whether a state exercises effective control over an area is determined primarily by reference to the strength of the state's military presence in the area and other indicators 'such as the extent to which its military, economic and political support for the local subordinate administration provides it with influence and control over the region'.[52] The Court also noted that where the fact of such domination is established, 'it is not necessary to determine whether the Contracting State exercises detailed control over the policies and actions of the subordinate local administration'.[53]

In any event, a simultaneous application of international humanitarian law and human rights law gives rise to questions as to whether and how competing obligations under two different legal regimes can be reconciled. The international legal techniques of resolving conflicting obligations such as *lex specialis* do not provide an immediate answer as to how particular rules apply in specific

---

48   *Loizidou v Turkey* (ECHR) (1997) 23 EHRR 513, 531 para. 56. See also, *Issa v Turkey* (ECHR) (2004) 41 EHRR 567, 589 para. 74 (although the application was rejected on the factual ground that Turkish troops were not found to have conducted operations in the area in question); *Ilascu v Moldova and Russia* (ECHR) (Grand Chamber) (2005) 40 EHRR 46, para. 316.

49   *Banković v Belgium and others* (2001) 11 BHRC 435; (2007) 44 EHRR SE5. The decision has been subject to extensive criticism. See, for example, Marco Milanović, 'From Compromise to Principle: Clarifying the Concept of State Jurisdiction in Human Rights Treaties', *Human Rights Law Review*, 8 (2008): 411; A. Rüth and M. Trilsch, 'International Decisions: Banković v. Belgium (Admissibility)', *American Journal of International Law*, 97 (2003): 168; Rick Lawson, 'Life After *Bankovic*: On the Extraterritorial Application of the European Convention on Human Rights', in F. Coomans and M.T. Kamminga (eds), *Extraterritorial Application of Human Rights Treaties* (Antwerp: Intersentia, 2004), p. 83; Matthew Happold, 'Bankovic v Belgium and the Territorial Scope of the European Convention on Human Rights', *Human Rights Law Review*, 3 (2003): 77.

50   *R (Al-Skeini and others) v Secretary of State for Defence* [2008] 1 AC 153 (House of Lords) (hereinafter *Al-Skeini* [HL]); *R (Al-Skeini and others) v Secretary of State for Defence* [2007] QB 140 (Court of Appeal) (hereinafter *Al-Skeini* [CA]). For discussion of the case, see for example, Tobias Thienel, 'The ECHR in Iraq: The Judgment of the House of Lords in *R (Al-Skeini) v. Secretary of State for Defence*', *Journal of International Criminal Justice*, 6 (2008): 115; Dominic McGoldrick, 'Human Rights and Humanitarian Law in the UK Courts', *Israel Law Review*, 40 (2007): 527.

51   *Banković v Belgium and others*, para. 71; *Al-Skeini* (HL), 202 para. 79 (Lord Rodger), 206 para. 97 (Lord Carswell), 214 para. 127 (Lord Brown).

52   *Al-Skeini and Others v The United Kingdom* (ECHR), Application No 55721/07, Judgment of 7 July 2011, para. 139.

53   Ibid., para. 138.

situations. No clear guidance or rule is yet to emerge, though different ideas have been expressed within academic debate.[54]

Non-International Armed Conflict

In non-international armed conflicts, warring parties – both states and armed opposition groups – are bound only by minimum provisions of protection under Common Article 3 of 1949 Geneva Conventions (except where 1977 Additional Protocol II is applicable, as will be elaborated later) and the customary international law applicable to non-international armed conflicts, unless a special agreement is concluded between the parties.[55] Non-international armed conflict is not restricted to internal armed conflicts that occur within the territory of a sovereign state, but may encompass transnational armed conflicts between a sovereign state and an armed group operating in the territory of a foreign state without overall control of that government or of a third country.

Common Article 3 does not provide the definition of 'armed conflict not of an international character', nor does it define the precise scope of application. Yet international jurisprudence developed on the applicability of Common Article 3 indicates that the law of non-international armed conflict requires a certain level of intensity of armed confrontation and a degree of organization that enables an armed group to carry out obligations under this provision.[56] The International Criminal Tribunal for the Former Yugoslavia (ICTY) in *Tadić* recognized that non-international armed conflicts existed because of the protracted nature of armed violence involving organized armed groups.[57] As clarified by the same

---

54 See, for example, the collection from 'Symposium: The Relationship Between International Humanitarian Law and International Human Rights Law', *Journal of Conflict & Security Law*, 14/3 (2010): 441–527; Roberta Arnold and Noëlle Quénivet (eds), *International Humanitarian Law and Human Rights Law: Towards a New Merger in International Law* (Leiden/Boston: Brill/Martinus Nijhoff, 2008); Alexander Orakhelashvili, 'The Interaction Between Human Rights and Humanitarian Law: Fragmentation, Conflict, Parallelism, or Convergence?', *European Journal of International Law*, 19 (2008): 161; Anthony E. Cassimatis, 'International Humanitarian Law, International Human Rights Law, and Fragmentation of International Law', *International and Comparative Law Quarterly*, 56 (2007): 623; collection in *Israel Law Review*, 40 (2007): 310–660.

55 For the author's view as to the legal status of organized armed groups and the legal basis upon which they are bound by the law of non-international armed conflict, see Hitoshi Nasu, 'Status of Rebels in Non-International Armed Conflict', in Jahid Hossain Bhuiyan, Louise Doswald-Beck and Azizur Rahman Chowdhury (eds), *International Humanitarian Law – An Anthology* (Dehli: LexisNexis, 2009), pp. 253–7.

56 See generally, Anthony Cullen, *The Concept of Non-International Armed Conflict in International Humanitarian Law* (Cambridge: Cambridge University Press, 2010).

57 *Prosecutor v Tadić* (Jurisdiction) (Appeals Chamber) (1997), 105 ILR 453, 488, para. 70; *Prosecutor v Akayesu* (ICTR) (Trial Chamber), ICTR-96-4-T, Judgment of 2 September 1998, paras 619–21.

tribunal in *Haradinaj*, the criterion of protracted armed violence has in practice been interpreted as referring to the 'intensity' of armed violence rather than its 'duration'.[58] The Inter-American Commission on Human Rights also considered fighting at the La Tablada military base, despite the brief duration, to be a non-international armed conflict in light of the carefully planned, coordinated nature of the hostile acts undertaken by the attackers as well as the nature and level of the violence.[59] More recently, the International Committee of the Red Cross expressed its view that the March 2011 violence between Libya's government forces and rebel forces constituted a non-international armed conflict.[60]

Additional Protocol II expanded and strengthened the scheme of civilian protection by developing and supplementing Common Article 3. Yet the scope of application was restricted with strict conditions to be fulfilled. Additional Protocol II is to be applied to all armed conflicts:

> which take place in the territory of a High Contracting Party between its armed forces and dissident armed forces or other organized armed groups which, under responsible command, exercise such control over a part of its territory as to enable them to carry out sustained and concerted military operations and to implement this Protocol.[61]

Those conditions constitute a positive definition of non-international armed conflict for the purpose of this protocol, setting the objective criteria for its application: the organizational character, the level of intensity of armed conflict, territorial control, and the capacity of implementing the protocol.[62]

It is generally agreed that Common Article 3, as well as the 'core' of Additional Protocol II provided in Articles 2(1) and 4, has become customary international law, irrespective of the nature of the armed conflict.[63] Thus, parties to a non-international armed conflict are prohibited from engaging in acts of violence, torture and degrading or inhumane treatment, discriminatory treatment, collective punishment, medical or scientific experiments, sexual violence, ethnic cleansing,

---

58   *Prosecutor v Haradinaj* (ICTY) (Trial Chamber), Case No. IT-04-84-T, Judgment of 3 April 2008, para. 49.

59   *Juan Carlos Abella v Argentina* (Inter-American Commission of Human Rights), Case 11.137, 18 November 1997, paras 155–6, http://www.cidh.org/annualrep/97eng/argentina11137.htm#_ftn17

60   'Libya Engulfed in Civil War as Casualties Rise: ICRC', *Reuters*, 10 March 2011, http://www.reuters.com/article/2011/03/10/us-tripoli-cross-idUSTRE72927N20110310

61   APII, Art. 1.

62   For details, see Nasu, 'Status of Rebels', pp. 251–2; Sylvie Junod, 'Additional Protocol II: History and Scope', *American University Law Review*, 33 (1983): 29, 36–8.

63   The customary international law status of various rules applicable to non-international armed conflict has been examined, for example, in *San Remo Manual on the Law of Non-International Armed Conflict with Commentary*, para. 1.2.4; Henckaerts and Doswald-Beck.

hostage taking, pillage and enslavement. The customary international law status of other rules found in Additional Protocol II, such as forced displacement of civilians,[64] remains in dispute.[65] Thus, civilians are not protected from internment by detailed requirements or procedural safeguards in non-international armed conflicts,[66] especially if they are not covered by Additional Protocol II.[67]

In addition, in the case of non-international armed conflict, a state party to the conflict continues to be under an obligation to protect human rights within its own territory or jurisdiction.[68] This is particularly the case when the matter concerns the protection of civilians from acts of violence and threats, as opposed to civilian protection in the conduct of warfare.

Unlike the situation of military occupation, the relationship between international humanitarian law and human rights law has not been seen as posing a sharp conflict. In purely internal armed conflict, international human rights monitoring bodies and regional human rights courts have been making findings of human rights violations without explicitly applying the rules of international humanitarian law.[69] The jurisprudence developed by the inter-American human rights bodies, which has made explicit reference to relevant rules of international humanitarian law, should be seen as an exception.[70] When the armed conflict is between a state and an organized armed group operating in a foreign country, on the other hand, the application of human rights obligations to the former appears to be less compelling. This is because the latter country is presumed to have the

---

64   APII, Art. 17.

65   See, for example, Lindsay Moir, *The Law of Internal Armed Conflict* (Cambridge: Cambridge University Press, 2002), pp. 143–4.

66   Dieter Fleck, 'The Law of Non-International Armed Conflicts', in Fleck, *The Handbook of International Humanitarian Law*, p. 628. Internment is widely practised as a means of exercising control over certain persons without bringing criminal charges against them. See, Jacob Kellenberger, *Strengthening Legal Protection for Victims of Armed Conflicts* (Geneva: ICRC, 21 September 2010), http://www.icrc.org/web/eng/siteeng0.nsf/html/ihl-development-statement-210910

67   Cf. APII, Art. 5.

68   See, for example, Peter Rowe, *The Impact of Human Rights Law on Armed Forces* (Cambridge: Cambridge University Press, 2006), Ch. 6.

69   See, for example, William Abresch, 'A Human Rights Law of Internal Armed Conflict: The European Court of Human Rights in Chechnya', *European Journal of International Law*, 16 (2005): 741. There are difficulties for human rights bodies to determine the application of international humanitarian law. See Françoise J. Hampson, 'The Relationship Between International Humanitarian Law and Human Rights Law from the Perspective of a Human Rights Treaty Body', *International Review of the Red Cross*, 90 (2008): 549.

70   See Liesbeth Zegveld, 'The Inter-American Commission on Human Rights and International Humanitarian Law: A Comment on the Tablada Case', *International Review of the Red Cross*, 38 (1998): 505.

primary obligation to protect and ensure respect for human rights,[71] unless a person comes within the total and exclusive control of the former state.[72]

Civilian Protection from the Effects of Attacks

An Expansive Interpretation of Common Article 1 of 1949 Geneva Conventions

In the context of international humanitarian law, states party to 1949 Geneva Conventions are required, under Common Article 1, not only to respect but also to ensure respect for the conventions in all circumstances. Some commentators rely on this provision to suggest a broader meaning of the obligation, encompassing positive duties to protect civilians from violence by other parties,[73] particularly in light of Article 89 of Additional Protocol I to the Geneva Conventions.[74] Yet, the original intention of this provision was to impose the legal obligation on a contracting state to ensure that the whole of its population respects the law in all circumstances.[75] An expansive interpretation of Common Article 1 is difficult to maintain in the absence of a clear development of subsequent state practice.

Often cited as an authoritative support for this expansive interpretation of Common Article 1 is the International Court of Justice's Advisory Opinion on the *Legal Consequences of the Construction of a Wall in the Occupied Palestinian Territory*. The Court observed that every state party to the Geneva Conventions 'is under an obligation to ensure that the requirements of the instruments in question

---

71   See *Amnesty International Canada and British Columbia Civil Liberties Association v Chief of the Defence Staff for the Canadian Forces, Minister of National Defence and Attorney General of Canada* [2009] 4 FCR 149 (Federal Court of Appeal), paras 24–6 (per Desjardins JA with whom Richard CJ and Noël JA agreed); [2008] 4 FCR 546, paras 187–301.

72   See, eg, *Al-Saadoon and Mufdhi v The United Kingdom* (EHCR), Application No 61498/08, Admissibility Decision of 30 June 2009, paras 86–9; Öcalan *v Turkey* (ECHR), Application No 46221/99, Judgment of 12 May 2005, para. 91. See also, *Lopez Burgos v Uruguay* (International Human Rights Committee), Communication No 52/1979, para. 12.3; *Celeberti de Casariego v Uruguay* (International Human Rights Committee), Communication No 56/1979, para. 10.3.

73   See, for example, Siobhán Wills, *Protecting Civilians: The Obligations of Peacekeepers* (Oxford: Oxford University Press, 2009), pp. 100–106; Laurence Boisson de Chazournes and Luigi Condorelli, 'Common Article 1 of the Geneva Conventions Revisited: Protecting Collective Interests', *International Review of the Red Cross*, 82 (2000): 67.

74   It provides: 'In situations of serious violations of the Conventions or of this Protocol, the High Contracting parties undertake to act, jointly or individually, in co-operation with the United Nations and in conformity with the United Nations Charter.'

75   See especially, Frits Kalshoven, 'The Undertaking to Respect and Ensure Respect in All Circumstances: From Tiny Seed to Ripening Fruit', *Yearbook of International Humanitarian Law*, 2 (1999): 3–61.

are complied with'.[76] Yet, in elaborating on this obligation, the Court referred to negative obligations, speaking of 'an obligation not to recognize the illegal situation' and 'an obligation not to render aid or assistance in maintaining the situation'.[77] Other obligations the Court referred to are general in nature, requiring states 'to see to it that any impediment ... to the exercise by the Palestinian people of its right to self-determination is brought to an end' and 'to ensure compliance by Israel with international humanitarian law',[78] as well as calling upon the United Nations to 'consider what further action is required to bring to an end the illegal situation'.[79] The crucial question is whether Common Article 1 extends to include a positive obligation to take action to prevent violations against civilians or to protect civilians outside one's own control.

It is highly contentious to suggest that this general obligation would encompass a positive obligation for contracting parties to protect local civilians from attacks or violence in order to ensure respect for the Geneva Conventions by other states.[80] Even if a broader reading of Common Article 1 is adopted, it does not provide what action a contracting party should and is authorized to take to prevent or respond to violations of international humanitarian law. Nor does it indicate whether a state is even required to take preventive action to protect civilians before serious violations of humanitarian law are committed.

Precautions against the Effects of Attacks

Article 58 of the Additional Protocol I provides a more explicit obligation that states parties must protect civilians under their control from the effects of armed attacks. This involves a positive obligation to take necessary precautions to protect civilian populations (including not only a state's own population but also foreigners, refugees and enemy civilians in occupied territories) to the maximum extent feasible, against the effects of armed attacks. This obligation applies not only to states parties to an international armed conflict,[81] but also to a state involved in a non-international armed conflict under customary international law.[82] Those provisions for the protection of local civilians arguably constitute the 'principles and spirit' of international humanitarian law to which the UN peacekeeping forces are bound.[83]

---

76   *Palestinian Wall Advisory Opinion*, 200 para. 158.

77   Ibid., 200 para. 159.

78   Ibid.

79   Ibid., 200 para. 160.

80   Carlo Focarelli, 'Common Article 1 of the 1949 Geneva Conventions: A Soap Bubble?', *European Journal of International Law*, 21 (2010): 125.

81   API, Art. 58.

82   Henckaerts and Doswald-Beck, Rule 22.

83   See T. van Baarda and F. van Iersel, 'The Uneasy Relationship Between Conscience and Military Law: The Brahimi Report's Unresolved Dilemma', *International Peacekeeping*, 9/3 (2002): 25, 39.

Precautions against the effects of attacks include three specific obligations:

1. to endeavour to remove civilians and civilian objects from the vicinity of military objectives;
2. to avoid locating military objectives within or near densely populated areas; and
3. to protect civilians and civilian objects against the dangers resulting from military operations.

Throughout the development of the law of armed conflict, little attention has been given to the responsibilities of national authorities to ensure the security of their civilian population from the effects of armed attacks.[84] In this context, those precautionary obligations have the great potential for encouraging and facilitating more active and robust precautionary measures to protect civilians during an armed conflict. Yet, there remains uncertainty about the scope of this obligation in two respects.

The first point of uncertainty concerns the temporary dimension of the application of precautions. One view is that those precautionary obligations require long-term planning even in peacetime by civil authorities as well as military authorities.[85] On the other hand, some states might argue that obligations under the Additional Protocol I apply only in armed conflicts. It is conceivable that measures such as the evacuation of civilians from the vicinity of military objectives are likely to be undertaken only in times of armed conflict. Yet, such evacuation plans need to be drawn up prior to the armed conflict, with the preparation of an adequate air-raid warning system and shelters in order to implement these precautionary obligations.[86] Thus, the precautionary obligation to protect civilians arises even before violence is actually committed by virtue of the nature of the obligation.

The second point arises from the fact that the scope of the obligations is qualified by language such as 'to the maximum extent feasible' and 'under their control'. This discretionary wording might significantly undermine the extent to which a state may be forced to take action in compliance with precautionary obligations. Kalshoven and Zegveld observe that the obligations to take necessary

---

84 A.P.V. Rogers, *Law on the Battlefield*, 2nd edn (Manchester: Manchester University Press, 2004), pp. 120–21.

85 Louise Doswald-Beck, 'The Value of the 1977 Geneva Protocols for the Protection of Civilians', in Michael A. Meyer (ed.), *Armed Conflict and the New Law* (London: British Institute of International and Comparative Law, 1989), p. 162.

86 Rogers, pp. 122–3. Alternatively, human rights law recognizes a positive obligation on the part of national authorities to take preventive operational measures to protect civilians. See *Demiray v Turkey* (ECHR) Application No. 27308/95, Judgment of 21 November 2000, para. 41.

precautions 'may be very difficult, if not impossible, to realize'.[87] Having regard to the statements made by some states that Article 58 was not to be regarded as a restriction on measures for the defence of their national territory, Parks goes as far as to state that this provision is not obligatory.[88] The fact that failure to take precautions against the effects of attacks does not constitute a grave breach of international humanitarian law[89] supports their observations. Yet, the wording can also be seen as simply illustrating the drafters' intention that military personnel are not required to do the impossible.[90]

It is important to note the positive nature of the precautionary obligations against the effects of attacks. These obligations are not meant to establish criminal liability for failures of compliance, but rather require states to take positive steps to achieve good outcomes or to prevent bad ones.[91] Those positive obligations do not specify the exact nature of the required act, leaving room for discretion and choice.[92] States are rather guided by teleological norms that oblige them to bring about or to prevent certain states of affairs.[93] Here, one might find scope for operationalizing the 'responsibility to protect' concept that emerged in 2001 and was unanimously adopted by world leaders in 2005,[94] which can be characterized as providing a positive duty to protect civilians.[95] The obligation to take precautionary measures against the effects of attacks can be interpreted in light of this development and its potential as a legal source of compassing a duty to protect civilians in a prospective and positive sense.

---

87   Frits Kalshoven and Liesbeth Zegveld, *Constraints on the Waging of War*, 3rd edn (Geneva, ICRC, 2001), p. 110 .

88   W. Hays Parks, 'Air War and the Law of War', *Air Force Law Review*, 32 (1990): 1, 159.

89   Cf. API, Art. 85.

90   See Yves Sandoz, Christophe Swinarski and Bruno Zimmerman (eds), *Commentary on the Additional Protocols of 8 June 1977 to the Geneva Conventions of 12 August 1949* (Geneva: ICRC, 1987), p. 692; J.-F. Quéguiner, 'Precautions Under the Law Governing the Conduct of Hostilities', *International Review of the Red Cross*, 88 (2006): 793, 809–10, 820.

91   See, M. Bovens, *The Quest for Responsibility: Accountability and Citizenship in Complex Organisations* (Cambridge: Cambridge University Press,1998), pp. 26–38.

92   D. Birnbacher, 'Philosophical Foundations of Responsibility', in Ann E. Auhagen and Hans-Werner Bierhoff (eds), *Responsibility: The Many Faces of a Social Phenomenon* (London/New York: Routledge, 2001), p. 10.

93   Ibid.

94   See generally, Alex J. Bellamy, *Responsibility to Protect: The Global Effort to End Mass Atrocities* (Cambridge: Polity Press, 2009); Gareth Evans, *The Responsibility to Protect: Ending Mass Atrocity Crimes Once and For All* (Washington, DC: Brookings Institution Press, 2008); C. Stahn, 'Responsibility to Protect: Political Rhetoric or Emerging Legal Norm?', *American Journal of International Law*, 101 (2007): 99.

95   Sandra Szurek, '*La responsabilité de protéger, nature de l'obligation et responsabilité internationale*', in *Société Française pour le Droit International* (ed.), *La responsabilité de protéger – colloque de Nanterre* (Paris: Editions Pedone, 2008), pp. 94–7.

Complying with the precautionary obligation even before the rules of international humanitarian law become applicable has significant implications for peacekeeping troops deployed in a conflict area. This is because even if peacekeepers are not engaged in an armed conflict and hence are not directly bound by the rules of international humanitarian law, those precautionary obligations would require troop-contributing states, for example, not to locate their military camps near densely populated areas,[96] to evacuate civilians from the vicinity of military objectives and even to establish protected zones to protect civilians against the dangers resulting from military operations.

International humanitarian law envisages different safety zones, which merits attention in the context of civilian protection:

- Safety zone: to shelter the wounded, sick, aged persons, children under fifteen, expectant mothers and mothers of children in a place far removed from military operations (by agreement for mutual recognition).[97]
- Neutralized zone: to shelter the wounded, sick and civilians in the region where fighting is taking place.[98]
- Undefended localities ('open town'): an inhabited place open for occupation by an adverse party.[99]
- Demilitarized zones: areas established by an agreement for no mobile military equipment, no use of fixed military installations, no act of hostility or no activity linked to military efforts.[100]

Protected zones as part of UN peacekeeping operations are distinguished from those types of safety zones in international humanitarian law, in that protected zones need not be based on the consent of the parties to the conflict and they are not required to have an exclusively civilian character.[101]

Conclusion

This chapter has revisited the rules of international humanitarian law relevant to the protection of civilians against violence and from the effects of military

---

96   This issue has been raised with the International Security Assistance Force (ISAF) as a major concern posing a security threat to civilians. See UN Assistance Mission in Afghanistan (UNAMA), *Afghanistan: Annual Report on Protection of Civilians in Armed Conflict 2009* (Kabul, 2010), p. 19.

97   GCI, Art. 23; GCIV, Art. 14.

98   GCIV, Art. 15.

99   Hague Regulations, Art. 25; API, Art. 59; APII, Arts 13–14.

100   API, Art. 60.

101   See generally, K. Landgren, 'Safety Zones and International Protection: A Dark Grey Area', *International Journal of Refugee Law*, 7 (1995): 436–58.

attacks. The extent to which civilians are protected from acts of violence and the effects of attacks under international humanitarian law or even by application of international human rights law differs depending on how the armed conflict is classified. It has also been highlighted that international humanitarian law provides not only negative obligations to protect civilians but also imposes on states parties positive obligations, for example, to ensure humane treatment of civilians and to exercise necessary precautions to protect civilian populations to the maximum extent feasible against the effects of attacks. Those positive obligations also have significant implications for peacekeeping forces even when they are not directly engaged in an armed conflict by virtue of the nature of those obligations.

It is thus conceivable that the obligation to protect civilians can be discharged not only by responding to the actual or potential violence with military force, but also by proactively engaging in various measures to facilitate the creation of a secure environment where peacekeepers can maximize their capabilities in information gathering, analysis and operational manoeuvres. One might consider that in light of the failure in Srebrenica,[102] protected zones are ineffective as a measure for the protection of civilians in the absence of sufficient political will and military capabilities. Lessons need to be learned from the past failure to defend protected zones for the purpose of maximizing their potential as a way of implementing the positive obligation to protect civilians from acts of violence and the effects of attacks and further to operationalize the responsibility to protect civilians from mass atrocities.

---

102 *Report of the Secretary-General Pursuant to General Assembly Resolution 53/35: The Fall of Srebrenica*, UN Doc. A/54/549 (15 November 1999).

Chapter 6
Discriminate Warfare: The Military Necessity–Humanity Dialectic of International Humanitarian Law

Michael N. Schmitt

International humanitarian law (IHL) affords individual civilians, the civilian population and civilian objects a wide range of protection from the effects of war. For instance, it constrains the activities of occupation authorities, facilitates delivery of humanitarian assistance and limits the involvement of children in hostilities. The touchstone of civilian protection is, however, the principle of distinction. Its modern lineage as a customary-law norm can be traced back to the 1868 St Petersburg Declaration's pronouncement that 'the only legitimate object which States should endeavour to accomplish during war is to weaken the military forces of the enemy'.[1] Article 48 of the 1977 Additional Protocol I to the 1949 Geneva Conventions codifies this principle: 'In order to ensure respect for and protection of the civilian population and civilian objects, the Parties to the conflict shall at all times distinguish between the civilian population and combatants and between civilian objects and military objectives and accordingly shall direct their operations only against military objectives.'[2]

This chapter examines the impact of the distinction principle on the 'conduct of hostilities' – a legal term of art referring to combat. Companion chapters examine other protections set forth in humanitarian law. As this book also explores moral and ethical issues surrounding the protection of civilians, it must be acknowledged (at the risk of revealing jurisprudential hubris) that the chapter is premised on the notion that IHL amounts to the formal 'rules of the game' for warfare and, therefore, only law can technically render acts on the battlefield impermissible. Law represents an anticipatory compact among states as to those actions that are either prohibited or obligatory during armed conflict. It is grounded in and encompasses not only morality and ethics, but also broader domestic and international politics, as well as operational common sense. When the conduct

---

1   *Declaration Renouncing the Use, in Time of War, of Explosive Projectiles Under 400 Grammes Weight pmbl.*, 29 November 1868, 18 Martens Nouveau Recueil (Ser. 1) 474.

2   *Protocol Additional to the Geneva Conventions of 12 August 1949, and Relating to the Protection of Victims of International Armed Conflicts, June 8, 1977*, 1125 UNTS 3 [hereinafter Additional Protocol I], Art. 48.

of hostilities raises concerns as to the adequacy of civilian protection, it is left to states to recalibrate the law accordingly.

The Nature of International Humanitarian Law

To grasp the scope and nuances of the principle of distinction, it must be placed into context. In the international normative architecture, states alone make law. They do so in two ways. First, states may conclude a treaty – the key ones in IHL being the four Geneva Conventions of 1949 and their two 1977 Additional Protocols.[3] Treaties bind only the parties thereto. Second, international law can be customary in nature. Customary law emerges from a general practice of states, which has been accepted as law (*opinio juris*).[4] At the risk of oversimplification, when most states, especially those which are 'specially affected', either engage in a particular practice or refrain from a certain activity over time, and do so out of a sense of legal obligation, customary law emerges to bind all states. Since customary law is unwritten, it is difficult to ascertain either its precise contours or the moment when a practice matures into customary law.

The relationship between the two types of law is complex. Some treaty norms become accepted as customary law over time and thereby bind all states irrespective of party status. In IHL, the classic example is the 1907 Hague Convention IV.[5] Other treaty provisions might amount to a restatement of existing customary IHL. It is well accepted that the principle of distinction and its subsidiary rules generally fall into this category – a reality recognized by the International Court of Justice's characterization of distinction as a 'cardinal' principle of international

---

3	*Geneva Convention for the Amelioration of the Condition of the Wounded and Sick in Armed Forces in the Field of August 12, 1949*, 6 UST 3114, 75 UNTS 31 (hereinafter GCI); *Geneva Convention for the Amelioration of the Condition of Wounded, Sick and Shipwrecked Members of Armed Forces at Sea, August 12, 1949*, 6 UST 3217, 75 UNTS 85 (hereinafter GCII); *Geneva Convention Relative to the Treatment of Prisoners of War, August 12, 1949*, 6 UST 3316, 75 UNTS 135 (hereinafter GCIII); *Geneva Convention Relative to the Protection of Civilian Persons in Time of War, August 12, 1949*, 6 UST 3516, 75 UNTS 287 (hereinafter GCIV]; Additional Protocol I; *Protocol Additional to the Geneva Conventions of 12 August 1949, and Relating to the Protection of Victims of Non-International Armed Conflicts, June 8, 1977*, 1125 UNTS 609 (hereinafter Additional Protocol II).

4	*Statute of the International Court of Justice, June 26, 1945*, 59 Stat. 1055, 33 UNTS 993, Art. 38.

5	*Legal Consequences of the Construction of a Wall in the Occupied Palestinian Territory (Advisory Opinion)*, 2004 ICJ 136 (9 July), para. 89; *Legality of the Threat or Use of Nuclear Weapons (Advisory Opinion)*, 1996 ICJ 226 (8 July), para. 79. The rules were also found to be customary by the Nuremberg Tribunal. *1 Trial of the Major War Criminals Before the International Military Tribunal* 254 (1947).

humanitarian law.[6] Indeed, although attacks on civilians remain tragically commonplace in armed conflict, states universally condemn them as unlawful; no state takes the position today that attacking civilians is lawful.

That states, and only states, make IHL explains the unique quality of its provisions. States have an interest in protecting civilians, especially their own. The interest might be driven by moral commitment, fulfilment of a 'social contract' or simply the desire of a government to retain its population's support. Ascertaining why states embrace norms designed to protect the civilian population is a task better left to the philosophers and political scientists contributing to this volume. What is clear, though, is that from ancient times states have accepted constraints on military activities in order to safeguard civilian populations.[7] Since World War II, treaties and customary law designed to enhance such protection have blossomed.[8]

Yet, rules affording civilians protection come at a cost. For instance, the 1907 Hague Convention IV provides that '[i]n sieges and bombardments all necessary steps must be taken to spare, as far as possible, buildings dedicated to religion, art, science, or charitable purposes, historic monuments, hospitals and places where the sick and wounded are collected, provided they are not being used at the time for military purposes'.[9] Militarily, the requirement to avoid harming the enumerated protected places complicates planning and execution. Nevertheless, states have agreed through the instrument of IHL to accept the costs associated therewith.

States have an equally compelling interest in being able to effectively prosecute military operations. Therefore, they carefully consider the military implications of potential IHL norms before accepting them, through either treaty or state practice. Only prospective norms that are perceived by affected states as allowing sufficient freedom of military action can survive to become law.

As a result, IHL represents the synthesis in a dialectical process involving the balancing of two seemingly contradictory concerns: military necessity and humanity. The aforementioned rule illustrates precisely this balance. Although acquiescing to some operational restrictions, states have not agreed to an absolute ban on actions that threaten the specified protected places. Instead, the limits on

---

6   *Legality of the Threat or Use of Nuclear Weapons*, para. 78. The other is unnecessary suffering – a norm that safeguards only combatants since it is forbidden in the first place to attack civilians.

7   Coleman Phillipson, *The International Law and Custom of Ancient Greece and Rome* (London: Macmillan, 1911), Vol. II, pp. 166–364; Michael Howard, George J. Andreopoulos and Mark R. Shulman (eds), *The Laws of War: Constraints on Warfare in the Western World* (New Haven, CT: Yale University Press, 1997).

8   In particular, through GCIV, Additional Protocol I and Additional Protocol II. For the position of the International Committee of the Red Cross (ICRC) on the extant customary norms of international humanitarian law, see Jean-Marie Henckaerts and Louise Doswald-Beck (eds), *Customary International Humanitarian Law* (Cambridge: Cambridge University Press, 2005), Vol. I.

9   *Convention Respecting the Laws and Customs of War on Land, October 18, 1907*, 36 Stat. 2277, 207 Consol. TS 277, Annex Art. 27.

sieges and bombardments apply only 'so far as possible' and not at all when the places are used for military ends. These caveats reflect the military necessity concerns of states.

Every rule of IHL is the product of an identical balancing of military necessity (the need for military effectiveness) and humanitarian considerations (the desire of states to scale back the destruction and suffering caused during warfare). Accordingly, the very label 'international humanitarian law' is imperfect, for it suggests a disproportionate emphasis on the humanitarian aspect of the balance. The purpose of IHL is not solely to extend protections to civilians and their property. It is instead to find a rational equipoise between that goal and the equally valid objective of conducting effectual military operations in pursuit of national interests. No principle or rule of IHL more clearly reflects this dynamic than that of distinction.

The Principle of Distinction

The principle of distinction is operationalized in a number of subsidiary rules that delineate who and what may be attacked, set conditions on attacks and proscribe certain methods of attack. Although codified in Additional Protocol I, most are considered customary in nature by non-party states such as the United States.[10] Each reflects the military necessity–humanitarian considerations balance in a very distinct way.

Prohibited Targets

Article 51.2 of Additional Protocol I sets forth the most basic prohibition regarding legitimate targets: 'The civilian population as such, as well as individual civilians, shall not be the object of attack.'[11] On the one hand, the rule explicitly bans attacks on civilians – recognition of the fact that since such attacks seldom

---

10 For documents referring to such recognition, see US Army Judge Advocate General's School, *Law of War Documentary Supplement* (2010), pp. 232–6.

11 See also *Rome Statute of the International Criminal Court, July 17, 1998*, 2187 UNTS 90, Arts 8(2)(b)(i) and (e)(i) (hereinafter *ICC Statute*); Henckaerts and Doswald-Beck, Rule 1. Case law has confirmed the norm. See, for example, *Legality of the Threat or Use of Nuclear Weapons*, paras 78–9; *Armed Activities on the Territory of the Congo (Democratic Republic of the Congo v Uganda)*, 2005 ICJ 168 (19 December), paras 208, 211. Many cases of the International Criminal Tribunal for the Former Yugoslavia (ICTY) are in accord. See, for example, *Tadic, Interlocutory Appeal* (1995); *Karadzic and Mladic, Review of the Indictments* (1996); *Martic, Judgement* (2007); *Blaskic, Judgement on Appeal* (2004); *Galic, Judgement* (2003) and *Judgement on Appeal* (2006); *Kordic and Cerkez, Judgement* (2004); *Kupreskic, Judgement* (2000); *Milosevic, 2d Amended Indictment* (2002); *Jokic, Sentencing Judgement* (2004); *Stugar, Judgement* (2005); *D. Milosevic, Judgement* (2007).

weaken the enemy's military wherewithal, there is no military value in conducting them; humanitarian considerations therefore prevail. But on the other, it implicitly acknowledges that it is generally legitimate to attack the enemy's forces because doing so is militarily necessary.

Civilians are defined in the negative as individuals who are not:

- Members of the armed forces of a Party to the conflict as well as members of militias or volunteer corps forming part of such armed forces.
- Members of other militias and members of other volunteer corps, including those of organized resistance movements, belonging to a Party to the conflict and operating in or outside their own territory, even if this territory is occupied, provided that such militias or volunteer corps, including such organized resistance movements, fulfil the following conditions: a) that of being commanded by a person responsible for his subordinates; b) that of having a fixed distinctive sign recognizable at a distance; c) that of carrying arms openly; [and] d) that of conducting their operations in accordance with the laws and customs of war.
- Members of regular armed forces who profess allegiance to a government or an authority not recognized by the Detaining Power.
- Inhabitants of a non-occupied territory, who on the approach of the enemy spontaneously take up arms to resist the invading forces, without having had time to form themselves into regular armed units, provided they carry arms openly and respect the laws and customs of war.[12]

Essentially, the category of civilians encompasses all those who neither comprise the enemy's military, however constituted, nor fall into the unique category of the *levee en masse* – civilians who rise up to confront an invading force and are therefore assimilated to the enemy's forces.

Two applicative norms highlight the humanitarian underpinnings of the prohibition on attacking civilians. First, the rule is violated even if an attack proves unsuccessful – for instance, due to a weapons malfunction or an error in delivery. Thus, it is based on acts, rather than consequences – an appropriately heightened safeguard in light of the fact that an attacker gains little militarily by attacking civilians.

Second – and more illustrative of the balancing – an attacker must treat a target as a civilian and refrain from attack should doubt exist as to his or her status.[13] This rule should not be overstated, lest the balance be thrown off kilter. It is not the existence of any doubt that precludes attack, for doubt is a normal incident of warfare. Rather, '[t]he degree of doubt necessary to preclude an attack is that which would cause a

---

12   Derived from Additional Protocol I, Art. 50.1; GCIII, Art. 4(A)(1-3, 6).

13   Additional Protocol I, Art. 50.1. See also Special Court for Sierra Leone (SCSL), *Fofana and Kondewa, Judgement* (2007), paras 134–5; ICTY, *Galic, Judgement* (2003), para. 50; ICTY, *D. Milosevic, Judgement* (2007), para. 946.

reasonable attacker in [the] same or similar circumstances to abstain from ordering or executing an attack'.[14] The presumption of civilian status is therefore both rebuttable and conditioned by military reasonableness. It is not absolute.

Civilians uninvolved in the hostilities may not be attacked even if doing so would seemingly benefit the other side. To take one example: purely political leaders may not be directly targeted even if doing so might benefit the other side by disrupting governance. But the principle of distinction nevertheless accommodates military necessity by withdrawing protection from attack 'for such time as [civilians] take a direct part in hostilities'.[15] Thus, civilians who take up arms become legitimate targets.

This rule, codified in Article 51(3) of Additional Protocol I, has been the subject of considerable recent attention within the IHL community. In 2003, the International Committee of the Red Cross (ICRC) convened a group of international experts to consider the issue of direct participation by civilians in hostilities. The result was its publication in 2009 of the controversial *Interpretive Guidance on the Notion of Direct Participation in Hostilities Under International Humanitarian Law.*[16] Virtually all criticism aimed at the document can be boiled down to a concern that the ICRC miscalculated the military necessity–humanity balance in interpreting the rule.[17]

There is much to recommend the *Guidance*. For instance, it treats organized armed groups belonging to a party to the conflict as 'armed forces' regardless of whether they meet the standards set forth earlier, thereby rendering them attackable

---

14   Program on Humanitarian Policy and Conflict Research, *Manual on International Law Applicable to Air and Missile Warfare* (Harvard University, 2009), p. 87.

15   Additional Protocol I, Art. 51.3 (international); Additional Protocol II, Art. 13.3 (non-international). See also Geneva Conventions I–IV, Art. 3; *ICC Statute*, Arts 8.2(b)(i) and 8.2(e)(i); International Criminal Tribunal for Rwanda (ICTR), *Bagilishema, Judgement* (2001); ICTY, *Simic, Judgement* (2003); ICTY, *Galic, Judgement* (2003); ICTY, *Kordic and Cerkez, Judgement* (2004); ICTY, *D. Milosevic, Judgement* (2007); SCSL, *Fofana and Kondewa, Judgement* (2007).

16   Nils Melzer, *Interpretive* Guidance *on the Notion of Direct Participation in Hostilities Under International Law* (Geneva: ICRC, 2009). The author was one of the experts who participated in the project.

17   Bill Boothby, '"And for Such Time As": The Time Dimension to Direct Participation in Hostilities', *New York University Journal of International Law and Politics*, 42 (2010): 741; W. Hays Parks, 'Part IX of the ICRC "Direct Participation in Hostilities" Study: No Mandate, No Expertise, and Legally Incorrect', *New York University Journal of International Law and Politics*, 42 (2010): 769; Michael N. Schmitt, 'Deconstructing Direct Participation in Hostilities: The Constitutive Elements', *New York University Journal of International Law and Politics*, 42 (2010): 697; Kenneth Watkin, 'Opportunity Lost: Organized Armed Groups and the ICRC "Direct Participation in Hostilities" Interpretive Guidance', *New York University Journal of International Law and Politics*, 42 (2010): 641; Michael N. Schmitt, 'The Interpretive Guidance on the Notion of Direct Participation in Hostilities: A Critical Analysis', *Harvard National Security Journal*, 1 (2010): 5.

at any time as if they were the enemy's military.[18] From a military perspective, such an approach makes great sense, since it should not matter whether, for instance, members of a group fighting your forces wear uniforms before you may treat them as the enemy.

Moreover, the *Guidance* provides useful criteria against which to assess whether activities civilians engage in constitute direct participation in hostilities such that they lose their protection from attack. According to the *Guidance*, an act qualifies as direct participation when it meets three cumulative criteria:

1. The act must be likely to adversely affect the military operations or military capacity of a party to an armed conflict or, alternatively, to inflict death, injury, or destruction on persons or objects protected against direct attack (threshold of harm).
2. There must be a direct causal link between the act and the harm likely to result either from that act, or from a coordinated military operation of which that act constitutes an integral part (direct causation).
3. The act must be specifically designed to directly cause the required threshold of harm in support of a party to the conflict and to the detriment of another (belligerent nexus).[19]

The issue of direct participation is dealt with directly in a companion chapter. Suffice it to say here that articulation of criteria by which a civilian's act deprives them of protection is exceptionally useful to forces in the field when determining whether lethal force may be used against that individual.

Yet, critics correctly argue that the *Guidance* exaggerates humanitarian considerations in a number of regards. For example, they suggest that there should be no 'belonging to a party' requirement for organized armed groups. Commanders are not concerned with whether there is a relationship between the group opposing their forces and the opposing belligerent state; they merely want to treat any organized armed group that attacks them as the enemy. The situation in Iraq during the international armed conflict phase of the war illustrates this predicament. Certain Shia militia and jihadists were unaffiliated with the regime, but posed a threat to Coalition forces on par with that of the regular Iraqi armed forces. To have imposed a requirement that they be treated differently would have run counter to military common sense.

The *Guidance* also provides that only those members of an organized armed group who have a 'continuous combat function' qualify as members of the group who are targetable at all times. Critics point out that this interpretation affords certain group members greater protection than the regular armed forces, who (with the exception of medical and religious personnel) are targetable regardless of their assigned duties.

---

18 Melzer, p. 22.
19 Ibid., p. 45.

Although most of the experts who participated in the ICRC project accepted the three cumulative criteria for direct participation, many disagreed with the examples proffered in the document. In particular, the *Guidance* cited assembly of improvised explosive devices (IED) and voluntary human shielding of military objectives as examples of *in*direct participation in the hostilities.[20] For the critics, both activities amount to clear instances of direct participation. They argue that it would defy logic to refrain from attacking civilians assembling the one weapon that has proven most deadly in Iraq and Afghanistan. As to voluntary human shielding, the critics acknowledge that there would seldom be any military benefit from directly attacking human shields, but assert that it would be insensible to have to consider harm to them when making proportionality calculations or determining what precautions to take in attack (see below), as would be required if they retain full civilian protections. After all, the very purpose of their voluntary shielding is to interfere with military operations. For the critics, the military necessity imperative in both cases is overwhelming, especially in light of the fact that the civilians concerned have of their own volition decided to become involved in the conflict without any right to do so.

The greatest concern over the *Guidance*'s interpretation of the direct participation standard came with regard to the 'for such time' aspect of the norm. For the ICRC, the deprivation of civilian protection extended only to '[m]easures preparatory to the execution of a specific act of direct participation in hostilities, as well as the deployment to and the return from the location of its execution'.[21] Critics responded that this standard was overly restrictive, for it created a 'revolving door'. By the ICRC interpretation, civilians participating in the conflict would regain their immunity from attack between each operation. From a military perspective, it makes little sense to know individuals are going to attack or otherwise become directly involved in the fighting, as they have in the past, but be unable to strike them until they are preparing to conduct the next operation. In many cases, you might not know when or where you are going to be attacked, but have reliable intelligence that particular individuals will be involved; to fail to act when the opportunity presents itself would be militarily irresponsible. As these examples illustrate, it is often one's assessment of how to balance military necessity and humanitarian considerations that drives interpretation and application of the IHL norms bearing on the protection of civilians in armed conflict.

In addition to the prohibition on directly targeting civilians, IHL forbids 'acts or threats of violence the primary purpose of which is to spread terror among the civilian population'. The rule is found in Article 51.2 of Additional Protocol I and in customary international law.[22] It is particularly noteworthy in humanitarian

---

20   Ibid., pp. 54, 56–7.

21   Ibid., p. 65.

22   Additional Protocol I, Art. 51.2; Henckaerts and Doswald-Beck, Rule 2. For cases dealing with the subject, see ICTY, *Dukic, Initial Indictment* (1996); ICTY, *Martic, Review of the Indictment* (1996); ICTY, *Kradzic and Mladic, Review of the Indictments* (1996);

terms, for it encompasses 'threats' that merely cause mental anguish. A recent example would be Muammar Gaddafi's claim that Libyan forces would 'come house by house, room by room' in their attack against the rebels' stronghold of Benghazi – a city with a population of 700,000.[23]

As with that on targeting civilians, the prohibition accommodates military considerations. Most importantly, only those acts or threats that are intended to terrorize are precluded, thereby allowing for operations against lawful targets that incidentally cause terror. It was essential from a military-necessity perspective to so limit the prohibition because many attacks often frighten the civilian population without that being their purpose. Additionally, the requisite intent must be the primary one. An attacker might understand that terror could result from an operation, and even relish the prospect of such an eventuality, but unless terrorization is the underlying objective, the operation is lawful.

This raises the issue of targeting civilian morale. It is a topic characterized by much misunderstanding. Civilian morale is neither a lawful nor an unlawful target *per se*. The legal question is whether the target that is attacked in order to affect civilian morale otherwise qualifies as a combatant, a direct participant in hostilities or a military objective. Except for terror attacks, motive is irrelevant so long as the person or object attacked is a lawful target; should they not be, the attack would be unlawful in any event. For instance, it is acceptable to target military objectives or personnel in the enemy's capital early in a conflict to demonstrate military supremacy and thereby demoralize the civilian population and diminish its support for the war effort. But it would be unlawful to strike civilians or civilian objects for the same purpose. The military necessity–humanitarian considerations balance has already been struck in international humanitarian law.

International humanitarian law also extends protection to civilian objects. Pursuant to Article 52.1 – a provision undoubtedly reflective of customary law – '[c]ivilian objects shall not be the object of attack'.[24] Civilian objects are those objects that are not military objectives, defined as 'objects which by their nature, location, purpose or use make an effective contribution to military action and whose total or partial destruction, capture or neutralization, in the circumstances ruling at the time, offers a definite military advantage'.[25]

The balance is again apparent. As with civilians who directly participate in hostilities, a civilian object may lose its protection from attack when its destruction (or other form of harm) is militarily necessary. By law, this happens

---

ICTY, *Blagogevich and Jokic, Judgement* (2005); ICTY, *Galic, Judgement on Appeal* (2006); ICTY, *D. Milosevic, Judgement* (2007); SCSL, *Fofana and Kondewa, Judgement* (2007); SCSL, *Brima, Judgement* (2007); SCSL, *Taylor, 2d Amended Indictment* (2007).

23 Dan Bilefsky and Mark Landler, 'Military Action Against Qaddafi is Backed by U.N.', *The New York Times*, 18 March 2011, p. A1.

24 See also Henckaerts and Doswald-Beck, Rule 7; *ICC Statute*, Art. 8.2(b)(ii); ICTY, *Blaskic, Judgement* (2000); ICTY, *S. Milosevic, 1st Amended Indictment* (2002).

25 Additional Protocol I, Art. 52.2.

when the civilian object has military significance because of its location (for example, a mountain pass through which enemy forces will pass), is being used militarily (for example, a minaret or church steeple used as a military observation post) or will be so used in the future (the 'purpose' criterion – for example, an apartment building being converted into military barracks). The legal conversion into a military objective is not unconditional. Before it occurs, the contribution to military operations must be 'effective'; in other words, actual; and the advantage gained through striking the object must be 'definite' – that is, more than merely 'potential, speculative or indeterminate'.[26]

Although the textual definition of 'military objective' is universally accepted,[27] its application is the subject of an ongoing debate – one that lies at the core of the balance between military necessity and humanitarian considerations. It is generally accepted that the definition encompasses any objects that are 'war fighting', such as military equipment, or 'war supporting', such as a factory producing munitions or a port used for military shipments. The United States, however, in its current law of armed conflict manual, *The Commander's Handbook on the Law of Naval Operations*, extends the definition to those entities that are 'war-sustaining'.[28] As an example, it notes that '[e]conomic objects of the enemy that indirectly but effectively support and sustain the enemy's war-fighting capability' may be attacked.[29]

The paradigmatic case would be oil production and transhipment facilities used to generate export revenue that finances the war effort. The facilities in no way directly enhance the military wherewithal of the state, yet but for the income from oil production, the state's ability to field a military over an extended period would be severely hampered. The Americans have concluded that the military necessity of denying the enemy such funds justifies including war-sustaining objects in the definition of military objectives. For many other nations, humanitarian considerations would dominate, such that attack on such objects would be prohibited even though their destruction would clearly, albeit indirectly, benefit the attacking side.

International humanitarian law imposes a number of additional prohibitions and restrictions on targeting objects that might place the civilian population at risk or otherwise negatively affect it. The precise parameters of the law vary. In some cases, the prohibition is absolute, whereas in others IHL merely restricts the nature of an attack. Although space does not permit a comprehensive catalogue of the prohibitions and restrictions, the reader's attention is drawn to the IHL

---

26   Yves Sandoz, Christophe Swinarski and Bruno Zimmerman (eds), *Commentary on the Additional Protocols of 8 June 1977 to the Geneva Conventions of 12 August 1949* (Geneva: ICRC, 1987), para. 2024.

27   Henckaerts and Doswald-Beck, Rule 8; Department of the Navy, *The Commander's Handbook on the Law of Naval Operations (NWP 1-14M)* (2007), para. 8.2. The United States is not a party to the protocol.

28   Department of the Navy, para. 8.2.

29   Ibid., para. 8.2.5.

provisions governing medical and religious personnel, units and transports, the natural environment, civil defence personnel, matériel and facilities, cultural property, objects indispensable to the civilian population, UN personnel, matériel and facilities and humanitarian aid.[30]

Each of these rules takes account of the military-necessity aspect of international humanitarian law. For instance, medical and religious personnel, units or transports may not be made the object of attack.[31] Should they engage in, or be used for, acts harmful to the enemy, however, protection ceases (although for units and facilities, such protection may be withdrawn only following an unheeded warning to desist).[32] The special protection of the natural environment, which is solely a matter of treaty law, comes into play only when an attack might be expected to cause 'widespread, long-term and severe damage' to the environment.[33] UN peacekeepers enjoy immunity from attack, but only so long as the United Nations or the states comprising UN forces are not a party to the conflict, in which case their military personnel qualify as combatants subject to attack.[34]

A highly controversial topic in the law governing targeting – and one that acutely exemplifies the complexity of balancing military necessity with humanitarian considerations – is that of reprisals. Reprisals are otherwise unlawful acts taken in response to the enemy's serious illegal acts. They are not retaliatory or vengeful in nature, but instead are intended to force the enemy back into compliance with the law. In essence, they allow for a relaxation of humanitarian considerations in order to achieve compliance by the enemy with the balance already set by the law.

Since reprisals might involve attacking persons or objects that are otherwise protected by IHL, they are subject to very strict conditions. These include notice that reprisals will be taken if the enemy does not desist in violating the law, exhaustion of other means to secure compliance with legal norms and proportionality between a reprisal and the offending act. Because they involve a deviation from generally applicable norms, reprisals are meant to be authorized only at the highest levels of government.

There is significant disagreement over who and what may be the subject of reprisals. Some states and commentators take a very narrow view, arguing that the law has evolved to a point where reprisals are prohibited. Others take a much broader view. Both sides point in justification to humanitarian considerations – the former arguing that it is incongruous to lower the shield of immunity from attack, the latter suggesting that doing so is the only viable means of ensuring compliance by the enemy with its humanitarian obligations. Despite the differences, consensus

---

30 See, for example, rules and commentary contained in Program on Humanitarian Policy and Conflict Research, ss. K, M, N and O.

31 GCI, Arts 19, 24, 25, 35; GCII, Art. 36; GCIV, Arts 18, 20, 21; Additional Protocol I, Arts 12, 15, 21, 24.

32 GCI, Art. 21; GCII, Art. 34; GCIV, Art. 19; Additional Protocol I, Arts 13(1), 21.

33 Additional Protocol I, Arts 35.3, 55.1.

34 Program on Humanitarian Policy and Conflict Research, p. 225.

exists that the following may not be the subject of reprisals as a matter of customary law: the wounded, sick and shipwrecked; medical personnel and chaplains; medical units, establishments and transports; prisoners of war; and persons and property protected under the Fourth Geneva Convention, in particular persons in occupied territory.[35] Additional Protocol I extends the protection (for states party thereto) to civilians and the civilian population, civilian objects, historical monuments, works of art or places of worship that constitute the cultural or spiritual heritage of peoples, objects indispensable to the survival of the civilian population such as foodstuffs, crops, livestock, drinking-water installations and supplies and irrigation works, the natural environment and works or installations containing dangerous forces – namely, dams, dykes and nuclear electrical generating stations.[36] The extent to which these treaty norms have matured into customary law is uncertain.

Some states party to the protocol qualify the prohibitions. Of particular note, the United Kingdom issued a statement on ratification to the effect that if the enemy makes 'serious and deliberate' attacks against the enumerated persons and objects, it 'will regard itself as entitled to take measures otherwise prohibited by the Articles in question to the extent that it considers such measures necessary for the sole purpose of compelling the adverse party to cease committing violations'.[37] Uneasy with the balance set by Additional Protocol I *vis-à-vis* reprisals, the United Kingdom has claimed a right to deviate from its strictures when necessary to restore the military necessity–humanitarian considerations balance.

Conditions on Targeting

Even when a planned attack is to be conducted against a lawful target, it must still comply with the rule of proportionality – a key component of the protection civilians enjoy during armed conflict. The rule – codified in Articles 51 and 57 of Additional Protocol I and reflective of customary international law – provides that attacks that 'may be expected to cause incidental loss of civilian life, injury to civilians, damage to civilian objects, or a combination thereof, which would be excessive in relation to the concrete and direct military advantage anticipated', are prohibited.[38] Everyone in the 'kill chain', especially those who plan, approve or execute an attack, shoulder the obligation. As an example, if a pilot reaches

---

35   GCI, Art. 14; GCII, Art. 16; GCIII, Art. 13; GCIV, Art. 33. See also UK Ministry of Defence, *The Manual of the Law of Armed Conflict* (London, 2004), para. 16.18.

36   Additional Protocol I, Arts 20, 51.6, 52.1, 53(c), 54.4, 55.2, 56.

37   Reprinted in UK Ministry of Defence, para. 16.19.1.

38   Additional Protocol I, Arts 51.5(b), 57.2(a)(iii), 57.2(b). See also *ICC Statute*, Art. 8.2(b)(iv); Henckaerts and Doswald-Beck, Rule 14; ICTY, *Kupreskic, Judgement* (2000); ICTY, *Galic, Judgement on Appeal* (2006); ICTY, *Kodic and Cerkez, Judgement on Appeal* (2004); ICTY, *D. Milosevic, Judgement* (2007); ICTY, *Martic, Judgement* (2007).

the target area only to discover the presence of unanticipated civilians, they must reassess whether the attack would be proportional in the attendant circumstances.[39]

The rule of proportionality is the paradigmatic exemplar of balancing military necessity and humanitarian considerations. No matter how important the target, striking it is unlawful when the likely collateral damage caused to civilians and civilian property will be excessive relative to the value of that target. On the other hand – and contrary to mistaken ICRC commentary on the rule[40] – there is no point at which the collateral damage, standing alone, prohibits an attack. Instead, an attack must always be assessed in light of what the attacker reasonably hopes to gain militarily. This is true even when the collateral damage is 'extensive'. Resultantly, there are situations in which light collateral damage will preclude attack because the anticipated military utility of the attack is so slight. For example, it would not be lawful to attack a single, unarmed low-level soldier in an urban area far from the battlefield if civilian lives were placed at serious risk. Conversely, in some situations a great deal of collateral damage will be lawful due to the exceptional significance of the target, as in the case of striking a target in order to severely disrupt enemy command and control.

The qualifiers 'expected' and 'anticipated' make clear that the assessment is based upon the reasonable expectations of the attacker as to both the military advantage to be gained and the collateral damage to be caused, not the operation's eventual consequences. The results of an attack are relevant as to the reasonableness of the attacker's expectations, but do not bear directly on the proportionality calculation itself.

This point is frequently missed. Drawing on recent events, for example, Predator attacks in Pakistan have been condemned as disproportionate on the basis that they have caused civilian casualties or that the individuals targeted were either not insurgents or absent at the time of the strike. Yet, the causation of civilian casualties is not in itself unlawful; the very existence of the rule of proportionality disproves any such claim. And misidentification of targets and the targets' absence raise questions as to whether sufficient steps were taken to identify the target. This is an issue of the adequacy of precautions in attack (discussed below), not proportionality.

Despite common misapplication of the rule of proportionality in this regard, there is absolute consensus as a matter of law that only the expected, vice actual, collateral damage factors into a proportionality assessment. What qualifies as collateral damage, however, is less certain. Two points of disagreement prevail; both reflect differences over how best to balance military necessity and humanitarian considerations.

It is generally agreed that the death of or injury to civilians or damage to or destruction of civilian objects does qualify. It is equally agreed that mere inconvenience for civilians does not. Between these extremes, there is no bright line. In particular, does non-physical suffering count and, if so, what degree and

---

39 Additional Protocol I, Art. 57.2(b).
40 Sandoz et al., para. 1980.

type of non-physical suffering? Consider an attack that is not intended to terrorize the civilian population (and thus is not prohibited *per se*), but nonetheless does so. Should the mental anguish count as collateral damage? The most defensible view is that it should not, for the *lex scripta* itself speaks of loss of civilian life, injury to civilians and damage to civilian objects.[41] States have arguably already agreed as to the type of harm that qualifies based on their determination of the appropriate balance between military and humanitarian concerns. An alternative view, however – one placing increased emphasis on humanitarian considerations – is that the type of qualifying harm should not be so narrowly construed, although where the line would be drawn by advocates of this approach is unclear.[42]

More problematic is the issue of indirect (or reverberating or knock-on) effects. All concur that any direct harm to civilians or civilian property, as in collapse of a civilian facility due to an adjacent blast, is collateral damage. There is also complete agreement that speculative harm or harm that was not reasonably foreseeable in the circumstances plays no part in proportionality analysis. Disagreement arises, however, over indirect harm, such as that caused during an attack on an electrical grid that deprives hospitals of electricity or interferes with the civilian emergency-response system, thereby indirectly resulting in civilian casualties. One school of thought holds that only directly caused damage factors into the proportionality calculation. The better position – and the one generally adopted by militaries – is that any reasonably foreseeable death of or injury to civilians or damage to or destruction of civilian property counts. That the harm must be 'reasonably foreseeable' alleviates any concern that this interpretation might unduly restrict military operations.

Even when an attack is properly directed against a lawful target and would not result in excessive harm to civilians and civilian property, the law still requires attackers to do everything reasonable in the circumstances to avoid collateral damage. This is the requirement to 'take precautions in attack'. A customary norm codified in Article 57 of Additional Protocol I, the rule requires attackers to take 'constant care … to spare the civilian population, civilians and civilian objects'.[43]

A number of specific precautions 'operationalize' the general requirement. Those who plan or decide on attacks must 'do everything feasible to verify that the objectives to be attacked are neither civilians nor civilian objects' or otherwise subject to any special protection, as with medical facilities.[44] They must also select

---

41   Program on Humanitarian Policy and Conflict Research, p. 91.

42   Knut Dörmann, 'Applicability of Additional Protocols to Computer Network Attack', Paper delivered at the International Expert Conference on Computer Network Attacks and the Applicability of International Humanitarian Law, Stockholm, 17–19 November 2004, www.icrc. org/web/eng/siteeng0.nsf/htmlall/68lg92?opendocument (in the context of cyber operations).

43   Additional Protocol I, Art. 57.1. See also Henckaerts and Doswald-Beck, Ch. 5; ICTY, *Kupreskic, Judgement* (2000); ICTY, *Galic, Judgement on Appeal* (2006).

44   Additional Protocol I, Art. 57.2(a)(1). See also Henckaerts and Doswald-Beck, Rule 16. The warning requirement for medical facilities is in GCI, Art. 21; Additional Protocol I, Art. 13.1.

weapons, tactics and targets that would minimize harm to civilians and civilian property whenever 'feasible'.[45]

The term 'feasible' in both rules indicates that attackers need not sacrifice possible military advantage, accept diminished likelihood of success or engage in otherwise militarily insensible operations to avoid civilian harm.[46] For example, a precision-guided munition must be used when readily available and its employment would lessen the risk of collateral damage. But if such weapons are in short supply, they may be withheld for subsequent operations in which their employment might enhance the probability of striking a higher-value target or be more beneficial in avoiding collateral damage. Similarly, if the objective is to disrupt rail traffic temporarily then tracks should be destroyed rather than a rail terminal in which civilian casualties might be high. If, however, the goal is long-term disruption then it may be acceptable to strike the terminal, assuming the rule of proportionality is satisfied.

The precautions in attack requirements also mandate an 'effective advance warning' when an attack 'may affect the civilian population, unless circumstances do not permit'.[47] Again, note how the requirement is conditioned by military practicalities. In order to maintain the element of surprise or limit risk to attacking forces, circumstances might justify only a general warning that attacks will take place or even no warning at all. This is especially so when attackers are seeking to kill a particular person, for the target would flee were they to receive an advance warning.

Prohibited Methods of Targeting

The principle of distinction also protects the civilian population by forbidding certain 'indiscriminate' forms of attack. States have agreed through IHL that the likely military benefits of such attacks, as they are indiscriminate, are too speculative and indeterminate to risk potential harm to civilians, civilian property and other protected persons and objects.

First, the law prohibits attacks that are 'not directed at a specific military objective'.[48] These attacks must be distinguished from those directed at protected

---

45   Additional Protocol I, Art. 57.2(a)(ii); Henckaerts and Doswald-Beck, Rule 17.

46   On ratification of Additional Protocol I, the United Kingdom stated that it understood 'feasible' to mean 'that which is practicable or practically possible, taking into account all circumstances ruling at the time, including humanitarian and military considerations'. Letter from Christopher Hulse, Ambassador for the United Kingdom to Switzerland (28 January 1998), http://www.icrc.org/ihl.nsf/NORM/0A9E03F0F2EE757CC1256402003FB6D2?OpenD ocument, reprinted in relevant part in UK Ministry of Defence, p. 59 (Fn 32). The same formula appears in the *Protocol on Prohibitions or Restrictions on the Use of Incendiary Weapons (Protocol III), October 10, 1980*, S. Treaty Doc. No. 105-1 (1997), 1342 UNTS 171, Art. 1(5); *Amended Protocol on Prohibitions or Restrictions on the Use of Mines, Booby Traps and Other Devices (Amended Protocol II), May 3, 1996*, S. Treaty Doc. No. 105-1 (1997), Art. 3(10).

47   Additional Protocol I, Art. 57.2(c). See also Henckaerts and Doswald-Beck, Rule 20.

48   Additional Protocol I, Art. 51.4(a). See also Henckaerts and Doswald-Beck, Rule 12.

persons and objects such as civilians and civilian objects. The prohibition bans un-aimed attacks, such as firing rockets blindly into a city in the mere hope of hitting a military objective or releasing bombs over enemy territory without aiming at any particular target.

Second, IHL bars the use of 'methods or means [tactics or weapons] of combat which cannot be directed at a specific military objective' or have uncontrollable effects.[49] The former prohibits use of weapons that cannot be reliably aimed at lawful targets, the standard example being V-2 rockets fired against England during World War II. At issue is the guidance system in the abstract. In other words, to be banned, there must be no reasonably foreseeable situation in which the weapon could be used effectively against enemy military objectives and personnel. Iraq's use of Scud missiles during the Gulf War of 1990–91 illustrates the distinction. Although the Scud has a rudimentary guidance system, the weapon was capable of discriminate use, as in attacking armoured formations in the desert or large, remote military bases. But this legally discriminate weapon was used indiscriminately when fired into population centres. Said use was unlawful because they were not directed against specific military objectives within the cities.

The other prohibition found in the weapons provision bans those having uncontrollable effects – that is, an attacker cannot limit their effects to lawful targets. Biological weapons, which are otherwise unlawful, exemplify the dynamic. Although biological contagions may be directed against enemy personnel, as in releasing them over a military base, it would be impossible to constrain the subsequent spread of many such contagions into the civilian population. In modern warfare, certain computer viruses intended to spread randomly throughout a particular military network could violate the norm if they are not designed to preclude likely transmission into civilian networks (assuming the requisite level of harm – death, injury, damage, destruction – was likely to eventuate).

Third, IHL prohibits 'an attack by bombardment by any methods or means which treats as a single military objective a number of clearly separated and distinct military objectives located in a city, town, village or other area containing a similar concentration of civilians or civilian objects'.[50] This rule bars area (or 'carpet') targeting, albeit only when not militarily necessary. Take a town in which a particular district has many military targets. This is often the case in capitals, where the military headquarters, supporting barracks and logistics facilities are located in close proximity to each other. If the attacker has the means of striking each of the facilities individually, and doing so is militarily feasible (for instance, enemy defences are not robust enough to hinder individual attacks), it would be unlawful to treat the entire area as one target. On the other hand, if individual

---

49   Additional Protocol I, Art. 51.4(b) and (c). See also Henckaerts and Doswald-Beck, Rule 12; *Legality of the Threat or Use of Nuclear Weapons*, paras 78–9; ICTY, *Martic, Judgement* (2007).

50   Additional Protocol I, Art. 51.5(a). See also *Amended Protocol II to the Convention on Certain Conventional Weapons*, Art. 3(9).

attacks were not feasible – for instance, due to the absence of sufficiently precise weaponry or heavy enemy defences in the target area – and attack would not be expected to cause excessive collateral damage, the military objectives may be treated as a single targetable area.

The Defender's Obligation

The principle of distinction bears primarily on the actions of attackers. Defenders also, however, shoulder obligations to protect the civilian population. These are found primarily in Additional Protocol I, Articles 51.8 and 58, which are generally accepted as reflective of customary law. The former prohibits the use of human shields 'to render certain points or areas immune from military operations, in particular in attempts to shield military objectives from attacks or to shield, favour or impede military operations'. It also forbids directing 'the movement of the civilian population or individual civilians in order to attempt to shield military objectives from attacks or to shield military operations'. No distinction is made between the use of voluntary and involuntary shields. It must be cautioned that an element of *mens re* is present. It would not be unlawful, for example, for troops to travel down the same road as fleeing civilians unless there was an intention to take advantage of the presence of the civilians to shield those troops from attack.

> Article 58 requires parties to a conflict, to the 'maximum extent feasible', to endeavour to remove the civilian population, individual civilians and civilian objects under their control from the vicinity of military objectives, avoid locating military objectives within or near densely populated areas [and to] take other necessary precautions to protect the civilian population, individual civilians and civilian objects under their control against the dangers resulting from military operations.

Again, this norm is subject to a feasibility caveat. As an example, in many cases it would not be militarily feasible to evacuate a large urban area in which military objectives are based since a massive evacuation might hinder the ability of the defending forces to manoeuvre or otherwise place manpower demands on the military that could not be met in the circumstances. Additionally, it is accepted that military objectives are often placed in the vicinity of civilians and civilian objects for good military reasons. National military headquarters, for instance, are typically based in the nation's capital. The defence of key cities also necessitates the presence of military forces and military assets are often located near key lines of communication, such as ports, major highways, rail lines and airports, for military logistical purposes. Application of the rule therefore demands sensible balancing of the goal of protecting the civilian population with valid military needs.

Concluding Thoughts

It should be clear that the law extending protection from the effects of warfare to the civilian population reflects a dialectical process during which states delicately balance military needs and humanitarian concerns. Therefore, neither aspect ever reigns fully supreme. At times, military necessity, although unambiguous and pressing, must yield to the greater demands of protecting civilians, civilian property and other protected persons and objects. At others, the law allows protected persons and objects to be placed at risk – even knowingly killed or destroyed – in order to attain important military goals. This agreed upon balance might shift over time with the emergence of new treaties of customary norms or through reinterpretation of existing law, but so long as warfare remains a reality of the human condition, the balancing will remain a constant.

Two cautionary notes are necessary. To begin with, beware those who would distort this carefully crafted balance. One might argue that IHL is overly restrictive, as often occurred in the aftermath of the attacks of 9/11. Alternatively, it might be proffered that IHL insufficiently protects the civilian population, as illustrated by the many efforts to ban specific weaponry. Overemphasizing one or the other element of the balance will, however, serve only to engender disrespect for the law – on the one hand by those who feel it might be losing sight of its humanitarian underpinnings or, on the other, by those who believe it unjustifiably limits their ability to employ force for legitimate ends.

It must equally be understood that law is never an end in itself, but instead reflects an agreement by states – and only states are empowered to craft international law – as to the appropriate accommodation of a wide variety of interests. To the extent that moral, political or other concerns surface regarding the conduct of hostilities, they are best responded to through law, for law contains within it the means for enforcement, imperfect as those means might be. In particular, law should not be counterpoised against ethics or morality; law is the very expression of these considerations. And it is, given the extant global construct, through law that they will best find their realization.

Chapter 7

Who is Protected Under International Humanitarian Law? Finding a Definition for 'Direct Participation in Hostilities'[1]

Helen Durham and Eve Massingham

Introduction

International humanitarian law (IHL) is one of the oldest areas of international law and can be found in every culture and community across the centuries.[2] International humanitarian law can be defined as a branch of international law that limits the use of violence in armed conflict by protecting those who do not or no longer directly participate in hostilities.[3] International humanitarian law also limits the methods and means of warfare, meaning it places restrictions upon weapons and tactics that may be used in the fighting.[4] Furthermore, the IHL regime restricts the amount of force used to what is necessary to achieve the military aim.[5] From both a practical and a theoretical point of view, no discussion on issues relating to the protection of civilians can avoid reflecting upon IHL This chapter aims to explore the role of the International Red Cross and Red Crescent Movement in IHL; it then briefly exposes the reader to the broader debate within the humanitarian sector on mechanisms to increase the protection of civilians and finally undertakes a case study of the important study by the International Committee of the Red Cross (ICRC) on finding a definition for 'direct participation in hostilities'. It concludes that whilst there continue to be challenges with ensuring the current IHL system

---

1   The authors would like to sincerely thank Mr William Taylor for his research and assistance with this chapter. All views are those of the authors and do not represent the Australian Red Cross in any way.

2   Geoffrey Best, 'The Restraint of War in Historical and Philosophical Perspective', in *Humanitarian Law of Armed Conflict – Challenges Ahead, Essays in Honour of Frits Kalshoven* (Dordrecht: M. Nijhoff, 1991), pp. 3–26.

3   *Protocol Additional to the Geneva Conventions of 12 August 1949, and Relating to the Protection of Victims of International Armed Conflicts (Protocol I) 1977*, 1125 UNTS 3 [hereinafter Additional Protocol I], Art. 48.

4   Ibid., Art. 35.

5   Protocol I, Art. 51.

is fully implemented and respected, it still holds great value in protecting civilians and must be central to any debate on this topic.

International Humanitarian Law and the International Red Cross and Red Crescent Movement

Whilst the concept of limiting suffering during war is ancient, the modern codification of this principle was the result of the vision of Henry Dunant. A Swiss businessman who witnessed a terrible battle in the mid-1800s, Dunant became the founder of the Red Cross/Crescent Movement and is credited with persuading states to create the first multilateral IHL treaty. From his urgings, the Swiss Government convened a diplomatic conference and the 1864 Geneva Convention for the Amelioration of the Wounded in Armies in the Field was adopted. In relation to other proposals, a small committee was created to give protection and relief to wounded soldiers. This was the precursor to the International Committee of the Red Cross (ICRC), the founding element of the International Red Cross and Red Crescent Movement.

The initial Geneva Convention continued to adapt for many years, affording rights to those wounded or injured at sea and prisoners of war, but until 1949 the protection of civilians was not a key focus. It was the during the aftermath of World War II, when reflection began on the changing nature of armed conflict and on the increased attacks upon civilians, that international laws were drafted to respond to this reality. The existing Geneva Conventions were updated and a final treaty was added to specifically provide civilians with protection. Today the four Geneva Conventions of 1949 are significant texts within IHL and provide a range of protections for civilians, which sadly are needed more than ever before.[6] With the adoption of the two Additional Protocols in 1977, increased protections were granted for civilians with greater attention given to the specific methods and means of warfare (such as the prohibition of attacking objects indispensable to the survival of the civilian population found in Article 54 of Additional Protocol I). Furthermore, adjusting to the growing number of internal (rather than international) armed conflicts, Additional Protocol II updated the IHL regime and extended the protections to times of non-international armed conflict.

Over the years, the ICRC has been constantly involved in the updating and development of IHL treaties and, within the laws themselves, the ICRC has a range of humanitarian activities it is mandated to undertake in an impartial manner. For example, during times of international armed conflict, the ICRC is able to visit detained civilians and prisoners of war under Article 142 of Geneva Convention IV

---

6   For example, today a large number of victims of conflict are civilians. The United Nations expressed 'deep regret that civilians continued to account for the vast majority of casualties in conflict situations' (UN Security Council Statement SC/10089, 22 November 2010).

and Article 126 of Geneva Convention III. Both the ICRC and national societies of the Red Cross or Red Crescent (such as the Australian Red Cross) are able to carry out humanitarian activities in favour of the victims of the conflict[7] and throughout the world the movement is one of the largest humanitarian organizations assisting civilians during war and violence today.[8] Even during times of non-international armed conflict, the ICRC and its national societies can offer their services of humanitarian assistance.[9] As well as practical and operational assistance to the civilian population, the ICRC and its national societies are obliged to disseminate IHL with the aim of developing knowledge about, and increased respect for, international humanitarian law. As noted previously, IHL plays a significant role in any attempts to protect civilians during times of armed conflict.

The Humanitarian Sector and the Protection of Civilians

In recent years the topic of the protection of civilians has become a main focus of attention not only for the Red Cross/Crescent Movement but also for the wider humanitarian sector. The ICRC recognizes that 'protecting people caught up in armed conflict and other situations of violence is a critical challenge'.[10] As one part of the solution to increase the protection of civilians, the ICRC has advanced the view that IHL has a crucial role to play. With the increased incidence of flagrant violations committed by parties to conflict around the world, the ICRC has stated that it 'firmly believes that the relevance and importance of IHL is reaffirmed rather than weakened'.[11]

Compared with the 1800s, when the Red Cross/Crescent Movement was established, today, the more complex battlefields bear witness to a broad range of humanitarian actors – many with the aim of engaging in the protection of civilians.[12] There are, however, different views on what protecting civilians actually entails. Even the definition of the parameters of 'protection activities' has

---

7   Protocol I, Art. 81.

8   For more information, see the ICRC web site: www.icrc.org

9   Common Article III to the Geneva Conventions of 1949, and *Protocol Additional to the Geneva Conventions of 12 August 1949, and Relating to the Protection of Victims of Non-International Armed Conflicts, June 8, 1977*, 1125 UNTS 609 [hereinafter Additional Protocol II], Art. 18.

10   International Committee of the Red Cross, *Professional Standards for Protection Work* (Geneva, 2009).

11   Statement by Yves Daccord, Director-General of the ICRC, UN Security Council, New York, 22 November 2010, http://www.icrc.org/eng/resources/documents/statement/protection-civilian-statement-2010-11-22.htm

12   For example, there are currently more than 3,400 non-governmental organizations (NGOs) with UN Economic and Social Council (ECOSOC) Consultative Status, many of whom are working on civilian protection in regions across the world (http://esango.un.org/paperless/Web?page=static&content=intro).

become contestable. There is a lack of consensus on 'what protection means, what it entails and which agents are best placed to provide it'.[13] Objectives could range from physical protection from imminent violence to provision of basic necessities through to establishing a protective environment that enhances the safety and supports the rights of civilians.[14]

One recent concept that has increasingly gained traction within the protection debate is the concept of the 'responsibility to protect' (R2P). R2P initially came about as a response to the humanitarian dilemma in repeated protection failures – in particular in Rwanda,[15] Bosnia[16] and Kosovo.[17] It is a principle 'born from a desire to protect the world's most vulnerable communities and populations from the most heinous international crimes'. For many in the humanitarian sector, it is about holding governments and authorities responsible for actions that impact upon the civilian population.[18] It is based on the idea that sovereignty is not a privilege, but a responsibility with a range of obligations to ensure that there is protection afforded to vulnerable populations. R2P focuses on preventing and halting four 'mass atrocity' crimes: genocide, war crimes, crimes against humanity and ethnic cleansing.

In February 2009, UN Secretary-General, Ban Ki-moon, issued his report on 'Implementing the responsibility to protect'. He suggested that R2P can be thought of as having three equally important and parallel 'pillars', including the protection responsibilities of the state, the responsibility of the international community to assist if the state is unable to protect its own citizens and the responsibility of the international community to intervene if a state is 'manifestly failing' to protect its citizens.[19]

Unlike IHL, R2P is not contained in any specific treaty and as such should currently be considered as a principle rather than a legally binding framework. In essence it provides the international community with the basis for certain actions relating to the protection of civilians.[20] Yet the obligations under the R2P umbrella are grounded in existing international law and international treaties such as the

---

13   Asia-Pacific Centre for the Responsibility to Protect, *Protecting Civilians in Uncivil Wars*, Working Paper No. 1 (University of Queensland, August 2009), p. 16.

14   Ibid.

15   In 1994: the mass murder of between 500,000 and 1 million people.

16   In 1995: the Srebrenica genocide, where more than 8,000 civilians were killed.

17   In 1998–99: the Kosovo conflict involved a highly controversial bombing campaign, prompted by fear of similar killings. There were mass killings of thousands of Kosovans and displacement of the population of Kosovo estimated to be close to 1 million people.

18   Oxfam, *NGOs and the Prevention of Mass Atrocity Crimes* (London, 23–24 November 2009), http://responsibilitytoprotect.org/Oxfam%20R2P%20workshop%20 outcome%20doc%20March%202010-2.pdf

19   For more details, see *Implementing the Responsibility to Protect*, Report of the Secretary General, UN Doc. A/63/677 (2009).

20   For example, see the reference to 'Responsibility to Protect' in Security Council Resolution 1973 relating to Libya.

Genocide Convention,[21] the Geneva Conventions and Additional Protocols[22] as well as crimes found listed in the Rome Statute of the International Criminal Court[23] such as crimes against humanity and ethnic cleansing.

In terms of the civilian protection framework, R2P is much narrower in scope than IHL, focusing on four mass-atrocity crimes. The UN Secretary-General characterized R2P as being 'narrow' in scope but 'deep' in response[24] – narrow in the sense that it is focused on the prevention of four crimes, but deep in that it needs to employ the wide array of prevention and protection instruments available to states, UN forums and other international and regional actors to assist states in meeting their primary responsibility to protect their populations. The introduction of the concept of R2P and debates about states' obligations to protect their own citizens have provided a rich area of discussion within the humanitarian discourse of how to best protect civilians.

Working within existing legal obligations under IHL and international criminal law, R2P provides a strong conceptual framework for specific protections afforded to civilians, and is continuing to evolve and gain traction.

The Notion of Direct Participation in Hostilities

As noted previously, a major element in the IHL framework is the requirement to provide protection to civilians. The laws of war are premised on there being two groups of people: combatants and civilians.[25] Whilst this publication is about the protection of civilians, it is important to understanding civilian protection to acknowledge that both combatants and civilians are protected under the law. These protections are against, for example, cruel and inhumane acts, outrages on personal dignity, unnecessary suffering and the denial of natural justice. The term 'combatant', however, denotes the right to participate directly in hostilities. That is, the privilege to kill the enemy in accordance with the laws of war, without repercussion, and the corollary: to be killed by the enemy acting in accordance with the laws of war. A combatant may therefore lawfully be the object of direct attack. As the Inter-American Commission on Human Rights has stated, 'the combatant's privilege … is in essence a licence to kill or wound enemy combatants

---

21   *Convention on the Prevention and Punishment of the Crime of Genocide* (1948).

22   For example, *Geneva Convention Relative to the Protection of Civilian Persons in Time of War, August 12, 1949* [hereinafter GCIV], Art. 1.

23   *Rome Statute of the International Criminal Court, July 17, 1998*, 2187 UNTS 90, Art. 8.

24   *Implementing the Responsibility to Protect*, p. 8.

25   For the purposes of the law on the conduct of hostilities, there is no gap. See, for example, K. Dormann 'The Legal Situation of "Unlawful/Unprivileged Combatants"', *International Review of the Red Cross*, 849 (2003): 45–74, at p. 72.

and destroy other enemy military objectives'.[26] Only combatants rendered *hors de combat* through injury, sickness or capture must be protected against attack. On the other hand, those without combatant status – civilians – are protected against attack. Civilians have no right to participate in the hostilities and as such enjoy the corollary: protection from attack. This protection of persons not taking part in the conflict is absolutely central to the foundations of international humanitarian law and the balance that international humanitarian law seeks to achieve between the military reality of humankind engaging in conflict and the humanity of seeking to protect those who are not taking part. That civilians benefit from protection against direct attack only 'unless and for such time as they take a direct part in hostilities' is, however, a binding rule of international humanitarian law.[27] That is, those civilians who take a direct part in hostilities lose their protection under international humanitarian law, for such time as they are directly participating.

That the distinction between those taking part in the fighting and those who are not is a constant one in international law is clear. Dating back to Grotius, under the law of war, not everything has ever been fair game in war.[28] The Leiber Code is early evidence that 'protection of inoffensive citizens of the hostile country is the rule',[29] suggesting that offensive citizens are not entitled to such protection. So what does it mean to be an offensive citizen or, in more modern language, a civilian 'directly participating in hostilities'?

The International Committee of the Red Cross Study

In May 2009, the ICRC published its *Interpretive Guidance on the Notion of Direct Participation in Hostilities Under International Humanitarian Law*. The *Guidance* seeks to provide a legal reading of the notion of 'direct participation in hostilities'. This concept is articulated in various ways in the Geneva Conventions of 1949 and their Additional Protocols.[30] Commissioned by the ICRC and the

---

26   Ibid., p. 46; Inter-American Commission on Human Rights, *Report on Terrorism and Human Rights*, OEA/Ser. L/-V/II.116 Doc. 5 Rev. 1 Corr., 22 October 2002, para. 68.

27   Common Article III to the Geneva Conventions of 1949; *Protocol Additional to the Geneva Conventions of 12 August 1949, and Relating to the Protection of Victims of International Armed Conflicts, June 8, 1977*, 1125 UNTS 3 [hereinafter Additional Protocol I], Art. 51(3); for the ICRC Customary Law Study, see Jean-Marie Henckaerts and Louise Doswald-Beck (eds), *Customary International Humanitarian Law* (Cambridge: Cambridge University Press, 2005), Rule 6.

28   Hugo Grotius, *The Law of War and Peace in Three Books* (1625) [*De Jure Belli ac Pacis Libris Tres*].

29   US War Department, *Instructions for the Government of Armies of the United States in the Field*, General Order No. 100 [Leiber Code].

30   Common Article III to the Geneva Conventions of 1949 (taking no active part in hostilities); and see Additional Protocol I, Art. 51(3) and *Protocol Additional to the Geneva Conventions of 12 August 1949, and Relating to the Protection of Victims of Non-*

TMC Asser Institute, the *Guidance* is the culmination of five meetings of some 40–50 legal experts from academic, military, governmental and non-governmental circles over the period 2003–08[31] and extensive work of the ICRC Legal Advisor, Dr Nils Melzer. The resulting document, whilst informed by the views of these experts expressed in their private capacities,[32] is solely an expression of the ICRC's views.[33] It is not legally binding, nor does it purport to change existing law.[34]

The *Guidance* approaches the issue of clarifying the notion of 'direct participation in hostilities' by examining three questions: who is considered a civilian for the purpose of the principle of distinction; what conduct amounts to 'direct participation in hostilities'; and what modalities govern the loss of protection against direct attack.[35] Each of these will be looked at in turn, with the most attention being paid to the notion of civilians.

Civilians

The *Guidance* effectively concludes that the definition of a civilian is everyone who does not have a 'continuous combat function'. In reaching this conclusion, the *Guidance* looks at the concept of a civilian in international and in non-international armed conflicts separately. It is first acknowledged that the definition of a civilian under the Geneva Conventions is a negative definition.[36]

A civilian is any person who does not belong to one of the categories of persons referred to in Articles 4A(1), (2), (3) and (6) of Geneva Conventions III and Article 43 of the Additional Protocol I.[37] In more detail, civilians are everyone who does not fall into the following categories:

International Armed Conflicts, June 8, 1977 [hereinafter Additional Protocol II], 1125 UNTS 609, Art. 13(3).

31 Nils Melzer, *Interpretive Guidance on the Notion of Direct Participation in Hostilities Under International Law* (Geneva: ICRC, 2009), p. 9.

32 Ibid., p. 9.

33 Ibid., p. 6. It should be noted that a number of the experts' opinions diverged from that of the ICRC during the process such that some experts did not remain on the panel throughout all consultations.

34 Melzer, p. 6.

35 Ibid., p. 13.

36 Ibid., p. 21; Additional Protocol I, Art. 50(1).

37 Additional Protocol I, Art. 50(1). This leaves a combatant being those persons referred to in Common Article III to the Geneva Conventions II, Art. 4A(1), (2), (3) and (6), and Additional Protocol I, Art. 43. The conditions for prisoner-of-war status can be derived from *Geneva Convention Relative to the Treatment of Prisoners of War, August 12, 1949*, 6 UST 3316, 75 UNTS 135 [hereinafter GCIII], Art. 4, and from Additional Protocol I, Arts 43 and 44. Prisoner-of-war status should not be confused, however, with combatant status. The criteria are not completely interchangeable (Melzer, p. 22).

4A (1) Members of the armed forces of a Party to the conflict as well as members of militias or volunteer corps forming part of such armed forces.

4A (2) Members of other militias and members of other volunteer corps, including those of organized resistance movements, belonging to a Party to the conflict and operating in or outside their own territory, even if this territory is occupied, provided that such militias or volunteer corps, including such organized resistance movements, fulfil the following conditions:

(a) that of being commanded by a person responsible for his subordinates;

(b) that of having a fixed distinctive sign recognizable at a distance;

(c) that of carrying arms openly;

(d) that of conducting their operations in accordance with the laws and customs of war.

4A (3) Members of regular armed forces who profess allegiance to a government or an authority not recognized by the Detaining Power.

...

4A (6) Inhabitants of a non-occupied territory, who on the approach of the enemy spontaneously take up arms to resist the invading forces, without having had time to form themselves into regular armed units, provided they carry arms openly and respect the laws and customs of war.[38]

In respect of those countries party to Additional Protocol I, and in so far as Article 43 in Additional Protocol I is customary international law,[39] this also includes:

The armed forces of a Party to a conflict consist[ing] of all organized armed forces, groups and units which are under a command responsible to that Party for the conduct of its subordinates, even if that Party is represented by a government or an authority not recognized by an adverse Party. Such armed forces shall be subject to an internal disciplinary system which, 'inter alia', shall enforce compliance with the rules of international law applicable in armed conflict.

Thus, in times of international armed conflict, a combatant is a member of the armed forces of a party to the conflict.[40] This includes all units under responsible command and all armed actors showing a sufficient degree of military organization and belonging to a party to the conflict.[41] Everyone else – save participants in a *levee en masse* – is a civilian.

---

38   Such persons are referred to as participants in a *levee en masse*.

39   Art. 43(1) is considered to be customary international law by the ICRC Customary Law Study (Henckaerts and Doswald-Beck, Rule 4, pp. 14–17).

40   Additional Protocol I, Art. 43(2).

41   Melzer, p. 23; see also Dieter Fleck (ed.), *The Handbook of International Humanitarian Law*, 2nd edn (New York: Oxford University Press, 2008), p. 304.

It is in respect of internal armed conflict that the path to a concluding paragraph such as the one immediately preceding this is not so clear. Guidance can be drawn, however, from Common Article 3 and Additional Protocol II, Articles 1, 4 and 13.

> Most notably, Article 3 GC I–IV provides that 'each Party to the conflict' must afford protection to 'persons taking no active part in the hostilities, including members of armed forces who have laid down their arms and those placed *hors de combat*'. Thus, both State and non-State parties to the conflict have armed forces distinct from the civilian population. This passage also makes clear that members of such armed forces, in contrast to other persons, are considered as 'taking no active part in the hostilities' only once they have disengaged from their fighting function ('have laid down their arms') or are placed *hors de combat*; mere suspension of combat is insufficient.[42]

> … According to the Protocol, 'armed forces', 'dissident armed forces', and 'other organized armed groups' have the function and ability 'to carry out sustained and concerted military operations'; whereas the 'civilian population and individual civilians shall enjoy general protection against the dangers arising from military operations' carried out by these forces 'unless and for such time as they take a direct part in hostilities'.[43]

As such, non-civilians (and therefore combatants) in times of internal armed conflict, arguably consisting of 'armed forces', 'dissident armed forces' and 'other organized armed groups', have the function and ability 'to carry out sustained and concerted military operations'. The *Guidance* notes that membership in irregular (or dissident) state armed forces 'can only be reliably determined on the basis of the same functional criteria that apply to organized armed groups of non-State parties to the conflict'.[44] Sufficient degree of military organization is key to this.[45] It is therefore the membership of 'other organized armed groups' that calls for further investigation.

The ICRC has chosen to adopt the view that the test for combatant status in respect of members of organized armed groups should be a test of 'continuous combat function':[46]

> For the practical purposes of the principle of distinction, therefore, membership in such groups cannot depend on abstract affiliation, family ties, or other criteria prone to error, arbitrariness or abuse. Instead, membership must depend on whether the continuous function assumed by an individual corresponds to that

---

42   Melzer, p. 28.
43   Ibid., p. 29.
44   Ibid., p. 31.
45   Ibid., p. 32.
46   Ibid., p. 33.

collectively exercised by the group as a whole, namely the conduct of hostilities on behalf of a non-State party to the conflict. Consequently, under IHL, the decisive criterion for individual membership in an organized armed group is whether a person assumes a continuous function for the group involving his or her direct participation in hostilities (hereafter: 'continuous combat function').[47]

Continuous combat function requires lasting integration into an organized armed group acting as the armed forces of a non-State party to an armed conflict. Thus, individuals whose continuous function involves the preparation, execution, or command of acts or operations amounting to direct participation in hostilities are assuming a continuous combat function. An individual recruited, trained and equipped by such a group to continuously and directly participate in hostilities on its behalf can be considered to assume a continuous combat function even before he or she first carries out a hostile act.

Individuals who continuously accompany or support an organized armed group, but whose function does not involve direct participation in hostilities, are not members of that group within the meaning of IHL.[48]

The phrase 'continuous combat function' has received criticism for the high threshold it imposes.[49] Interpreting the term 'combat function' too narrowly could exclude many members of the organized armed group who, had they served in state armed forces, would be legitimate targets because they would be considered combatants. It could be argued that, although the focus of the *Guidance*, and some of the criticism, is on the idea of '*continuous* combat function', the answer to where is the line between 'combat function' and 'non-combat function' is perhaps even more vital to find agreement on.

Combat function is not defined in the *Guidance*; however, the intended meaning can be discerned from the examples given. The *Guidance* notes that

> recruiters, trainers, financiers and propagandists may continuously contribute to the general war effort of a non-State party, but they are not members of an organized armed group belonging to that party unless their function additionally includes activities amounting to direct participation in hostilities.[50]

This suggests that the ICRC takes the view that 'combat function' is synonymous with 'direct participation in hostilities'. The difference therefore between a combatant, as a member of an organized armed group belonging to a party to a

47   Ibid., p. 33.
48   Ibid., p. 34.
49   K. Watkin, 'Opportunity Lost: Organised Armed Groups and the ICRC "Direct Participation in Hostilities" Interpretive Guidance', *Journal of International Law and Politics*, 42/3 (2010): 641 at p. 659.
50   Melzer, p. 34.

non-international armed conflict, and a civilian, who is directly participating in the hostilities, is continuity of the activity.[51]

Direct Participation

The study notes that 'direct participation in hostilities ... refers to a specific act carried out by individuals as part of the conduct of hostilities between parties to an armed conflict'.[52]

Three constitutive elements of direct participation in hostilities are outlined:

1. The act must be likely to adversely affect the military operations or military capacity of a party to an armed conflict or, alternatively, to inflict death, injury or destruction on persons or objects protected against direct attack (threshold of harm).
2. There must be a direct causal link between the act and the harm likely to result either from that act or from a coordinated military operation of which that act constitutes an integral part (direct causation).
3. The act must be specifically designed to directly cause the required threshold of harm in support of a party to the conflict and to the detriment of another (belligerent nexus).[53]

As such, *likely* harm (that is, harm reasonably expected to result in the prevailing circumstances)[54] of a sufficiently grave nature (threshold of harm), which has a specific connection to the conflict (belligerent nexus), is required for a specific act to constitute direct participation in the hostilities. This is relatively straightforward. It is the second constitutive element – direct causation – that is a little less straightforward.

It is proposed by the ICRC that the question of what is a war-sustaining effort, which is traditionally considered indirect participation, and what is direct participation, can be resolved by reference to whether the 'act in question may be expected to directly – in one causal step – cause harm that reaches the required threshold'.[55] By this, the *Guidance* makes it clear that the test is not an act that is 'indispensable',[56] but rather an act that itself causes the harm or constitutes an integral part of an operation that itself directly causes the harm.[57]

The one causal step test is perhaps best explained by the improvised explosive device (IED) example offered in the *Guidance*:

---

51 See also ibid., Recommendation II, p. 16.
52 Ibid., p. 43.
53 Extracted from ibid., p. 46.
54 Ibid., p. 47.
55 Ibid., p. 58.
56 Ibid., p. 54.
57 Ibid., p. 54.

the assembly and storing of an [IED] in a workshop, or the purchase or smuggling of its components, may be connected with the resulting harm through an uninterrupted causal chain of events, but, unlike the planting and detonation of that device, do not cause that harm directly.[58]

The *Guidance* cites the Commentary to Additional Protocol I where it notes that

to restrict this concept to combat and to active military operations would be too narrow, while extending it to the entire war effort would be too broad, as in modern warfare the whole population participates in the war effort to some extent, albeit indirectly.[59]

As such, conduct that 'merely builds up or maintains the capacity of a part to harm its adversary ... is excluded'.[60]

Interested readers might wish to explore the numerous examples provided in the *Guidance* for further detail on what is envisioned by the one causal step test:[61] 'Measures preparatory to the execution of a specific act of direct participation in hostilities as well as the deployment to and the return from the location of its execution constitute an integral part of that act.'[62]

Loss of Protection against Direct Attack

The loss of protection against direct attack is 'for such time as' the civilian directly participates in hostilities. The suspension of protection lasts exactly as long as the corresponding engagement by the civilian. As the ICRC points out, this necessarily entails that the so-called revolving door of civilian protection – that is, the fact that civilians may pop in and out of protective status on a continuing basis due to their conducting separate specific acts of direct participation on multiple occasions – remains a feature of international humanitarian law. The ICRC asserts that the revolving door of civilian protection is by no means a 'malfunction' of IHL, but rather that it does, and it is intended to, protect civilians at any time during which they do not represent a military threat. As frustrating as this might be for opposing armed forces, as the ICRC points out, 'it remains necessary to protect the civilian population from erroneous or arbitrary attack'.[63]

---

58   Ibid., p. 54.
59   Yves Sandoz, Christophe Swinarski and Bruno Zimmerman (eds), *Commentary on the Additional Protocols of 8 June 1977 to the Geneva Conventions of 12 August 1949* (Geneva: ICRC, 1987), p. 1679; see also Melzer, Fn. 113.
60   Melzer, p. 53.
61   See ibid., pp. 51–8.
62   Ibid., p. 65.
63   Ibid., p. 71.

Other key points made in the study include that principles of precaution and proportionality continue to apply in both determining whether a person may be attacked and the conduct of the attack.[64] Further, it is noted that civilians regain full civilian protection when they cease to directly participate in the hostilities. Such persons may, however, be prosecuted for their participation in the hostilities.[65]

As has been flagged above, some of the concern expressed to date relates to the 'continuous combat function' test adopted by the ICRC in determining membership of an organized armed group[66] for the purposes of establishing who is a combatant. Concerns have also been expressed about the 'confusing' nature of the one causal step test[67] and the failure of the study to prevent the revolving door of actors coming in and out of direct participation in hostilities.[68] Despite any concerns expressed, the fact the ICRC has started the conversation on this topic is commendable and necessary to ensure IHL remains relevant and vibrant. As guardian and custodian of the Geneva Conventions, the ICRC is well placed to start this conversation and has a mandate to engage with states on matters of the understanding of international humanitarian law. As in any topic to be debated, some, including states, will have concerns over some of the conclusions drawn by the ICRC. In the constant attempt to balance military necessity with the principle of humanity, the document is unashamedly an ICRC view with a focus upon ensuring civilians are protected to the strongest extent possible but also taking into account the realities of a complex and fast-moving battlefield. What is now clear is that the ICRC *Guidance* document has mobilized many different voices to enter this debate – for example, it has been proposed that an analysis of state practice in this area would be useful.[69]

As General McChrystal's April 2010 comments at a virtual town hall make clear, nations ask a lot of their young service people at checkpoints: 'they're asked to make very rapid decision[s] in often very unclear situations.'[70] As such, to ensure civilian protection, providing soldiers with easily interpretable criteria for direct participation in hostilities, which can be distilled into their rules of engagement and orders for opening fire, is imperative.

---

64   Ibid., pp. 74–82.

65   Ibid., pp. 83–4.

66   P Alston, *Study on Targeted Killings: Addendum to the Report of the Special Rapporteur on Extrajudicial, Summary or Arbitrary Executions* (A/HRC/12/24/Add.6), pp. 65–6; Watkin, pp. 655 and 691.

67   M. Schmidt, 'Deconstructing Direct Participation in Hostilities: The Constitutive Elements', *Journal of International Law and Politics*, 42/3 (2010): 697, at p. 728.

68   B. Boothby, '"And for Such Time As": The Time Dimension to Direct Participation in Hostilities', *Journal of International Law and Politics*, 42/3 (2010): 741, at p. 757.

69   Alston proposes the convening of state representatives, together with the ICRC and experts in the field, under the auspices of the High Commissioner for Human Rights (Melzer, p. 69).

70   J. Elliot, 'Gen McChrystal: We've Shot "an amazing number of people" Who Were Not Threats' (2 April 2010), quoting transcripts provided by *Sholtis*.

Conclusion

Reports suggest that at the 1859 Battle of Solferino, very few civilians were killed. Some 30–40,000 combatants lay dead and dying on that battlefield. Many note that on the modern battlefield those figures can be reversed. Whilst civilian casualty numbers are notoriously hard to estimate and corroborate, we know the modern-day battlefield is often in urban environments, and that unfortunately in many conflicts around the world civilians are deliberately targeted. As noted previously, the protection of civilians has, unfortunately, become the perennial IHL issue. Asymmetrical warfare, technology (including unmanned drones firing on predetermined targets from on high) and new developments in methods of warfare are challenging international humanitarian law. The challenges of new technological developments are particularly evident. Non-lethal weapons technology provides an example of where the potential for justifications being put forward to sidestep the principle of distinction are significant. As Mayer notes,

> the concept of noncombatant immunity prohibits the intentional targeting of noncombatants. The availability of non-lethal weapons may weaken this prohibition, especially since using non-lethal weapons against noncombatants may, in some cases actually save ... lives.[71]

Mayer continues, however:

> requiring soldiers to use lethal weapons, when this may potentially cause greater harm to the non-combatants, seems to violate non-combatant immunity. However, when due care is taken to minimize non-combatant causalities ... directly attacking ... with lethal weapons is the course of action most in line with non-combatant immunity.[72]

Article 36 of Additional Protocol I requires that in the development of new weapons, means or methods of warfare, high contracting parties are under an obligation to consider whether their employment would violate international humanitarian law. Perhaps unsurprisingly, international lawyers with the ICRC and the wider Red Cross/Crescent Movement advocate without apology for the maintenance of the primacy of the principle of distinction as at least a significant part of the solution:

> In order to ensure respect for and protection of the civilian population and civilian objects, the Parties to the conflict shall at all times distinguish between the civilian

---

71   C. Mayer, 'Nonlethal Weapons and Noncombatant Immunity: Is it Permissible to Target Noncombatants?', *Journal of Miltiary Ethics*, 6/3 (2007): 221.

72   Ibid., p. 227.

population and combatants and between civilian objects and military objectives and accordingly shall direct their operations only against military objectives.[73]

The principle of distinction does not just underpin modern-day international humanitarian law. 'There is remarkable consistency between age-old moral principles and the modern rules of international law.'[74] Christian just-war theory provided that militaries could not use force internationally against civilians. Traditional societies have also always had the principle of distinction at the heart of their rules about the conduct of warfare. In Tuvalu, for example, 'a man must only attack another man of equal strength'; 'to kill women and children [is] considered an immensely shameful thing to do as a man'.[75] The principle of distinction has served humankind well. As Fidler points out, 'rapid technological change will continue to stress international law on the development and use of weaponry, but in ways more politically charged, legally complicated and ethically challenging than the application of IHL in the past'.[76] We must hold on to the fundamental principles of IHL more strongly than ever if we are to protect the civilians of future wars.

---

73   Additional Protocol I, Art. 48.

74   D. Fidler, 'Non-Lethal Weapons and International Law: Three Perspectives on the Future', *Medicine, Conflict and Survival*, 17 (2001): 195.

75   International Committee of the Red Cross, *Under the Protection of the Palm: Wars of Dignity in the Pacific* (Geneva: ICRC, 2009), p. 41.

76   D. Fidler, 'The Meaning of Moscow: "Non-Lethal" Weapons and International Law in the Early 21st Century', *International Review of the Red Cross*, 87/859 (2005): 552.

Chapter 8

Protecting Civilians in Armed Conflict Through Rules of Engagement

Rob McLaughlin[1]

Introduction

The start point in any discussion of the utility of rules of engagement (ROE) in protecting civilians must always be that the issue is well hedged with options – and in many cases, requirements – for relative assessments and discretionary decision making. In armed conflict, there are many occasions when there is lawful scope – and indeed often obligation – to seek a balance between the competing requirements to achieve the mission efficiently and effectively, whilst simultaneously protecting civilians from the vagaries of armed conflict to the utmost extent possible. Mark Martins expressed this conundrum most accurately and acutely in his 1994 article 'Rules of Engagement for Land Forces: A Matter of Training, Not Lawyering'.[2] Discussing the dangers inherent in the absence of an effective and coherent method for ROE training, he observed that

> at least two dangers to military missions become more imminent. The first danger is that troops will respond tentatively to an attack, thereby permitting harm to themselves, to fellow soldiers, or to some mission facility. The second, opposite, danger is that troops will strike out too aggressively, thereby harming innocents.[3]

As Martins goes on to explain, 'the first criterion recognizes that a military force must protect itself to accomplish its objective. The second acknowledges that use of excessive force could jeopardize claims to legitimacy and frustrate both short-term and long-term goals.'[4] An updated, Afghanistan and counterinsurgency-focused assessment of this fundamental dichotomy in assessing use of force for

---

1 I wish to record my deep gratitude for comments provided on an earlier draft by Phil Drew (Canadian Forces), Dr Ian Henderson (Royal Australian Air Force) and Andrew Murdoch (Royal Navy). All errors, of course, are mine alone.

2 Mark S. Martins, 'Rules of Engagement for Land Forces: A Matter of Training, Not Lawyering', *Military Law Review*, 143 (1994): 1.

3 Ibid., pp. 4–5.

4 Ibid., pp. 13–14.

mission accomplishment, as against the imperative for protection of civilians, is provided by Matthew Beran:

> [C]ounterinsurgency operations are inherently different [from operations focused on the 'conventional' goal of complete or partial submission of the enemy] because the mission focuses not on destruction of the enemy but on providing for the safety and security of the local population, making safety and security the military advantage[s] to be gained. Consequently, civilian casualties (both civilian deaths and civilian injuries) and civilian property damage in counterinsurgency operations necessarily detract from the military advantage to be gained and may result in mission failure.[5]

Protecting civilians through lawful, defensible and contextually sensitive ROE is but one component of a system that must be seen as an integrated whole. Rules of engagement are not intelligence; ROE are not tactics; ROE are not weaponeering; ROE are not a foolproof guarantee against either mistake or misconduct. But ROE do provide one (hopefully accessible) means by which a certain degree of discipline and guidance can be brought to complex decision making, which requires the short-notice, incomplete and often contestable fusing of information, capacity, context and assessment in relation to use of force and the protection of civilians.

Rules of engagement are, therefore, a positive statement of intent, underpinned by legal, policy, capability and operational factors that are specific to that particular theatre of operations.[6] In both armed conflict and non-armed conflict (or 'law enforcement') operations, ROE are a formal attempt to centralize in a practical way the imperative – legal, moral, ethical, political, doctrinal and operational – to protect civilians. But they do so within a field of endeavour where this imperative cannot always deliver unambiguous results in terms of protection of civilians. This is precisely because (in the context of armed conflict) the imperative itself makes sense only if understood as connected to, and assessed in comparison with, its counterpart concept of expeditious and effective mission accomplishment. It is important to recognize at the outset that the very existence of this balancing requirement precludes any guarantee of universal or complete civilian protection from the vagaries of war – as Tony Rogers noted from the crucible of the Kosovo campaign, zero-casualty warfare does not exist.[7] Similarly, as Yoram Dinstein observed:

---

5   Matthew L. Beran, 'The Proportionality Test Revisited: How Counterinsurgency Changes "Military Advantage"', *The Army Lawyer* (August 2010): 4, at p. 5.

6   See, for example, Beran's argument that the concept of LOAC proportionality has to be re-envisioned and redefined for counterinsurgency contexts. Beran, pp. 7–10.

7   A.P.V. Rogers, 'Zero-Casualty Warfare', *International Review of the Red Cross*, 837 (2000), http://www.icrc.org/eng/resources/documents/misc/57jqcu.htm

One has to constantly bear in mind that war is war; not a chess game. There is always a price-tag in human suffering. Admittedly, Kosovo is not a very appropriate backdrop for such a point to be made, inasmuch as the war was conducted on NATO's part on the assumption of zero casualties (although that meant zero casualties to NATO) ... but in the long run civilian suffering cannot be utterly avoided ...

The current disproportion of the civilian/combatant ratio of casualties is totally unacceptable ... Nevertheless, the realistic goal is to minimise civilian casualties, not to eliminate them altogether. There is no way to eliminate civilian deaths and injuries due to legitimate collateral damage, mistake, accident and just sheer bad luck.[8]

In armed conflict it is inevitable – indeed it is essentially a precondition for the legal relationship of armed conflict to exist – that people, be they civilian or military, will be killed or injured.

Outline

This short analysis will attempt to illustrate how ROE can assist militaries to articulate, in practical terms, the manner by which they will achieve the balance required between the imperative to protect civilians to the utmost and the imperative to expeditiously and effectively accomplish the mission. In seeking to achieve this aim, it must be stressed at the outset that the methodology adopted is overtly and unapologetically practical as opposed to more deeply theoretical – a simple reflection of the fundamental nature of the subject matter (ROE) as it currently stands. The analysis will begin by detailing a series of definitions of ROE and will then move from this contextually vital background into an examination of the elements of rules of engagement. The next progressive step will be an assessment as to the purposes of ROE and then – vitally – a review of what ROE are not, for this is a fundamental issue in understanding the role ROE can, and cannot, play in the protection of civilians. The analysis will then proceed to assess in finer detail two discrete examples of ROE that could be said to have a protection-of-civilians focus, but within a general scheme of indicating some of the limitations that dictate the extent to which such ROE can contribute to this aim. To this end, the analysis will focus upon the issues of self-defence and protection of others and identification of targets.

---

8   Yoram Dinstein, 'Targeting: Discussion', in Andru E. Wall (ed.), *Legal and Ethical Lessons of NATO's Kosovo Campaign*, *International Law Studies*, 78 (2002): 211, at p. 219.

Rules of Engagement: A Definition

Academic assessment and publicly available documentation relating to ROE are relatively slim – primarily because ROE profiles for actual operations are generally classified. What is available, however, nevertheless provides a sound and solid foundation for analysis.[9] The following definitions and descriptions – all available in the public domain – certainly provide some indication as to the general development, coherence, and consistency of approach and understanding that underpin the concept:

• '[Rules of engagement] specify in detail the circumstances under which fire may be opened.'[10]

---

9   Apart from the articles by Martins and Beran, noted above, publicly available academic/practitioner analyses relating to ROE include: D.P. O'Connell, *The Influence of Law on Seapower* (Annapolis, Md: Naval Institute Press, 1975), Ch. XII; J. Ashley Roach, 'Rules of Engagement', *Naval War College Review* (January–February 1983): 46; Richard J. Grunawalt, 'The JCS Standing Rules of Engagement: A Judge Advocate's Primer', *Air Force Law Review*, 42 (1997): 245 (Joint Chiefs of Staff Standing ROE); John G. Humphries, 'Operations Law and the Rules of Engagement in Operations Desert Shield and Desert Storm', *Airpower Journal* (Fall 1992), http://www.airpower.maxwell.af.mil/airchronicles/apj/apj92/fall92/hump.htm (Iraq/Kuwait, 1991); F.M. Lorenz, 'Forging Rules of Engagement: Lessons Learned in Operation United Shield', *Military Review* (November–December 1995): 17 (Somalia, 1992–95); Dale Stephens, 'Rules of Engagement and the Concept of Unit Self Defence', *Naval Law Review*, 45 (1998): 126 (ROE and unit self-defence); Peter Rowe, 'The Rules of Engagement in Occupied Territory: Should They be Published?', *Melbourne Journal of International Law*, 8/2 (2007): 327; Alan Cole, Philip Drew, Rob McLaughlin and Dennis Mandsager, *Rules of Engagement Handbook* (San Remo: International Institute of Humanitarian Law, 2009), http://www.iihl.org/iihl/Documents/Sanremo%20ROE%20Handbook%20(English).pdf Gary Solis provides a very fine summative history of the concept, from a US perspective: Gary D. Solis, *Law of Armed Conflict* (Cambridge: Cambridge University Press, 2010), pp. 490–5. There are also a number of publicly available national doctrine publications that incorporate ROE matters – for example, the US Navy's *Annotated Supplement to the Commanders Handbook on the Law of Naval Operations* (http://www.usnwc.edu/Research---Gaming/International-Law/RightsideLinks/Studies-Series/documents/Naval-War-College-vol-73.aspx). There is some (albeit limited) public availability of actual ROE profiles – for example, the Chairman of the Joint Chiefs of Staff (US) Standing Rules of Engagement (2000) at http://www.fas.org/man/dod-101/dod/docs/cjcs_sroe.pdf; and two serials of the ROE for the UN Transitional Administration in East Timor (UNTAET) Peacekeeping Force, which have been published in *Law and Military Operations in East Timor (UNTAET) Feb 2000 – May 2002* (Australian Defence Force Military Law Centre/Asia Pacific Centre for Military Law, 2003), Annexure X (ROE for the Military Component of UNTAET, 28 April 2000, MPS/3633) and Annexure Y (UNTAET PKF HQ ROE Issue 2, 27 March 2000).

10   O'Connell, p. 169.

- 'The purpose of these SROE [standing rules of engagement] is to provide implementation guidance on the application of force for mission accomplishment and the exercise of the inherent right and obligation of self-defense.'[11]
- 'Rules of Engagement are directives to military forces (including individuals) that define the circumstances, degree, and manner in which force, or actions which might be construed as provocative, may, or may not, be applied. ROE are not used to assign tasks or give tactical instructions.'[12]
- 'ROE are designed to ensure that the activities of military personnel remain within the law and are consistent with Government policy; they are not a comprehensive statement of either the law or policy, although they take account of both. ROE define the constraints placed upon military activity, as well as the freedoms permitted, and they reflect the operational context in which it is envisaged that force may be used.'[13]
- 'ROE are orders issued by military authority that define the circumstances, conditions, degree, manner, and limitations within which force, or actions which might be construed as provocative, may be applied to achieve military objectives in accordance with national policy and the law.'[14]

---

11   From CJCS Instruction CJCSI 3121.01A (15 January 2000), *Standing Rules of Engagement for US Forces*, Enclosure A, para. 1(a), http://www.fas.org/man/dod-101/ dod/docs/cjcs_sroe.pdf The Standing Rules of Engagement were updated in 2005 and further detail can be found in the publicly available Judge Advocate General's School, US Army, *Operational Law Handbook* (2010), http://www.loc.gov/rr/frd/Military_Law/pdf/ operational-law-handbook_2010.pdf, pp. 73–102.

12   Quoted NATO definition, from *NATO Rules of Engagement*, MC 362/1, in the USAF TJAG publication *Air Force Operations and the Law*, 2nd edn (2009), p. 235, http:// www.afjag.af.mil/shared/media/document/AFD-100510-059.pdf

13   UK Ministry of Defence, *British Defence Doctrine*, 3rd edn (London: August 2008), JDP 0-01, para. 168, http://www.mod.uk/NR/rdonlyres/CE5E85F2-DEEB-4694-B8DE-4148A4AEDF91/0/20100114jdp0_01_bddUDCDCIMAPPS.pdf See also (for a different 2008 formulation of the concept), Ben F. Klappe, 'International Peace Operations', in Dieter Fleck (ed.), *The Handbook of International Humanitarian Law*, 2nd edn (Oxford: Oxford University Press, 2008), para. 1320: 'ROE define the degree and the manner in which force may be applied and are designed to ensure that the application of force is controlled and legal. They inform commanders of the constraints imposed and the degrees of freedom they have, in the course of carrying out their mission.' This is one of a series of maxims on ROE that Klappe presents.

14   *Use of Force for Canadian Forces Operations* (August 2008), CFJP 5.1, para. 205.1. See also, *Canadian Military Doctrine* (2009), CFJP 01, para. 0241, http://dsp-psd. pwgsc.gc.ca/collection_2010/forces/D2-252-2009-eng.pdf. For an earlier iteration of the CF definition, see Canadian definition, recorded in the 1997 *Report of the Somalia Commission of Inquiry*, http://www.forces.gc.ca/somalia/vol2/v2c

'[T]he term rules of engagement (ROE) refers to the directions guiding the application of armed force by soldiers within a theatre of operations.'22e.htm

- 'ROE are issued by competent authorities and assist in the delineation of the circumstances and limitations within which military forces may be employed to achieve their objectives.'[15]
- '[Rules of engagement are] directives issued by competent military authority that delineate the circumstances and limitations under which United States forces will initiate and/or continue combat engagement with other forces encountered.'[16]

As will be clear from the selection above, there are a number of core elements to most definitions of ROE, as well as a clear trend towards greater breadth and scope. The two core elements explicit or implicit in each definition are: that ROE are directives from some higher authority to military forces; and that ROE concern, as a minimum, the regulation of use of force.

The definitions above also clearly evidence three trends in rules of engagement. The first is that some states – in this case, the United States – have traditionally maintained a minimalist formal definition that is focused upon the use of force in armed conflict. This is the essence of the current US doctrinal definition of rules of engagement. This *prima facie* reading must be tempered, however, with a recognition of the fact that the US Standing Rules of Engagement – which do envisage use of force outside armed conflict (such as self-defence) – are clearly now an integral component of a broader US concept of ROE, applicable both within and outside armed-conflict contexts. This said, however, it is clear from the US definitions that the United States doctrinally prefers a generally minimalist approach to ROE, which is focused upon use-of-force issues.

The second trend that is immediately evident is that some definitions take a broader contextual view of ROE, indicating that ROE as a concept is applicable and useful in both armed conflict and non-armed conflict contexts. The UK, Canadian, NATO and International Institute for Humanitarian Law (IIHL) definitions all indicate this broader applicability.

The third trend is that some definitions are quite explicit that whilst ROE will always deal with their traditional concern of use of force, they are increasingly used to manage military activity more broadly than just use of force. The UK, NATO, recent Canadian and IIHL definitions, for example, all refer to a broader concept of 'employment of military force' or 'armed force' as opposed to the more narrow concept of 'use of force'. As a concept, armed force/military force is generally considered to include a wider ambit of conduct and activity than use of force – presence (and the latent threat carried thereby) or search and detention operations, for example. As the IIHL *Rules of Engagement Handbook* notes: 'Whatever their

---

15   Cole et al., p. 1.

16   US Department of Defense, *Dictionary of Military and Associated Terms* (http://www.dtic.mil/doctrine/dod_dictionary/), also available as *Dictionary of Military and Associated Terms* (12 April 2001, as amended through 30 September 2010), JP 1-02, http://www.dtic.mil/doctrine/new_pubs/jp1_02.pdf, p. 404.

form … [ROE] provide authorisation for and/or limits on, among other things, the use of force, the positioning and posturing of forces, and the employment of certain specific capabilities.'[17]

The Elements of Rules of Engagement

As will be evident from the outline above, there are, consequently, four key elements in most definitions of ROE: direction, addressees, function and subject matter. Each repays brief examination.

Direction

Rules of engagement are clearly directions from a higher authority to military commanders and forces. As the IIHL *Rules of Engagement Handbook* notes, 'in some nations, ROE have the status of guidance to military forces; in other nations, ROE are lawful commands'.[18] This is a critical point and is fundamental to the nature of most ROE: they reflect the law; they are not law themselves. Thus a military member who is prosecuted for a 'breach of ROE' may be subject to this process for either or both of the following reasons: because they breached the legal norm that underpins a particular rule within the ROE; or because they breached an order, where that order happened to be in the form of ROE. This is an important issue, for it is not infrequent that the relevant higher authority may limit the freedom of action of a military force to a collection of actions or conduct that is more limited or restrictive than the underpinning law requires. Take, for example, a rule from the IIHL *Rules of Engagement Handbook* (with the 'SPECIFY' defined) such as: '30B: Non-destructive attack on enemy force communications facilities is permitted.'[19]

There are two immediately relevant aspects to this rule: the military order and the underlying laws of armed conflict (LOAC) requirements to attack only military objectives and only where there is a military advantage in doing so. If a subordinate commander disregarded this rule of engagement and attacked an enemy force's communications installation with kinetic, destructive force (such as a bomb) rather than with a non-destructive attack (such as by jamming the transmissions from the installation) then the commander has breached the order that is encapsulated by the rules of engagement. But the commander has, arguably, not breached the law underlying the rules of engagement. Under LOAC, it is almost inevitable that an enemy force's communications installation would be properly defined as a legitimate military objective and its destruction would clearly offer a significant military advantage. It is also a very strong likelihood – assuming that

---

17   Cole et al., p. 1.
18   Ibid., p. 1.
19   Ibid., p. 38.

the installation is not near civilian objects and people, and thus there is no collateral damage balance to be assessed – that the military advantage in destroying the installation would of course outweigh the very limited likelihood of, and level of, collateral damage. The ROE, however, prohibit this otherwise lawful action (destructive force against the communications installation). Thus the limitation encapsulated by the ROE serves an operational or policy purpose, not one based in law. Such an operational or policy purpose might have been, for example, that a deception operation was under way, spreading false operational plans that the enemy force was intended to intercept through use of its communications capabilities. It was therefore vital that these capabilities remain available to the enemy force. Thus the prosecution of a subordinate commander for breaching this rule of engagement would be on the basis of his or her having breached an order, not having breached the underlying law of armed conflict norm.

Addressees

The second element of most definitions of ROE is that they are explicitly addressed to military commanders and, ultimately, to each sailor, soldier and airperson who must operate in accordance with the rules of engagement. It is a general maxim of ROE that a subordinate commander may – for operational, policy or capability reasons, for example – further limit the ROE, but may not expand them: 'While commanders may restrict the use of issued ROE measures, they cannot authorize their forces to exceed them.'[20]

Function

The function of ROE, as is evident in the definitions noted above, is to govern the actions of the military force, either through imperative, direct orders or by providing guidance. Some ROE are clearly expressed as prohibitions or absolute requirements. An example of a rule of engagement that is a direct, unambiguous order (in this case, a prohibition) is: '23A: Firing of warning shots is prohibited.'[21]

There is no 'guidance' or choice indicated by the rule; it is unambiguous, simple and non-discretionary. There are, however, equally occasions when ROE will seek to leave broad discretion in the hands of the commander/decision maker, not only because this is what the law permits or requires, but also because this is what is operationally necessary and sensible. Often, such ROE are expressed as general permissions – an authority to act, if required. On such occasions, ROE may operate by establishing decision-making parameters as guidance for the exercise of discretion, rather than by providing simple non-discretionary orders.

'93G: Non-compliant boarding [a boarding where the target vessel's agreement to the boarding has not been obtained] of merchant vessels where

20   Ibid., p. 7.
21   Ibid., p. 35.

there are reasonable grounds for suspecting that the vessel is engaged in piracy is permitted.'[22] The essence of this rule is that the commander is given a broad envelope of guidance as to what to take into account when determining if and how to exercise the discretionary action (what the commander determines to be reasonable grounds for suspicion), as well as a direct discretion as to the action itself (to conduct a non-compliant boarding of a vessel suspected of being engaged in piracy or not to conduct such a boarding).

Subject Matter

As noted previously, ROE are increasingly cast in terms of governing the use of military force or military forces, rather than the more traditional and narrowly cast subject of use of force *per se*. A rule of engagement governing the use of force, for example, might be: '21B: Use of non-deadly force, to prevent interference with the freedom of movement of persons belonging to [one's own] Force, is permitted.'[23]

There is also room for differential characterizations as to whether a particular rule of engagement is considered as governing the use of force or as governing military force more broadly. For example, it will fall primarily to an individual state's legal assessments and operational doctrine as to whether warning shots constitute an actual use of force or are simply 'military force' – for example, where warning shots are characterized as a 'signal' rather than as a 'use of force'. Finally, there are ROE that clearly cannot be characterized as relating to a 'use of force', but which are equally clearly intended to govern 'military force'. An example (with a scenario made organic to the rule) is: '70B: Carrying of weapons by members of the force on guard duty at entrances to the Force base is permitted.'[24]

This rule might be necessary because the military force – perhaps participating in a humanitarian assistance/disaster relief operation on the territory of another state – has no general authority or legal immunity with respect to carriage of weapons in the territory of that state. In the status of forces arrangements (SOFA) that underpin the military force's presence in the host state, the host state might have agreed, however, that the military force may arm its guards at the entrance to the base, for the purpose of providing a credible deterrent so that instructions to stop and be searched prior to entry to the base can be adequately enforced. Clearly, this is a matter as to the governance of 'military force' (in this case, presence and latent threat) as opposed to 'use of force'.

---

22   Ibid., p. 53.
23   Ibid., p. 34.
24   Ibid., p. 48.

The Purpose of Rules of Engagement

The purpose of ROE is clearly evident in most definitions of rules of engagement. As noted above, each of the definitions quoted either explicitly or implicitly refers to the concept of control of military force and military forces. What is less evident, but equally important in making ROE useful – that is, in ensuring that they achieve 'fit' with their context – is that they reflect not only legal permissions and limitations, but also political, operational, capability and other contextual authorizations, limitations and factors.[25] This is why discrete campaigns generally require discrete ROE; generalized or generic ROE are not sufficiently context sensitive to achieve this 'fit'. NATO ROE for counter-piracy operations off the coast of Somalia are fundamentally unsuitable for NATO use in stabilization operations in Afghanistan. Rules of engagement for the UN Peacekeeping Force in East Timor will not be readily transferrable to the UN force in Sudan. Several examples will serve to illustrate this point. The first example, cited by Lorenz from the Somalia experience, concerns ROE on 'security zones'. Whilst the ROE properly reflected the applicable law, to be credible and thus useful, it was essential that they equally reflected operational capability and strategic context:

> For security zones to be effective, the defending force must have the capability and will to enforce them. In a situation such as that in Somalia, local aggressors will instinctively push ROE limits. They will not be deterred by warnings or signs but by immediate and effective ROE enforcement.[26]

Lorenz's point is critical: if ROE create the operational option of a 'security zone' simply because there is a legal potential for such zones, but this option is not matched by either capability (too few forces to police them) or political/strategic will to enforce them (that is, to ultimately use force if the security zone is flouted), the consequence can be catastrophic in terms of the credibility of the force and, consequently, its ability to achieve the mission. The experience with 'UN safe areas' in Bosnia-Herzegovina is tragically testamentary of this point.[27]

A second example of the fundamental importance of the broader (that is, not merely legal) context that underpins and informs ROE is Beran's previously

---

25   See, for example, Roach, pp. 47–9 (political, military and legal purposes); Grunawalt, pp. 256–7 (ROE must be dynamic, influenced by mind-set and tailored to the user).

26   Lorenz, p. 24.

27   See *Report of the Secretary-General Pursuant to General Assembly Resolution 53/35: The Fall of Srebrenica*, UN Doc. A/54/549 (15 November 1999), s. XI, http://www.un.org/peace/srebrenica.pdf The BBC reported that the report clearly indicated the UN Secretary-General's assessment of the experience of the Srebrenica 'safe area': 'In his report, UN Secretary-General Kofi Annan said "safe areas" should never be established again without credible means of defence' ('Srebrenica Report Blames UN', *BBC*, 16 November 1999, http://news.bbc.co.uk/2/hi/europe/521825.stm).

noted argument (centred upon a legal concept often given practical expression and limitation through ROE) that 'excessive' must be understood differently in a counterinsurgency context than in a traditional armed conflict context.[28]

A third example, cited by Martins, is a US ROE limitation, based upon an executive order, which prohibits use of riot-control agents and herbicides without presidential approval – in the US view, a policy-based decision as opposed to a legal limitation.[29] Yet another rule of engagement – again cited by Martins but as an example of a capability/operational direction (and in this case without any immediate legal underpinnings) – is 'the common requirement on ground operations that the artillery tubes organic to a unit will not fire beyond a designated fire support coordination line, which ensures an efficient division of labour between fires controlled at one level and those controlled by higher levels of command'.[30] Martins' examples also highlight a further salient point in relation to operating within a coalition under a single coalition ROE profile, in that each coalition partner's own national ROE (reflecting their own particular legal, policy and operational pressures and permissions) will generally be considered to 'trump' the coalition ROE to the extent of any inconsistency.

A final example is offered by the IIHL *Rules of Engagement Handbook*, Rule Series 53, on relative positioning of own-force units 'in relation to other forces or assets'. One rule option, for example, is Rule 53A: 'Approaching closer than (SPECIFY distance/range) to (SPECIFY forces/contacts of interest) is prohibited.'[31] Certainly there are legal issues that might come into play in such a rule of engagement – what legitimately constitutes a 'threat of use of force', for example – but the fundamental driver and designated limitations that stand behind these ROE would clearly be politically, operationally and capability oriented.

What Rules of Engagement Are Not

It is also important to be aware of what ROE are not. Roach perhaps best sums this up, discussing the US doctrinal definition (in 1983):

> ROE should *not* delineate specific tactics, should *not* cover restrictions on specific system operations, should *not* cover safety-related restrictions, should *not* set forth service doctrine, tactics or procedures. Frequently these matters are covered in documents called ROE. ROE should never be 'rudder orders', and

---

28   Beran.

29   Martins, p. 24. Military forces are (in general) not permitted to employ riot-control agents (RCA) in actions related to and governed by LOAC. See *Chemical Weapons Convention 1993*, Art. 1(5): 'Each State Agent undertakes not to use riot control agents as a method of warfare' (http://www.opcw.org/chemical-weapons-convention/articles/).

30   Martins, p. 25.

31   Cole et al., p. 43.

certainly should never substitute for a strategy governing the use of deployed forces, in a peacetime crisis or in wartime.[32]

It is also salient, at this point, to note that ROE should not necessarily – or at least, in the absence of further corroboration and explicit indications, they should not – be taken as reflecting a state's interpretation of the underpinning law. As noted above, states will often limit the scope of action available to their military forces, through ROE, to a subset of what is nonetheless permissible in law. They might do this for policy reasons (such as pursuing a population-centric strategy, which might be reflected in ROE that very tightly limit lawful attack options in urban areas) or for military-operational reasons (such as excluding certain infrastructure from targeting with destructive force so that it can be exploited by one's own force as part of a broader plan). Two illustrations are found in COMISAF's Tactical Directive (6 July 2009, as publicly released), which aimed to further reduce the incidence of civilian casualties, collateral damage to civilian property and alienation of the civilian population in the course of International Security Assistance Force (ISAF) operations in Afghanistan. The tactical directive specifies – in a manner intended to guide the understanding and implementation of the relevant ROE – that '[n]o ISAF forces will enter or fire upon, or fire into a mosque or any religious or historical site except in self-defence'.[33]

It is essential that this ROE limitation not be read as the new, much more limited baseline for ISAF troop-contributing states, and now relevant to all their operations, as to what LOAC permits in terms of attack upon such places. It is permissible under LOAC to fire upon a place of religious worship – for example, where it is being used as an enemy command and control facility or to store military material. Article 53 of Additional Protocol I (1977) to the Geneva Conventions (1949) certainly provides that 'it is prohibited ... to commit any acts of hostility directed against the historic monuments, works of art or places of worship which constitute the cultural or spiritual heritage of people'.[34] Below this threshold, other (less historically or culturally significant) places of worship are subject to the general protection afforded to civilian objects.[35] Such civilian objects – including places of worship – may, however, be attacked if they are determined to be a

---

32   Roach, p. 46. By 'rudder orders', Roach is referring to the detail of instructions as to executing a task – such as changes of course and so on. Rules of engagement should not, and are not designed or equipped to, take on such a role.

33   North Atlantic Treaty Organization (NATO), *COMISAF Tactical Directive*, 6 July 2009, http://www.nato.int/isaf/docu/official_texts/Tactical_Directive_090706.pdf

34   *Protocol Additional to the Geneva Conventions of 12 August 1949, and Relating to the Protection of Victims of International Armed Conflicts, June 8, 1977*, 1125 UNTS 3 [hereinafter Additional Protocol I], Art. 53(a), in Adam Roberts and Richard Guelff, *Documents on the Laws of War*, 3rd edn (Oxford: Oxford University Press, 2003), p. 450.

35   Additional Protocol I, Art. 52(1).

'military object' in accordance with the LOAC test.[36] Thus the COMISAF Tactical Directive limitation in relation to attacks on places of worship must be understood for what it is – an operationally sensitive, strategically specific policy and military limitation as to authorized scope of action. The enabling ROE should not be read as a universal statement by ISAF troop-contributing states that the LOAC rule is now understood to mean that places of worship may be 'attacked' only in self-defence.

The second illustration from the tactical directive concerns capability and the potential for strategically focused and contextually sensitive capability limitations to be incorrectly universalized. The issue is that such innovations can be misunderstood as indicating a new, broader (legal) limitation across that capability, applicable in all theatres of operation because it reflects or expresses a new baseline or interpretation of the relevant LOAC rule. The tactical directive states:

> The use of air-to-ground munitions and indirect fires [broadly, fire delivered on a target that is not itself used as a point of aim for the weapons or the director] against residential compounds is only authorised under very limited and prescribed conditions (specific conditions deleted due to operational security).[37]

Clearly, this direction must be read as a highly discrete and contextual ROE limitation – imposed for strategic reasons and to meet a strategic purpose. It should not be read as evidence that these 'very limited and prescribed conditions' now constitute the general interpretative baseline for determining permissibility under LOAC when considering use of air-to-surface munitions in relation to attacks on residential compounds that otherwise meet the military objective test.

A third illustration of a case where ROE should not be understood as setting a new interpretative baseline with respect to the applicable law – also drawn from Afghanistan – relates to a very specific collateral damage mitigation initiative. In July 2010, the US Army reported that a US artillery regiment had 'crafted a way to fire non-exploding training rounds in the adjustment phase, and then switch to a lethal round in the fire-for-effect phase. Using this method, fewer live rounds are fired, reducing collateral damage and civilian casualties.'[38] This innovation – clearly and explicitly focused upon 'meeting objectives that support

---

36   Ibid., Art. 52(2) and (3). The test is 'those objects which by their nature, location, purpose or use make an effective contribution to military action and whose total or partial destruction, capture or neutralization, in the circumstances ruling at the time, offers a definite military advantage'.

37   *COMISAF Tactical Directive*, 9 July 2009. The definition of 'indirect fire' in square brackets is from the US Department of Defense, *Dictionary of Military and Associated Terms*.

38   Staff Sergeant Bruce Cobbledick, 'Innovation Aims to Reduce Collateral Damage in Afghanistan', 7 July 2010, http://www.army.mil/-news/2010/07/07/41913-innovation-aims-to-reduce-collateral-damage-in-afghanistan/

the counterinsurgency or COIN doctrine' – is described in terms of being an ROE innovation: 'Our rules of engagement have been a challenge, because our enemy knows when we use artillery in a conventional firefight there remains a very real possibility of unintended collateral damage.'[39] But this innovation is highly particular – to its strategic context, to the serendipity of a correlation between the ballistics of the training round and the high-explosive round in the conditions prevailing in Afghanistan, and so on. It is an ROE initiative made possible in Afghanistan; it should not be understood as a new universal baseline requiring that LOAC be understood to mean that training rounds be used for the test and adjust phase of all fire-support missions or that this is the minimum that 'all feasible precautions in the choice of means and methods of attack'[40] now requires.

A final illustration is provided by Fenrick, in his analysis of 'Operation Allied Force' (Kosovo, 1999). Fenrick records that a 'soft bomb', used on 2 May 1999 over Serbia, temporarily knocked out power across 70 per cent of the country. The 'soft bomb', he continues, dispensed graphite powder, which shorted out the electrical grid without the long-term damage that would have accompanied a conventional high-explosive bomb.[41] What is important to recognize is that whilst this choice of munition would have had ROE links and implications, it was primarily a weaponeering and targeting choice, adopted for that particular operation and to achieve a particular targeted purpose. It should never be read as having established a new 'maximum' permissible under LOAC when considering the targeting of an electrical distribution system.

Protecting Civilians through Rules of Engagement: Two Illustrative Rules

It is quite evident that ROE certainly play an important (but not singular) role in ensuring the protection of civilians in armed conflict. Although ROE – as noted previously – are not task orders or 'the mission', they operate to spell out the permissions and prohibitions that govern the military force's conduct whilst carrying out tasks aimed at accomplishing the mission. In order to analyse both the capacities and the limitations of ROE in this role, the most illuminating course of action is to descend into detail – in this case, by examining two specific rules of engagement that have direct implications for the protection of civilians. In particular, it repays attention to look at these rules with a view to determining what protection-of-civilian factors feed into and fall out from each rule. These issues are what will most directly point to the practical capacities and limitations of ROE in their protection-of-civilians role. These rules are drawn from the IIHL *Rules of Engagement Handbook*.

---

39   Ibid.

40   Additional Protocol I, Art. 57(2)(a)(ii).

41   William J. Fenrick, 'Law Applicable to Targeting and Proportionality After Operation Allied Force', *Yearbook of International Humanitarian Law*, 3 (2000): 53, at p. 74.

Self-Defence and the Protection of Others

'12C: Use of force, up to and including deadly force, for the protection of civilians is permitted.' There are two preliminary issues that must be dealt and dispensed with at the outset when considering this most apposite rule. The first is that this rule is most generally conceived of as a rule based in the legal and operational concept of self-defence, and as such transcends the legal paradigmatic distinction between armed conflict and non-armed conflict contexts. Self-defence is a right that is applicable across all forms of operation and (under most legal systems) resides in all people – civilian and military. The second preliminary issue is that the form of self-defence referred to in this rule is 'individual' self-defence, not 'UN Charter Article 51 national self-defence'.[42] That is, the legal basis for this rule is best understood as being the domestic criminal law of self-defence applicable to the ROE actor (in Australia, Section 10.4 of the *Commonwealth Criminal Code*, for example),[43] not the international-law based concept of a nation's right to defend itself from armed attack (as encapsulated in Article 51 of the UN Charter).

With this background in mind, it is readily apparent that a rule such as 12C above creates opportunities for the protection of civilians. The rule does, however, raise a fundamental issue: which civilians may the military force use lethal force to protect? All civilians encountered? Civilian members of their own force? UN personnel? Local and/or international non-governmental organization staff? Local civilians? Local police?[44] This is a critical question and any *legal* answer is hostage to a number of legal vagaries. Assume the following scenario: a group

---

42   *Charter of the United Nations 1945*, Art. 51: 'Nothing in the present Charter shall impair the inherent right of individual or collective self-defence if an armed attack occurs against a Member of the United Nations' (http://www.un.org/en/documents/charter/chapter7.shtml).

43   *Criminal Code Act 1995* (Cwlth), s. 10.4 (http://www.comlaw.gov.au/ComLaw/Legislation/ActCompilation1.nsf/current/bytitle/2EF9353C62DC16D9CA257801000 7D95E?OpenDocument&mostrecent=1). There is an associated debate as to the precise jurisprudential nature of the 'next step up' in self-defence – unit self-defence – but it is not relevant for the purposes of this particular discussion. For the general parameters of this debate, see, for example, Stephens. Stephens therein explores the debate as to whether unit self-defence is simply a collective of the several individual rights of self-defence accruing to each person in the unit (and thus is jurisprudentially sourced from the domestic-law right of individual self-defence) or that unit self-defence is an independent right accruing to the unit itself (drawing its authority and substance from customary international law).

44   See, for example, *Use of Force for CF Operations*, CFJP 5.1, para. 204.2: 'Personal, Unit or Force Self-Defence. Both international law and Canadian domestic laws recognize the authority to use appropriate force in self-defence, up to and including deadly force. Without further written or oral direction CF personnel are entitled to use force in self-defence to protect: a. oneself; b. other members of the Canadian Forces; and c. non-Canadian military personnel who are attached or seconded to a Canadian force against a hostile act or hostile intent.'

of villagers in country Alpha is being terrorized by a local criminal gang. Military forces from country Bravo are part of a regional stabilization force, operating in the territory of Alpha with the consent of the Alphan Government. There is an armed conflict afoot within Alpha, but the criminal gang is *not* an organized armed group participating in the armed conflict – it is simply a gang of thugs who take advantage of the chaos attendant upon the armed conflict to harass and exploit vulnerable villagers for private gain. To what extent may Bravan forces use lethal force against the criminal gang to defend the villagers – the civilians in need of protection (noting that the criminals themselves are also 'civilians' under LOAC) – in the exercise of a right of self-defence against the criminal gang?

The first question, therefore, must be: what law of self-defence applies? If a Bravan force member kills a criminal gang member who was holding a villager hostage at gunpoint, by what law is the Bravan force member's condut to be assessed? It is highly likely that Bravan criminal or military law will apply to the Bravan force member (unless the application of that Bravan law is excluded through some jurisdictional exemption for the military or some territorial or other jurisdictional exemption relating to the fact that the conduct took place on the territory of another sovereign state and thus Bravan law does not operate). What does Bravan law say about self-defence of others – that is, what does Bravan law say about a stranger (A) intervening in a situation where they themselves are not threatened, but they use lethal force to defend a person (B) who is threatened by an assailant (C)? Clearly, Australian law on self-defence would permit A to use lethal force against C in defence of B, where B was faced with death or serious injury; there is, in general, no territorial limitation on an Australian Defence Force member exercising this right in a third state and in favour of a national of that third (or any other) state. This might not, however, universally be the case. Some states may limit the application of their law on self-defence to their own territory or to their own nationals. If this were the case then it is possible that the Bravan force member may not have any domestic Bravan legal authority to use force in self-defence against an Alphan national, in the protection of another Alphan national, on Alphan territory.

Another limb of this question – again, highly relevant to understanding the capacities and limitations inherent in ROE with respect to protection of civilians – is to determine whether the local Alphan law applies and, if so, whether it has been displaced in terms of application to Bravan forces, and, if not, what does it say about the Bravan conduct? Clearly, Alphan law on self-defence will apply to the Alphans involved in this situation: B, the hostage villager, and C, the criminal gang member. The general default position would naturally be that as the conduct took place on Alphan territory, the Alphan law would also apply to the Bravan force member (A) who killed the assailant (C). This would, in the normal course of events, create a protection-of-civilians ROE conundrum: in the absence of either a good handle on the applicable Alphan law or a slick plan to extract A from Alphan territory or jurisdiction until things become clearer, is Bravo happy to authorize its forces, through a rule of engagement such as that above, to use lethal force against Alphan civilians in defence of other Alphan civilians? Often, of course, this issue is mitigated through the existence of some form of SOFA or analogous arrangement – such as a memorandum of understanding or exchange of letters – by which Alpha indicates that it accepts that Bravo will have primacy of jurisdiction over Bravan force members (generally for acts committed in the course of duties, as opposed to acts committed whilst on 'a frolic of their own') or will not exercise its own jurisdiction over Bravan forces.[45]

The second question flowing from this rule, which is again directly relevant to the protection-of-civilians objective, is: protection from what? Again, the parameters of the legal concept of self-defence – and more importantly, which state's domestic vision of that legal concept is at play – are central to this issue. For some states (Australia, New Zealand and the United Kingdom, for example), lethal force may be used only to protect someone from death or serious injury. Lethal force may not be used to defend someone from minor injury and may not be used to defend property alone. Certainly, proportionate non-lethal force may be used in such situations, but not lethal force. For other states (in some US jurisdictions, for example),[46] and as an ROE option under UN ROE, there are occasions when lethal force may be used to protect property alone. Indeed, the UNTAET PKF ROE applicable in East Timor contained a rule authorizing the use of lethal force in defence of certain mission-critical property: 'UNTAET PKF Rule No 1.5: Use of force, up to and including deadly force, to protect United Nations installations, area or goods designated by the SRSG [Special Representative of the Secretary-General] in consultation with the Force Commander, against a hostile act, is authorized.'[47]

Such complexities in relation to self-defence are but one example of the often misunderstood need for national caveats to be attached to multinational rules of engagement. For Australian, New Zealand and UK forces, for example, operating in a multinational force, where the multinational force's collective ROE included a rule such as this, it would be necessary to caveat their obligations in relation to

---

45   See, for example, Bruce Oswald, Helen Durham and Adrian Bates, *Documents on the Law of United Nations Peace Operations* (Oxford: Oxford University Press, 2010), Ch. 2 (the Model UN SOFA). Paragraph 47(a) of the Model UN SOFA states: 'Military members of the military component of the United Nations Peace-keeping operation shall be subject to the exclusive jurisdiction of their respective participating States in respect of any criminal offences which may be committed by them in [host country/territory].' For a different example of a similar provision in an operation-specific SOFA, see *Coalition Provisional Authority (CPA) Order No. 17 (Iraq)*, s. 2 (http://www.iraqcoalition.org/regulations/20040627_CPAORD_17_Status_of_Coalition__Rev__with_Annex_A.pdf).

46   On the use of lethal force in defence of certain property, under the US Uniform Code of Military Justice, see the explanations in Department of the Army Pamphlet 27-9, *Military Judges' Benchbook*, September 2002, pp. 778–9.

47   *Law and Military Operations in East Timor (UNTAET) Feb 2000 – May 2002*, Annexure X (ROE for the Military Component of UNTAET, 28 April 2000, MPS/3633), Rule No. 1.5.

such a rule so that their operational partners clearly understood this limitation or interpretation.[48] Another example of the possible need for such explanatory caveats might be found in the Canadian Force's use-of-force doctrine, which clearly and succinctly articulates the issue:

> During operations other than law enforcement, CF [Canadian Force] members will not have a mandate to provide law enforcement assistance. As a result, the chain of command will not have the legal authority to order individual members of the CF to intervene to stop the commission of crimes. However, the law permits, but does not require, members of the CF to intervene to stop the commission of a crime if they come across such an event during the course of their duties. That is, CF members have the same right as every Canadian citizen to intervene to stop crimes. However, the CF should not be seen to be supplanting the authority of the civilian police forces. Therefore, CF personnel performing non-law enforcement duties should not routinely intervene in stopping any crime that they may encounter. They should limit any interventions to serious crimes involving any acts endangering the life of anyone where it is reasonably likely that the person committing or about to commit the act intends that it will cause immediate death or serious injury.
>
> It must be clearly understood that during non-law enforcement operations, the decision to intervene is that of the individual witnessing the crime. The chain of command cannot order that CF personnel intervene to stop crimes and the law does not impose an obligation to intervene. CF personnel should not expose themselves to a risk of death or serious injury when coming to the assistance of a victim of crime. Nevertheless, CF members should be prepared to deal with the Canadian public's expectation that their military forces will intervene to assist them in cases of need involving crimes. CF members must therefore clearly understand the limits on the use of force permitted by the law when intervening to prevent crimes during non-law enforcement operations.[49]

Clearly, if the concept of protection of civilians is cast in such a way as to include routine protection of civilians from criminal violence and/or the protection

---

48   See, for example, Marc Houben, 'Making Waves and Building Bridges: Dutch Experiences in the Arabian Sea', *RUSI Defence Systems* (June 2007): 82 (http://www. rusi.org/downloads/assets/Houben,_Making_Waves_and_Building_Bridges.pdf):   'On top of this every nation had its own Rules of Engagement (ROE) set. It appeared to [the Dutch Task Force Commander] that the primary task of the commander of a multi-national force is not, as one would expect, to lead the coalition; instead, the primary process can be characterized as a matching process. The commander has to match the task at hand with available national capabilities, the national caveats placed upon these assets and the geographical area/position of the respective ships. Making the coalition work means taking these national caveats and constraints seriously and facilitating the participating countries to work within these constraints.'

49   *Use of Force for CF Operations*, CFJP 5.1, paras 308.2–308.3.

of civilian property from criminal acts then understanding the legal limitations, expressed (in this case) through ROE, is essential to understanding whether (and how) ROE can make a contribution to this purpose and what limitations may attend action targeted at achieving this purpose. Rules of engagement, as noted previously, are not law and adherence to ROE that are not consistent with the law (generally unintentionally, if this were the case) will rarely offer succour to the charged sailor, soldier or airperson. As was starkly illustrated in the UK House of Lords decision in *R v Clegg* (1995) – a case involving use of force by British forces in Northern Ireland – ROE on the 'yellow card' issued to the force (which was effectively assessed by the Lords as exceeding the law) did not assist Private Clegg as they had no legal force and provided no form of defence or excuse.[50]

Another element of this question, where the issue of 'protection' is more broadly cast than direct defence of individual civilians from death or serious injury, is the protection of civilians from crimes not necessarily characterized by physical injury or assault. Obviously, a Bravan force member who encountered C raping B or about to shoot B or about to set fire to B's house might normally be authorized to step in and use force to protect B. But what of serious crimes that do not involve threats to life (such as burglary) or lesser crimes and situations, where any intervention to 'protect' a civilian from a deleterious result – such as a simple theft with no overt violence (such as pickpocketing) or an argument that is becoming heated – might only serve to exacerbate the situation and create opportunities for escalation where resort to lethal force might then become necessary. This is, of course, a conundrum routinely faced by police forces, but for deployed military (and police) forces operating in an alien cultural milieu, the uncertainties, unpredictabilities and risks of intervention are manifestly greater.

It is thus axiomatic that a rule of engagement along the lines of 'use of force, up to and including deadly force, for the protection of civilians is permitted' should not be glossed over as a 'statement of the obvious'; such rules must be understood in their legal and operational context. In most situations, the issues outlined above would be explicitly addressed within the ROE context – for example, by listing categories or adding caveats within the rule itself or through scenario-based training to ensure that the limitations inherent in the rule are operationalized and understood. Such ROE are clearly very useful for and targeted at protection of civilians, but they are not without limitations and complications. It is vital that this be borne in mind when assessing the capacity or adequacy of any ROE in this role. An uninformed reading of a rule *simpliciter* will mislead and might give rise to quite unjustified criticism that a military force did not act to 'protect civilians' in a given situation because it *would not*. An authorization in ROE must be read within its context; it would defy all dictates of commonsense and operational effectiveness that a platoon of infantry (perhaps 30 individuals) providing security for a small medical detachment treating and evacuating wounded from a massacre in a refugee camp should be required to step in to separate the machete-wielding

---

50   *R v Clegg* [1995] WLR 80.

sides, numbering in the thousands, even though the ROE permit such a course of action.[51] It might also be the case that, despite what a rule of engagement appears on its face to say, the force actually *could not* intervene because the applicable law, when properly understood in its context, does not actually support such action by providing either a positive authorization or a defence that otherwise justifies or excuses the inevitable use of force.

Identification of Targets

In some ways, the issue of target identification is at the very apex of the ROE–protection-of-civilians relationship. But, as observed at the outset of this chapter, it is essential that this aspiration does not obscure the fact that mistakes will happen and that some degree of collateral damage is often lawful because it is unavoidable to the achievement of militarily necessary outcomes. It might be that a collateral damage estimate of 10 civilians is considered acceptable if the target is the militarily irreplaceable leader of the insurgency, whereas this level of collateral damage would be considered excessive if the target is a mid-level local insurgent commander. With this general note in mind, however, it is nevertheless correct to assert the intimacy between target identification and protection of civilians when analysing 'attack' ROE applicable in armed conflict. Clearly – and placing to the side malfeasance, malfunction and legitimate collateral damage – the greater the fidelity in target identification, the less is the likelihood of mistakes whereby civilians are injured or killed or civilian property damaged through direct (but mistaken) targeting. To this end, the following rule of engagement might be said to significantly enhance the prospects for the protection of civilians: '31A: Identification of targets must be by visual means.'

This rule of engagement is immediately attractive as a means of buttressing the protection of civilians through requiring visual observation and identification of all targets. But, of course, the eye is connected to the brain and the brain is not infallible. This is an important issue in understanding that even a strict targeting rule of engagement such as 31A is no panacea for the protection of civilians. Clothing, conduct, carriage of weapons – these overt and readily observable indicators are highly contextual and situational. The individual moving in an apparently tactical manner through a crop field whilst talking on a mobile phone as you are patrolling along a path that is approaching a choke point where previous patrols have been ambushed might be a farmer trying to stay out of your line of sight so as not to mistakenly draw your fire, whilst calling home to tell his wife that there is a patrol approaching so get the children inside. Or he might be the spotter assigned to the local organized armed group element, who is phoning in intelligence on your movements to the ambush team ahead. It is this conundrum – actually working out whether what you are seeing is 'civilian' or 'tactical' conduct and whether who

---

51   See, for example, the Kibeho incident in Rwanda (http://www.awm.gov.au/wartime/39/bravery.asp).

you are seeing is a 'civilian' or a 'fighter member of an organized armed group' – that cannot be adequately expressed in rules of engagement. The ROE assessments required are highly contextual and situational and the ROE mechanism utilized (identification criteria) must be understood in terms of its actual purpose – that is, to achieve a desired level of certainty.

Rules of engagement may, as a consequence, be crafted so as to require combinations of identification tools in an attempt to ensure even greater fidelity – in effect, requiring corroboration from other sources so as to further buttress, or to at least achieve, the necessary level of certainty. Such a rule of engagement might be: '31C: Identification of targets must be by visual means and one of the following … Thermal imaging.'

Assume that a person is observed, through night-vision equipment, digging a hole beside a road in the middle of the night. The road passes through farmland. Is the individual a farmer, digging an irrigation channel in the cool of the evening as opposed to the fierce heat of the day (a routine local practice known to the observers) or a fighter member of an organized armed group who is digging in an improvised explosive device (IED) along a route on which one of your logistics convoys will travel in the morning? Thermal imaging indicates that there is a battery power source located in an object the person has placed nearby as he digs the hole. Is it the battery pack for the IED that is destined for the hole or is he listening to the radio as he digs the irrigation channel? Rules of engagement cannot, and are not designed to, answer such questions. This is (once again) the fundamental point about the utility of ROE in the protection of civilians that must always be borne in mind: ROE are very useful, and indeed today arguably essential, to the objective of protecting civilians in armed conflict, but they must be understood as subject to the same vagaries of human agency as any other mechanism serving this purpose.

Conclusion

It is clear that ROE do indeed contribute to the protection of civilians in armed conflict. They distil legal, political, strategic, capability, operational and other factors into context-sensitive permissions and prohibitions that seek to establish – where they are in competition – the necessary balance between the need to expeditiously and effectively accomplish the mission and the need to ensure the protection of civilians from the vagaries of armed conflict to the fullest extent practicable. But ROE are a highly context-sensitive tool, not a universal guarantee. Certainly, ROE can very successfully facilitate protection of civilians if they are clear, understood, legally sound and followed. Rules of engagement might even assert – for political, military or other reasons – stricter and tighter controls over such issues as acceptable collateral damage than are legally required, building into the conduct of operations even stronger mandates for the protection of civilians to prevail over what would otherwise be legitimate and lawful, although destructive, conduct. There are also other ROE-related options that might yet further enhance the protection-of-civilians role they serve. Peter Rowe, for example, has argued persuasively that it might be prudent, in territory under occupation, to publish some aspects of the ROE used by the occupying force in an attempt to reduce instances of misunderstanding. This, of course, carries with it the inherent risk of disclosing to the enemy operational information that they can exploit in their attacks upon the military force or the civilian population, but it is possible to strike a balance between these two competing interests.[52] Similarly, Randall Bagwell's analysis of the 'threat assessment process' (TAP) used by military forces at traffic-control points and similar locations is indicative of an ROE-related process that might prove even more facilitative of the protection of civilians if more widely publicized and understood amongst the civilian population.[53] People might, however, consciously commit atrocities against civilians; ROE will not change that. People might make mistakes that lead to civilian deaths; ROE will not change that. Equipment might malfunction; ROE will not change that. Rules of engagement are an indispensable component in systems established by military forces to maximize the protection of civilians, but they are only one such component. Their effectiveness as a protection-of-civilians tool will always be subject to their integration and 'fit' within these broader systems.

52 Rowe.
53 Randall Bagnall, 'The Threat Assessment Process (TAP): The Evolution of Escalation of Force', *The Army Lawyer* (April 2008): 5.

Chapter 9

Educating for Ethical Behaviour? Preparing Military Leaders for Ethical Challenges

David W. Lovell[1]

Introduction

Formalized rules surrounding both the conditions for waging a just war and the appropriate conduct of combatants within war were an artefact of modernizing Europe and its growing conceit about its 'civilization', despite the fact that ancient societies as well as other cultures had highly developed conventions for honourable conduct by warriors. The classic theoretical exposition for formalizing such rules was developed by Hugo Grotius in the seventeenth century; the classic treaties regulating conduct towards non-combatants in warfare are embodied in the Geneva Conventions of 1949 and their Additional Protocols. The notions that there are rules of war and that they are universal have become widely accepted, even if not honoured; in 2002 the International Criminal Court (ICC) received its mandate to deal with trying, among other things, suspected war criminals. There are good reasons for making ethical choices in war, and not just to avoid the reach of the ICC. Such choices might be defended on consequentialist grounds, as the best basis for prosecuting a war and confronting and settling its underlying causes, or they might be defended on deontological grounds, as befitting an honourable cause. However this might be, unethical decisions have proven damaging in recent years in Iraq and Afghanistan – conflicts in which Australians have been engaged and to which the rhetoric of 'winning hearts and minds' has been central. The spectre of the abuses in Abu Ghraib Prison in Iraq under the control of US forces remains a salutary lesson in losing the moral high ground in a conflict in which the overarching narrative – leaving aside the false trail of 'weapons of mass destruction' – was civilization versus Ba'athist Party barbarism, but it constitutes just one entry in a sad litany of Coalition abuses of non-combatants. Such abuses weaken the case that these wars are legitimate and threaten the fragile political alliances that allow coalition forces to continue operations as liberators rather than occupiers, irrespective of the murderous and unethical behaviour of their adversaries. Early in 2010, when he

---

1   I would like to thank Dr Stephen Mugford, Visiting Fellow in Military Sociology at the Australian Defence College's Centre for Defence Leadership and Ethics, for his comments on an earlier version of this chapter.

was head of US Central Command, General David Petraeus endorsed the 'concept of living our values'. He added: 'Whenever we have taken expedient measures, they have turned around and bitten us in the backside.'[2]

Our armed forces rely upon men (and increasingly women) who are young and relatively inexperienced, yet who in a very important sense represent our country, its values and aspirations. Their moral development is unlikely to be complete. Their moral compass, such as it is, will likely have been set by a conventional 'Western' upbringing, supplemented by strong loyalties to their newly acquired military 'family' – those with whom they share the day-to-day experiences and dangers of war. There might even be doubt about whether they are able to 'read' this compass; the relatively commonplace activities of their peers concerning binge drinking, casual sex and petty criminality related to theft, drugs and illegal Internet downloads might not be perceived by them as creating any moral dilemmas. How, then, can we best prepare them for the ethical challenges of war? Their bodies can be honed by training in ways we have long understood; their reactions to danger can become almost instinctive by the procedures instilled by drill. But their minds, and especially their ethical sense of what is right and wrong in war, need to be developed and exercised in different ways.

This chapter asks whether the teaching of ethics alone is sufficient to equip combatants for their ethical and lawful duty to protect civilians, especially in the complex counterinsurgency operations in which Australians have recently been involved.[3] While nothing can guarantee virtuous decision making by people placed under extraordinary pressures, their ability to empathize with others is a critical faculty and is developed not just through ethical awareness, but also through both inter-cultural and cross-cultural understanding and a better feel for the battlefield, sharpened primarily by studying history and literature. But we must note two important caveats at the level of individual soldiers. First, the ability of young men and women to rise to the emotional and ethical demands of battle, including empathizing with others, is partly a function of cognitive *development* and not simply of *education*.[4] Second, while we cannot teach the frustrations, fatigue and emotional pain of a military campaign, imaginative anticipation through the study of history and literature is no certain inoculation against the 'temporary autism' (as Malcolm Gladwell has put it)[5] induced by enormous stress. There are, in addition, broader issues impacting upon the ethical climate within which our soldiers operate. For those who lead our troops and for those who make

---

2   Mark Dodd, 'Allies Target Volatile Province', *The Australian*, 23 February 2010.

3   While my remarks focus on the Australian experience, this question is common to other Western militaries and challenges their approaches to the professional development of their combatants also.

4   Robert Kegan, *In Over Our Heads: The Mental Demands of Modern Life* (Harvard, MA: Harvard University Press, 1994).

5   Malcolm Gladwell, *Blink: The Power of Thinking Without Thinking* (New York: Little, Brown and Company, 2005), pp. 221–2.

overarching decisions of strategy, ethical considerations need to be factored into decision making. The increasing technical capability to be at one or more removes from direct action – operating a drone over Afghanistan from a control room in a distant country or sitting in an aircraft at 30,000 ft dropping ordnance onto a battle zone you will never enter – puts even more responsibility on soldiers and leaders to be dispassionate, thoughtful and ethically aware of their actions.

Civilian Casualties and the War on Terrorism

Whatever else they are, wars are about the use of force in which the prospect of people killing and being killed is both inherent and likely. No matter how repellent we find such a prospect, we distinguish the killing in war from simple murder,[6] especially by trying to separate   both conceptually and physically combatants from non-combatants. The distinction is reinforced in international law. Paragraphs 2b and 2c of Article 8 of the Statute of the International Criminal Court (which covers 'war crimes'), for example, prohibit intentional attacks against civilian populations and property. The distinction is easier to maintain when civilian populations and armed forces are kept apart during conflict. But while the term 'field of battle' once meant something, since at least World War II things have changed: 'Previously, armed forces and civilian populations were reasonably distinct. Now … whole populations come more and more to be regarded as legitimate objects of annihilation.'[7] And because war is generally played for the highest of stakes – including the freedom of a state or the pursuit of some absolutist ideological or religious cause – victory is pursued at almost any cost. Gray argued in 1970 that war 'has lost its former character of a deadly game, and becomes increasingly a struggle for national survival, in which all moral principles except the one concerning victory are strategic instruments'.[8] In this process, civilians have become the biggest losers.

The issue of civilian casualties in war has become an increasingly salient ethical issue, by virtue of the numbers involved, the clearer links between civilian safety and the achievement of war aims and the nature of irregular warfare. The Canadian Security Intelligence Service sketches the historical context: 'at the beginning of the twentieth-century, between 85 and 90 per cent of war deaths were military. However, by the end of the twentieth-century about three-quarters of war deaths were civilians.'[9] For our purposes, the scale and causes of civilian deaths in

---

6   J. Glenn Gray, *The Warriors: Reflections on Men in Battle* (New York: Harper & Row, 1970 [1959]), pp. 131–2.

7   Ibid., p. 132.

8   Ibid., p. 133.

9   Canadian Security Intelligence Service, 'Conflicts Between and Within States', *Perspectives*, Report # 2000/06 (Canadian Security Intelligence Service Publication, 2000), http://www.csis-scrs.gc.ca/eng/miscdocs/200006e.html.2000, p. 2.

Afghanistan are worth noting. A recent report by the Afghanistan Rights Monitor shows that about 1,074 civilians were killed and more than 1,500 injured in armed violence and security incidents in the first half of 2010.[10] This is a slight increase in the number of civilian deaths compared with the same period in the previous year. But the number of civilians killed by insurgents was significantly higher than those killed by pro-government Afghan and foreign forces. The indiscriminate and widespread use of improvised explosive devices (IEDs) caused more deaths and misery to Afghan civilians than any other tactic, while suicide attacks came second; both have resulted in hundreds dead and hundreds maimed. Likewise, the Centre for Strategic and International Studies estimates that since January 2007 insurgents have caused 80 per cent of civilian casualties in Afghanistan. In Iraq, actions in the continuing insurgency, mostly by the insurgents, kill on average about a dozen civilians every day, though US combat forces completed their withdrawal from the country in August 2010.

The actions of coalition troops in a counterinsurgency against this sort of enemy bring to the fore important ethical questions. But the increasing use of defence assets and personnel to respond to a range of non-traditional security threats, such as the Royal Australian Navy interdicting unauthorized arrivals to Australia's shores, also raises ethical issues about how to deal appropriately with civilians. The stress of turning around rickety boats full of asylum-seekers, mixed with genuine concern about the safety of these civilians, is something that deeply affects the sailors involved.

There is no need to rehearse here the evil acts against civilians that soldiers have done in wars. Perhaps each generation needs to be shocked anew, as my own generation was shocked by the My Lai massacre in Vietnam in March 1968. But such acts are frequent enough to confirm that the use and abuse of power are things about which we need to be constantly vigilant. Instead, we tend to see cycles of abuse and reaction. The torture and death of a civilian detainee in Somalia in 1993 by Canadian soldiers on a humanitarian mission was one of a number of incidents that led eventually to the disbanding of the Canadian Airborne Regiment. The allegations against a group of marines in Haditha, Iraq, of the murder of innocents in November 2005 is another; it led the US general in charge in Iraq, General George W. Casey jr, to call for immediate ethics training for his troops.

The Australian Defence Force and Ethics Education

The Australian Defence Force (ADF) takes its responsibilities to its uniformed personnel very seriously across the spectrum of professional development. It established the Australian Defence Force Academy (ADFA) in 1984 to provide tertiary education and military training for officer cadets and midshipmen of its

---

10   Afghanistan Rights Monitor (ARM), *ARM Mid-Year Report. Civilian Casualties of Conflict. January–June 2010* (Afghanistan Rights Monitor, 2010), arm.org.af/file.php?id=2

three uniformed branches. Likewise, its overarching Australian Defence College (ADC) structure also supports the professional education of mid-career and senior defence personnel through its Centre for Defence Leadership and Ethics.

In Australia, the stress on ethical preparation for war is relatively recent – not for us the soul-searching amongst Americans after the Vietnam War. A decade after that war ended, for example, Richard Gabriel published an important work based on the premise that 'the [US] military [had] discovered that its performance was seriously flawed, and it experienced a breakdown not only in its professionalism, but also in its ethical content'.[11] Developments in the Iraq war, however, have prompted a much wider re-evaluation of ethics education among Coalition partners. Revelations about prisoner abuse by US forces in the Abu Ghraib Prison in Iraq, which began to surface in April 2005, led to the introduction in ADFA in 2006 of the first of a number of courses on ethical issues. In teaching applied ethics to future military leaders at ADFA, the focus is largely on identifying ethical decisions and analysing them in terms of their significance and cogency. Students are introduced to ethical theory and debate, encouraging the self-awareness on which ethical decision making turns, and an ability to justify and defend a decision in ethical terms. Furthermore, the conditions of *jus ad bellum* (going to war) and of *jus in bello* (particularly discrimination, proportionality and weapons and targets) are analysed. Surveys of ethical theories alone do little to help students engage with the moral dilemmas they will and do confront. That explains the development of problem-oriented courses in ethics. The value of such courses is that they bring to the fore issues with which military leaders will likely have to deal and the consequences of their decisions. Identifying ethical issues (before they confront them in the real world) is one aim of such courses; another is to develop the faculty of reasoning about such issues. Instilling and enforcing a military code of conduct and the rules of engagement remain responsibilities of the ADF.

Soldiers, of course, are people of action and ethicists are primarily thinkers. Some of the former tend to suspect the latter of being logic-choppers with a penchant for fine distinctions and a dislike of the decisive; they suspect that moral reasoning is inconclusive, perhaps inherently so. They see reasoning not as guiding action, but as frustrating it. (Winston Churchill is reported once to have asked, in exasperation, for a one-handed economist, since the advice he generally received from economists took the form 'on the one hand, this; on the other hand, that'.) Nevertheless, given the awful finality of the decisions our soldiers are asked to make in combat, an appreciation of their ethical dimensions is vital. As Gabriel has argued, '[o]nly ethics can place the destruction of warfare in perspective and prohibit men from using violence beyond reason. Without ethics the horror of human combat becomes even greater.'[12] But there is a further element to this preparation that is worth stressing. As we explore ethical theories

---

11   Richard A. Gabriel, *To Serve With Honor: A Treatise on Military Ethics and the Way of the Soldier* (Westport, CT: Greenwood Press, 1982), p. 3.

12   Ibid., p. 227.

and problems with our officer cadets and midshipmen in the classroom, we need to remember that none of us knows how, precisely, they will respond to unknown and unpredictable situations, such as combat. John Keegan, the celebrated historian of war who taught at the Royal Military Academy, Sandhurst, addressed precisely this point in the 1970s.

Keegan reflected on the characteristics and deficiencies of life at Sandhurst, in particular as it affects the question: how can we know about war, so that we can prepare for its challenges? As he wrote, his own

> teaching on such subjects as strategic theory, national defence policy, economic mobilisation, military sociology and the like – subjects which, vital though they are to an understanding of modern war, nevertheless skate over what, for a young man training to be a professional soldier, is the central question: 'What is it like to be in a battle?'[13]

When discussions amongst cadets turned to this subject, and in particular to the question 'How would *I* behave in a battle?', Keegan says that they became

> a noisy mixture of slightly unconvincing bombast, frank admissions of uncertainty and anxiety, bold declarations of false cowardice, friendly and not-so-friendly jibes, frequent appeal to fathers' and uncles' experience of 'what battle is really like' and heated argument over the how and why of killing human beings.[14]

Nevertheless, the very 'atmosphere and surroundings' of Sandhurst and perhaps any military academy – serene and orderly – 'are not conducive to a realistic treatment of war'; the knowledge of war among cadets is 'theoretical, anticipatory and second-hand'.[15] In trying to take the emotion out of a highly emotive subject, the conduct of war is presented as 'a set of rules and a system of procedures', which misleadingly makes 'orderly and rational what is essentially chaotic and instinctive'.[16] Procedures and simulations cannot capture the experience of war and the feelings of stress, grief and rage that confront soldiers constantly.

Keegan argues that '[h]istory ... can be pressed into the service of familiarising the young officer with the unknown'.[17] This is the starting point for his excellent analysis of good and bad military history. And it is the foundation for my view that one of the keys to developing a sense of the realities of war amongst future officers is the development of imagination and self-awareness – both important aspects of a balanced and liberal education.

---

13   John Keegan, *The Face of Battle* (London: Folio, 2007 [1976]), p. 3.
14   Ibid., p. 4.
15   Ibid., p. 5.
16   Ibid., p. 6.
17   Ibid., p. 8.

Imagination and the Experience of War

It is not just history that is an important preparatory discipline for officers. Literature, memoirs, reportage, theatre, photographs and cinema should also be studied. Indeed, Aristotle can be deployed – without too much violence – to make the case that such products have a priority over history in this respect. For Aristotle argued that

> the poet's function is to describe, not the thing that has happened, but a kind of thing that might happen ... Hence poetry is something more philosophic and of graver import than history, since its statements are of the nature rather of universals, whereas those of history are singular.[18]

Like those of us who support the role of teaching literature at military academies, so Elizabeth Samet, who teaches literature at West Point, gently confronts the notion that literature has no relevance to the curriculum of a military academy. She notes the 'mistrust of literature (especially poetry) [within the military] as an effete civilian pastime'.[19] Samet would doubtless be pleased to read the words of Admiral James Stavridis of the US Navy, currently Supreme Allied Commander Europe. Stavridis recently recounted both his love of fiction and the encouragement he gives his staff to build 'a reading list and a well-rounded personal collection of works';[20] he particularly advises officers to learn another language, so as to have access to an even greater wealth of literature. Samet relates how ideas and feelings – such as loyalty, courage and fear – can be explored in literature. This lends itself to ethical exploration, which requires imaginatively putting oneself into another's position and embracing – rather than denying – complexity. Samet's book *Soldier's Heart* is a wonderful account of the ways her students use the literature, poetry and films they have studied to prepare for, and make sense of, their experiences of war. Such students have acquired an ability to cut through the clichés of heroism, the infantile patriotism and the crude appeals to 'sacrifice' that surround modern wars, whatever their merits or justice. Soldiers, in short, need to imagine war to help prepare them for the realities they will face and the challenges they will encounter.

There are two objections to this view on which I would like to comment briefly. The first is that the impressions gained by an imaginative foray into war are partial. But while there is nothing like the direct experience of combat, that experience, too, is incomplete. The second is that the technical details of military life tend to be inauthentic in novels and movies and that reality is often simplified or otherwise distorted for dramatic effect; but the 'truth' of such representations is not so much

---

18   Cited in Elizabeth D. Samet, *Soldier's Heart: Reading Literature Through Peace and War at West Point* (New York: Farrar, Strauss and Giroux, 2007), p. 67.

19   Ibid., p. 75.

20   James Stavridis, 'Let Us Dare', *Australian Defence Force Journal*, 181 (2010): 72–8, at p. 72.

in their technical detail but in the sureness of their human grasp. Perhaps the real problem with the accounts of war we read and see is not so much in their intrinsic partiality, but in their imposing a coherent narrative upon the events they relate. As an Iraqi veteran perceptively 'blogged' about the Academy Award-winning film *The Hurt Locker* – which focuses on the activities of a US bomb-disposal squad in Iraq – '[f]rom the street level, there is no plot in war, just a series of unrelated missions that fit in The Big Picture on some PowerPoint presentation. Especially in EOD units where there literally is no mission, just bomb interdiction ... Over and over like *Groundhog Day*.'[21]

Since the Homeric poems, wars have been the catalyst for literature – some of it profound. In a brief survey of recent war literature, Ben Macintyre notes that the wars in Iraq and Afghanistan have produced some fine non-fiction reportage, but as yet no major novelists: 'no modern Joseph Heller or Evelyn Waugh to mock the absurdities of war; no Norman Mailer or Ernest Hemingway to portray the horrors of conflict, nor even a Rudyard Kipling or a G.A. Henty to fictionalize wartime sacrifice and heroism.'[22] This might simply point to the delay between events and great writing about them. After all, Erich Maria Remarque's *All Quiet on the Western Front* first appeared in 1929; Karl Marlantes's recently published and critically acclaimed novel about Vietnam, *Matterhorn*, took 35 years to appear. The 'defining account' of the Gulf War, Macintyre argues, is Anthony Swofford's memoir, *Jarhead*, published in 2003. The difference between literature and reportage remains a significant one: '[Sebastian] Junger's *War* may help us to understand war; but a novel such as Mailer's *The Naked and the Dead* can make you feel war.'[23]

Since the advent of cinema, films, too, have played an important role in telling the stories of war. If this was, at first, for patriotic effect, film has become a place to explore the complexities of conflict. There are, of course, good and bad films. On one side stand films such as *Winged Victory* (1944) and *Thirty Seconds Over Tokyo* (1944), along with the British film *In Which We Serve* (1942). On the other, there have been dozens of morale-boosting pot-boilers. Film director and Vietnam veteran Oliver Stone directed *Platoon* (1986) and *Born on the Fourth of July* (1989) – both about the Vietnam War and both disproving his view that 'films about war are recruiting posters'. The Iraq and Afghanistan Wars, too, have had their share of films: *Green Zone* (2010), *Lions for Lambs* (2007), *In the Valley of Elah* (2007), *Stop-Loss* (2008), *Rendition* (2007), *The Men Who Stare at Goats* (2009), among many others. As films, not all of them are strong. Many betray an overbearing political message, generally anti–President George W. Bush, which – whatever the value of the case – tends to diminish their artistry.

21   ArmyofDude (2009), http://armyofdude.blogspot.com/2009/06/most-entertaining-movie-review-ever.html

22   Ben Macintyre, 'All Quiet on the Afghan–Iraqi Fiction Front', *The Times*, 10 August 2010.

23   Ibid.

Ethics Education And Its Limits

It is important to understand the limits to what ethics education can do. I do not see its purpose as creating virtuous people – the so-called 'virtue ethics' approach. In Plato's dialogue *Meno*, Socrates declares that 'virtue is neither natural nor acquired, but an instinct given by God to the virtuous. Nor is this instinct accompanied by reason … virtue comes to the virtuous by the gift of God.' While we might agree with Socrates that people cannot be educated to have a virtuous character, they can nevertheless be assisted in making good ethical decisions by studying the origins of and approaches to the discipline of ethics and exploring ethical dilemmas in a range of scenarios they are likely to encounter.

The teaching of applied and professional ethics in this way is relatively new. In the 1970s, Derek Bok, then President of Harvard University, argued for the importance of formal ethics education:

> [I]t does seem plausible to suppose that the students in these courses will become more alert in perceiving ethical issues, more aware of the reasons underlying moral principles, and more equipped to reason carefully in applying these principles to concrete cases. Will they behave more ethically? We may never know.[24]

The teaching of ethics has two elements. The first concerns the ability to reason ethically: to understand which part of a situation has ethical implications and how one might go about evaluating the appropriate ethical course of action in that situation. The second concerns the ethical foundation on which decisions are ultimately based, offering a range of ethical perspectives. The formulation and understanding of professional 'codes of conduct' are in some respects the lowest common denominator of the ethics education process. As Gabriel argued: 'A man who observes a code without knowing these reasons [why one ought to do some things and not others] and without understanding them cannot be said to be acting ethically. He can only be said to be obeying a set of precepts that he does not understand.'[25]

Codes of conduct alone are unlikely to sustain a soldier through prolonged ethical challenges. Admiral James B. Stockdale, a prisoner of the North Vietnamese from 1965 to 1973, including four years of solitary confinement, faced enormous pressures from his captors to inform on his comrades and betray his country. He did not submit, finding guidance in the stoicism of Epictetus, a philosopher whose writings he had encountered in his postgraduate education. Reflecting in 1974 on how to prepare for the physical and mental strains of political imprisonment, he wrote:

---

24 Derek C. Bok, 'Can Ethics Be Taught?', *Change*, 8/9 (October 1976): 26–30, at p. 30.

25 Gabriel, p. 27.

> I think the best preparation for an American officer who may be subjected to political imprisonment, is a broad, liberal education that gives the man at least enough historical perspective to realize that those who have excelled in life before him were, in the last essence, committed to play a role.[26]

Ethical action involves making choices. What ought one to do; what ought one not to do? Sometimes – perhaps often – we are confronted with choices that do not easily fit the precepts, where there is a choice between conflicting obligations. Ethical choice means choosing between these competing obligations. And the latter involves making a judgment. The important thing for professional ethics is that this is a judgment that we can defend to others and we believe would be made by others if they were faced with the same circumstances.

On the basis of Canadian experience, Walker argues that soldiers can be prepared for the ethical challenges of the asymmetrical battlefield by a military ethics program, 'which articulates an internalized combat ethos (Warrior's code) that defines how we fight no matter "how vile" the enemy or how amoral the battlefield'.[27] And as Adam Smith put it in his *The Theory of Moral Sentiments*,[28] the ability to empathize with others is a major foundation of moral sensibility. But there is only so much that an intellectual and imaginative preparation for war can do. One can easily empathize with others and make calm decisions when one is safe, comfortable and well fed. In the battle space itself, good judgment – especially about the enemy – becomes much more difficult.

How capable are the students of our ethics education of absorbing the lessons and developing the complex reasoning capacities that battle will demand of them? Psychologists Lawrence Kohlberg[29] and Robert Kegan,[30] among others, have raised such issues at the broadest level. While their approaches differ, both point to the importance of understanding the developmental stages of individuals as they move from a lower to a higher stage of moral reasoning – development that is not simply a product of maturation or age. The conclusion we might draw from their work is that although we expect sophisticated moral reasoning to emerge from those who have been provided with a high-quality ethics education, some individuals might simply not be ready – and some might never be ready – to perform the

26   James B. Stockdale, *A Vietnam Experience: Ten Years of Reflection* (Stanford, CA: Hoover Institution Press, 1984), p. 8.

27   Richard J. Walker, 'Quarter and *Jus in Bello*: Meeting the Challenge of Ethical Uncertainty Within the Asymmetrical Battlespace', in Daniel Lagacé-Roy and Bernd Horn (eds), *The War on Terror – Ethical Considerations: Proceedings from the 7th Canadian Conference on Ethical Leadership* (Kingston, ON: Canadian Defence Academy Press), Vol. 1, pp. 133–59, at p. 156.

28   Adam Smith, *The Theory of Moral Sentiments*, eds D.D. Raphael and A.L. Macfie (Oxford: Oxford University Press, 1976 [1759]).

29   Lawrence Kohlberg, *The Psychology of Moral Development: The Nature and Validity of Moral Stages* (San Francisco: Harper & Row, 1984).

30   Kegan.

reasoning our military missions require. In connection with the prisoner abuses at Abu Ghraib, for example, Bartone makes the following observation:

> Kegan's model implies that most soldiers, like other young adults, are functioning at the Stage 3 developmental level [conformist, as distinct from Stage 4: autonomous], making them rather more susceptible to group influences, for good or ill. In fact, recent studies on Army officers and cadets suggest this developmental framework applies very closely within the military.[31]

The developmental literature presents a profound challenge to the ethics educators' mission – one we have yet to appreciate fully.

Theory into Practice: The Importance of Context

Even if soldiers have developed the capacity for complex moral reasoning, the experience of war – especially contemporary war – is enormously stressful. Soldiers are fearful for their own lives and those of their comrades, whatever their bravado. They fight in a terrain that is unfamiliar, in short, sharp bursts, against an enemy that specializes in ambush and melts into the surrounding population with relative ease. The levels of frustration and stress under these circumstances are palpable and have health and other consequences long after deployment. It has been reported that a study by the Australian Defence Department into the health of Afghanistan veterans reveals soldiers addicted to prescription drugs and taking illicit substances; post-deployment marriage break-ups and suicides also seem to have increased.[32]

To get some sense of the realities that have confronted our soldiers in recent years, it is useful to survey the reportage of Sebastian Junger and David Finkel – two of the very best observers. Junger, a journalist embedded on five occasions between mid-2007 and mid-2008 with a group of American soldiers from the Battle Company of the 173rd Airborne Brigade, writes about the American military mission in the Korengal Valley in Afghanistan. His *War*, according to one reviewer, is 'a combat classic'.[33] His insights are not new: we have known since at least World War II, for example, that soldiers are motivated largely by loyalty to their immediate group of comrades-in-arms. But the immediacy of his writing is powerful.

Death for the Americans in the Korengal Valley was unexpected: 'Pretty much everyone who died in this valley died when they least expected it, usually shot in

---

31   Paul T. Bartone, 'Preventing Prisoner Abuse: Leadership Lessons of Abu Ghraib', *Ethics and Behaviour*, 20/2 (2010): 161–73, at p. 167.

32   Sean Parnell and Rory Callinan, 'Soldiers' Despair Confronts Defence', *The Weekend Australian*, 10–11 July 2010.

33   Peter Wilson, 'A Combat Classic', *The Australian Literary Review*, 2 June 2010: 5.

the head or throat ... The men just never knew, which meant that anything they did was potentially the *last* thing they'd ever do.'[34] Tiredness is a major factor, impairing judgment. Group loyalty becomes overwhelming. On discovering a dead comrade, a soldier says: 'I just wanted to kill everything that came up that wasn't American. I actually didn't care who came up – man, woman, child, I still would've done something.'[35] The randomness of death due to IEDs also generates fear: 'The enemy now had a weapon that unnerved the Americans more than small-arms fire ever could: random luck'.[36] But the picture is nuanced, with Junger also capturing the excitement felt by soldiers: 'The machinery of war and the sound it makes and the urgency of its use and the consequences of almost everything about it are the most exciting things anyone engaged in war will ever know.'[37] The adrenalin highs of combat are one factor that makes the integration of soldiers back into quotidian life so very difficult.

Finkel's *The Good Soldiers* is reportage of 'the surge' in the Iraq war of 2007–08. It follows the deployment of the Second Battalion, Sixteenth Infantry Regiment, of the Fourth Infantry Brigade Combat Team, First Infantry Division of the US Army, known as the 2-16, as it deployed from Fort Riley, Kansas, to a forward operating base called Rustamiyah in eastern Baghdad. Four hundred and twenty days later, having taken a number of casualties, including 14 soldiers killed – but, more importantly, having undergone some profoundly unsettling experiences and changes – the 2-16 left Iraq. Like Junger, Finkel notes that soldiers' nerves were set on edge both by a lull in fighting and by a series of low-level attacks. In mid-2007, he recounted: There were also the frustrations of putting in infrastructure only to watch it being destroyed:

> A year before, when [Brent] Cummings had first seen Kamaliyah and peered into a hole in the ground at the cadaver named Bob, he had talked of the goodness here and the need to act morally. 'Otherwise we're not human,' he had said. Eight months before, when he had bent some rules to get Izzy's [the interpreter] injured daughter into the aid station and had watched her smile as Izzy kissed her, he had said, 'Man, I haven't felt this good since I got to this hellhole.' Now, watching the water geyser [created by a missile that had missed their convoy but severed a water main], he simply said, 'Stupid people. I hate 'em. Stupid fucking scumbags.'[38]

Finkel's underlying theme is the disintegration of good people under the stresses of war – or, at least, this war – because their hopes of making a difference had been dashed.

34　Sebastian Junger, *War* (London: Fourth Estate, 2010), p. 57.
35　Cited in ibid., p. 106.
36　Ibid., p. 142.
37　Ibid., p. 144.
38　Ibid., p. 245.

The difficult conditions under which our soldiers are operating can be gained from numerous sources, particularly correspondence from colleagues and former students; they confirm the accounts already cited. A former PhD student in my school, and former Lieutenant Colonel in the Australian Army, based with the International Security Assistance Force (ISAF) at Kandahar International Airfield, painted a vivid picture of the conditions under which he worked. Direct threats were rare, except at a local level for short periods; rockets were a major problem, but the other threats included all types of IEDs, attacks by suicide bombers and small-arms attacks against vehicles and aircraft. Casualties were taken every day. It was, he says, never quiet: constant aircraft noise was supplemented by the engines of military trucks, civilian semi-trailers from Pakistan and hundreds of four-wheel-drive vehicles. A field of diesel power generators, located next to the camp, ran day and night. It was blistering hot or icy cold – and it smelled of human waste: 'As always with operational deployments, we are all tired all of the time. Red Bull stimulant drinks and black coffee are used to make up for missed and broken sleep'.[39]

Under these pressures, making good ethical decisions becomes harder. The unconventional nature of the enemy and the irregular combat with which ISAF soldiers have to deal make this a difficult place for judicious decision making. So how different is the conflict in which we are currently engaged and should our ethical approach be adjusted?

The Ethical Challenges of Asymmetrical Warfare

The current conflict in Afghanistan has the character of both an 'asymmetrical' struggle, with forces of very different types and technical capabilities confronting each other (or not), and a 'counterinsurgency', where the imperatives of 'shape, clear, hold and build' apply. Each of these creates crucial practical and ethical challenges. In particular, the soldiers' image of 'the enemy' is important for their approach to the ethical treatment of them.[40] It is clear that the insurgent is not a military professional; they might be an ideological or religious zealot, but they might just as likely be an opportunist. If they are denigrated by racist, cultural or other stereotypes, there is a danger of considering them subhuman – the terrible consequences of which approach were evident during World War II and the Vietnam War.

How to deal with an enemy who does not play by the rules, is thoroughly opportunist in its approach to inflicting casualties and will target non-combatants with impunity? When the enemy takes prisoners – which is not often – they become hostages for ransom and propaganda purposes. The enemy is able to merge into the local population to seek sanctuary and to terrorize the local population into supporting them. For insurgents, controlling territory is relatively unimportant,

---

39 Personal email, 22 June 2010.
40 Gray, pp. 131–69.

state borders are minor inconveniences and traditional concepts of winning or losing do not apply.[41] By operating in complex urban terrain, such as major towns and cities, or in forbidding natural terrain, such as mountains, they blunt the traditional 'big-war' technologies.[42] This is a very difficult type of warfare for conventionally trained armies to confront.

Walker argues that in the asymmetrical battle space, Western soldiers expect from the law of armed conflict a reciprocity of honourable practice, but find that there is sometimes little to distinguish friend from foe. They go into counterinsurgency struggles with a conventional-war culture: 'just how are [these] soldiers ... expected to cope with the new asymmetry within the spatial, functional, and moral dimensions, when faced by an enemy armed with the certainty that human slaughter is both business and religious fulfilment?'[43] The uncertainties of the asymmetrical battlefield tend to give rise to rash decisions. 'Recent allegations of atrocities committed by British and American forces in Iraq identify "soldier uncertainty" as the key cultural variable and officer cover-up as the common denominator.'[44] Britain's Defence Minister, John Reid, even argued in April 2006 that 'all the conventions, declarations, laws, rules and protocols created after World War II ... are inadequate to cover the world that exists now'.[45]

Leaving aside the issue of the justice of the wars in Iraq and Afghanistan, soldiers who have been directed by their government to fight must conduct themselves appropriately, for operational, legal and ethical reasons. The two key issues in this domain of just conduct remain the identification of legitimate targets and the appropriate application of force against them – discrimination and proportionality. The ability to discriminate between combatants and non-combatants is often problematic. Combatants, especially in asymmetrical warfare, do not always wear uniforms and are unlikely to announce themselves. Pinpointing such enemies with precision and then attacking them with military force become difficult, impractical and arguably unethical, particularly when a civilian population forms part of their camouflage.[46] Even wounded and surrendered combatants create problems when they use their new status to come to close quarters with an enemy and inflict casualties. But there is a further complication, brought on by the fact that those who shoot the guns need to be supported: is the population that enfolds the insurgents

---

41   Peter K. Manning, 'Policing new social spaces', in James Sheptycki (ed.), *Issues in Transnational Policing* (London: Routledge, 2000), p. 177.

42   Carol J. Fitzgerald, 'Changing the face of Urban Warfare: DoD Advanced Concept Technology Demonstration Evaluates City-Fighting Technologies', *Armed Forces Journal International*, 138 (February 2001): pp. 18–19; Robert H. Scales, 'Urban Warfare: a Soldiers View', *Military Review*, January-February 2005: 9–18, at p. 9.

43   Walker, p. 141.

44   Ibid., p. 141.

45   Cited in ibid., p. 146.

46   P. Robinson, 'Introduction: Ethics Education for Irregular Warfare', in Don Carrick, James Connelly and Paul Robinson (eds), *Ethics Education for Irregular Warfare* (Farnham: Ashgate, 2009), p. 4.

also a legitimate target or the financiers who make their struggle possible or the arms-dealers who sell them weapons? Are immediate non-combatants 'innocents'?

The principle of discrimination also goes to the issue not just of who are legitimate targets, but whether the weapons used against them are appropriately discriminatory. Bombs of the aerial and roadside variety – both of which play an important role in the current insurgencies – are amongst the least discriminatory. It is one reason the UN convention banning the use of anti-personnel landmines was signed in 1997 and why the Convention on Cluster Munitions was adopted in 2008. In terms of the appropriate application of force, just conduct in war means that an offensive action should be proportional to the objective sought. Destruction and casualties should be minimized. This principle is broadly utilitarian in seeking to minimize overall suffering, but it can also be understood from other moral perspectives, including the Christian perspective of mercy. Proportionality supports the distinction between a battle and a massacre. But proportionality does not come with a distinctive set of agreed metrics.

There are legitimate grounds for disagreement about the ethical treatment of one's adversaries in counterinsurgency and counter-terrorist operations. Kasher, for example, argues that the traditional doctrine of just war is difficult if not impossible to apply to all the challenges of terrorism. He proposes instead a new 'principle of distinction' that includes a 'scale of involvement' in hostilities.[47] The scale of involvement goes from the most direct, military-style involvement, where an individual represents an immediate threat and is therefore a legitimate target, through a dozen categories to the 'individuals that *exercise* political, social or religious leadership of an organization that supports terrorists'.[48] These and other distinctions give guidance to the appropriate ethical response to terrorists, whether predominantly military (injury) or policing (minimum injury). He concludes by arguing that 'the notion of "military necessity" should play a much more important role in ethical and moral considerations of military activities of fighting terrorists'.[49] For his part, Amitai Etzioni has argued that '[t]he onus for avoiding collateral damage altogether is on the terrorists. They have to stop exploiting their status as civilians, stop using civilians as human shields, and homes – as headquarters, as locations to store ammunition and for snipers to ply their deadly trade.'[50] And Dick Couch has proposed a new 'tactical ethic' for conduct in the insurgent battle space.[51]

---

47   Asa Kasher, 'Problems in Military Ethics of Fighting Terrorism', in Daniel Lagacé-Roy and Bernd Horn (eds), *The War on Terror – Ethical Considerations: Proceedings from the 7th Canadian Conference on Ethical Leadership* (Kingston, ON: Canadian Defence Academy Press, 2008), Vol. 1., pp. 1–14, at p. 9.

48   Ibid., p. 11.

49   Ibid., p. 14.

50   Personal communication, 31 March 2010.

51   Dick Couch, *A Tactical Ethic: Moral Conduct in the Insurgent Battlespace* (Annapolis, MD: Naval Institute Press, 2010).

But while the contemporary challenges of counterinsurgency might differ from those in previous conflicts, they are not fundamentally different in kind. The current 'war on terror' and the counterinsurgencies it has generated raise ethical issues in warfare that have long been with us. And in counterinsurgency, in particular, the protection of civilians is key to success. This goes to the heart of what it means to 'win' a counterinsurgency, where body counts are not a measure of success. General Stanley McChrystal, at the time he was ISAF Commander in Afghanistan, put considerable emphasis on winning over and protecting civilians as his contribution to turning around the war. Early in February 2010, McChrystal explained that '[t]his is all a war of perceptions. This is not a physical war in terms of how many people you kill ... This is all in the minds of the participants.'[52]

We do not need to develop within our soldiers an 'unconventional-war culture' to respond to the ethical challenges they face in counterinsurgency. Rather, their understanding of their longstanding legal and ethical obligations in combat must be deepened by a subtle grasp of the motivations, perspectives and likely responses of their adversaries, by an appreciation of the physical and mental challenges they will confront in this type of combat, and by a fundamental acknowledgement of the humanity of their enemy. Education, rather than training, is the key to this outcome.

Conclusions

Being a soldier requires that one puts oneself 'in harm's way' as and when required by one's government. In its best sense, it is one of the highest acts of citizenship. It also permits the deliberate taking of life under special circumstances. Bearing arms for one's country is consequently a great responsibility. An ethical appreciation of soldiers' difficult and demanding roles is central to undertaking and making sense of them. It is not simply that the injunction to protect the lives of civilians serves a utilitarian purpose in war itself, especially in counterinsurgencies; it also gives soldiers a sense of proper purpose, of retaining their own equilibrium and self-esteem.

The dedicated teaching of ethics to soldiers is increasingly and properly recognized as being an appropriate part of professional military development. But I have suggested in this chapter that neither an abstract nor an applied approach to the teaching of ethics – though both have merit when done well – can *by themselves* prepare soldiers for the ethical challenges they will confront on the battlefield. In addition, an appreciation of history and literature, in particular those related to combat, provides an opportunity imaginatively to enter the battle space, with its confusion, panic and pain. Even – perhaps especially – against adversaries who do not respect the rules of war or who deliberately attempt to provoke an intemperate

52   Christina Lamb, 'McChrystal's Publicity Blitzkrieg', *The Australian*, 15 February 2010.

and indiscriminate response these rules must be upheld. The terrible events of 11 September 2001 do not justify the use of any and all means against the terrorist challenge. Moving down this track has led the United States to tarnish its ideals and lose the international goodwill it gained in response to 9/11; it has led to wars in which civilian casualties are high, and which have created the sort of instability in which terrorism thrives.

Larger issues remain. In the ethical education of soldiers, we must be more conscious of their level of psychological development and consequently their ability to make the sorts of mature ethical calculations we expect. And soldiers' ethical development must be reinforced by a climate of ethical behaviour in the broader defence organization into which they fit and through which they will journey – some of them, ultimately, to the top. 'Leaders have the responsibility to create an ethical command climate where soldiers are not afraid to voice their opinions and more importantly tell the truth.'[53] The soldier is also, and ultimately, a citizen. If the conditions for entering a war are seriously contested or if the overall planning of a war is seriously awry – as is arguably the case in both Iraq and Afghanistan – a soldier's motivation to behave ethically is undermined. Professionalism and ethics education, no matter that they cannot guarantee ethical behaviour in combat, are sorely tested in the service of a campaign that is muddled or incoherent.

Michael Ignatieff declared that '[t]he decisive restraint on human practice on the battlefield lies within the warrior himself, in his conception of what is honourable or dishonourable for a man to do with weapons'.[54] This conception must be taught, not just by formal ethics courses, but by a broad program of familiarization with the 'known unknowns' of combat. If we are to continue to see the task of fighting wars – however unpleasant the prospect – as something that is honourable then we need to give our future military leaders a proper education in military ethics, the proper support when they are in the field and a just cause. What is at stake is the ability of the defence force to do the job requested of it.

---

53   Janis L. Karpinski, 'Ethical Behaviour and Ethical Challenges in the Complex Security Environment', in Daniel Lagacé-Roy and Bernd Horn (eds), *The War on Terror – Ethical Considerations: Proceedings from the 7th Canadian Conference on Ethical Leadership* (Kingston, ON: Canadian Defence Academy Press, 2008), Vol. 2, pp. 93–105, at p. 100.

54   Michael Ignatieff, *The Warrior's Honour: Ethnic War and the Modern Conscience* (London: Chatto & Windus, 1998), p. 118.

Chapter 10

First Do No Harm: Refugee Law as a Response to Armed Conflict

Penelope Mathew

Introduction

In times of armed conflict, the significance of international refugee law's palliative[1] role is heightened. As third countries discuss military responses to a conflict, under the auspices of 'responsibility to protect',[2] for example, refugee law reminds us of the Hippocratic oath: first do no harm.[3]

Responsibility to protect is broad enough to encompass *non-refoulement* – the obligation not to return a refugee.[4] Given the dangers of military intervention, it is arguable that *non-refoulement* is in fact the first line of defence for war victims. Responsibility to protect is, however, not yet sufficiently focused on the needs

---

1 See James C. Hathaway, 'New Directions to Avoid Hard Problems: The Distortion of the Palliative Role of Refugee Protection', *Journal of Refugee Studies* (1995): 288, 293–4. I will not delve into the debate about whether the phrase 'first do no harm' should be attributed to Hippocrates or whether it forms part of an oath pledged by medical practitioners. In my defence, I plead that I am a lawyer, not a doctor.

2 The concept of responsibility to protect ('R2P') has evolved to address cases of genocide, war crimes, crimes against humanity and ethnic cleansing. In such cases, the United Nations has accepted that the international community has a responsibility to intervene, including militarily under UN auspices. See *2005 World Summit Outcome*, UNGA Res. A/Res/60/1, 24 October 2005, paras 138–9. R2P has implicitly been invoked by the Security Council in the case of Sudan (UNSC Res. 1706 [2006]) when it referred to the relevant paragraphs of the *World Summit* document, and explicitly in the case of Libya (UNSC Res. 1973 [2011]), where it refers to the possibility that Muammar Gaddafi's regime has committed crimes against humanity, that Libya bears primary responsibility for protection of its citizens and that parties to the conflict also bear responsibility for protection of civilians.

3 Cf. Michael Baruticiski's point about the UN High Commissioner for Refugees' in-country operations: Michael Barutciski, 'Opinion: A Critical View on UNHCR's Mandate Dilemmas', *International Journal of Refugee Law*, 14 (2002): 365, 379–80.

4 The Secretary-General has included becoming party to the Refugee Convention as an aspect of responsibility to protect: *Implementing the Responsibility to Protect*, Report of the Secretary-General, A/63/677, 12 January 2009, para. 11.

of refugees[5] and, indeed, refugee-hood is a challenge to the authority of states and the international community as envisaged by the doctrine of responsibility to protect[6] because it is an option of self-help – an expression of an individual's political agency.

There are also deep controversies about the application of the primary 'universal' instruments of refugee law – the 1951 Convention relating to the Status of Refugees ('Refugee Convention')[7] and the 1967 Protocol relating to the Status of Refugees[8] – to persons fleeing from war torn countries. This chapter singles out three controversies for examination, all of which go to the question at the core of refugee protection: is it permissible to send this person home to danger or, on the other hand, are the risks so serious that we cannot contribute to them through forcible return? These controversies also speak to a fear that the oppressive or chaotic situations from which asylum-seekers flee will travel with them, indeed, are somehow embodied by asylum-seekers, and threaten, by force of numbers and/or supposed non-assimilability, to overwhelm the order prevailing within state borders. This fear finds a comfortable home in the Refugee Convention's failure to go beyond *non-refoulement* and explicitly provide for entry to state territory.

The first controversy, examined in the second section, is the application of the definition of a refugee to people fleeing from civil wars or internal armed conflicts or violence. The second issue, dealt with in section three, is the role and scope of complementary protection – that is, protection that falls outside the Refugee Convention – for victims of violence that is generalized or 'indiscriminate'. Even the terminology is difficult. 'Indiscriminate' is a term that is particularly fungible in that violence is usually intended, but its impacts can indeed go well beyond intended targets and results. The meaning of the term in the two areas of law most relevant to this chapter – international humanitarian law and refugee and asylum law – might sometimes diverge. The final problem, discussed in section four, is the question of exclusion from refugee status of participants in outlawed forms of armed conflict (for example, war crimes) and what consequences might follow from exclusion.

---

5   See Susan Harris Rimmer, 'Refugees, Internally Displaced Persons and the "Responsibility to Protect"', *New Issues in Refugee Research*, Research Paper No. 185 (Geneva: UNHCR, March 2010).

6   As Anne Orford writes, in the *World Summit Outcome* document's vision of responsibility to protect, '[t]he vocabulary of "responsibility" works ... as a language for conferring authority and allocating power rather than as a language for imposing binding obligations and commanding obedience'. Anne Orford, *International Authority and the Responsibility to Protect* (Cambridge: Cambridge University Press, 2011). She argues that the concept of responsibility to protect has 'authoritarian tendencies'.

7   *Convention Relating to the Status of Refugees, July 28, 1951*, 189 UNTS 137 (hereinafter Refugee Convention).

8   *1967 Protocol Relating to the Status of Refugees, January 31, 1966*, 606 UNTS 267.

The Refugee Convention and 'War Refugees'

As is well known, the Refugee Convention adopted a narrow definition of a refugee. According to Article 1A(2) of the convention, a refugee was a person outside their country of origin as a result of events that occurred prior to 1 January 1951 and who was unable to avail themselves of the protection of that state owing to a 'well-founded fear of being persecuted for reasons of race, religion, nationality, membership of a particular social group or political opinion'. Parties to the convention also had the option of limiting their obligations to refugees fleeing events in Europe. In 1967, the protocol lifted the temporal and geographic restrictions on the definition, but it did not touch the other stringent elements of the definition such as the requirement of 'persecution' and a nexus to the five convention grounds. Consequently, extended definitions of refugee-hood have been adopted in the Americas and Africa in order to capture the experience of 'generalized' or 'indiscriminate' violence in the Americas and Africa (as will be discussed later in this chapter).

Strict as it is, the Refugee Convention definition is capable of being applied during times of armed conflict. The term 'persecution' is widely accepted as encompassing violations of human rights.[9] Clearly, persecution might occur in the context of an armed conflict and we might refer to general human rights law and/or to international humanitarian law (IHL) as an aid in the construction of the term persecution.[10] Sometimes there might be interesting questions concerning the extent to which IHL is *lex specialis*, but it is important to remember that the *lex specialis* applies against the backdrop of general human rights law and that general human rights law is not simply ousted from consideration because of the context of an armed conflict.[11] It might, however, be difficult in some conflict situations to show that the harm feared was a violation of human rights law as opposed to so-called 'collateral damage' or that the violation had a sufficient connection with the convention's grounds of persecution.

The UN High Commissioner for Refugees (UNHCR) handbook, last updated in 1992, has this to say on the subject of what it calls 'war refugees':

> Persons compelled to leave their country of origin as a result of international or national armed conflicts are not normally considered refugees under the 1951 Convention or 1967 Protocol ... However, foreign invasion or occupation of all or part of a country can result – and occasionally has resulted – in persecution

---

9   For a detailed discussion of the 'human rights approach' to the meaning of persecution, see Michelle Foster, *International Refugee Law and Socio-Economic Rights: Refuge From Deprivation* (Cambridge: Cambridge University Press, 2007), Ch. 2.

10   See Hugo Storey and Rebecca Wallace, 'War and Peace in Refugee Law Jurisprudence', *American Journal of International Law*, 95 (2001): 349.

11   *Legal Consequences of the Construction of a Wall in the Occupied Palestinian Territory (Advisory Opinion)* [2004], ICJ Rep. 136, paras 105–6.

for one or more of the reasons enumerated in the 1951 Convention. In such cases, refugee status will depend upon whether the applicant is able to show that he has a 'well-founded fear of being persecuted' in the occupied territory and, in addition, upon whether or not he is able to avail himself of the protection of his government, or of a protecting power whose duty it is to safeguard the interests of his country during the armed conflict, and whether such protection can be considered to be effective.[12]

These paragraphs recognize that all wars are fought for political reasons, but this does not make everyone fleeing a war a refugee. To some extent, nearly everyone is at risk during a time of armed conflict. A remote connection to the convention's grounds will not suffice for the purposes of refugee status.[13]

The changing nature of war, however – in particular the fact that we tend not to be concerned with classic interstate conflicts undertaken for 'reasons of state' but civil conflicts that involve political, religious and/or ethnic cleavages – has led to cases in which it is fairly easy to identify violations that are linked to one of the five grounds, as opposed to generalized or indiscriminate harm. Furthermore, in the civil wars we witnessed in the late twentieth century, it has sometimes been meaningless to rely on obligations imposed by IHL such as those concerning safety zones as a protective device. As Jennifer Hyndman has written of safe spaces such as safety zones implemented under the Geneva Conventions[14] or the safe havens negotiated during the Bosnian war:

---

12   *UNHCR Handbook on Procedures and Criteria for Determining Refugee Status Under the 1951 Convention and the 1967 Protocol Relating to the Status of Refugees*, 2nd edn (Geneva: UNHCR, 1992), paras 164–5.

13   The UNHCR takes the position that 'it is sufficient that the Convention ground be a relevant factor contributing to the persecution. It does not have to be the sole, or even dominant, cause.' *UNHCR Position on Claims for Refugee Status Under the 1951 Convention Relating to the Status of Refugees Based on a Fear of Persecution Due to An Individual's Membership of a Family or Clan Engaged in a Blood Feud* (Geneva: UNHCR, 17 March 2006), http://www.unhcr.no/Pdf/Position_countryinfo_papers_06/Membership_ clan_family_blood_feud.pdf. The *Michigan Guidelines* present the predicament-based approach to the convention grounds: *Michigan Guidelines on Nexus to a Convention Ground* (http://www.refugeecaselaw.org/documents/Nexus.pdf). They state that 'the convention ground need not be shown to be the sole or even the dominant cause of the risk of being persecuted. It need only be a contributing factor to the risk of being persecuted. If, however, the convention ground is remote to the point of irrelevance, refugee status need not be recognized' (*Michigan Guidelines*, para. 13). Participants in the colloquia that led to the adoption of the *Michigan Guidelines* have been a mix of 'eminent publicists' and more junior colleagues in the field of refugee law, meaning that the guidelines might be appropriately referred to as a guide to interpreting the Refugee Convention.

14   For example, see *Geneva Convention for the Amelioration of the Condition of the Wounded and Sick in Armed Forces in the Field*, 74 UNTS 31 [hereinafter GCI], Art. 23,

The rules of war and the safe spaces they create, as inscribed in humanitarian law, are less and less relevant as warring factions ignore these consensual arrangements. Dutch peacekeepers in Srebrenica assisted Bosnian Serbs in creating lists of men of fighting age, believing Serb claims that those detained would be questioned as prisoners of war in accordance with the Geneva Conventions. In the end, these lists were used to systematize the murder of between seven and eight thousand Bosnian Muslim men.[15]

International humanitarian law might still play a very valuable role in refugee protection, as pointed out by Brett and Lester, who argue, *inter alia*, that IHL rules concerning detention of combatants might play an important role in determining what should happen to persons who need to be separated from the rest of a refugee population during a mass influx and who may be excluded from refugee protection.[16] The 'surrogate protection' of refugee law, however – the protection provided by the international community in the absence of national protection – is increasingly important in the context of civil wars.

Modern case law generally reflects the position that the context of armed conflict does not divest decision makers of the responsibility of applying the refugee definition. For example, in *Knezevic v Attorney-General*, the US Court of Appeals (Ninth Circuit) had no difficulty in determining that Serbs who had fled ethnic cleansing by Croats in the context of the Bosnian civil war were refugees.[17] In some other cases, however, the fact that almost everyone is at risk during wartime has led to strained jurisprudence.

A very famous example is the House of Lord's decision in *Regina v Secretary of State for the Home Department, ex parte Adan*.[18] In this case, which involved armed conflict among the clans in Somalia, the court required that there be a showing of some differential risk over and above that of other clan members or

---

and *Geneva Convention Relative to the Protection of Civilians in Time of War*, 75 UNTS 287 [hereinafter GCIV], Art. 14.

15   Jennifer Hyndman, 'Preventive, Palliative, or Punitive? Safe Spaces in Bosnia-Herzegovina, Somalia and Sri Lanka', *Journal of Refugee Studies*, 16 (2003): 167, at p. 182. Hyndman's point is illustrated most recently by the Sri Lankan Government's herding of Tamil civilians into 'no-fire zones', which were then fired upon. International Crisis Group, 'War Crimes in Sri Lanka', *Asia Report*, 191 (17 May 2010), http://www.crisisgroup.org/~/media/Files/asia/south-asia/sri-lanka/191%20War%20Crimes%20in%20Sri%20Lanka.ashx.

16   Rachel Brett and Eve Lester, 'Refugee Law and International Humanitarian Law: Parallels, Lessons and Looking Ahead', *International Review of the Red Cross*, 83 (2001): 713.

17   *Knezevic v Attorney-General* 367 F.3d 1206; 2004 US App. LEXIS 10162. For other examples, see *Mengstu v Holder*, 560 F3d 1055; 2009 US App. LEXIS 6988; and *S---P--- v INS*, 1996 BIA LEXIS 25.

18   *Regina v Secretary of State for the Home Department, ex parte Adan* [1999] 1 AC 293 (hereinafter *Adan*).

members of other clans.[19] Clearly, the court was concerned by the prospect that with 'everyone fighting everyone', all Somalis could claim refugee status.

In fact, the stringent nature of the refugee definition means that this concern is unfounded. Indeed, when the difficulties of escaping the country of origin, let alone travelling as far as the United Kingdom, are taken into account, some would find it more troubling that asylum-seekers might be returned to danger because they fall outside the Refugee Convention definition.

The court might have found comfort in looking to IHL to assist in the definition of persecution under refugee law (while noting that international criminal law has its own concept of persecution that might diverge from the interpretation of persecution in refugee law).[20] For example, the court could have looked to rules of IHL and considered whether non-combatant clan members were targeted in violation of the principle of distinction.[21] The *lex specialis* of IHL could narrow down the category of violent deaths that would be considered 'persecution' as opposed to 'generalized' or 'indiscriminate' violence. It could also have referred to the exclusion clauses in the refugee definition as a reassurance that combatants engaged in war crimes are excluded from refugee status.[22]

The court did not go down this path. The lead judgment delivered by Lord Lloyd of Berwick doubted whether 'in the context of clan warfare in Somalia, it is realistic to think in terms of rules of war, or the conventional distinction between civilians and members of the armed forces. Mr Adan's own evidence was that most of the population is armed.'[23] With respect, this suggests that the violence in Somalia is so 'tribal' that it cannot meet Western standards of warfare and therefore it cannot even *fail* 'civilized' standards governing armed conflict that might be called in aid to determine whether persecution is occurring.[24]

In any case, the court reasoned that differential risk was required because otherwise both sides fighting the civil war would be entitled to protection and innocent bystanders would be the only ones not protected as refugees.[25] So certain

---

19   Ibid., 311B, per Lord Lloyd of Berwick.

20   See the *Rome Statute of the International Criminal Court, July 17, 1998*, 2187 UNTS 3, Art. 7(1)(b).

21   See *1977 Protocol Additional to the 1949 Geneva Conventions Relating to the Protection of Victims of International Armed Conflicts (Protocol I)*, 1125 UNTS 3, Art. 51.

22   See Justice McHugh's opinion in *Minister for Immigration and Multicultural Affairs v Hussein Mohamed Haji Ibrahim* (2000) 204 CLR 1, pp. 71–2 (hereinafter *Haji Ibrahim*). The exclusion clause in Art. 1F of the Refugee Convention is discussed *infra* in section four of this chapter.

23   *Adan*, 308H – 309A, per Lord Lloyd of Berwick.

24   Cf. Justice Kirby's opinion in *Haji Ibrahim*, where he stated that '[c]onduct may be "unsystematic" when compared to the generally methodical persecution and the elimination of Jews and others in Nazi Germany. Yet it may still amount to "persecution" in the context of the lives of the victims in a country such as Somalia.' *Haji Ibrahim*, per Kirby J (dissenting), para. 194.

25   *Adan*, 308G, per Lord Lloyd of Berwick.

was the court that civil wars were a different category, requiring different rules, that Lord Lloyd of Berwick even stated that '[w]hat I have said ... applies only so long as the state of civil war continues. Once the victors have restored order, then the picture changes back again. There is no longer any question of both sides claiming refugee status.'[26]

The Lords' decision in *Adan*'s case throws the issue of defining persecution in the context of a civil war situation in the too-hard basket. From the perspective of a refugee lawyer, the argument that in a civil war everyone is fighting someone is *not* a good basis for determining that a person is not a refugee. The New Zealand Refugee Status Appeals Authority has criticized the ruling in *Adan*'s case and said:

> The inquiry mandated by Article 1A(2) of the Refugee Convention in civil war situations is no different from that required in other situations. What must be borne in mind, however, is that the factual inquiry may be more complex and there is a need to ensure that what the refugee claimant faces is not generalized violence, but a specific risk of harm 'for reason of' one of the Convention reasons.[27]

Further, while we might all have some sympathy for the *Adan* court's expression of concern for innocent bystanders caught in the cross-fire, this is not a valid basis for determining that someone who falls within the refugee definition is not a refugee. In fact, had the court recognised that some military actions are going to fall within the laws of war and therefore preclude their classification as persecution, the court might have been able to see that, regrettably, it is precisely the innocent bystanders who are simply in the wrong place at the wrong time who show us that there are limits to the Refugee Convention. *They* are the 'war refugees' referred to in the UNHCR handbook who are not covered by the Refugee Convention.

Non-refoulement Beyond the Refugee Convention

The limited basis for the Refugee Convention's scheme of protection can be defended on the basis that it is about cases of disenfranchisement – *de facto*

---

26   *Adan*, 311C, per Lord Lloyd of Berwick.

27   Refugee Appeal No. 71462/99, para. 77. See also *Ali v Canada* (FC) [1999] FCJ No. 63. For analysis of Canadian jurisprudence subsequent to *Ali v Canada*, see Olugbenga Shoyele, 'Armed Conflicts and Canadian Refugee Law and Policy', *International Journal of Refugee Law*, 16 (2004): 547–83. In *Haji Ibrahim*, the Australian High Court effectively reinstated a decision by the Refugee Review Tribunal, which appeared to apply *Adan*, however, the lead judgment of Justice Gummow rejects the reasoning of the House of Lords in *Adan*. *Haji Ibrahim*, per Gummow J, paras 144–7. Justice Gummow characterizes the differences between the Full Federal Court and the Refugee Review Tribunal as differences in the appreciation of the facts, rather than reviewable errors of law (*Haji Ibrahim*, para. 149).

statelessness caused by something about a person that they cannot or should not be required to change (that is, one of the five convention grounds of persecution).[28] It seems unsatisfactory, however, to argue that other victims can simply be turned away at the border on the basis that the Refugee Convention deals with a narrow case of disenfranchisement when the state is dysfunctional in terms of the protection it offers any of its citizens and might even have lost the recognizable characteristics of statehood – namely, a government in control of territory. The desire or need to include the 'innocent bystander' referred to in *Adan*'s case has led to the extension of the refugee definition in regional instruments and to the concept of complementary protection – protection outside the strict confines of the refugee definition.

Expanding Non-refoulement *Through Human Rights and Complementary Protection*

The principle of *non-refoulement* has shifted from the discrete context in which it was first adopted – the protection of a defined category of 'refugees' – and become associated with other human rights norms, particularly the prohibition on torture and other cruel, inhuman or degrading treatment or punishment, the right to life and, most recently, the prohibition on enforced disappearances.[29] 'Complementary protection' – that is, protection that is complementary to the Refugee Convention – might be required for persons on the basis of this extended norm of *non-refoulement*.

Of particular relevance to the context of armed conflict is the European Court of Human Rights' dictum that in 'the most extreme cases of general violence, where there is a risk of ill-treatment simply by virtue of an individual being exposed to such violence on return',[30] the protection and related ill-treatment

---

28   In the course of expounding his theory of interpretation concerning the otherwise nebulous convention ground 'membership in a particular social group', Hathaway has described the other four grounds – race, religion, nationality and political opinion – as encompassing either something immutable or something so fundamental to personality that a refugee should not be required to change the characteristic. James C. Hathaway, *The Law of Refugee Status* (Toronto: Butterworths, 1991), pp. 160–61.

29   Express *non-refoulement* clauses are contained in *Convention Against Torture and Other Cruel, Inhuman or Degrading Treatment or Punishment*, 1465 UNTS 113 [hereinafter Convention Against Torture), Art. 3; and *International Convention for the Protection of All Persons from Enforced Disappearance*, A/RES/61/177, Art. 16. Prohibitions against *non-refoulement* have also been read into *European Convention for the Protection of Human Rights and Fundamental Freedoms*, ETS 005, Art. 3; *International Covenant on Civil and Political Rights*, 999 UNTS 171 [hereinafter ICCPR], Arts 6 and 7; and *Convention on the Rights of the Child*, 1577 UNTS 3, Arts 6 and 37.

30   *Case of NA v The United Kingdom* (Application No. 25904/07), 17 July 2008, para. 115.

under Article 3 of the European Convention on Human Rights[31] may be violated. (Clearly, the protection of the right to life in Article 2 is also implicated, but the court tends to deal with these issues under the rubric of Article 3 instead.) The dictum has recently been applied in *Sufi and Elmi v. the United Kingdom*.[32] In this case, the Court ruled that the Somali asylum seekers could not be returned. After an extensive review of country information,[33] the Court found that the evidence

> overwhelmingly indicates that the level of violence in Mogadishu is of sufficient intensity to pose a real risk of treatment reaching the Article 3 threshold to anyone in the capital. In reaching this conclusion the Court has had regard to the indiscriminate bombardment and military offensives carried out by all parties to the conflict, the unacceptable number of civilian casualties, the substantial number of persons displaced within and from the city, and the unpredictable and widespread nature of the conflict [34]

The Court then turned to consider whether relocation elsewhere in Somalia was a possibility. It found that if a person without recent experience of living in Somalia was required to live in or travel through an al-Shabaab-controlled area, relocation would not be possible,[35] and that if forced to live in a camp for internally displaced persons or in the Dadaab refugee camp in Kenya, the treatment there would also violate Article 3.[36]

The threshold set by the court is very high. This is not surprising as the philosophical underpinnings of *non-refoulement* beyond the Refugee Convention are not entirely clear and there are unanswered questions as to when return engages responsibility for violation of human rights. The absolute nature of some human rights norms, such as the prohibition on torture, suggests that to return someone to such treatment amounts to an impermissible derogation from these norms.[37]

---

31 *European Convention for the Protection of Human Rights and Fundamental Freedoms*, ETS No. 005 (as amended).

32 *Case of Sufi and Elmi v. The United Kingdom* (Applications Nos. 831/07 and 1149/07) 28 June 2011 (hereinafter, '*Sufi and Elmi*').

33 Ibid, paras 80–195.

34 Ibid, para. 248. The Court noted a possible exception for persons well-connected to those in power, however.

35 Ibid, para. 277.

36 Ibid, para. 292.

37 See, for example, Manfred Nowak's report prepared in the context of the drafting of the *International Convention for the Protection of All Persons from Enforced Disappearances*, E/CN.4/2002/71. His report simply states that 'in view of the particularly serious nature of the crime of enforced disappearance … [t]he prohibition on refoulement shall also apply to the danger of being subjected to enforced disappearance' (para. 82). It is notable, however, that only torture – not the related forms of ill treatment – is included in the *non-refoulement* norm of Article 3 of the Convention Against Torture, even though cruel, inhuman or degrading treatment or punishment is also non-derogable.

The precise contours of this *non-refoulement* norm, however, including the human rights to which it applies[38] and the reach of those human rights norms to which we know it applies, are unclear.

Article 3 of the European Convention on Human Rights, for example, tends to focus the judicial mind on active or direct 'treatment'. It has been construed by the UK House of Lords in such a way that violations of socioeconomic rights require some discriminatory element before an Article 3 violation is established. In the *Limbuela*[39] decision, the court was prepared to rule that homelessness created by the discrimination against asylum-seekers violated Article 3, but some members of the court clearly excluded other cases of homelessness.[40] There is also some uncomfortable jurisprudence concerning health care: the decisions of the European Court of Human Rights in *D v United Kingdom*[41] and *N v United Kingdom*.[42] Both involved HIV/AIDS sufferers. D would have been homeless in his country of origin and he had no family to assist him. The court ruled unanimously that it would be a violation of the prohibition on inhuman treatment to return the acutely ill man home to die alone and on the streets.[43] While D was allowed to die in dignity on British soil, Ms N was returned to her country, even though her life expectancy could be cut in half because she might be unable to secure the drugs available in the United Kingdom that supported a reasonable life expectancy.[44] The majority took the view that while transporting a person on their deathbed[45] (D's case) is in and of itself a violation of Article 3, transporting someone to an early death after acute mental and physical suffering (N's case) was not.[46]

The lack of clarity or indeterminacy emanates from a clash of principles. On the one hand, if human rights are universal, interdependent, indivisible and

---

38   See, for example, *R v Special Adjudicator, ex parte Ullah* [2004] 2 AC, paras 24–5, per Lord Bingham, suggesting that it is possible that all the rights in the European Convention on Human Rights carry a *non-refoulement* norm.

39   *Regina v Secretary of State for the Home Department (Appellant), ex parte Adam (FC)(Respondent); Regina v Secretary of State for the Home Department (Appellant), ex parte Limbuela (FC)(Respondent); Regina v Secretary of State for the Home Department (Appellant), ex parte Tesema (FC)(Respondent)(conjoined appeals)*, [2005] UKHL 66 (hereinafter *Limbuela*).

40   Ibid., para. 7, per Lord Bingham; para. 66, per Lord Scott.

41   *D v United Kingdom*, ECHR Appl. No. 30240/96 (2007) (hereinafter *D v UK*).

42   *N v United Kingdom*, ECHR Appl. No. 26565/05 (27 May 2008) (hereinafter *N v UK*).

43   *D v UK*, paras 52–4.

44   The majority's approach to the facts was that they involved a 'degree of speculation': *N v UK*, paras 47–50. The minority accepted the UK court's findings that Ms N's health would be adversely affected: para. 9, per Tulkens, Bonello and Spielmann JJ (dissenting).

45   Ibid., para. 20, per Tulkens, Bonello and Spielmann JJ.

46   Ibid., para. 23, per Tulkens, Bonello and Speilmann JJ.

interrelated then they should be borderless.[47] Arguably, people should be free to move in order to ensure that their rights are respected, protected and fulfilled. We live in a world divided into sovereign states, however, on which the obligations to respect, protect and fulfil rights are imposed. Therefore, beyond the relatively clear confines of refugee status, where we accept that there is an obligation of surrogate protection imposed on the international community, there has been uncertainty and confusion about the extent of *non-refoulement* and a tendency to draw the line at extreme and direct threats to the integrity of the human person that involve 'positive' action by the state.

Importantly, in *Sufi and Elmi*, the Court analogized the case not to *N's* case, but to another recent decision in *M.S.S. v Belgium and Greece*[48] in which it had found that a refugee applicant returned to Greece from Belgium would be subjected to a violation of Article 3 because he would be wholly dependent on state support, but faced with 'official indifference in a situation of serious deprivation or want incompatible with human dignity'.[49] (In Greece, asylum seekers were regularly detained, or rendered street homeless, the rates of refugee recognition are extremely low and they are at risk of return to their countries of origin.) In *Sufi and Elmi*, the Court reasoned that the conditions in Somalia were not 'solely or even predominantly attributable to poverty or the States' lack of resources to deal with a naturally occurring phenomenon … .'[50] Rather, the crisis was due to 'the direct and indirect actions of the parties to the conflict' which involved indiscriminate warfare and al-Shabaab's obstruction of international aid efforts.[51]

Expanding the Content of 'Refugee-Hood' and the Reach of Complementary Protection

In addition to the expansion of the *non-refoulement* norm that has occurred under particular human rights principles, two regional instruments apply the norm of *non-refoulement* quite explicitly to 'war refugees'. The African Union's convention governing the specific aspects of refugee problems in Africa provides an extended definition of a refugee:

> The term 'refugee' shall also apply to every person who, owing to external aggression, occupation, foreign domination or events seriously disturbing public order in either part or the whole of his country of origin or nationality,

---

47   For arguments concerning open borders and whether states would exist in an ideal world where human rights did not even need assertion and protection, see Joseph H. Carens, 'A reply to Meilaender: Reconsidering Open Borders', *International Migration Review*, 33/4 (1999): 1082–97.

48   *M.S.S. v Belgium and Greece* (Application No 30696/09) 21 January 2011.

49   *Sufi and Elmi*, para. 292.

50   Ibid, para. 282.

51   Ibid.

is compelled to leave his place of habitual residence in order to seek refuge in another place outside his country of origin or nationality.[52]

The Americas have also adopted an extended definition of a refugee. The Cartagena Declaration, adopted by 10 South and Central American states and then endorsed by the General Assembly of the Organization of American States, provides that

> the definition or concept of a refugee to be recommended for use in the region is one which, in addition to containing the elements of the 1951 Convention and the 1967 Protocol, includes among refugees persons who have fled their country because their lives, safety or freedom have been threatened by generalized violence, foreign aggression, internal conflicts, massive violation of human rights or other circumstances which have seriously disturbed public order.[53]

An alternative to expanding the definition of a refugee is to extend the reach of complementary protection. An example is the European Qualification Directive

---

52   *Convention Governing the Specific Aspects of Refugee Problems in Africa, September 10, 1969*, 1001 UNTS 45, Art. 1(2). Interestingly, the main reason for the adoption of the African Union convention's expanded definition was not the need to deal with internal conflicts and generalized violence, although it is now applied to such situations. Rather, as Okoth-Obbo explains, it was to deal with the freedom fighters seeking refuge from countries that were still colonized or under white minority rule. George Okoth-Obbo, 'Thirty Years On: A Legal Review of the 1969 Refugee Convention Governing the Specific Aspects of Refugee Problems in Africa', *Refugee Survey Quarterly*, 20/1 (2001): 79, at p. 112. He also explains that the expanded definition does not imply that the Refugee Convention has no application to civil wars (pp. 117–18). Unfortunately, there are few published decisions applying this definition in individualized refugee-status determinations, even though individual refugee-status determination is increasingly carried out in Africa. See Alice Edwards, 'Refugee Status Determination in Africa', *African Journal of International and Comparative Law*, 14 (2008): 204.

53   *Cartagena Declaration on Refugees, Colloquium on the International Protection of Refugees in Central America, Mexico and Panama, November 22, 1984, Annual Report of the Inter-American Commission on Human Rights*, OAS Doc. OEA/Ser.L/V/II.66/doc.10 (1984–85), Rev. 1, pp. 190–93. As of December 2009, the UNHCR reported that 10 countries in Latin America had incorporated an extended definition of refugee status based on the Cartagena Declaration in their national laws. These countries are Argentina, Brazil, El Salvador, Guatemala, Honduras, Nicaragua, Panama, Paraguay, Uruguay and Venezuela. See UNHCR, *Refugee Protection and International Migration in the Americas: Trends, Protection Challenges and Responses*, Background Document (Geneva: UNHCR, December 2009), p. 43, N. 81. The most recent Mexican refugee law, the *Ley Sobre Refugiados Y Proteccion Complementaria*, of 27 January 2011, includes an expanded definition of refugees in Art. 13(II).

(which uses the term 'subsidiary' instead of 'complementary').[54] This EU instrument provides in Article 2(e) that a

> person eligible for subsidiary protection means a third country national or a stateless person who does not qualify as a refugee but in respect of whom substantial grounds have been shown for believing that the person concerned, if returned to his or her country of origin, or in the case of a stateless person, to his or her country of former habitual residence, would face a real risk of suffering serious harm.

Serious harm is defined in Article 15 as the death penalty or execution, torture or inhuman or degrading treatment or punishment or 'serious and individual threat to a civilian's life or person by reason of indiscriminate violence in situations of international or internal armed conflict'. Thus complementary protection in the European context is based in part on well-established human rights principles (as explored above in the section 'Expanding *non-refoulement* through human rights and complementary protection'), but it may also extend to cases that go beyond the currently accepted reach of these human rights norms, as the separation of indiscriminate violence from cases involving the death penalty or the prohibition on torture suggests.[55]

The category of 'indiscriminate violence', dealt with in Article 15(c), has the broadest scope for war refugees, although its drafting is infelicitous.[56] Does the reference to 'international or internal armed conflict' incorporate definitions from international humanitarian law? Does the threshold 'serious and individual threat' require a person to be 'singled out' or might there be situations so violent that simple presence of the individual would be enough, as the European Court of Human Rights has confirmed is the case with respect to Article 3 of the European Convention on Human Rights?

A considerable jurisprudence is developing concerning the meaning of Article 15(c). The Court of Justice of the European Union (CJEU) has clarified the meaning of Article 15(c) in the *Elgafaji* case to some degree.[57] Interestingly for present purposes, the court did not refer to IHL in order to define an 'armed conflict', but sidestepped the issue since clarification of the term was not requested by the

---

54   *Council Directive 2004/83/EC of 29 April 2004 on Minimum Standards for the Qualification and Status of the Third Country Nationals or Stateless Persons as Refugees or as Persons Who Otherwise need International Protection and the Content of the Protection Granted*, OJ L 304, 30 September 2004, pp. 0012–23.

55   In *Sufi and Elmi*, the European Court of Human Rights indicates that Article 3 and Article 15(c) could be viewed as offering comparable protection, para. 226.

56   Cf. *QD (Iraq) and AH (Iraq) v Secretary of State for the Home Department* [2009] EWCA Civ. 620, para. 19 (per Lord Justice Sedley on behalf of the court) (hereinafter *QD*).

57   *Elgafaji v Staatssecretaris van Justitie*, C-465/07 (European Court of Justice, 17 February 2009).

parties.[58] It has been argued by the eminent refugee law scholar Guy Goodwin-Gill that IHL should not be used to define the term 'armed conflict' for the purposes of the Qualification Directive.[59] He points to the different purposes of refugee law and international humanitarian law, and some lack of clarity in IHL when it comes to defining non-international armed conflicts.[60] Goodwin-Gill argues that IHL 'may be illustrative, but … it cannot be determinative' and that Article 15(c) of the Qualification Directive includes all forms of armed conflict as defined by the *Oxford English Dictionary*: 'an encounter with arms … fighting, contending with arms, martial strife.'[61]

Jane McAdam has made a similar argument that 'it is in respect of individual risk that the intensity or duration of a conflict is relevant, rather than as indicia of the conflict's nature'.[62] Consequently, she argues that relevant instruments to be considered when interpreting Article 15(c) include the Organization of African Unity (OAU) Convention, the Cartagena Declaration and the European Union's Temporary Protection Directive.[63] She refers to the history of the European Union's Temporary Protection Directive and points out that

> for legal and logical consistency, article 15(c) ought to protect people fleeing individually or in small groups from situations which, in a mass influx, would result in protection – especially since article 15(c) was originally intended to protect those who, but for the fact that they arrived individually rather than as part of a mass influx, would fall within the scope of the Temporary Protection Directive.[64]

English case law – clearly taking a purposive approach, as suggested by these scholars – has adopted the approach that for the purposes of Article 15(c), armed conflict is not defined by international humanitarian law.[65] In particular, the English Court of Appeal has held that 'the phrase "situations of international or internal armed conflict" in article 15(c) has an autonomous meaning broad enough to capture any situation of indiscriminate violence, whether caused by one or more armed factions or by a state, which reaches the level described by

---

58   See discussion in Jane McAdam, 'Individual Risk, Armed Conflict and the Standard of Proof in Complementary Protection Claims: The European Union and Canada Compared', in James C. Simeon (ed.), *Critical Issues in International Refugee Law* (Cambridge: Cambridge University Press, 2010), p. 59, at p. 72.

59   See Guy S. Goodwin-Gill, *Challenges to the Protection of Refugees and Stateless Persons – Compliance with International Law* (London: Blackstone Chambers, March 2009), http://www.blackstonechambers.com/news/publications/protection_refugees.html

60   Ibid., paras 5–7.

61   Ibid., para. 10.

62   McAdam, 'Individual Risk', p. 75.

63   Ibid., pp. 76–7.

64   Ibid., p. 79.

65   *QD*, paras 15–18.

the CJEU in *Elgafaji*.[66] In contrast, German courts have opted for an 'orientation towards international humanitarian law', but modified by the protective purpose of the convention.[67] Consequently, and very importantly, this means that military action resulting in 'unforeseeable collateral damage' and which therefore does not violate IHL may still be grounds for the application of Article 15(c).[68] After a false start,[69] the UK Upper Tribunal (Immigration and Asylum Chamber) has adopted a similar approach, finding that the principle of distinction in IHL does not define the content of the term 'indiscriminate violence'.[70]

Moving to the question of satisfying the relevant threshold, the CJEU in *Elgafaji* also held that the words 'serious and individual threat' do not require the applicant to 'adduce evidence that he is specifically targeted by reason of factors particular to his personal circumstances'.[71] Further, in cases of a particularly high level of indiscriminate violence, it might be that a civilian would face a real risk 'solely on account of his presence'.[72]

The CJEU did not indicate how the level of violence should be measured. Helene Lambert and Theo Farrell make a strong argument for measuring the intensity of the conflict by reference to civilian casualties rather than relying solely on combatant or battle casualties, which is highly relevant in the context of Afghanistan, for example.[73] They also argue for reference to the concept of human security,[74] which would encompass situations of chronic state failure and indirect

---

66   Ibid., para. 35.

67   *German Federal Administrative Court, Judgment of the Tenth Division of 27 April 2010*, BverwG 10 C 4.09.

68   Ibid., para. 34.

69   *GS (Article 15(c): indiscriminate violence) Afghanistan CG*, [2009] UK AIT 00044, 19 October 2009, especially para. 105.

70   See *HM and Others (Article 15(c)) Iraq CG* [2010] UKUT 331 (IAC) (hereinafter *HM and Others*). In this decision, the Upper Tribunal (Immigration and Asylum Chamber), which has replaced the Asylum and Immigration Tribunal, stated: 'In our judgment the nexus between the generalized armed conflict and the indiscriminate violence posing a real risk to life and person is met when the intensity of the conflict involves means of combat (whether permissible under the laws of war or not) that seriously endanger non-combatants as well as result in such a general breakdown of law and order as to permit anarchy and criminality occasioning the serious harm referred to in the Directive. Such violence is indiscriminate in effect even if not necessarily in aim' (para. 80).

71   *Elgafaji, dispositif.*

72   Ibid., *dispositif.*

73   Helene Lambert and Theo Farrell, 'The Changing Character of Armed Conflict and the Implications for Refugee Protection Jurisprudence', *International Journal of Refugee Law*, 22 (2010): 237–73, at pp. 261–3.

74   Ibid., p. 258. Human security, unlike national security, means protecting the rights of individuals and linking 'freedom from want, freedom from fear, and freedom to take action on one's own behalf'. Commission on Human Security, *Human Security Now*, Final Report of the Commission on Human Security (New York, 1 May 2003), pp. iv–v. For discussion of the concept with respect to refugee protection, see Alice Edwards, 'Human

impacts on sustainability of life (such as food shortages), and that population movements themselves should be taken as a measure of the severity of an armed conflict.[75]

Interestingly, despite the 'orientation' towards IHL definitions of armed conflict, the German judiciary appears to have adopted elements of Lambert and Farrell's approach, particularly the element of civilian casualties, suggesting that in addition to a finding of an armed conflict, it is necessary to have

> at least an approximate quantitative determination of the total number of civilians living in the area concerned, on the one hand, and on the other hand, the number of acts of indiscriminate violence committed by the parties to the conflict against the life or person of civilians in this region, as well as a general assessment of the number of victims and the severity of the casualties (deaths and injuries) among the civilian population.[76]

Lambert and Farrell's reference to population displacement as a measure of the severity of the conflict has also found favour with the UK Upper Tribunal (Immigration and Asylum Chamber).[77] It is an attractive approach because it recognizes that people do not flee war because they are 'economic migrants' in search of a 'better life'. Rather, life itself is often precarious to the point of unsustainability during war. Instead of second-guessing the motives of applicants for protection in this situation, the population flow itself is indicative of the necessity of movement and therefore protection. The 'asylum–migration' nexus, in which 'underdevelopment, impoverishment, poor governance, endemic conflict and human rights abuse are closely linked [and these] conditions lead both to economically-motivated migration and to politically-motivated flight',[78] flat-lines in the way that a life-support monitor flat-lines in the absence of vital signs. The economic and the political become one and the response should be a humanitarian response concerned to ensure the survival of the people concerned. This requires action by the international community. If war has rendered the concept of home-state protection meaningless, the international community should offer surrogate protection.

Security and the Rights of Refugees: Transcending Territorial and Disciplinary Borders', *Michigan Journal of International Law*, 30 (2009): 763.

75   Lambert and Farrell, pp. 257–73.

76   *German Federal Administrative Court, Judgment of the Tenth Division of 27 April 2010*, BverwG 10 C 4.09, para. 33.

77   *HM and Others*, paras 91–2. The Upper Tribunal observed that all the factors suggested by Lambert and Farrell could be taken into account, subject to the proviso that there be a sufficient causal nexus to the violence. On the facts, the tribunal found that current population displacement was not of the broad civilian population but of targeted groups (para. 276).

78   Stephen Castles and Mark J. Miller, *The Age of Migration: International Population Movements in the Modern World*, 3rd edn (New York: The Guilford Press, 2003), p. 32.

Needless to say, however, fear of the floodgates opening is likely to be heightened when complementary protection is proposed on this basis. In Australia, it seems impossible to even have a debate about complementary protection that explicitly encompasses generalized or indiscriminate violence,[79] because we have difficulty accepting any unauthorized onshore applicants for refugee status, as evidenced by the pronouncements about changes in circumstances in Afghanistan and the steep turn around in recognition rates.[80]

In the case of Afghanistan, about one-sixth of its population – which is estimated to be larger than Australia's, at about 26 million – has been displaced over the course of the 30 years of war.[81] Yet Afghans have been given temporary and precarious refuge in neighbouring states, most of whom are not party to the Refugee Convention. In particular, Pakistan has hosted millions of Afghans. It has recently been grappling with one of the largest internally displaced person (IDP) populations in the world because of the recent floods. Iran is a party to the convention, although it does not always comply with it, and has also sheltered a million Afghans.[82] Legally and politically, the situation for Afghans in those countries is not secure, and these front-line states should not be expected to bear the entire burden of externally displaced Afghans because countries such as Australia are not prepared either to recognize those Afghans who arrive without a visa as refugees or to extend complementary protection to them.[83]

---

79 A complementary protection bill was introduced into Parliament in 2009 and reintroduced after the federal election in 2010. The Bill does not explicitly extend to victims of generalized violence, but is limited to meeting Australia's obligations under the Convention Against Torture and Article 6 of the International Covenant on Civil and Political Rights. If passed, the Bill will insert into the *Migration Act* new, alternative criteria for a protection visa – namely, arbitrary deprivation of life, imposition of the death penalty, torture or cruel, inhuman or degrading treatment or punishment. Migration Amendment (Complementary Protection) Bill 2011, Cl. 12 and 14. The Bill contains an express exclusion from complementary protection where 'the risk faced by the person is faced by the population of the country generally and not by the person personally': proposed s. 36(2B)(c) (Cl. 14 of the Bill). For discussion, see Elibritt Karlsen, *Bills Digest*, No. 79 (2010–11), Migration Amendment (Complementary Protection) Bill 2011, pp. 19–20.

80 Paul Maley, 'Successful Asylum Claims Plummet', *The Australian*, 21 July 2010, p. 3.

81 At least 5 million people have been displaced and currently the UNHCR says that the return of 5 million has enlarged the population by 20 per cent: UNHCR, *Country Operations Profile – Afghanistan* (Geneva: UNHCR, 2011), http://www.unhcr.org/cgi-bin/texis/vtx/page?page=49e486eb6

82 For the numbers of Afghans in Iran, see UNHCR, *Country Operations Profile – Iran* (Geneva: UNHCR, 2011), http://www.unhcr.org/cgi-bin/texis/vtx/page?page=49e486f96

83 For a recent example of the literature relating to burden or responsibility sharing, see Tally Kritzman-Amir and Yonatan Berman, 'Responsibility Sharing and the Rights of Refugees: The Case of Israel', *George Washington International Law Review*, 41 (2011): 619. They make an interesting argument concerning the responsibility of countries most capable of protecting refugees.

Exclusion from Protection or Status

The changed nature of war in the late-twentieth and early twenty-first centuries has ramifications not only for the inclusive clauses of the refugee definition and the concept of complementary protection, but also for the refugee definition's exclusion clauses. Not only is there a perception that 'everyone is fighting everyone else', but there is a fear 'they' might bring the fight with them. In Australia, for example, some of the debate about Sri Lankan boat arrivals has centred on the 'links' between asylum-seekers and the Tamil Tigers. An article in *The Australian* newspaper quoted the Sri Lankan Government's assessment that between 25 and 50 per cent of Tamil asylum-seekers in Australia had links to the Tigers[84] – a group that the Sri Lankan Government official compared with Al Qaeda.[85]

The point was made that the Tigers have not been listed as a proscribed terrorist group in Australia.[86] Listing would bring into play various offences, including knowing membership of a listed terrorist organization,[87] whether or not that offence occurred in Australia,[88] which could then have consequences for refugee status under either the exclusion clauses in Article 1F or Article 33(2)[89] of the Refugee Convention, although the significance of listing was not properly unpacked in the article. The uncritical emphasis on listing of terrorist groups steers public attention away from the issue of what sort of humanitarian protection is due to individual asylum-seekers and assists in the perception that immigration control is linked with national security, while ignoring the protections against dangerous asylum-seekers that are already provided within the Refugee Convention, and conveniently ignoring the dilemmas with which such asylum-seekers confront us.[90]

---

84   Sally Neighbour, 'Half of Sri Lankan Arrivals Have Ties to Tigers', *The Australian*, 14 July 2010, http://www.theaustralian.com.au/news/nation/half-of-sri-lankan-arrivals-have-ties-to-tigers/story-e6frg6nf-1225891388934

85   Ibid.

86   Ibid. For the listing provision in the Commonwealth Criminal Code, see s. 102.1(1) (b), (2), (3) and (4). For discussion of the listing provisions, see Russell Hogg, 'Executive Proscription of Terrorist Organisations in Australia: Exploring the Shifting Border Between Crime and Politics', in Miriam Gani and Penelope Mathew (eds), *Fresh Perspectives on the War on Terror* (Canberra: ANU E Press, 2008), p. 297.

87   Commonwealth Criminal Code, s. 102.3.

88   See Commonwealth Criminal Code, s. 102.9.

89   Article 33(2) of the Refugee Convention provides that 'the benefit of the present provision [the principle of *non-refoulement*] may not … be claimed by a refugee whom there are reasonable grounds for regarding as a danger to the security of the country in which he is, or who, having been convicted by a final judgment of a particularly serious crime, constitutes a danger to the community of that country'.

90   See, for example, Greg O'Regan, Letter to the Editor, *The Canberra Times*, 17 July 2010, http://www.canberratimes.com.au/news/opinion/letters/general/letters-to-the-editor/1888087.aspx?storypage=0# See also, Comment by 'PS4' on 10 November 2009

Three important points need to be made here. First, the Refugee Convention does not oblige Australia or any other party to the convention to accept terrorists as refugees. Second, a 'link' to a group that engages in terrorist activity, whether listed or not, is insufficient as a matter of *international law* to exclude an asylum-seeker from protection as a refugee. Finally, in the context of a civil war characterized by war crimes and crimes against humanity on both sides, and in which the government prevailed solely because of the brutal measures it deployed,[91] the situation of excluded asylum-seekers raises pressing ethical questions.

The framers of the Refugee Convention were alive to the possibility that persecutors fleeing prosecution might claim refuge. As a result, Article 1F of the convention contains an exclusion clause, as follows:

> The provisions of this Convention shall not apply to any person with respect to whom there are serious reasons for considering that:
>
> (a) he has committed a crime against peace, a war crime, or a crime against humanity, as defined in the international instruments drawn up to make provision in respect of such crimes;
> (b) he has committed a serious non-political crime outside the country of refuge prior to his admission to that country as a refugee;
> (c) he has been guilty of acts contrary to the purposes and principles of the United Nations.

Terrorist activities or offences may be captured by all three of the categories of excluded acts. In its guidelines on the exclusion clauses, the UNHCR recommends the use of Article 1F(b) for terrorism cases. The Security Council, however, in Resolution 1373, appears to encourage a shift towards Article 1F(c).[92] Article 1F(c) might be attractive to states for a number of reasons. For example, it avoids the debate about terrorist action potentially being viewed as 'political' as well as the question of what should count as a 'serious' crime, both of which are questions that arise under Article 1F(b).[93] Whichever of the clauses is used, however, mere membership of an organization should *not* be grounds for exclusion.[94]

---

in response to Penelope Mathew, 'The Myth of Border Control', *The Drum Unleashed* (Sydney: Australian Broadcasting Corporation), which stated that the criminal background of a spokesperson for asylum-seekers on board the *Oceanic Viking* was 'the best argument yet to continue offshore processing' (http://www.abc.net.au/unleashed/stories/s2736660.htm).

91   International Crisis Group.

92   UNSC Res. 1373 (2001), [3](f) and (g), and [5].

93   For further discussion, see Penelope Mathew, 'Resolution 1373 – A Call to Pre-Empt Asylum Seekers? (Or "Osama the Asylum Seeker")', in Jane McAdam (ed.), *Forced Migration, Human Rights and Security* (Portland, Ore.: Hart Publishing, 2008), p. 19.

94   UNHCR guidelines suggest that voluntary membership of an organization that engages in violent activities might raise a rebuttable presumption of responsibility for those activities, but 'decision-makers must have regard to actual activities of the group, its

With regard to the specific case of the Tamil Tigers, the UNHCR's Eligibility Guidelines for Assessing International Protection Needs of Asylum-Seekers from Sri Lanka[95] nominate suspected links with the Tigers as potential grounds for refugee status as it appears that the Government has created a particular social group of persons who might or might not have any real involvement in terrorism.[96] The guidelines also note that there might be cause for exclusion in some cases.[97] In the case of voluntary membership in the Tamil Tigers, the UNHCR is even prepared to concede a presumption of responsibility with regard to 'those having held senior positions of authority in the organization'.[98] The guidelines urge caution, however, and go on to state that:

> For exclusion to be justified, individual responsibility must be established in relation to a crime within the scope of Article 1F. Such responsibility flows from a person having committed or participated in the commission of a criminal act, or on the basis of command/superior responsibility for persons in positions of authority. Applicable defenses, if any, as well as considerations related to proportionality, apply. As such, LTTE [Liberation Tigers of Tamil Eelam] membership is not a sufficient basis in itself to exclude an individual from refugee status, particularly in light of the well documented practices of forced recruitment, particularly of children. It is necessary to consider whether the individual concerned was personally involved in acts of violence or other excludable acts, or knowingly contributed in a substantial manner to such acts. A credible explanation regarding the individual's non-involvement with or disassociation from any excludable acts, should absent reliable evidence to the contrary, remove the individual from the application scope of the exclusion clauses.[99]

---

organizational structure, the individual's position in it, and his or her ability to influence significantly its activities'. UNHCR, *Guidelines on International Protection: Application of the Exclusion Clauses: Article 1F of the 1951 Convention Relating to the Status of Refugees*, UN Doc. HCR/GIP/03/05 (4 September 2003), pp. 19, 26. For a discussion of the case law in five common-law jurisdictions, see Joseph Rikhof, 'War Criminals Not Welcome: How Common Law Countries Approach the Phenomenon of International Crimes in the Immigration and Refugee Context', *International Journal of Refugee Law*, 21 (2009): 453–507.

95   UNHCR, *Eligibility Guidelines for Assessing International Protection Needs of Asylum-Seekers from Sri Lanka*, HRC/EG/SLK/10/03, 5 July 2010 (hereinafter *UNHCR Eligibility Guidelines for Sri Lanka*).

96   Ibid, p. 5.

97   Ibid.

98   Ibid, pp. 12–13. As Rikhov explains, in some jurisdictions – for example, Canada and the United Kingdom – it will be accepted that some organizations have a 'limited, brutal purpose', meaning that membership may constitute complicity in international crimes committed by the organization. Rikhof, pp. 466 – 2 (Canada), pp. 488 – 9 (United Kingdom).

99   *UNHCR Eligibility Guidelines for Sri Lanka*, p. 12.

Consequently, 'links' with the Tigers may found a claim to refugee status and will not necessarily suffice to exclude someone from refugee status.

If a person *is* excluded, on the basis of something more than a 'link' to the Tigers, the risks to the person as a result of return to Sri Lanka might mean that *non-refoulement* obligations attaching to the prohibition on torture or the right to life, or, possibly, the right to a fair trial,[100] are relevant. The International Crisis Group recommends that in the absence of guarantees of humane treatment and fair trial, domestic prosecutions should be used as an alternative to return to Sri Lanka.[101] Moreover, the useful role of granting asylum to those who merit protection is noted in light of the need to preserve evidence should the possibility of prosecutions occur.[102]

Unfortunately, there is little likelihood of trials of Sri Lankan war criminals at the International Criminal Court,[103] the UN Secretary-General's panel of experts met with opposition from Sri Lankan authorities[104] and Sri Lanka has gone ahead with its own 'Commission on Lessons Learned and Reconciliation'.[105] Given these unhelpful developments, it is vital that countries such as Australia do not step into line with the Sri Lankan Government's propaganda. Sri Lanka has always looked unfavourably on asylum claims by its citizens, claiming that asylum is abused by people wishing to fuel terrorism in Sri Lanka, and it has proudly boasted to the

---

100   The European Court of Human Rights has consistently said that it 'does not exclude that an issue might exceptionally be raised under Article 6 [the European Convention on Human Rights provision concerning fair trial] by an expulsion decision in circumstances where the person being expelled has suffered or risks suffering a flagrant denial of a fair trial in the receiving country, particularly where there is the risk of execution'. See *Soering v United Kingdom*, ECHR 7 July 1989, Series A, No. 161, p. 45, § 113; *Mamatkulov & Askarov v Turkey*, Nos 46827/99 and 46951/99, 2005-I, §§ 90 and 91. The requirement that there be a flagrant violation as opposed to simply that the trial is considered unfair arguably raises dilemmas of a similarly acute nature as to the question of when Article 3 is violated in cases concerning health treatment. (See the discussion of *D's* case and *N's* case in Note 41 above and accompanying text.) Is it possible to have a 'bit of an unfair trial'? In cases involving the death penalty, the court has made clear that stringent fair-trial standards apply. See *Ocalan v Turkey* 2005-IV; 41 EHRR 985 [166 GC].

101   International Crisis Group, p. 36.

102   The International Crisis Group report states that '[g]overnments should be willing to grant asylum or emergency visas to witnesses to alleged war crimes to ensure evidence is preserved. Given the longstanding history of abuses against witnesses in Sri Lanka, it is vital that more governments adjust policies to accommodate emergency cases.' Ibid., p. 36.

103   This is because Sri Lanka is not a party to the Rome Statute and the UN Security Council might be unlikely to refer the matter. Ibid., p. 34.

104   See Report of the Secretary-General's Panel of Experts on Accountability in Sri Lanka, 31 March 2011: http://www.un.org/News/dh/infocus/Sri_Lanka/POE_Report_Full. pdf

105   Charles Haviland, 'Sri Lankan War Inquiry Commission Opens Amid Criticism', *BBC News, Sri Lanka*, 11 August 2010, http://www.bbc.co.uk/news/world-south-asia-10934663

Counter-Terrorism Committee that it is not party to the Refugee Convention.[106] In the aftermath of the civil war, the Sri Lankan Government has reason to be particularly shrill in its objections about granting asylum to Tamil asylum-seekers because these asylum-seekers might have witnessed the atrocities committed by Sri Lankan forces. If the international community is committed to a resolution of the root causes of the Sri Lankan problem and refugee flows, it will, as the International Crisis Group suggests, have to support justice and reconciliation, rather than handing asylum-seekers over so that the Government's crimes might be covered up.

Conclusion

Armed conflicts present refugee-receiving states with ethical dilemmas. If we are true to our own stated values – in particular, human rights values – then the foreigner fleeing armed conflict has a claim on us. If they meet the definition of a refugee then the ethical dilemma is resolved for us by the Refugee Convention. There is an obligation not to return them and they are entitled to surrogate protection as defined by that convention and any other human rights treaties to which the state is a party that complement the protection conferred by the Refugee Convention.[107]

If however, their claim is not based on disenfranchisement on the basis of a protected characteristic, which is what the convention's refugee definition is about, but rather, their claim is that the state is failing most of its citizens because indiscriminate violence is rife, similar ethical dilemmas arise. There is a strong case for complementary protection in this situation; however, fear of the floodgates opening might prove an obstacle to this solution.

The exclusion cases also cause difficulties for refugee-receiving states. These are, however, problems of a prosaic, practical kind, reflecting domestic political concerns, as opposed to deep philosophical matters. If we are true to our values then we will pursue prosecution and other justice mechanisms over return to a place of persecution. This is particularly true in a situation such as Sri Lanka where return of those offenders who are also witnesses to violations of human rights abuses by the Sri Lankan Government is likely to feed a cycle of violence and contribute to new streams of forced migration. The obstacles to this path are practical and political. For example, how do we ensure successful prosecutions in a forum that is removed from many of the primary sources of evidence? And how does a government defend national prosecutions in the post-9/11 world? Terrorism

---

106   See Mathew, 'Resolution 1373 – A Call to Preempt Asylum Seekers?', p. 51.

107   An example is provided by the right to work, which is partially enshrined in the Refugee Convention, but also covered by the *International Covenant on Economic, Social and Cultural Rights*, 993 UNTS 360, Art. 6. For discussion of the relationship of various protections of the right to work in the refugee context, see the 'Michigan Guidelines on the Right to Work', *Michigan Journal of International Law*, 31 (2010): 289–91.

anywhere is now viewed as a threat to everyone,[108] no matter how localized and particular the grievances and actions of the particular terrorists involved. But return to a place of persecution in the form of unfair prosecutions or summary executions will feed the grievances that fuel terrorism. In prosecuting the 'war on terror', we disregard the maxim 'first do no harm' at the expense of our own best interests.

---

108   See Mathew, 'Resolution 1373 – A Call to Pre-Empt Asylum Seekers?', p. 37.

Chapter 11

Private Military and Security Companies and the 'Civilianization' of War

Andrew Alexandra

Grounding Civilian Immunity

The term 'the ethics of war' applies to two different kinds of enterprises. What might be called the positive ethics of war is a descriptive enterprise, aiming to provide an account of the body of broadly accepted and implemented rules governing the reasons for and means by which wars may be fought; normative ethics of war, on the other hand, aims to assess the moral status of those rules and, if necessary, suggest revisions to them. From the perspective of positive ethics the twinned principles of combatant liability to, and civilian immunity from, attack during war are central to the ethics of war. These principles are affirmed by international law and popular opinion and paid at least lip service by political and military leaders.

From the perspective of normative ethics, on the other hand, the moral status of the two principles is contestable, indeed increasingly contested. The source of that contestation is the apparent tension, if not outright conflict, between these principles and other, more basic and general moral principles – in particular, the principle that positive or negative moral liability should track moral responsibility. In the case of non-combatants, it seems that some are likely to be (very) morally culpable – those who incite or set out to profit from a war that they know, or could and should have known, was unjust, for example. Nevertheless, according to the principle of non-combatant immunity, such morally culpable persons retain their right not to be attacked in virtue of their non-combatant status. In the case of combatants, on the other hand, it seems that some, perhaps even most, will not be morally culpable in virtue of their participation in the fighting. On the just side – if there is one – far from doing wrong, combatants might be acting in a morally admirable way; nevertheless, the principle of combatant liability holds that they may be attacked, even if those who attack them are fighting in an unjust war. And even on the unjust side(s), many combatants may at least be morally excused for their participation – because they hold non-culpable false beliefs about the justness of their country's cause, for example, or because they are unwilling conscripts.[1] Again, despite their lack of moral culpability, according to the principle of combatant liability, in virtue of their combatant status, these people are not immune from attack.[2]

Broadly speaking there are two possible kinds of responses[3] to this apparent incompatibility between the basic moral principles governing the relationship between liability and responsibility, on the one hand, and general civilian immunity from, and combatant liability to, attack in war. Firstly, it might be claimed that the incompatibility is *only* apparent. Michael Walzer, for example, has attempted to reconcile the ordinary moral principle with those at the heart of the ethics of war by placing the responsibility for determining the justice of a war in the hands of political leaders, thereby removing it from both combatants and civilians and with it the possibility of their moral culpability. Secondly, it might be held that the basic moral principles governing the relationship between liability and responsibility, on the one hand, and general civilian immunity from, and combatant liability to, attack in war are in fact incompatible. In turn, there are two kinds of responses available to those who acknowledge this incompatibility. It may be seen as a bad thing, to be overcome by (presumably) recasting the rules of war to bring them into line with ordinary moral principles positive. Jeff McMahan, for example, has made an influential response along these lines.[4] Alternatively, it may be claimed that there are good reasons for maintaining the principles of civilian immunity from, and combatant liability to, attack in war, despite their incompatibility with moral principles governing the relationship between liability and responsibility which normally apply. It is this claim which I attempt to defend and explain here.

A satisfactory ethics of war must be sensitive to the specific features of war. Though war is in some ways *sui generis*, it can be situated in the class

---

1   For a useful summary of criticisms of arguments that see the principles of civilian immunity from, and combatant liability to, attack as resting on fundamental differences in the moral status of members of the two groups, see Aaron Xavier Fellmeth, 'Questioning Civilian Immunity', *Texas International Law Review*, 43 (Summer 2008): 455–97.

2   The liability to attack of non-culpable combatants, and non-liability of culpable civilians, is not the only example of this (apparent) disjunction between the ordinary presumption of responsibility for seriously immoral behaviour and the non-applicability of that presumption in the laws of war and the principles of just-war theory. Just as soldiers of a state that has unjustly invaded another state are not held accountable for killing their non-culpable foes, they are not held to account for participating in the unjust invasion, even when they knew, or should have known, that the invasion was wrong.

3   Assuming the soundness of the principle that positive or negative moral liability should track moral responsibility. As far as I am aware none of those who have written on this issue have denied that principle.

4   Jeff McMahan, *Killing in War* (Oxford: Oxford University Press, 2009); cf. Igor Primoratz, 'Michael Walzer's Just War Theory: Some Issues of Responsibility', *Ethical Theory and Moral Practice*, 5/2 (2002): 221–43.

of emergencies, where an emergency is a token of a type of event that has the following features:[5]

1. it is a temporally discrete event – it has a beginning and a (possible) end;[6]
2. it is an uncontrolled divergence from a state of normality;
3. it is reasonable to believe that the divergence can be overcome and the state of normality re-established;
4. it has the potential to cause severe harm;
5. it will cause such harm unless rapid action is taken;
6. the action to be taken can be effective – or will be most effective – only if both those taking action and those who stand to be harmed act in a coordinated manner.

Features 1–3 mean that emergencies are, by their nature, *provisional* rather than of permanent or indefinite duration. Features 4–5 mean that they are *acute* – that is, that taking effective action is a matter of *urgency*. Features 4–6 mean that the need to take action is *overriding* – in the sense both that those involved in emergencies[7] must give precedence to dealing with them over other considerations and that they must act in ways that are likely to prevent or mitigate the harm caused by the emergency, even when this means accepting restrictions on the exercise of normal rights and the imposition of special burdensome obligations.

Emergencies *qua* natural disasters such as bushfires, floods and epidemics would seem to be an inherent part of the human condition, while the development of complex social organizations has brought with it the possibility of various kinds of social emergencies, such as systemic financial failure, civil disorder and riots, as well as rebellions, sieges, blockades and invasions.

Modern societies have a number of specialized organizations dedicated to confronting emergencies – 'emergency services' – such as fire brigades, ambulance services and the police. Such organizations typically aim to prevent emergencies from occurring, to mitigate their effects when they do occur and to end the emergency and restore the *status quo ante* as quickly as possible. The emergency services, and more broadly the institutional arrangements put in place to deal with emergencies, are of purely instrumental value; they are valuable to the extent to which they reduce the evils that would occur without their operation. To say that they are of instrumental rather than intrinsic value is, however, not to deny that they are of great value.

---

5   Here I largely follow Oren Gross's account of the nature of emergencies in 'What "Emergency" Regime?', *Constellations*, 13/1 (2006): 74–88.

6   Emergencies can be seen as a species of crisis. Some crises are not emergencies, however, since it is not reasonable to think that the *status quo ante* can be restored. Climate change is perhaps currently an emergency, which will shortly become simply a crisis.

7   'Those involved in emergencies' include, at least, those who are likely to be harmed by them, as well as those who have the duty to assist them.

The ethics which apply in emergencies will often diverge from those which hold during normalcy. Normally, there is a wide range of circumstances in which people can legitimately hold and act on differing views about what counts as (the most) reasonable action and what rights and obligations, if any, they have. In emergencies, however, the overriding need to address the divergence from normalcy often requires convergence on choice of action. One way in which such convergence can be achieved is through the development of a system of rules of sufficient simplicity and obviousness that each person can know, and know that others know, what they are. Those desiderata might mean that the rules that apply in emergencies require actions that diverge, to some extent, from those that would be appropriate in normal cases.[8] These rules include guidance as to who has the power to determine what should be done in situations where that is otherwise unclear. Hence, there is often a radical simplification, centralization and extension of authority, with officials being granted extraordinary powers (such as the power to prevent residents from leaving or returning to their homes, to suspend *habeas corpus*, to confiscate property, to shoot looters, and so on) and, correlatively, the suspension of many ordinary rights of those involved.

With the outlawing of aggressive war following World War II, I believe that war should now be counted as an emergency and the armed forces seen as providers of an emergency service. The triggers for their use (the emergency) are certain kinds of egregious rights violations, especially foreign attempts to usurp political power, invasion or systematic abuse of vulnerable populations by states. Peace – the state of normalcy that provides the baseline against which emergency is measured – is thus a condition where rights are (sufficiently) respected. The purpose of armed forces is to deter the violation of rights, to limit such violations if they nevertheless occur and to restore the state of peace as soon as possible. Armed forces, then, as institutions dedicated to the provision of legitimate violence, are by their nature guardians. The ideal world is one in which there is no violation of rights and hence no need for violence. The best possible world is the one in which as much as possible of what would happen in the ideal world still happens; it is to the realization of this world that institutions of state violence, and the regulatory framework within which they operate, are dedicated. There are thus two overriding desiderata for such institutions: the first, obviously, is effectiveness in preventing and limiting violence and other rights violations; the second, perhaps less obviously, is what might be called neutrality. The thought here is that these institutions should operate in ways that impinge as little as possible on the legitimate activities of the public they protect, and that allow the resumption of normal life as fully and quickly as possible.

---

8   Think, for example, of the 'women and children first' rule that applies in shipwrecks and the like. This is a simple, widely acknowledged rule that allows for generally unambiguous application, though clearly there might be less reason to save some particular woman, say, than some particular man.

In light of the this desideratum of neutrality, those people living the normal life the preservation, protection and resumption of which is the purpose of war – civilians – should to the greatest extent possible be shielded from its harms and retain the rights they already possess, including the right to immunity from attack. That immunity does not simply imply a prohibition of intentional targeting of civilians by belligerents. In *Just and Unjust Wars* Michael Walzer drew attention to the place of what he called the 'doctrine of double intention'[9] (DDI) in war. According to this doctrine, not only should belligerents not attempt to harm civilians, they should attempt not to harm them. A good deal of the subsequent discussion about the DDI has focused on its tactical application, with debate about whether and the extent to which soldiers must assume risks to prevent harm to civilians. The doctrine of double intention also, however, has clear application to high-level policy decisions, regarding the organizational arrangements that are put in place in undertaking military activity, and the laws that govern that activity when it does occur. Indeed, a good deal of the development of the positive ethics of war over the past couple of centuries can be understood as attempting to give effect to the doctrine.

Institutionalizing Civilian Immunity

The laws of war[10] draw a categorical distinction between combatants and civilians in countries involved in war. These categories are both exhaustive – there is no other applicable category – and exclusive: if a person is in one category, they are excluded from the other. A person is classified as a civilian by default – that is, has civilian status unless they satisfy the conditions for being a combatant. Combatants either are members of a belligerent's armed forces, which are:

> all organized and armed forces, groups and units which are under a command responsible to that Party for the conduct of its subordinates ... subject to an internal disciplinary system which *inter alia* shall enforce compliance with the rules of international law applicable in armed conflict.[11]

or are

---

9   Michael Walzer, *Just and Unjust Wars* (New York: Basic Books, 1977), p. 156; cf. Steven Lee, 'Double Effect, Double Intention, and Asymmetric Warfare', *Journal of Military Ethics*, 3/3 (2004): 233–51.

10   See International Committee of the Red Cross, *International Humanitarian Law – Treaties & Documents* (Geneva: ICRC), http://www.icrc.org/ihl.nsf

11   *Protocol Additional to the Geneva Conventions of August 1949, and Relating to the Protection of Victims of International Armed Conflict*, 16 ILM 1391 (1977) [hereinafter 'Protocol 1'], Art. 43.3.

members of other militias and members of other volunteer corps ... belonging
to a party to the conflict ... provided that [they] fulfil the following conditions:

a)   that of being commanded by a person responsible for his subordinates;
b)   that of having a fixed distinctive sign recognizable at a distance;
c)   that of carrying arms openly;
d)   that of conducting their operations in accordance with the laws and customs
     of war.[12]

Very different rights, duties and immunities attach to members of these
two categories. Combatants have the (liberty) right to participate in hostilities,
while civilians do not; combatants have the right to intentionally target hostile
combatants, but no right to intentionally target civilians; combatants have the
(claim) right to be accorded prisoner-of-war status if apprehended by the enemy,
while civilians do not,[13] even if in fact they have taken part in hostilities; and
combatants are immune from prosecution for their role in hostilities provided they
have fought according to the laws of war, while civilians are liable to criminal
prosecution for such actions.

Civilians enjoy immunity from attacks during international armed conflict.
Those who do directly participate may be legally targeted and their injury or death
does not bear on such issues as proportionality or precautions in attack. While
civilians are legally forbidden from 'direct participation' in hostilities, by, for
example, taking up arms, obviously they might in fact participate. If they do, they
are classified as 'unlawful combatants' and forfeit their immunity from attack,
but only 'unless and for such time as they take a direct part in hostilities'.[14] Two

---

12   *Geneva Convention (III) Relative to the Treatment of Prisoners of War (1949)*,
6UST, 3316 (1956), Art. 4(A).
13   Unless they are in the special category of 'civilians accompanying the armed
forces'.
14   Protocol 1, Art. 51.3. What counts as taking direct part? The Third Geneva
Convention explicitly excludes certain authorized 'persons who accompany the armed
forces without actually being members thereof, such as civilian members of military aircraft
crews, war correspondents, supply contractors', from being seen as directly participating in
hostilities in virtue of their role, and implies that other persons undertaking similar functions
should also be excluded. On the other hand, the conditions for being counted as directly
participating are, perhaps inevitably, much vaguer. The *Commentary on the Additional
Protocols of 8 June 1977* explains that the term 'hostilities' refers to 'acts of war which are
intended by their nature or their purpose to hit specifically the personnel and materiel of the
armed forces of the adverse Party'. Claude Pilloud, Yves Sandoz, Christophe Swinarski,
Bruno Zimmermann and International Committee of the Red Cross, *Commentary on the
Additional Protocols of 8 June 1977 to the Geneva Conventions of 12 August 1949* (Leiden:
Martinus Nijhoff, 1987), s. 1679, p. 519. While conceding that '[u]ndoubtedly, there is
room here for some margin of judgment: to restrict this concept to combat and to active
military operations would be too narrow, while extending it to the entire war effort would

comments are in order here. First, the term 'unlawful combatant' is potentially misleading, implying as it does a third legal category, somewhere between that of (lawful) combatant and civilian. 'Unlawful combatants' are rather civilians whose illegal actions have caused them to forfeit their immunity temporarily and to incur criminal liability.[15] Secondly, even though unlawful combatants forfeit their immunity only temporarily, the presumption is that once a civilian has directly participated in hostilities, they remain an unlawful combatant, until it is put beyond doubt that they not will engage in further hostilities, either by an extended period of non-participation or by explicitly affirming their withdrawal.[16] The idea, for example, that a farmer may engage in guerilla activities at night, becoming liable to attack when he does so, but regain his immunity during the day when he takes up his hoe, should be resisted. Supposing that our nocturnal guerilla regains immunity when he is not actively engaged in fighting is to invite his enemies to disregard the doctrine of civilian immunity when they realize that it is being used as a shield for their enemies to hide behind.

Legal requirements that combatants wear distinctive uniform or other distinctive signs visible at a distance and carry weapons openly aim to make it clear which category people in a conflict zone belong in. These laws, along with prohibitions on 'weapons of mass destruction' such as nuclear bombs,[17] and the development of precision weapons, as well as such institutional arrangements as the siting of military installations away from civilian population centres, help make it possible, at least, that wars can be fought in ways that respect the combatant/ civilian distinction and in particular protect civilians from being targeted.

Importantly, the combatant/civilian distinction has been embodied in the development of national armed forces. While the status of members of insurgent groups and guerrilla forces remains a matter of debate, membership of national armed forces has served as a clear criterion for distinguishing combatants from civilians for citizens of countries involved in international conflict: those who serve in those forces are combatants, and those who do not, are not. Moreover, the authority relations that apply to members of the armed forces – with the

---

be too broad, as in modern warfare the entire population participates in the war effort to some extent', the *Commentary* holds that '[d]irect participation in hostilities implies a direct causal relationship between the activity engaged in and the harm done to the enemy at the time and place where the activity takes place'. Given the inherent indeterminacy in the applicability of the concepts of causation, particularly in highly mediated and complex actions, and of time and place in many instances, the advice that 'there is room here for some margin of judgment' is well taken.

15   See M. Schmitt, 'Humanitarian Law and Direct Participation in Hostilities by Private Contractors or Civilian Employees', *Chicago Journal of International Law*, 5 (2005): 511–46, especially pp. 523–4.

16   Ibid. p. 536.

17   International Court of Justice, *Legality of the Threat or Use of Nuclear Weapons (Advisory Opinion)*, 1996 ICJ 226 (8 July), http://www.icj-cij.org/docket/index.php?p1=3 &p2=4&k=e1&case=95&code=unan&p3=4

military being directed by, and at the service of, civil authority and a strictly hierarchical chain of command within the military – mean that there are clear loci of responsibility and accountability for breaches of the laws of war, including in particular those stemming from non-combatant immunity from attack.

Increasingly, however, in such conflicts, functions that were previously undertaken by members of national armed forces are being allocated to employees of private military and security companies (PMSCs). The services that PMSCs provide to national forces include logistical support, training, guarding personnel and installations, operation of weapons systems and gathering of intelligence.[18] Here the focus is on their use in war.

Private Military and Security Companies and the 'Civilianization' of War

The emergence and rapid growth of PMSCs is clearly one of the most significant developments in military affairs over the past two decades since the end of the Cold War. While PMSCs came to public attention with the military involvement of groups such as Sandline International and Executive Outcomes in conflicts in Sierra Leone and Angola in the 1990s, the major PMSCs are domiciled in First-World countries, which are also their principal clients. With estimated annual revenues of more than US$100 billion, PMSCs – including such substantial corporations as DynCorp, Northrop Grumman, Xe Services LLC (formerly Blackwater) and KBR (formerly Kellogg Brown & Root) – have come to play a significant role in the military activities of states, especially the United States.

The rise of PMSCs, and their central involvement in theatres of conflict, has generated a range of responses. Some think that PMSCs are unacceptable in principle, as corporatized incarnations of morally discredited mercenary forces,[19] or as usurpers of 'inherently governmental functions'.[20] On the other hand, arguably PMSCs provide services that make it more likely that[21] Western states will be willing and able to engage in interventions to protect civilian populations in times of crisis. The events occasioning such interventions are generally unpredictable, in timing or location, or both.[22] Not even the most powerful state can maintain

---

18   Singer, ibid., quotes an estimate that 60 per cent of US intelligence operations are now outsourced.

19   See, for example, Uwe Steinhoff, 'What Are Mercenaries', in A. Alexandra, D. Baker and M. Caparini (eds), *Private Military and Security Companies: Ethics Policies and Civil–Military Relations* (Abingdon: Routledge, 2008).

20   See John R. Luckey, Valerie B. Grasso and Kate M. Manuel, *Inherently Governmental Function and Department of Defence Operations: Background Issues, and Options for Congress* (Washington, DC: Congressional Research Service, 2009).

21   Doug Brooks and Matan Chorev, 'Ruthless Humanitarianism: Why Marginalizing Private Peacekeeping Kills People', in Alexandra et al.

22   At the time of writing, for example, NATO forces were enforcing a 'no-fly zone' in Libya in an attempt to prevent the Gaddafi regime from targeting civilian supporters of an

armed forces possessing the full range of resources and capabilities needed across the possible range of situations that they might face. Calling on the services of PMSCs, however, increases states' capacity to provide swift, effective responses to situations requiring humanitarian intervention.

Even if PMSCs are not in principle unacceptable, however, there are obvious reasons to be concerned about their operations in practice, and in particular about the problems they are posing for the viability of the combatant/civilian distinction and associated norms. Those concerns are the focus of the rest of this chapter. I look particularly at the role of PMSCs employed by the US Government in two conflicts in which they have played a major role: the second Iraq war and the war in Afghanistan. I do so for two reasons. First, PMSCs have become central to US – and hence to global – military activity. For example, in the first Gulf War in 1991 the ratio of members of US state forces to contractors is estimated to have been in the order of 50:1; in the second Gulf War and in the US-led war in Afghanistan, the ratio is close to 1:1.[23] Second, the activities of PMSCs in these wars have been relatively well scrutinized, so there is enough information to provide the basis for reasonable comment on their implications for the morality of war and particularly on their effects on the protection of civilians.

Even though, as indicated above, members of PMSCs employed by the US Government in Iraq and Afghanistan have taken on many of the tasks traditionally assumed by members of the armed forces, they do not thereby necessarily come to have the status of combatants. In determining what their status actually is, it is helpful to look at the structure and function of PMSCs. P.W. Singer influentially suggested a 'tip of the spear' typology of PMSCs, with military provider firms (MPFs) offering front-line command and combat operations at the offensive tip of the spear, followed by military consultancy firms (MCFs) providing training and advisory programs and then military support firms (MSFs) offering logistical support services.[24] The larger PMSCs typically will be able to offer services of all three kinds, although military consultancy and military support are the most important of their functions.

In terms of this typology, clearly members of MPFs in conflict zones will count as (lawful or unlawful) combatants. Military provider firms are, however, a relatively minor part of the PMSC industry and the operations of PMSCs in the conflicts in Iraq and Afghanistan do not involve MPFs.

---

uprising that was prompted by an eruption of popular discontent in Egypt and Tunisia and that led to the downfall of longstanding regimes there. The Western powers clearly did not anticipate this train of events.

23   Peter W. Singer, *The Regulation of New Warfare* (Washington, DC: The Brookings Institution, 2010), http://www.brookings.edu/opinions/2010/0227_defense_regulations_ singer.aspx

24   P.W. Singer, *Corporate Warriors* (Ithaca: Cornell University Press, 2004), pp. 88–100.

Contractors undertaking military consultancy and military support roles may become lawful combatants in one of two ways. First, states can make it a condition of granting contracts to PMSCs that members who undertake certain functions enlist as reservist members of the armed forces, becoming part of the military chain of command when on active service. The United Kingdom has done this in its 'Sponsored Reserve' scheme.[25] Second, Protocol 1 to the Geneva Conventions allows that a 'paramilitary or armed law enforcement agency' (which could include PMSCs) may be incorporated in the armed forces of a party to a conflict, provided that the party doing so notifies the opposing side.[26]

The United States, at least, chooses not to take either of these routes to bestowing combatant status on its contractors in conflict zones. Such contractors are not enlisted in the armed forces, nor are they in the military chain of command; they remain employees under the direction of companies that have a contractual relationship with the state. Hence, given the dichotomous nature of the combatant/civilian distinction, and the current criteria for drawing that distinction, it is at least *prima facie* plausible that, as US policy documents state, '[c]ontractors accompanying the armed forces ... are considered civilians accompanying the force'.

Since members of PMSCs working for the United States are not lawful combatants, they are civilians. That fact, together with the vastly increased role of contractors in conflict situations, has led the American legal theorist Michael Schmitt to speak of the 'civilianization of conflict'.[27] Assuming the general desirability of the civilian/combatant distinction and the norms supporting it, there are at least three aspects of this process of civilianization that are concerning.

First, the actions of members of PMSCs in a combat zone tend to endanger other civilians.[28] Figures for civilian casualties in Iraq and Afghanistan are speculative and highly contested[29] and there seems no reliable way of working out the relative contributions of contractors and uniformed troops to those casualties. There have been, however, a number of well-publicized cases of contractors injuring and killing civilians without just cause, such as the 'Nisoor Square Massacre', in which Blackwater employees escorting a convoy of State Department vehicles shot dead 17 Iraqi civilians in Baghdad.[30] According to the American journalist

---

25   Elke Krahmann, 'Controlling Private Military Companies in the UK and Germany: Between Partnership and Regulation' (2003), http://www.mercenary-wars.net/private-military-companies/index.html, p. 6.

26   Protocol 1, Art. 43.3.

27   Schmitt, p. 511.

28   See Schwartz, p. 14, for details and references; 'Catalogue of terror, torture ... and how the US tried to keep it all quiet', *New Zealand Herald*, 25 October 2010, http://www. nzherald.co.nz/world/news/article.cfm?c_id=2&objectid=10716234

29   See the estimates and discussion at http://www.unknownnews.net/casualties.html

30   Joe Burgess, Ahmad Fasam, Kareem Hilmi, James Glanz, Sabrina Tavernise and Archie Tse, 'An Account of the Shootings at Nisour Square', *The New York Times*, 21 September 2007, http://www.nytimes.com/interactive/2007/09/21/world/middleeast/0921-blackwater-nisour-square.html; David Johnston and John M. Broder, 'F.B.I. Says Guards

Scott Horton, '[d]ozens of incidents ... comparable to the Nisoor Square case have been referred to [the] Justice [Department]'.[31]

There is a variety of plausible reasons for the tendency of contractors to use unjustified deadly force against civilians, including inadequate screening of recruits, poor training, lack of local knowledge, and so on. To some extent at least, however, it stems from the incentive structures within which PMSCs operate. Consider the situation confronting Blackwater in providing personal security services to Paul Bremer in his role as Head of the Coalition Provisional Authority (CPA) in Iraq in 2003–04. This was a period of extreme disorder in Iraq (arguably exacerbated by some of Bremer's own decisions, such as dissolving the Iraqi Army) and Bremer was a highly visible and attractive target for forces hostile to the US occupation, with Osama Bin Laden offering '10,000 grams of gold to whoever kills the occupier Bremer'[32] and Bremer himself recounting that a US Secret Service survey had reckoned him to be 'the most threatened American official anywhere in the world'.[33] At a time when the market opportunities for PMSCs in Iraq were rapidly expanding, preventing a successful attack on Bremer became a commercial imperative for Blackwater. As the man charged with reconstructing the Iraqi armed forces, Colonel Thomas Hammes, put it:

> You may lose an ambassador in an insurgency – that's a fact; the British did in Malaya – but you have other ambassadors ... But if Blackwater loses a principal, they're out of business, aren't they? Can you imagine being Blackwater, trying to sell your next contract, saying, 'Well, we did pretty well in Iraq for about four months, and then he got killed.' And you're the CEO who's going to hire and protect your guys. You'll say, 'I think I'll find somebody else.' ... For the military, if the primary gets killed, that's a very bad thing. There will be after-action reviews, etc., but nobody's going out of business.[34]

Unsurprisingly, Blackwater staff were prepared to be extremely aggressive in protecting their charge, trying to ensure that his progress from place to place would be unimpeded, for example, by forcing other vehicles off the road or even shooting at them. Blackwater fulfilled their brief in protecting Bremer, but did

---

Killed 14 Iraqis Without Cause', *The New York Times*, 14 November 2007, http://www.nytimes.com/2007/11/14/world/middleeast/14blackwater.html?ex=1352696400&en=4d3e7a7a4fbc5721&ei=5088&partner=rssnyt&emc=rss

31   Scott Horton, 'Getting Closer to the Truth About the Blackwater Incident', *Harpers*, November 2007, http://harpers.org/archive/2007/11/hbc-90001669

32   Quoted in Jeremy Scahill, *Blackwater: The Rise of the World's Most Powerful Mercenary Army* (New York: Nation, 2007), p. 73.

33   Ibid., p. 74.

34   'Interview: Marine Col. Thomas X. Hammes (Ret.)', *Frontline*, 21 June 2005, http://www.pbs.org/wgbh/pages/frontline/shows/warriors/interviews/hammes.html

so in a way that alienated locals and arguably actually set back the overall US mission. According to Hammes:

> Their interests are fundamentally different than ours ... Blackwater's an extraordinarily professional organization and they were doing exactly what they were tasked to do: protect the principal. The problem is in protecting the principal they had to be very aggressive, and each time they went out they had to offend locals ... making enemies each time they went out. So they were actually getting our contract exactly as we asked them to and at the same time hurting our counterinsurgency effort.[35]

More generally, there is likely to be, at best, only an accidental coincidence between the broad politico/strategic goals of the state that employs a PMSC and the much narrower ones the PMSC is tasked to achieve.

Second, members of PMSCs in conflict zones are at a high risk of injury. In itself, that is hardly surprising: contractors work in an inherently dangerous environment on behalf of, and to further the cause of, an occupying power that faces violent opposition. Moreover, though contractors do not have combat functions *per se*, many of them undertake tasks – such as protection of personnel and installations – that have traditionally been undertaken by members of the armed forces, are of strategic value and predictably involve them in deadly confrontations. What is perhaps surprising is that risk of injury to members of PMSCs has been steadily climbing through the course of the Iraq and Afghan conflicts to the point where they have become even more likely than uniformed personnel to be casualties. In the period from June 2009 to November 2010, for example, contractors in Afghanistan were 2.75 times more likely to be casualties than US uniformed personnel,[36] while in Iraq in the period from January 2009 to June 2010, there were 204 contractor fatalities and 188 US troop fatalities.[37] Again, explanations of the causes of high rates of contractor casualties relative to that of uniformed troops are to some extent necessarily speculative: they might indicate the relative lack of training and equipment among PMSCs, as well as the recognition of their vulnerability by insurgents.

But, again, we can point to more deep-seated structural causes. Here, it is useful to consider the similarities between the organizational articulation of PMSCs, as described, for example, in Singer's tip-of-the-spear typology of PMSCs, and that of modern armies. It will be recalled that in Singer's typology military provider firms (MPF) offering front-line command and combat operations are placed at the

---

35 Ibid.

36 Moshe Schwartz, *Security Contractors in Afghanistan: Background, Analysis and Options for Congress* (Washington, DC: Congressional Research Service, 2011).

37 Steven L. Schooner and Collin D. Swan, 'Contractors and the Ultimate Sacrifice', *Service Contractor* (September 2010): 16–18. Schooner and Swan point to reasons for thinking that rates of contractor casualties are under-reported.

offensive tip of the spear, followed by military consultancy firms (MCF) offering training and advisory programs and then by military support firms (MSF) offering logistical support services. Singer's distinctions track similar distinctions between the main functional division arms of the armed forces – known respectively as the combat arm, the combat support arm and the combat support service.[38] The combat arms are (in army terms) infantry and armour – those elements of the army that aim to engage with and fight the enemy. Combat support covers those elements that directly help the combat arms close with and kill the enemy; engineers, artillery, air and intelligence fall under this category. Finally, combat service support encompasses those areas (logistics, signals, medical services, and so on) that support the overall military effort. The metaphor describing the relationship between the combat arm and the other arms is that of 'tooth to tail'.

While fighting is primarily the mission of members of the combat arms, all members of the armed forces bear arms,[39] have had at least basic combat training, are expected to engage in combat if required and are counted as combatants. The status of members of armed forces as combatants is, it seems to me, over-determined. An armed force engaged in ongoing conflict is a kind of corporate entity, all of whose members share a common animating end. It is composed of a number of interacting sub-units (such as the artillery and the intelligence units), which are defined by the different specialized means they use to help realize their common goal. The interdependence of the various sub-units means it is a tactical matter as to where resistance to achievement of their common goal is best focused and the form it takes. That is, resistance at any time may or may not take the form of the exercise of violent force (it might, for example, take the form of a denial of material support) and, if violence is used, it might be most effectively directed at units other than those that belong to the combat arms. It might be wiser to attack 'the tail' than 'the tooth'. At the same time, the functional divisions within the armed forces are not rigid; if necessary, any member can be called on to engage in combat (or other tasks). Potentially, at least, all members are both liable to, and capable of, attack.

Though US Government contractors in conflict zones have not been integrated into the command structure of the armed forces, they nevertheless fit into the corporate structure described in the previous paragraph, sharing a common goal with the armed forces and interacting with elements of it to achieve that goal. According to official US doctrine, 'contractor employees *cannot* lawfully perform military functions and should not be working in scenarios where they might be conceived as combatants' (emphasis added).[40]

---

38   John Whiteclay Chambers II, 'Combat Support', in *The Oxford Companion to American Military History* (New York: Oxford University Press, 2000), http://www.highbeam.com/doc/1O126-CombatSupport.html

39   With a few insignificant exceptions, such as chaplains.

40   Joint Chiefs of Staff, *4-0 Doctrine for Logistics Support of Joint Operations* V-1(d) (2000), www.aschq.army.mil/gc/files/JP4-0.pdf, pp. 64–5.

It is true that, as civilians, contractors may not legally take 'direct part' in hostilities. But when they are as integral a part of the military mission as they have been in Iraq and Afghanistan, it is fanciful to think that they will not be conceived and treated as combatants, not simply by opposition forces, but by the state for which they work. Consider two well-documented chains of events in Iraq in 2004. The first was sparked by the notorious killing of four Blackwater employees in the city of Fallujah, which had become one of the principal centres of resistance to the US occupation and the scene of fierce and ongoing fighting, with significant civilian casualties. The local population greeted the killing of the Blackwater employees with jubilation. According to *The New York Times*, '[m] any people in Falluja said they believed that they had won an important victory on Wednesday'.[41] The US Government and armed forces were concerned that the killings could undermine US resolve in Iraq, as the downing of Black Hawk helicopters had in Somalia in 1993, and embolden the resistance, unless there was a large and successful display of US force in response. The second began with a fire-fight in the holy city of Najaf, with followers of the cleric Muqtada Al-Sadr on one side and US soldiers and Blackwater employees guarding the Coalition Provisional Authority headquarters on the other. It is uncertain who was responsible for initiating the fire-fight,[42] but it is clear that not only did the Blackwater employees play a leading role, including directing the actions of the soldiers, but three Blackwater helicopters were given permission by CPA staff to deliver ammunition and evacuate a wounded marine during the course of the fight.[43] In both cases, US forces soon engaged in full-blown, bloody assaults on the towns – assaults that were clearly precipitated by, and responding to, the events involving Blackwater staff.

In a situation in which contractors are becoming involved in large-scale fire-fights alongside uniformed troops, are directing and providing material assistance for such troops and where targeting contractors is an effective tool in influencing enemy tactics, it is hard to maintain that they are not combatants.

Either employees of PMSCs in these sort of cases are combatants, in which case they are illegal combatants, or they are not, in which case their targeting is contrary to the laws of war. In either case, the arrangements currently in place are fostering a subversion of respect for and adherence to the laws of war regarding the immunity of civilians as are, of course, the incentives for PMSCs to place the fulfilment of short-term mission goals above concern for respect for civilian life. This is the final cause for concern about the so-called civilianization of war consequent to the widespread use of PMSCs.

---

41   Scahill, p. 109.

42   Ibid., p. 125.

43   Dana Priest, 'Private Guards Repel Attack on U.S. Headquarters', *Washington Post*, 6 April 2004.

Conclusion

The discussion in this chapter has shown that current arrangements for the use of PMSCs in conflict zones by the US government compromise respect for civilian immunity in a number of ways. One possible response to the shortcomings of those arrangements would, of course, be to radically curtail the role of PMSCs. This seems both unlikely and, for reasons alluded to above, not necessarily desirable. A more practicable response would be to follow the British example and make PMSC employees in conflict zones members of the armed forces, falling under the military chain of command. They therefore become unequivocally lawful combatants, whose actions may be directed to conform to the overall strategic goals of the armed forces. There have, in fact, been some significant, albeit insufficient, developments in the direction of integrating PMSC employees into the US armed forces – for example, the 2006 amendment of the *Military Extraterritorial Jurisdiction Act* to permit the court-martialling of contractors[44] and the inclusion of contractors in the official account of US forces.[45]

---

44   But see the concerns about the possible lack of validity and effectiveness of that amendment in David L. Snyder, 'Civilian Military Contractors on Trial: The Case for Upholding the Amended Exceptional Jurisdiction Claims of the Uniform Code of Military Justice', *Texas International Law Review*, 44/65: 65–97, especially p. 68.

45   *Army Regulation 530-1 'Operations Security'* (Washington, DC: Department of Army, 2007), para 2.1.

Chapter 12

Remote Killing and Drive-By Wars

David Whetham

There is often somewhat of a knee-jerk reaction by many observers, particularly ethicists, to any new military technological development. Each new technology is met with objections and criticisms while potential benefits and advantages are often downplayed or simply dismissed out of hand without sufficient scrutiny. Perhaps this is simply a reaction to the boundless enthusiasm of the 'techno advocates' who are often guilty of hype and overstating the massive revolutionary changes their favourite new bit of Gucci kit will inevitably bring to the world. This chapter will try to present a brief, hopefully balanced account of some of the ethical implications of recent developments in military technical affairs.[1]

The 'remote killing' referred to in the title of this chapter is directed at the type of weapon systems proliferating throughout the militaries of the technologically capable states, which separate the 'shooter' from the effect. Sometimes these are referred to as 'standoff' weapons. In its simplest contemporary form this could be a sniper with a long-range rifle. The sniper can be intimately aware of their target, perhaps reading the target's newspaper over their shoulder, and still be thousands of metres away when the trigger is pulled and the shot taken. The spectrum of standoff goes from a thrown stone at one end all the way to a fully autonomous weapon system sent off without external control in order to complete a mission completely on its own at the other end. In many ways, however, the current generation of unmanned military vehicles – particularly the ubiquitous Predator and now the Reaper Hunter Killer Unmanned Aerial Vehicle (UAV), often piloted and controlled from more than 10,000 km away from where they actually operate most visibly in the deserts and mountains of Afghanistan and Pakistan – pose some very interesting and challenging questions about warfare in general and about the role of and impact upon civilians in those wars.

---

1   This chapter builds on and develops certain core ideas the author first started engaging with in 2006. See 'Ethics and Military Technology', in Dr Emily Spencer and Dr Daniel Lagacé-Roy (eds), *Ethical Decision-Making in the New Security Environment. Proceedings from the Canadian Conference on Ethical Leadership* (Kingston, On.: Canadian Defence Academy Press, 2008), Vol. 2. See also D. Whetham (ed.), *Ethics, Law, and Military Operations* (Basingstoke: Palgrave, 2010), Ch.1.

Background

The first flight of the Curtiss-Sperry Aerial Torpedo, employing the twin technologies of inertial navigation and radio control, took place in March 1918. It was effectively the first cruise missile, but neither it nor its competitors proved viable as anything more than realistic target drones for other weapon systems to practise against.[2] The technology was revisited and refined over the rest of the century and developed into two separate areas: guided missiles designed to be controlled on to a specific target and UAVs, which were not themselves a weapon but rather a remotely piloted platform from which other things could be achieved. Occasionally this role, too, was offensive, but far more widely (and effectively) UAVs were equipped with cameras or other data-gathering equipment to carry out observation roles in theatres where piloted vehicles were unsuitable or simply too vulnerable. The adaptation from UAV surveillance craft into a genuine offensive missile platform, bringing the two paths of technology back together again, took place as an improvisation in 2002 under the last Bush administration. This otherwise impressive ability to watch and track suspected hostile targets had proved frustrating for those who could see exactly what was going on but lacked any mechanism for being able to do anything about it. Arming such assets, initially with *ad-hoc* weapon systems, to provide such an ability was therefore a natural development. While the technology might have been introduced before his time, US President Barack Obama really takes credit for the enthusiastic embrace of the ubiquitous armed drone as the centrepiece of US counterterrorism operations. He has hugely expanded their use in an effort to, in the words of his State of the Union address, 'take the fight to Al Qaeda'.[3] The questions this technology raises are, however, certainly not limited to the United States or even to the West. Everybody seems to be at it – from the Israelis on the one hand to Hezbollah on the other. The Iranians unveiled their own 'Karrar' bomber drone in August 2010, with President, Mahmoud Ahmadinejad, saying that the new plane would serve as a 'messenger of death' (but added comfortingly that its key message was one of friendship).[4]

The Advantages of Precision Standoff

First of all, then, to the considerable advantages such weapon systems can offer us. Of course, it is necessary to put the caveat that just because something is capable of being used in a particular way that does not mean that it actually

---

2   Thomas Parke Hughes, *American Genesis: A Century of Invention and Technological Enthusiasm 1870–1970* (Chicago: University of Chicago Press, 2004), pp. 130–31.

3   'State of the Union Address', *BBC News*, 28 January 2010, http://news.bbc.co.uk/1/hi/8484451.stm

4   'Iran Unveils First Bomber Drone', *BBC News*, 22 August 2010, http://www.bbc.co.uk/news/world-middle-east-11052023

will be. In that sense, however, contemporary UAVs are exactly the same as any other military technological development throughout history: anything is potentially open to abuse or can be put to use in pursuit of illegitimate ends.[5] Many of the advantages of such precision standoff weapons, used appropriately, appear obvious. The same result can be achieved with fewer and smaller weapons due to their improved accuracy; it is no longer necessary to saturate a target in order to have confidence in its destruction. The resulting reduction in foreseeable but unintended and unwanted civilian death and destruction – collateral damage – is therefore significant. For example, in World War II, it took 108 planes to successfully prosecute each target. In Afghanistan 60 years later, each individual aircraft could be expected to successfully engage more than four different targets per sortie.[6] If fewer weapons are required to achieve an effect, this also means that fewer platforms are required to deliver them. Therefore, fewer pilots need to put their lives at risk. If a UAV can be employed then no pilots need to put their lives at risk at all, as the platform can be controlled far from the theatre of operations. 'Such weapons can therefore help to preserve life from both perspectives (and are more financially efficient into the bargain).'[7]

It is not just in an offensive capacity that life can be preserved using such tools. For example, it is a notoriously dangerous task to resupply forward operating bases in hostile territory. Despite the dangers, the need for material and logistical support is huge and this is not a demand that is going to go away anytime soon. In Afghanistan, the US Marines alone consume 800,000 gallons of fuel a day.[8] Civilian contractors, many from neighbouring Pakistan, often do such resupply, but while the pay is understandably good, the cost in life is high. If that resupply can be carried out using unmanned vehicles – aerial or land based – some of those risks to human life can be reduced.[9] The ability to generate 'round the next corner' or 'over the next building' images and information can also be essential for

---

5 The contentious policy of 'targeted killing' or 'assassination in self-defence' employing standoff weapons is beyond the scope of this chapter, as although it is at present heavily associated with drones and UAVs, there is no logical reason that it cannot be accomplished using less remote tools. For an exploration of some of the moral issues specifically relating to this, see Michael Gross, *Moral Dilemmas of Modern War: Torture, Assassination and Blackmail in an Age of Asymmetric Conflict* (Cambridge: Cambridge University Press, 2010), particularly Ch. 5.

6 P.W. Singer, *Wired for War: The Robotics Revolution and Conflict in the 21st Century* (New York: Penguin, 2010), p. 100.

7 David Whetham, 'Ethics, Law and Conflict', in David Whetham (ed.), *Ethics, Law and Military Operations* (Basingstoke: Palgrave, 2010), p. 20.

8 Swiss Federal Institute of Technology, *Are ISAF's Tenuous Supply Lines Sustainable?* (Zurich, 2 March 2011), http://www.isn.ethz.ch/isn/Current-Affairs/ISN-Insights/Detail?ln g=en&id=127187&contextid734=127187&contextid735=127186&tabid=127186

9 'USMC Moves Closer to Deciding on Unmanned Resupply for Afghanistan', *flightglobal.com*, 17 February 2010, http://www.flightglobal.com/articles/2010/02/17/ 338476/usmc-moves-closer-to-deciding-on-unmanned-resupply-for.html

successful counter–improvised explosive device activity as well. As Honeywell's Micro Air Vehicle program manager puts it: 'every time a T-Hawk goes down it means a human didn't.'[10]

The effects of these different types of technologies can combine to reduce the fear of what is often referred to as the 'CNN effect', where public support is expected to fall away as civilian casualties mount and friendly forces become casualties in increasing numbers. If both of these considerations can be minimized, public resolve can be maintained – an essential consideration when democracies want to use military force, particularly where vital national interests are not obviously at stake. By lowering the potential political costs, this can, in turn, make it easier to intervene militarily where it might simply have been impossible to do so before. For example, US President Bill Clinton was able to reassure the American public that no US personnel would be put at risk by the decision to intervene and stop the ethnic cleansing that was happening in Kosovo in 1999. Precision airpower could be employed to do the job from the air, without fear of another Mogadishu coming to haunt the American conscience.[11] Very similar considerations were also obviously at play as the United States, European powers and some Arab states debated getting involved with enforcing a no-fly zone over Libya in early 2011 to help prevent, or at least hamper, Gaddafi's attacks on the civil population. In another earlier case, the political cost of using a Predator to kill the Al Qaeda leader Qaed Senyan al-Harthi, thought to be responsible for the October 2000 bombing of the *USS Cole*, would probably have been much higher had this involved the invasion of Yemen in order to do it.[12] While US Predator drone strikes in Pakistan are no doubt unpopular, they do not arouse quite the same level of outrage as actually invading across the border with troops to assault Taliban havens, as was attempted in September 2008 (unfortunately with disastrous consequences).[13] Of course, sometimes, the political cost is deemed to be worth it anyway, as was demonstrated with the US Special Forces mission into Pakistan against Bin Laden himself in 2011 (with slightly more success from a US perspective).[14] However, for the type of operations that do not directly involve the mastermind of 9/11 and that therefore may be harder to justify or 'sell' to a skeptical domestic and global audience, precision standoff weapons offer policy

---

10   Andrew Simms, 'A Magnificent Man and His Flying Machines', *Soldier Magazine* (October 2010), p. 37.

11   This was after the US raid in Somalia to apprehend two clan officials, which resulted in the death of 18 soldiers and the body of a dead American being dragged through the streets. Mickey Kaus, 'What *Black Hawk Down* Leaves Out', *Slate*, 21 January 2002, http://www.slate.com/id/2060941/

12   'CIA "Killed al-Qaeda Suspects" in Yemen', *BBC News*, 5 November 2002, http://news.bbc.co.uk/1/hi/2402479.stm

13   'U.S. Confirms Incursion into Pakistan', *MSNBC*, 3 September 2008, http://www.msnbc.msn.com/id/26522492/ns/world_news-south_and_central_asia/

14   'Bin Laden raid: Barack Obama describes 'huge risks'', *BBC News*, 9 May 2011, http://www.bbc.co.uk/news/world-us-canada-13331762

makers an option for direct action that would simply not be present, or at least realistic, using more conventional tools in the military toolbox.

Accountability

By highlighting the potentially huge distances between what is happening on the ground and the person directing it, it is easy to raise the question of accountability of those people for their actions. The person who has been targeted by a UAV will probably remain completely unaware of the weapon system, let alone the operator, until their world, quite literally, comes crashing down, while the marine squad on the ground has no idea who is controlling the faceless drone in the skies above them when they call in fire support. What happens if something goes wrong? It is not as if one can just jot down a name from an ID badge. While it is of course always a question of how the technology is employed in practice, the very nature of this technology actually offers a much higher degree of oversight than in virtually any other area of military activity. Many of this author's conversations with military personnel recently returned from operations in Afghanistan highlight the complete lack of scrutiny in theatre; no journalists are foolhardy enough to be embedded on long-range patrols so there is no media presence and such teams can be out of contact with their own people for extended periods. It is easy to see how what happens in the desert might well stay in the desert as a result.[15] Every movement of a UAV's joystick, however, every frame of camera footage and therefore every decision (or indeed hesitation or omission) of the operator are recorded and can be pored over at great length following any incident. There is nowhere to hide from a bad decision if the military wishes to use that information (and recent experience suggests that if they do not, Wikileaks will ensure that action is taken eventually).

That on its own would appear to offer a profound restraint on any trigger-happy behaviour; however, it goes further than this. While recognizing that the study was done in very particular circumstances in Iraq and that a great deal of work has been done to correct these attitudes since, the 2006 Mental Health Advisory Team (MHAT) IV research showed that 45 per cent of soldiers and 60 per cent of marines surveyed stated that they would not report a fellow unit member for killing an innocent non-combatant. These figures rise to 57 and 70 per cent respectively for not reporting a fellow unit member for unnecessarily destroying private property.[16] Adequate oversight – fear of being caught – is one

---

15   For a disturbing account of what can happen when effective oversight is lacking, see Mark Boal, 'The Kill Team', *Rolling Stone*, 27 March 2011, http://www.rollingstone.com/kill-team

16   Mental Health Advisory Team IV, *Operation Iraqi Freedom 05-07: Final Report*, 17 November 2006, p. 37, http://www.armymedicine.army.mil/reports/mhat/mhat_iv/MHAT_IV_Report_17NOV06.pdf

of the ways that such attitudes and behaviour can be adapted and changed.[17] While the thought of UAVs being used to spy on friendly forces as well as hostile ones is not necessarily palatable to everyone, the fact that the whereabouts of such assets is generally unknown but that when they are there they are perfectly capable of seeing events on the ground in intimate detail means that there is at least a chance of having misdemeanours captured on film. Knowing or even thinking that there is a small chance of someone watching might help improve questions of accountability far beyond just the operator of the UAV itself.

Of course, the question of accountability when considering all the actions of a fully autonomous weapon system is somewhat more complicated than this. The current UK position is clear: 'A fully autonomous system would have to be capable of making the qualitative assessments currently required by the Law of Armed Conflict, until this is possible, the human must remain within the decision-making process.'[18] Given the technical limitations currently faced by even the most ambitious projects, this appears to still be a little way off in practice.[19]

Moral Disconnection

There is an innate reluctance in many, if not most, people to kill. This inhibition – necessary for civilized society to function – has to be overcome by military training to allow individuals to achieve emotional distance from their enemies and thus enable the individual to kill.[20] One of the tools that has traditionally been employed to get people to kill each other is dehumanization – the promotion of a sense of 'otherness' in the group that is deemed to be a threat. Those who fall into such a group can then be perceived as 'non-entities, expendable or undeserving', making the act of killing them easier to carry out.[21] How much easier, then, must this be if the person 'pulling the trigger' is 8,000 km away to begin with? There is no need to look anyone 'in the eye'; they are just pixels on a screen. Does this make the act of killing using drones or other standoff weapons easier as far as one's conscience is concerned? Grayling notes that Royal Air Force (RAF) bomber crews in World

---

17   See Paolo Tripodi ('Understanding Atrocities', pp. 173–88) and the chapter by General Wall in Whetham, *Ethics, Law and Military Operations*, pp. 221–9.

18   Wing Commander Alison Mardell, 'Unmanned Aerial Vehicles – The Legal Perspective', *Air Power UAVs: The Wider Context* (Northolt, UK: Ministry of Defence, 2009), p. 82.

19   For example, see the debate between Singer, Arkin and Sharkey in 'Special Issue: Ethics and Emerging Military Technologies', *Journal of Military Ethics*, 9/4 (2010).

20   See Dave Grossman, *On Killing: The Psychological Cost of Learning to Kill in War and Society* (Boston: Little Brown, 1996).

21   Susan Opotow, 'Moral Exclusion and Injustice: An Introduction', *Journal of Social Issues*, 46/1 (Spring 1990). See also Edward Tick, *War and the Soul: Healing Our Nation's Veterans from Post-Traumatic Stress Disorder* (Wheaton, Ill.: Quest Books, 2005), pp. 82 ff.

War II could unleash their bombs from 20,000 ft and knowingly kill hundreds or even thousands of women and children. If, however, you gave the same bomber crew a knife and told them to slit the throats of the family in the room next door, they would not be able to do it.[22] Physical separation appears to also provide some moral distance in order to make such actions easier to carry out, even to the extent of making terrible things possible. Interviews with contemporary military pilots with combat experience show that they tend to agree that 'not only are decisions to kill [from the air] rarely perceived as emotionally charged, the death of friendly, yet physically distant combatants is emotionally dulled'.[23]

It would appear that the process of alienation of each side from the other due to reliance upon remote killing might be enhanced by the lack of actual contact. Whether this is a roadside improvised explosive device (IED) for which people bid money over the Internet to win the right to detonate the bomb and watch the results on a web-link, or a UAV operator wasting tiny avatars on a computer screen, it is difficult to see how you can have the essential mutual respect that combatant equality – the bedrock of the law of armed conflict – requires. If a faceless enemy can be so demonized, it is easy to see how lines get blurred and civilians can come to be seen as just another target. Not everyone who is physically distant, however, can emotionally separate themselves from their actions or other events on the ground. An American World War II veteran recalled his first mission over Europe as he opened his aircraft's bomb-bay doors: 'He felt terrible resistance, nausea, sickness, headaches, despair. He couldn't do it, but his crew chief screamed at him, "Now! Now!" If he didn't, the mission would be a failure and it would be his fault. He finally pushed the button. Then he vomited.'[24]

Of course, this refers to an act that was part of a total war in which large-scale, devastating attacks on civilian populations were common rather than the type of highly accurate, precision-targeting policies of wars of choice in the contemporary age. Still, the moral comfort that distance can provide might not extend as far as many would think. Just because the target is being viewed through a TV screen rather than a rifle sight that does not mean that taking life has no effect on the person pulling the trigger. Perhaps surprisingly, there are examples of post-traumatic stress disorder (PTSD) among UAV pilots who have never even set foot in the theatre of military operations.[25]

One wonders if operating a UAV for offensive missions in the contemporary operating environment might actually be closer to the experience of military

---

22   For a fascinating and balanced discussion of these issues, see A.C. Grayling, *Among the Dead Cities* (London: Bloomsbury, 2006).

23   Tucker-Lowe, *Does the Advent of Uninhabited Systems Fundamentally Affect the Ethical Landscape of Contemporary Conflict?*, Defence Research Paper (Unpublished Defence Studies MA Dissertation, King's College, London, July 2010), p. 11.

24   Tick, p. 91.

25   For example, see Jane Mayer, 'The Risks of a Remote-Controlled War', *National Public Radio*, 21 October 2009. This is also discussed in Singer, *Wired for War*.

snipers. Snipers, too, are separated by distance, but can also be intimately aware of their target, much like the UAV operator with their real-time video feeds who might be tracking a target for hours before the decision is taken to strike. A sniper deployed in Iraq recalls:

> Theoretically, sniping was supposed to be a matter of clinical, dispassionate killing. 'Even when we were in Iraq, killing Iraqis, it was target one, target two. Target one's on the left; target two's on the right. OK, scan target one. Target one's down. Scan target two. Fire. Target two's down. That's it. They're just targets; you try to convince yourself of that.' [However] imagining a man purely as a target was not easy when you had to aim specifically at him and fire and then watch him fall over, screaming and arching his back in agony.[26]

Unmanned aerial vehicle footage can be just as graphic and one wonders whether the geographic dislocation is actually providing moral dislocation at all, or at least any dislocation greater than that experienced by a sniper.[27]

On the other hand, even if it is not clear that the geographic disconnection actually makes killing (or at least dealing psychologically with the results of killing) any easier, it has to be the case that the absence from the physical situation has some clear implications for the effectiveness of the UAV operator. Because the operator is not directly at risk, they have a number of options that a person physically in harm's way can probably not afford. For example, they can wait until fired upon before returning fire, engaging only those who are actually armed and dangerous rather than having to assume that anything that is potentially threatening needs to be engaged before it is too late.[28] This detachment provides time and space for decision making that is, quite literally, a world away from that experienced by those soldiers on the ground or even pilots in hostile airspace. The ability to remain cool, calm and detached arguably allows better decisions to be taken in the heat of battle. There are undoubtedly situational awareness issues linked to available bandwidth, potential time delays and the physical limitations of the information feeds, but these are all technical issues that are constantly being minimized or ameliorated. At the same time, one might expect that the quality of the decisions being made should be getting better and better. For example, the Mental Health Advisory Team report cited above makes a strong correlation

---

26   Jeff Sparrow, *Killing: Misadventures in Violence* (Carlton, Vic.: Melbourne University Press, 2009).

27   This emphasizes the idea introduced above that, in many ways, remote killing is in reality a spectrum rather than sharp differentiation. There is a connection between the Lancaster bomber crews in World War II and the English and Welsh archers at Agincourt in 1415.

28   Indeed, under UK law in which defence of property alone does not justify the use of lethal force, in some combat situations, returning fire when it is only a piece of unmanned hardware at risk may actually be legally unwarranted anyway.

between anger and the mistreatment of non-combatants. It also suggests that soldiers and marines who were members of units that had suffered casualties were more likely to treat civilians in negative ways.[29] If there is some emotional distance between the UAV operator and the events on the ground, presumably, such factors will have less influence on behaviour. 'Once fear for their own safety is not a pressing concern, one would assume the operator would be more capable, not less, of behaving justly.'[30] Tripodi argues that the ability to remain slightly detached from one's immediate situation is one of the attributes of a good commander.[31] If so, the enforced detachment of the UAV operator might well be a positive thing.

Grossman, in his powerful book *On Killing: The Psychological Cost of Learning to Kill in War and Society*, notes that it is those who do not dehumanize their opponents who are most likely to be able to deal with the aftermath of war and go on to lead happy and productive lives. If it is true that the innate (or at least the socially programmed) inhibitions do not need to be overcome in the same way for UAV operators as they do for, say, infantry who need to be prepared to close with and then kill the enemy, the psychological repercussions of war might be significantly reduced. It will be interesting to see if incidences of PTSD among UAV operators in the longer term turn out to be significantly different to those who are physically present in the battle space. At the same time though, one does wonder whether the removal of risk made possible by standoff capabilities comes at a different kind of price. A Predator unit might work the same hours as soldiers in theatre – seven days a week, 12 hours a day, split into two shifts – but at the end of the working day, 'you walk out of the deployment and walk back into the rest of life in America'.[32] That is obviously very different from the experience of those in theatre.

The distance between the UAV and the operator can also raise the question of whether the operator needs to be a combatant at all or whether civilians can undertake such roles. Whilst it is not necessarily unlawful for a civilian to take direct part in hostilities, they do lose their immunity from attack while doing so. That means they may be directly targeted and, if captured, they will not be recognized as combatants or receive the protection of prisoner-of-war status.[33] Of course, if the civilian operator is in a different country to the actual military operation, this might seem to be a small or acceptable risk to take but it needs also to be remembered that civilians employing lethal force that is not in direct self-defence may be charged with murder. 'Therefore, allowing civilians to operate UAVs during armed conflict may have significant implications for them if their activity amounts to a direct part in hostilities.'[34]

---

29   Mental Health Advisory Team IV, pp. 38–9.

30   B.J. Strawser, 'The Duty to Employ Uninhabited Aerial Vehicles', *Journal of Military Ethics*, 9/4 (2010): 353.

31   Tripodi, 'Understanding Atrocities', pp. 185–6.

32   Singer, *Wired for War*, p. 330.

33   Mardell, p. 79.

34   Ibid.

Does the removal of physical risk mean that UAV operators are not really at war at all? Are even those in uniform actually fellow combatants? Apart from these existential questions, this also raises some interesting dilemmas over the nature of direct and indirect participation in conflict that the geographic separation from the battlefield might appear to cloud a little. If a man drives his brother to plant an IED, he might be a civilian, but he is facilitating the planting of the device and is therefore presumably directly participating in hostilities at that time. If a husband on the morning school run drops his officer wife at work at an airforce base in Nevada where she will be piloting a UAV employed in offensive operations, doesn't he, too, become a direct participant in hostilities while acting as chauffeur? Presumably, little Billy on the back seat of the car could be considered acceptable collateral damage in such circumstances. If the wife is actually a civilian rather than an officer, 'there is also the risk that by employing civilians in ambiguous roles, the wider protection of them may be compromised, not least if confusion as to who is and who is not participating in the hostilities is created'.[35]

The Paradox of Precision

Of course, sometimes things do go wrong. Any system is only as good as the information that goes into it. Accidents and mistakes do happen – from accidentally destroying the Chinese Embassy in Belgrade in 1999 through to bombing wedding parties, such as in Wech Baghtu, Afghanistan, in 2008.[36] One report that looked at the use of UAVs in Pakistan's remote tribal areas concluded that '32 per cent of those killed in drone attacks since 2004 were civilians'.[37] While civilian deaths caused by such accidents are obviously highly regrettable, the fact that they took place at all leads some to the idea that they must have been intended in the first place. The argument is that if the weapons are as accurate as we make out, surely, whatever those weapons hit must be the intended target – the paradox of precision.[38] The importance of managing expectations and not creating an erroneous mythology surrounding the West's ability to carry out attacks with pinpoint accuracy is essential, as is an understanding by policy makers that just because the technology has the potential to be extremely accurate that does not

35   Ibid., p. 80.

36   'Embassy Strike "A Mistake"', *BBC News*, 8 May 1999, http://news.bbc.co.uk/1/hi/world/europe/338557.stm; 'Karzai Says Air Strike Kills 40 in Afghanistan', *Reuters*, 5 November 2008, http://www.reuters.com/article/2008/11/05/us-afghan-violence-idUSTRE4A44EW20081105

37   'One in Three Killed by US Drones in Pakistan is a Civilian, Report Claims', *The Telegraph*, 4 March 2010, http://www.telegraph.co.uk/news/worldnews/asia/pakistan/7361630/One-in-three-killed-by-US-drones-in-Pakistan-is-a-civilian-report-claims.html

38   Whetham, 'Ethics, Law and Conflict', p. 21.

mean that there will not be civilian casualties. Despite what propaganda might claim, warfare has never been clinical in this sense and is unlikely to suddenly become so as long as the fog of war and friction – all of the factors out of one's control that stop things working in the way one intends – persist. The situation is exacerbated when an opponent deliberately seeks to 'draw the foul', as it is known in basketball: placing themselves in a situation from which to do harm when they know that any military response will either violate, or be perceived as violating, the rules of *in bello* by creating substantial numbers of civilian casualties.[39] The decision to abort an attack with Storm Shadow missiles on a recent mission over Libya rather than risk killing civilians allegedly being used as 'human shields' illustrates this dilemma only too well.[40] Of course, as with so many other issues, this is not a problem unique to standoff weapons, but rather an issue for all military activity in the contemporary operating environment.

Asymmetrical Implications of Standoff

Another area of military activity in which standoff weapons might create a particular ethical issue is with the potential mismatch between opponents. The asymmetrical threat normally focuses attention on those hostile agents who seek to turn the tables on the sophisticated military machines they oppose by not playing the same game. This can range from adopting hit-and-run-style guerrilla attacks that prevent the preponderance of military power being brought to bear through to using IEDs against dismounted troops or their vehicles. It is important to recognize, however, that there is another side to this asymmetrical reality: using remotely piloted drones against those who cannot counter them is just as asymmetrical as using IEDs. This does not seem to me to be particularly controversial, rather it is just recognizing that one normally seeks to exploit an opponent's weakness rather than attacking their strength. Conducting a war from thousands of metres in the air without even being in the same hemisphere as the weapon might be seen, however, to be taking such an asymmetry to the extreme. Any military activity carried out by a technologically sophisticated protagonist against a less sophisticated one is inherently asymmetrical. Singer notes Arthur C. Clarke's observation that '[a]ny

---

39   See Michael Skerker, 'Just War Criteria and the New Face of War: Human Shields, Manufactured Martyrs, and Little Boys with Stones', *Journal of Military Ethics*, 3/1 (2004): 28. That lessons are being learnt might be indicated by the apparent reduction in civilian deaths associated with drones. For example, see Ken Dilanian, 'CIA Drones May Be Avoiding Pakistan Civilians', *The Sacramento Bee*, 7 March 2011, http://www.sacbee.com/2011/02/21/3419750/cia-drones-may-be-avoiding-pakistan.html

40   Ian Dury, 'Mission Aborted on Orders of SAS', *HMForces.co.uk*, 22 March 2011, http://www.hmforces.co.uk/news/articles/6375-mission-aborted-on-orders-of-sas

sufficiently advanced technology is indistinguishable from magic'.[41] Is it even ethical to use such magic on those who cannot employ it themselves? Münkler suggests: 'The pilot of a fighter-bomber or the crew of a man-of-war from which Tomahawk rockets are launched are beyond the reach of the enemy's weapons. War has lost all features of the classical duel situation here and has approached, to put it cynically, certain forms of pest control.'[42]

This feeling – beautifully captured here – is a common concern when determining the proportionality of one's response within the criteria provided by the *in bello* category of the just-war tradition. War can become 'like playing God from afar, just with unmanned weapons substituted for thunderbolts'.[43] Disturbing though these images might be, the question is, however, fundamentally misguided if it is motivated by a concern to create a level playing field: 'the principle of proportionality is not about being fair, it is about not using more force than is necessary to achieve the required ends.'[44] It would be morally perverse to avoid any weapon that one's opponent did not have access to, thereby eschewing precision munitions and causing additional and unnecessary death and destruction out of some misguided notion of fair play.

In fact, the moral imperative might well work in precisely the other direction. If one has access to precision munitions, in some situations one is obliged to employ them rather than a less sophisticated and therefore less accurate 'dumb' bomb. This might not apply to every situation, of course. For example, where civilian collateral damage might not be an issue due to the location of the target, the ethical concern about limiting the additional harm might not be as pressing. A commander also needs to take into account operational reality and the marshalling of scarce resources; using up all of one's available precision-guided munitions (PGMs) on targets that did not really require them might mean that when they would be genuinely useful for limiting civilian collateral damage, they are no longer available. Therefore, the larger picture must be taken into account. What this also makes clear is that such decisions are simply not a concern for an opponent who does not have access to precision munitions. If one has only conventional munitions and the expected collateral damage using these is acceptable in relation to the military necessity of destroying the target, and one does not have a choice of reducing that collateral damage further by selecting an alternative weapon, one is not obliged to cease the attack because, hypothetically, a weapon exists that

41   P.W. Singer, 'The Ethics of Killer Applications: Why is it So Hard to Talk About Morality When it Comes to New Military Technology?', *Journal of Military Ethics*, 9/4 (2010): 310.

42   H. Münkler, *Die neuen Krige* (Hamburg: Rowohlt, 2003), quoted and translated in U. Steinhoff, 'Torture: The Case for Dirty Harry and Against Alan Dershowitz', *Journal of Applied Philosophy*, 23 (2006): 337–53.

43   Singer, *Wired for War*, p. 324.

44   See David Whetham, 'The Just War Tradition: A Pragmatic Compromise', in Whetham, *Ethics, Law and Military Operations*, p. 21.

could do the same job with less unwanted damage. Therefore, proportionality calculations are, to some extent, relative to the capabilities of the actors involved and the side with the more sophisticated equipment might be held to a higher standard than a less sophisticated actor.

It would also be just as perverse, surely, to insist on using a manned platform because that is all one's opponent can employ. Why would you put your own personnel at risk in this way and claim it was ethically preferable to not putting them at risk? In fact, there might be a moral imperative at work here that compels the West to pursue and deploy this type of technological development in greater numbers. Strawser suggests that the principle of unnecessary risk is a demand that we should not order someone to take unnecessary risks when there are alternative methods available that can achieve the same results but are less risky for those taking part.[45] Stawser claims that this is uncontroversial and, on the face of it, it is difficult to disagree with this assessment (although I will attempt to do so below).

Conclusions

All things being equal, such standoff precision military technologies do indeed appear to offer some genuine comfort to those concerned with protecting civilians in situations of violent conflict. In terms of precision, numbers of weapons employed, a reduction in collateral damage, potential for improved outcomes through detached and rational decision making, accountability and a reduction in risks to our own forces as well, it is easy to see that there are potentially some real advantages when it comes to reducing risks for nearly everyone concerned. There is, however, an issue in the way that standoff weapons might be used that means that all things are not equal. An over-reliance on remote killing can create a dangerous perception in both parties that might undermine all of those other advantages and put more civilians at risk in the long run. As suggested above, the lowering of political risk that standoff weapons offer political leaders means that they are able to consider employing military force in situations where public support would simply have made such decisions impossible in the past. Kosovo in 1999 is a case in point and, while it is still unfolding as I write this chapter, the coalition operations to police a no-fly zone and degrade Muammar Gaddafi's ability to harm Libyan civilians seems to be another. Both were initiated against a backdrop of political promises of 'no boots on the ground'.[46]

Is, however, this lowering of the political threshold in employing lethal force actually a good thing? Can one imagine President Obama promising to engage

---

45   B.J. Strawser, 'Moral Predators: The Duty to Employ Uninhabited Aerial Vehicles', *Journal of Military Ethics*, 9/4 (2010): 342–68.

46   Paul Richter, 'U.N. Security Council Authorizes Action Against Moammar Kadafi', *Los Angeles Times*, 18 March 2011, http://articles.latimes.com/2011/mar/18/world/la-fg-un-libya-20110318

terrorists in Pakistan with or without the support of the Pakistan Government if it still required squadrons and squadrons of aircraft, suppression of enemy air defences and so on? 'We're not really violating Pakistan's sovereignty; it's only a drone.' This attitude can lead to the promotion of wars in which there is no real moral commitment to the struggle. As was darkly joked in 1999 when NATO was willing to bomb to stop a massacre, but only as long as pilots were not put at risk by flying below 15,000 ft, 'the life of one NATO soldier is worth 20,000 Kosovars'.[47] 'Are we on the eve of a new age of "drive-by" wars, in which American power can strike anywhere, in near certainty that neither its civilians nor its soldiers will ever be put at risk?'[48]

The reduction or even elimination of risk offered by precision standoff means that it *is* easier to resort to the use force and this risks making what should be a tool of last resort a first or at least early response to any crisis. This has to be profoundly worrying. Strawser argues that even if this argument at first appears to be 'intuitively plausible', it ultimately fails as a valid objection because it does not negate the moral imperative to use UAVs or other standoff weapons when they are available and equally effective.[49] I accept that at the tactical and operational level there might indeed be a moral imperative to reduce the risk to our own personnel where it is possible to do so. It is indeed 'wrong to command someone to take on *unnecessary* potentially lethal risks in an effort to carry out a just action for some good'.[50] The very reduction in that risk might, however, actually contribute to failure at the strategic level resulting in the conclusion that taking some risk might be necessary to achieve one's political aims. Why should the 'losing side' accept their defeat? Perhaps there is a lesson to be drawn from the experience of the Sunni Triangle in Iraq: 'the future hotbed of rebellion wasn't occupied until weeks after Baghdad fell in 2003, and local would-be insurgents instead got the signal that they had never been defeated.'[51] New generations of standoff weapons seem to demonstrate 'an ability to kill *but little or no willingness to die* for the West's causes'.[52] Technological advantages might actually be sending a message of a fundamental lack of resolve to see an issue through to the end. It is, after all, the 'willingness to take mortal risk [that] is what makes military deterrence believable'.[53] In Beirut, those on the receiving end of unmanned targeting and the 'all-seeing eye in the sky' saw the result as a 'spurring of mass identity politics ... as an antidote to the technology discrepancy ... they [Israelis and American] don't want to fight us like real men, but are afraid to fight. So we just have to kill a few of

---

47   Singer, *Wired for War*, p. 324.

48   Michael Ignatieff, 'To Fight But Not to Die', *The World Today*, February 2000, p. 21.

49   Strawser, *Moral Predators*, p. 358.

50   Ibid., p. 344.

51   Singer, *Wired for War*, p. 308.

52   Whetham, *Ethics, Law and Conflict*, p. 22.

53   Ignatieff, p. 23.

their soldiers to defeat them.'[54] It was not the bombing from above a safe distance of 15,000 ft that led to success in Kosovo, it was the eventual credible threat of substantial numbers of boots on the ground combined with real political pressure from the international community – a demonstration of both credible means and genuine resolve. We might well find ourselves getting into future situations more easily because of the apparent low cost of action only to find that we have started something that we do not have the stomach or the tools to finish.

The removal of our own military personnel from harm's way wherever possible might also have other implications for our own civilian population. Going further than just the risks about creating ambiguity over civilian status when having contractors or civilians involved in operating, maintaining or supplying standoff weapon systems, there is also the risk that the broader civilian population might themselves be seen as legitimate targets. It seems a small jump to go from targeting a family car carrying a UAV operator to work, to building a justification for attacking other civilian targets in a country. If it is impossible to hurt a state's military assets due to it relying on standoff tools, how does one fight back against that state? If there are no legitimate targets for you to strike, does that mean you may broaden the permitted range of targets if the stakes are high enough? Does this justify the breaking of the normal rules due to the creation of some sort of 'supreme emergency' where an effective response within the normal rules of *in bello* is simply impossible?

The term 'supreme emergency' was coined by Winston Churchill to depict the terrible situation that Britain found herself in early in 1941: faced with imminent invasion and with only RAF Bomber Command as an effective offensive weapon. There was little doubt regarding the terrible cost of defeat to the Nazi powers and the existential crisis was seen to justify using those bombers against the only target that could be struck given the limits of technology at the time: German cities and the German people.[55] This supreme emergency passed as other theatres of operation opened up, new allies joined the struggle, technology improved allowing more accurate targeting and, most importantly, the threat of the imminent invasion of Britain passed. As the emergency passed, the deliberate bombing of German civilians became increasingly difficult to justify on moral grounds (although, of course, it continued anyway).[56] The existential test for supreme emergency and the contentious leeway it offers is a very hard one to pass, if it can be passed at all, but it is easy to see how such arguments can be made to sound convincing to those who feel powerless in the face of overwhelming technological superiority. Once this feeling of impotence is combined with rhetoric that convinces a population that they are being 'exterminated' by a faceless enemy that is impossible to counter, taking the war to that enemy's undefended homeland and targeting the

---

54 Rami Khouri, an 'Arab moderate', quoted in Singer, *Wired for War*, pp. 308–9.

55 See Michael Walzer, *Just and Unjust Wars: A Moral Argument with Historical Illustrations* (New York: Basic Books, 2000), pp. 251–68.

56 See Grayling.

civilian population there in order to stop the attacks on your own homeland seem much easier to justify.

The lowering of the political threshold to using military force promoted by the ability to conduct standoff wars in a way that minimizes risks to non-combatants might well make the occurrence of war more frequent but also more difficult to resolve without the will to put our own people in harm's way. At the same time, getting involved more often in other people's affairs while relying overwhelmingly on military tools that reduce or eliminate risk to our combatants, ironically, might actually increase the risk to our own civilian population. Some see robots as our 'answer to the suicide bomber',[57] but what if a reliance on that remote approach to war becomes the very thing that inspires them?

---

57   US Navy researcher Bart Everett, quoted in Singer, *Wired for War*, p. 62.

Chapter 13
Discrimination and Non-Lethal Weapons: Issues for the Future Military

Stephen Coleman

Traditionally, the military might of a state was properly employed only in open warfare against the military power of another state. In more recent times, however, and particularly since the end of the Cold War, the military forces of a large number of states have been employed in a range of international operations other than war: in counterinsurgency operations on behalf of other states, in peacekeeping, peacemaking and peace-enforcement operations, in humanitarian interventions launched for the purpose of protecting the rights of civilians in other states, and so on. This new range of military operations has led to a number of difficulties for the military personnel involved, since the methods that they have been trained to employ and the pieces of equipment that they have been issued with and trained to use are designed for use in interstate warfare and not for modern irregular conflicts, for 'war amongst the people'.[1] These difficulties have led a large number of people to suggest (or even to demand) that military personnel be equipped with a range of non-lethal weapons that would allow them to act more appropriately in the situations they face when engaged in such operations. While there are many reasons why it might be attractive to equip military personnel with non-lethal weapons, I believe that there is also a range of issues involved with such a move; the aim of this discussion is to highlight some of these issues and, where possible, to suggest some ways in which they might be minimized.

The term 'non-lethal weapon' is itself rather controversial and in fact other terms have been used to describe the sorts of weapons that I will discuss. They have, for example, been described as 'soft-kill weapons', as 'less-than-lethal weapons', as 'sub-lethal weapons', and so on.[2] All of these terms are somewhat problematic for various reasons, chief of which is the fact that virtually any weapon can have lethal effects in some situations. In this discussion, I will use the term 'non-lethal weapons' (or NLWs) since it is a term in general use, while at the same time recognizing that the term itself is rather problematic. To be clear, in this discussion when I refer to

---

1   This term was coined by General Sir Rupert Smith. See Rupert Smith, *The Utility of Force: The Art of War in the Modern World* (London: Allen Lane, 2005) p. xiii.

2   See David A. Koplow, *Non-Lethal Weapons: The Law and Policy of Revolutionary Technologies for the Military and Law Enforcement* (Cambridge: Cambridge University Press, 2006), pp. 9–10.

NLWs I am using the term to describe weapons whose effects are intended to be temporary, relatively minor and reversible. Thus this definition includes weapons that are intended to have non-lethal effects but are known to be lethal if used in some circumstances, but it specifically excludes weapons that are intended to cause permanent damage of some sort, such as weapons intended to cause permanent blindness or weapons whose intended effect is to maim, but not kill, their target.

As I mentioned earlier, it is the manner in which military forces are now being used that has led for calls for them to be equipped with NLWs. There are many situations that modern military personnel face where their traditional military skills and equipment might not be appropriate. The operations undertaken by the military forces of the United States since the end of the Cold War are a good example of this. Over the past couple of decades, US forces have been engaged in a remarkable range of operations in a large number of different countries, very few of which can easily be characterized as traditional wars. In a lot of those situations, US personnel have been involved in operations where the protection of local civilians has been an imperative, such as in humanitarian interventions or so-called 'hearts and minds' campaigns. Such operations have sometimes involved an attempt to dramatically reduce the level of collateral damage produced by military attacks or even to eliminate collateral damage altogether. But despite the increased use of precision-guided munitions, reducing collateral damage is difficult when one is forced to rely on traditional methods of warfare, which are based on the use of firearms and explosives. During their overseas deployments, US military personnel have also been required to perform a number of tasks that, in the US domestic sphere, would be routinely undertaken by police officers, such as constructing and manning vehicular checkpoints, conducting house-by-house searches for individual persons of interest, detaining those suspected of having committed offences, and so on. Military personnel have often had difficulty carrying out such tasks effectively, which is perhaps unsurprising since the training and equipment given to the police who routinely carry out those tasks in other jurisdictions are quite different from the training and equipment of US military personnel.

The suggestion of the advocates of military use of NLWs is that issuing military personnel with such weapons would allow those personnel to take more appropriate actions in these types of situations, to give military personnel an option between 'shout' and 'shoot'. There are of course many situations that modern military personnel face where it does appear likely that NLWs would be useful. The many military checkpoints that were established by Western forces in Afghanistan after 2001 and in Iraq after 2003 provide good examples here. On many occasions the military personnel manning those road-blocking checkpoints were faced with a difficult choice when they observed a car speeding towards them. Was this car being driven by a suicide bomber, intending to crash into the checkpoint and detonate the vehicle, in which case the troops ought to shoot the car and stop it as soon as possible? Or was it simply being driven by a local civilian who, for one reason or another, had not realized they were required to stop, in which case the troops ought to hold their fire and hope that the driver would see the checkpoint and realize they had to stop? Having access to some NLWs, which would allow these personnel to stop the car some distance from the checkpoint – thus ensuring their own safety, without having to shoot (and thus risk harming) the occupants of the car if they were actually innocent civilians – would make such a choice much easier. In fact, NLWs would be useful for military personnel in any situation where it is difficult, for whatever reason, to distinguish between combatants and non-combatants, and checkpoints are simply one specific example of this type of problem. Another example of this sort of situation would be those times when enemy combatants effectively use non-combatants as human shields, either intentionally or non-intentionally. If the only response option for military personnel is lethal force then it is likely either that there will be a large number of collateral casualties or that the military personnel will simply be unable to defend themselves since the risk of collateral damage is so high. Having access to NLWs might enable military personnel to respond more effectively in such cases.[3]

There is a range of NLWs that might be (and in some cases, has been) issued to military personnel and research is being actively undertaken to develop more options as well. Examples of currently existing NLWs that could be of use to the military in some situations include:

- Flash-bang (stun) grenades, which as their name suggests are designed to produce a temporarily blinding flash and a stunning loud noise.[4]
- Dazzling laser devices, which are designed to disorientate or temporarily blind their target.[5]
- Chemical irritants and riot-control agents (RCAs), including tear gas and various forms of pepper spray, which are designed to cause irritation to the eyes and nasal passages, leading to temporary blinding, coughing and incapacitation.
- Non-lethal firearm rounds (for example, rubber bullets), which are designed to produce pain and bruising when fired at a person, but not to kill.
- Acoustic devices, which can emit an extraordinarily loud oscillating tone along a relatively focused beam, causing disorientation and nausea to those affected. Such devices can often also be used to deliver warning messages to suspect individuals at long ranges.

---

3   One other possibility, which I will not explore further here, is that NLWs might be used on autonomous military robots. The idea is that if such military robots are going to be deployed into the field where they will make targeting decisions without human involvement then it might be better to equip them with NLWs rather than with lethal weapons, so that if these robots make mistakes in targeting the results will not be as serious.

4   Flash-bangs are used by the military special forces of a number of countries.

5   Dazzling laser devices have been used by some military personnel, but mainly for the purposes of attracting attention (for example, to make a driver aware that they are approaching a checkpoint) rather than to incapacitate.

- Electro-muscular disruption devices (commonly known as Tasers though strictly speaking this is simply the name of the main company that manufactures such devices), which transmit an electric shock to the target, which temporarily interrupts the ability of the brain to control the muscles in the body.
- The Active Denial System, which is being developed by the US Department of Defense's Non-Lethal Weapons Program. The Active Denial System (ADS) is essentially a heat ray, mounted on the back of a truck or a Humvee, which 'projects a focused beam of millimeter waves to induce an intolerable heating sensation on an adversary's skin, repelling the individual with minimal risk of injury'.[6] As of the time of writing, the ADS had not been officially deployed, but had been tested through more than 11,000 exposures to the beam on more than 700 volunteers, including journalists and representatives of Human Rights Watch.[7] Attempts are apparently also under way to construct a lower-powered but human-portable version of the device.

General Problems with Non-lethal Weapon Use by the Military

While it seems obvious that there are quite a number of situations where the availability of a non-lethal option would be of benefit to modern military operations, I would argue that there are also a number of problems associated with the military use of these weapons. Some problems arise out of the nature of the weapons themselves; these can be problems either with NLWs in general or with a specific type of NLW. Other problems arise out of the way that NLWs might be used in the field, which again can be problems with NLWs in general or specific to a certain type of NLW. Some problems perhaps only arise out of a unique combination of the problems attributable to the actual weapons and problems attributable to the people who use them.

One of the more general problems for use of NLWs by the military is the fact that effective NLWs are not yet available for many situations where military personnel really need them. The military checkpoints in Iraq and Afghanistan, which I mentioned earlier, are a good example of this problem. While it would certainly be extremely helpful for military personnel to have access to NLWs that would be able to stop suspect vehicles a safe distance from such a checkpoint, such weapons do not yet exist. There are various devices that do exist that are capable of stopping vehicles, such as a range of different types of tyre spikes and arresting

---

6   From the web site of the US Department of Defense Joint Non-Lethal Weapons Directorate, https://www.jnlwp.usmc.mil/ads.asp
7   Ibid.

nettings and barriers,[8] however, most of these are designed either for use in police pursuits (and thus require personnel to deploy them immediately in front of the pursued vehicle when their use is required) or to minimize the damage caused by out-of-control vehicles by slowing these vehicles and thus preventing high-speed impacts. What is required at checkpoints is a device that can be activated with (at most) only a few seconds' notice that would safely stop a vehicle travelling at high speed. The best prospect for such a device is something that would stop a vehicle's engine by disabling all the onboard computers and other electronics,[9] but such a device is unlikely to be effective against older vehicles, making it much less useful in economically disadvantaged countries such as Iraq and Afghanistan where older vehicles are much more common than they are in more affluent Western countries.

Another problem for military use of NLWs is that this use might violate current international law in some circumstances. The 1993 Chemical Weapons Convention, for example, bans the use of riot-control agents as weapons of war,[10] though not for use in law enforcement, including domestic riot-control situations.[11] This situation was actually commented on by then Secretary of Defense Donald Rumsfeld, who complained in testimony to the House Armed Services Committee that 'in many instances our forces are allowed to shoot somebody and kill them, but they're not allowed to use a non-lethal riot control agent'.[12] It could perhaps be argued, however, that the use of RCAs is actually permitted in military operations short of war, such as operations launched for humanitarian purposes or peacekeeping, peacemaking and peace-enforcement operations. The reason the Chemical Weapons Convention bans the use of RCAs as a weapon of war is almost certainly due to another concern with the military use of NLWs – that these weapons might be used as lethal force multipliers rather than lethal force avoiders, that they might be used in combination with the use of lethal force thus increasing, rather than decreasing, the lethality of the military operations in which NLWs are used.

There are also issues for military use of NLWs with regard to the *jus in bello* considerations of discrimination and proportionality. Consider the issue of proportionality. Rumsfeld noted that it seems odd that military personnel may be allowed to shoot someone, but not use a non-lethal agent, and this certainly does seem counterintuitive, to say the least. So intuitively it might seem to be the

---

8   Some devices of this type are described in US Department of Defense Joint Non-Lethal Weapons Directorate, *Non-Lethal Weapons for Today's Operations: DoD Non-Lethal Weapons Program Annual Report 2010 & DOD Non-Lethal Weapons and Capabilities 2011* (Washington, DC, 2011), pp. 10–11, https://www.jnlwp.usmc.mil/public_affairs/annual_report.asp

9   Ibid., pp. 20–1.

10   *Convention on the Prohibition of the Development, Production, Stockpiling and Use of Chemical Weapons and on their Destruction* (1993), Art. 1, Point 5 ('Each State Party undertakes not to use riot control agents as a method of warfare').

11   Ibid., Art. 2, Point 9(d).

12   Quoted in Brad Knickerbocker, 'The Fuzzy Ethics of Nonlethal Weapons', *Christian Science Monitor*, 14 February 2003.

case that if it is considered proportional to shoot someone then it must also be proportional to use any non-lethal agent; if it is proportional to kill someone then it must also be proportional to use a weapon that is not intended to kill. The mere fact that a weapon is not intended to kill its target does not mean, however, that the weapon does no harm, and some weapons that are intended to have non-lethal effects have been banned by other international conventions on the grounds that the use of these weapons does actually cause disproportionate harm. The use of permanently blinding laser weapons, for example, has been banned under Protocol IV of the Convention on Certain Conventional Weapons;[13] these weapons are considered to cause disproportionate harm despite the fact that the effects of such weapons are non-lethal. Thus problems related to the proportionality of non-lethal weapons cannot simply be ignored; it cannot simply be assumed that all non-lethal weapons will meet the requirements of proportionality in any case where the use of lethal force would be considered to be proportional.

Even more serious with regard to the use of NLWs by military personnel are the problems with regard to discrimination. When the principle of discrimination is applied to the use of lethal force, it is always applied before the use of that force; military personnel are simply not permitted to deliberately target non-combatants. Many advocates of NLWs seem, however, to advocate their use in a manner that applies the principle of discrimination *after* the use of force rather than before. The following quotation from Michael Gross is a good example of this:

> Unlike the use of ordinary weapons, non-lethal weapons deliberately target civilian noncombatants so that the harm they suffer is no longer incidental but intentional. Targeting civilians in this way requires that one subject the principle of noncombatant immunity to a 'lesser evils' test that compares a small amount of intentional harm with a greater level of non-intentional harm that comes from using high explosives. If the former is significantly less than the latter, then there are moral grounds to targeting civilian noncombatants with non-lethal weapons.[14]

Unlike many of the other possible problems I have highlighted in this discussion, there is an actual example of indiscriminate use of NLWs that can be examined

---

13   The full name of this treaty is the *Convention on Prohibitions or Restrictions on the Use of Certain Conventional Weapons Which May Be Deemed to Be Excessively Injurious or to Have Indiscriminate Effects*. Since permanently blinding laser weapons are not by their nature indiscriminate, it is obvious that the reason for the inclusion of such weapons in this treaty is that they may be deemed to be 'excessively injurious' – that is, that they cause disproportionate harm to their targets. Protocol IV, regarding permanently blinding laser weapons, was adopted in October 1995.

14   Michael L. Gross, 'The Second Lebanon War: The Question of Proportionality and the Prospect of Non-Lethal Warfare', *Journal of Military Ethics*, 7 (2008): 1–22, at pp. 15–16.

here: the Russian response to the Moscow theatre siege.[15] On 23 October 2002, 40–50 armed Chechens, claiming allegiance to the militant Islamic separatist movement in Chechnya, seized control of a crowded theatre in Moscow, about 4 km south-east of the Kremlin. While some of those in the theatre managed to escape, the Chechens succeeded in securing some 850–900 hostages, threatening to kill these hostages unless Russian military forces immediately withdrew from Chechnya. During negotiations over the next few days, the Chechens released approximately 200 hostages, including children, pregnant women, foreigners and those requiring medical care, but the Chechens repeated their threat to start executing other hostages if their demands were not met. Early in the morning of Saturday 26 October, members of the Russian Federal Security Service surrounded and stormed the building, after first pumping a large quantity of a still unidentified aerosol anaesthetic into the theatre's ventilation system. This gas rendered many hostages and some of the Chechen hostage takers unconscious. After a fierce gun battle, the Special Forces blew open the front door and entered the auditorium, directly engaging those Chechens who remained conscious. None of the Chechens was taken alive. After regaining control of the theatre, the security forces began bringing out the dead and unconscious bodies of hostages who had been overcome by the gas. Almost all the hostages required medical care due to their inhalation of the gas, but those treating the hostages were not told what sort of gas had been used in the assault and apparently were not told that gas was even used until after the event and were thus completely unprepared for the mass casualties they had to treat. Two days after the siege ended, some 118 hostages had been confirmed dead and, of the 646 former hostages who remained hospitalized, 150 were still in intensive care and 45 were in critical condition. At least 33 of the hostage takers and 129 hostages died during the raid or over the following days. Despite official Russian Government claims that none of the hostages died due to poisoning, it appears that almost all of the hostages died as a result of exposure to the gas rather than from injuries sustained during the exchange of gunfire between the Chechen hostage takers and the Russian security forces.

The Russian Special Forces used NLWs in almost exactly the manner that Michael Gross has advocated. The Russian forces could have simply relied on conventional weapons when they decided to storm the theatre, and if they had done so it is highly likely that a number (possibly a very large number) of the hostages would have died, killed either directly by the hostage takers or by being caught in the crossfire. If such an assault is considered in purely military terms then it would appear to follow the principle of discrimination, since even if the

---

15 I recognize that it is open to debate as to whether or not this case actually illustrates the *military* use of NLWs, as it can certainly be argued that the Russian forces involved were not actually military personnel or even if they were that this was a law-enforcement situation and not a military one. Whether this is an actual example of military use of NLWs or not, I think it still serves as a good illustration of some of the issues that military use of NLWs might raise.

Russian forces killed some of the hostages in the process of assaulting the theatre, they would have been directly targeting only the Chechen hostage takers. What actually happened of course was that the Russian forces used a NLW, in the form of the anaesthetic gas that they pumped into the theatre's ventilation system. If the actual assault is considered in purely military terms then it seems to fail the principle of discrimination; since an anaesthetizing gas is an indiscriminate weapon, the best way to characterize the situation seems to be to say that all the occupants of the theatre were targeted by this NLW. While the intention in using NLWs is to decrease the overall level of harm, if NLWs are routinely used in an indiscriminate manner then it is perfectly possible that using NLWs might actually result in an *increased* overall level of harm.

As well as being a reasonable example of the problems that might be caused by lack of discrimination, the Russian response to the Moscow theatre siege is perhaps a good illustration of one of the other concerns about the use of NLWs, which I mentioned earlier: that NLWs might be used as lethal force multipliers. I noted in the case that when the Russian Special Forces stormed the theatre none of the Chechens was taken alive. This was despite the fact that some of the hostage takers were rendered unconscious by the gas in the same way that many of the hostages were. It appears that rather than taking these people into custody, the Russian Special Forces simply executed them while they were unconscious.

The Use and Testing of Non-lethal Weapons

One particular problem for the use of NLWs by military personnel relates to the differences in the way that NLWs are actually used in comparison with the way that they are tested. When NLWs are being developed, they are extensively tested. Such tests occur, however, on healthy individuals, with continual monitoring and in a controlled environment. The manufacturers of such weapons stress the various precautions that must be taken in order to use these weapons safely and when they start to advertise the weapons for sale such precautions will be an important part of the sales pitch. Even video clips that are released into the public domain in order to advertise these NLWs, and to emphasize how safe they are to use, will almost inevitably include warnings about safety requirements. For example, an official Taser video advertisement on YouTube ends with the following statement: 'WARNING: These demonstrations were performed under strict safety guidelines. Consult a certified TASER instructor for safety instructions before attempting any such tests.'[16] In the actual video, every person who is shot with a Taser falls onto a padded mat when they lose muscle control, is caught by another person so as to ensure they are not injured when they hit the ground, or both. Even when there is a desire to exhaustively test a new type of NLW, there will, however, still be various limits that might be imposed on those tests. So while the Active Denial System

---

16   Found at http://www.youtube.com/watch?v=cNpT-IZLC4A

might have been tested thousands of times on hundreds of different individuals, there are legal requirements at play that prevent it being tested on certain groups of people, such as children or people with a range of pre-existing medical conditions.[17]

Of course, when NLWs are actually used in the real world the situation is very, very different. While military personnel do not have a lot of access to NLWs at the moment, there are a lot of paramilitary organizations that do use NLWs, especially police forces and security companies. The NLWs used by such organizations are employed on people of varying levels of health and in an environment that is far from controlled. In the real world there are very rarely padded mats for people to fall on or other people around who will ensure that those targeted by NLWs will not hurt themselves. Nor are careful checks performed to ensure that the target of a NLW does not have a medical condition that will be exacerbated by the use of a particular non-lethal weapon. Thus it is no surprise that people have been killed after being targeted with NLWs, in some cases due to existing medical conditions that, had they been known, might have precluded the use of the particular weapon against that individual,[18] in other cases due to injuries sustained while falling.[19]

These problems are probably compounded by the fact that many organizations do not do a great deal to monitor the way that their employees actually use NLWs. If the use of NLWs is monitored, the level of scrutiny is inevitably at its highest when a particular type of NLW is first introduced. The level of detail that is recorded about the frequency and manner of use of NLWs almost inevitably declines as use of that particular type of NLW becomes accepted; this effect is most obvious in the records of many larger organizations such as the big police departments in the United States, the United Kingdom and Australia. A good example of the manner in which record-keeping standards for documented use of NLWs tend to decline over time can be seen with regard to the use of Oleoresin Capsicum (OC) spray in the Australian State of Victoria.[20] Oleoresin Capsicum spray was first introduced in 1998, when stringent records were kept of all uses. The Victorian Office of Police Integrity examined the use of OC spray in 2009. Police officers were still required to report uses of OC spray, but evidence collected in the inquiry

---

17   Panel discussion with Susan LeVine, Principal Deputy, Strategy and Policy, Department of Defense Joint Non-Lethal Weapons Directorate, at the 2010 McCain Conference of Service Academies, Annapolis, MD.

18   See Anthony Dowley and Matt Schultz, 'OC Spray Man Dies in Police Van on Way to Dandenong Police Station', *Herald Sun*, 22 December 2009.

19   Inman Morales died after being shot with a Taser by members of the New York Police Department and falling, head first, more than 3 m to the pavement below. See 'Statement From the New York City Police Department', *The New York Times*, 25 September 2008.

20   Police services in Australia are organized rather differently than is the case in countries such as the United States. Rather than having different police departments for each city or county, each Australian State has one police force that provides law enforcement across the entire State; thus Australian police departments are among the largest in the English-speaking world. The State of Victoria has a population of more than 5 million and its police force employs more than 11,000 sworn officers.

suggested the possibility of massive under-reporting in some regions. The inquiry examined, amongst a mass of other data collected, records regarding the use of force by officers from six individual police stations, which included both the number of reported uses of OC spray and the amount of OC spray ordered by the police station over a four-year period. The massive discrepancies shown in the ratio between the reported uses of OC spray and the quantity of OC spray ordered between the six stations studied suggested significant under-reporting of OC spray use. Ringwood Station, for example, ordered almost exactly the same quantity of OC spray as Werribee Station over the four-year period: 239 cans compared with 242. Ringwood, however, reported less than half the number of uses of OC spray as Werribee: 106 uses compared with 216.[21]

Another issue that often arises when NLWs are introduced is perhaps best characterized as a form of mission creep, in that the weapons are intended for use in certain cases – for example, as an alternative to the use of deadly force (sometimes described as an option between 'shout' and 'shoot') – but once they are available they are used in a much broader range of cases, such as to compel non-violent persons to comply with directions. Good examples of this phenomenon are the introduction of OC spray in the Australian State of Queensland[22] and the introduction of Tasers to police departments in the United States.

Oleoresin Capsicum spray was issued to general-duties police officers in Queensland in 2000 following a successful one-year trial by specialist police. At the time, this was sold to the public as an important step since it would give police an alternative to the use of deadly force. This introduction was a voluntary one and was not forced upon the Queensland Government and police by a public outcry over a spate of police shootings; there had been a total of 25 police shootings across the whole of Australia in the previous five years.[23] Given that OC spray had been explicitly introduced as an alternative to the use of deadly force one might expect that the spray would be used in only a few cases a year – that is, those where police officers would have resorted to the use of a firearm if OC spray had not been available. This was, however, clearly not the case. Between January 2001 and December 2002, Queensland police officers reported use of OC spray on 2,226 occasions.[24] According to an analysis of a representative sample of those cases, the target of the OC spray was armed in about only 15 per cent of

---

21   See Office of Police Integrity, *Review of the Use of Force By and Against Victorian Police* (Melbourne: Government of Victoria, 2009), p. 42.

22   Queensland has a population of more than 4.5 million people and its police service employs more than 10,000 sworn officers.

23   This includes people who were shot by police and people who shot themselves in the presence of police from 1995 to 1999. See Jane Curnow and Jacqueline Joudo Larsen, *Deaths in Custody in Australia: National Deaths in Custody Program 2007* (Canberra: Australian Institute of Criminology, 2009), p. 51.

24   Crime and Misconduct Commission, *OC Spray: Oleoresin Capsicum (OC) Spray Use by Queensland Police* (Brisbane: Government of Queensland, 2005), p. 14.

cases.[25] In fact, as was made clear in a study conducted by the Queensland Crime and Misconduct Commission, despite the fact that OC spray had apparently been introduced for use only as an alternative to the use of lethal force, the spray was being used routinely to deal with a large number of violent and potentially violent offenders, whether or not they were actually armed. In addition, the spray was often being used on those who were simply non-compliant, as opposed to actually being violent. In simple terms, this NLW had been introduced for police to use in one specific, and indeed very uncommon, situation but having been found to be effective it was now being used in a large number of other situations.

If the intention was to limit the use of OC spray to those situations where lethal force would otherwise have been used then this ought to be reflected in the guidelines for the use of this weapon. The *Queensland Police Operational Procedures Manual* makes it very clear, however, that the use of OC spray is not limited to those situations.[26] In fact, the guidelines for the use of OC spray do not limit its use to cases where it is an alternative to the use of deadly force or even to cases were OC spray is an alternative to the use of other types of non-deadly force, but allow its use in some situations where police, prior to its introduction, might well have resolved the situation without resorting to the use of force at all. Even in situations where the use of OC spray might be thought to be contraindicated, the manual does not actually forbid its use, but rather 'strongly discourages the use of OC spray in certain circumstances'.[27] Such circumstances include using OC spray:

- against people offering passive resistance (for example, sitting down and refusing to comply with instructions);
- as a crowd-control measure (for example, for crowd dispersal at a demonstration or industrial dispute);
- against the driver or occupants of a vehicle where there is a danger of the vehicle going out of control and injuring the occupants or other people;

---

25   Ibid., pp. 26–8. Even in cases where the subject was armed, in only 3 per cent of cases was this with a firearm – that is, less than 0.5 per cent of all uses of OC spray in this period were directed at a suspect armed with a gun.

26   According to the *Queensland Police Operational Procedures Manual*, examples of situations where it is considered appropriate to use OC spray include the following:

- incidents where police officers are required to defend themselves or other people if they fear physical injury to themselves or others and they cannot reasonably protect themselves or others less forcefully;
- arrest situations, if they believe on reasonable grounds that the offender poses a threat of physical injury and the arrest cannot be effected less forcefully;
- incidents where a person is acting in a manner likely to seriously injure themselves and the incident cannot be resolved less forcefully;
- to deter attacking dogs.

Quoted in Crime and Misconduct Commission, p. 4.

27   Ibid.

- against juveniles, except in extreme circumstances where there is no other reasonable option to avoid the imminent risk of injury.

Some of these situations are particularly problematic. The use of any form of violence at all could be deemed to be an excessive use of force when dealing with passive protests, for example. At the other end of the spectrum, far from being an alternative to the use of deadly force, using OC spray might actually *be* a use of deadly force if the spray is used against the driver of a vehicle in cases where it is reasonably foreseeable that they might crash the vehicle and fatally injure themselves or other occupants of the vehicle. Overall, these instructions do make it clear that despite the fact that OC spray was introduced as an alternative to the use of lethal force, its perceived effectiveness in a wide range of cases meant that its 'mission' was rapidly broadened to allow its use in a host of other situations beyond this original application.[28]

The widespread use of Taser weapons by police in various jurisdictions in the United States seems to be another example of this phenomenon. As was the case in Queensland, in the United States this type of NLW was usually introduced to provide an additional option to police, especially to give them an alternative to the use of deadly force. Given the number of different police departments in the United States that now use these weapons it is obviously impossible to provide any sort of overview of the ways in which they are used. It is, however, a relatively simple matter to find examples of situations where police officers in the United States have resorted to the use of the Taser despite it being clear that there is no risk of violence against anyone, yet where this use has been considered justified under the local police regulations for use of the weapon. This includes cases such as the use of a Taser on:

- a diminutive seventy-two-year-old woman who argued with a police officer after being pulled over for speeding in Texas in June 2009;[29]
- a fan who ran onto the field during a break in a major league baseball game in Philadelphia and waved a towel to the cheering crowd while attempting to run away from security staff in June 2010;[30]

---

28   Being sprayed with OC can be quite painful, especially if a significant quantity of the spray gets into the victim's eyes or if there is a delay in providing post-spray care (that is, washing the OC spray out of the eyes and off the face of the victim). Given this fact it is obviously possible for OC spray to be misused, as would be the case if a police officer were to use it as a punishment inflicted upon a fully restrained person. The cases I am discussing here, however, are not cases of this type, but rather are ones where the use of OC spray is seen to be both legal and justified, despite the fact that OC spray is now being used in a huge range of situations where the use of firearms would not even be remotely considered.

29   See Jerome Tuccille, 'Texas Cop Tasers Great-Grandmother', *Examiner*, 2 June 2009, http://www.examiner.com/civil-liberties-in-national/texas-cop-tasers-great-grandmother

30   See http://www.cbsnews.com/video/watch/?id=6461150n

• a twelve-year-old girl who tried to run away from a police officer in Miami in November 2004 – a case that is especially notable since the officer stated that he never had any intention of actually arresting the girl.[31]

Police associations and police departments often argue in favour of the introduction of new NLWs on the grounds that increased options will reduce the likelihood of police officers needing to use deadly force and thus will reduce the level of risk of harm faced by members of the community. The procedures for the use of these NLWs suggest, however, that in many cases the concern is not so much about reducing the level of risk faced by those the police are dealing with as reducing the level of risk to which the police officers themselves are exposed.[32] It is significant to note that while the availability of such NLWs might actually reduce the level of risk faced by police officers, the availability of NLWs simultaneously reduces the perceived level of risk to which such officers can acceptably be exposed. In simple terms, the availability of a particular NLW leads to an imperative to use it, often in a much wider range of circumstances than was intended when that NLW was originally issued. Thus NLWs come to be used in situations that would previously have been resolved with the use of less force or even without the use of any force at all. Reviews of the misuse of the various types of NLWs available to police officers also suggest that the more inexperienced and/ or less highly trained an officer is, the more likely they are to either use NLWs inappropriately or resort to the use of NLWs before such use is really necessary.[33]

Conclusions

Though a number of people have called for military personnel to be issued with NLWs, at the moment such personnel have few, if any, NLWs to call upon. The lessons learned from the use of NLWs in other areas, such as by police forces around the world, can, however, quite reasonably be applied to the situations

---

31   http://articles.cnn.com/2004-11-14/us/children.tasers_1_taser-international-police-car-officers?_s=PM:US

32   One of the aims of the study of the use of OC spray by Queensland Police was to see if the introduction of OC spray had reduced the number of injuries suffered by police. While the study concluded that there was no statistical evidence to suggest that the use of OC spray had reduced the number of assaults on police or the number of injuries suffered by police, it also noted that officers *believed* that the introduction of OC spray had reduced the injuries suffered by police. Crime and Misconduct Commission, p. xi.

33   See, for example, Crime and Misconduct Commission; NSW Ombudsman, *The Use of Taser Weapons by New South Wales Police Force* (Sydney: Government of New South Wales, 2008); Office of Police Integrity, *Review of the Use of Force By and Against Victorian Police* (Melbourne: Government of Victoria, 2009); and Federation of Community Legal Centres, *Taser Trap: Is Victoria Falling for It?* (Melbourne), http://www.communitylaw.org.au/cb_pages/taser_trap_.php

likely to be faced by military personnel who might be armed with NLWs in the future, especially since the situations in which military personnel are most likely to be equipped with NLWs (that is, in counterinsurgency, peacekeeping and humanitarian operations and the like) are themselves very similar to the situations often faced by police officers in domestic law-enforcement contexts. With these thoughts in mind, it seems reasonable to engage in a little 'crystal-ball gazing' and predict some of the likely results of issuing military personnel with NLWs.

I think it is highly likely that if reliable long-range NLWs (that is, suitable for use at military checkpoints and so on) are developed and if such NLWs are routinely issued to general military personnel then they will be used on a routine basis. Specifically, these NLWs will *not* be used only in situations where those personnel might open fire if NLWs were not available, but instead they will be used far more often than firearms would have been. To suggest than NLWs might be used hundreds of times more often than firearms currently are in such situations does not seem at all unreasonable; psychologically speaking, it is obviously going to be much easier for military personnel to open fire with a NLW than with a firearm, simply because the effects of NLWs are not intended, or expected, to be lethal. Given this fact, it is reasonable to conclude that the willingness to use such NLWs will actually lead to civilian deaths that could have (and perhaps should have) been avoided.

I also think that if relatively reliable anaesthetizing NLWs are developed at some stage in the future then this type of NLW might well be used on civilian populations in a relatively indiscriminate manner, in violation of current principles of non-combatant immunity but in line with the suggestions made by writers such as Michael Gross. This is particularly likely to occur in situations where military personnel know that enemy forces are present, but these forces are hidden within large civilian populations. If this sort of use of NLWs does occur then it is also likely that the overall level of harm caused to those civilian populations by such operations will actually be higher than current operations using conventional weapons. In actions against enemy forces, such NLWs are also likely to be used as lethal force multipliers, as occurred in the Moscow theatre case.

The last point I would like to make is perhaps an obvious one, but is nonetheless extremely important. Many companies around the world are engaged in various forms of research into NLWs and the holy grail of such research is to develop the perfect NLW – one whose effects are temporary and reversible without any medical intervention, but are unpleasant enough to ensure compliance with the directions of the user. Groups such as Amnesty International already worry about the potential for existing NLWs to be used for purposes such as torture,[34] so it should never be forgotten that the perfect NLW is also likely to be perfect for abuse, enabling painful punishment to be inflicted on the victim by an unscrupulous

---

34   See, for example, Amnesty International, *Amnesty International's Concerns About Taser Use: Statement to the US Justice Department Inquiry into Deaths in Custody* (London, 1 October 2007), http://www.amnesty.org/en/library/info/AMR51/151/2007/en

user with minimal risk of detection. Given the stressful situations that military personnel are often placed in, the risk to life and limb that they might face and the tendency of such personnel to dehumanize their enemies, it is a near certainty that some types of NLWs would be misused by military personnel if they were to be issued with them. This is one final reason to be wary about the use of NLWs by military personnel.

Chapter 14

Surviving in a War Zone: The Problem of Civilian Casualties in Afghanistan

William Maley

In August 1985, an Afghan woman in the vicinity of the northern city of Mazar-e Sharif had an encounter with a Soviet search party that no mother could ever be expected to forget: 'They asked me if I knew where the *mojahedin* were hiding. I had my little boy in my arms. I said I didn't know. So they took a *kalashnikov* and just shot my little boy in front of me.'[1] Twenty-five years later, 1 March 2011 proved to be a bad day for the village of Nanglam in the Afghan Province of Kunar. A group of young boys had been sent out to gather firewood to warm their houses against the bitter cold of winter. Nine of the boys did not make it back. They were mistaken for insurgents, NATO helicopters were soon hovering above them and, by the time the helicopters left, the boys were dead. 'Some of the dead bodies were really badly chopped up by the rockets', reported the uncle of one of the victims. 'The head of a child was missing. Others were missing limbs.'[2] NATO subsequently apologized for the mistake.[3] To some, the two cases might seem to have little in common. The slaying of the child in August 1985 was indubitably a war crime, whereas the deaths in March 2011 could be seen as the result of a horrible mistake. Yet somehow such neat distinctions fail to capture the emotional parallels between the two situations. In each case, the use of force left behind grieving and traumatized parents and relatives, and if the aim of counterinsurgency is to win hearts and minds, NATO in 2011 surely failed just as spectacularly as did the USSR in 1985.

Many will be familiar with Thomas Hobbes's[4] famous depiction of war in which the life of man is 'solitary, poore, nasty, brutish and short', but this is merely a modern version of what is a much more ancient insight. In the Old Testament Book of Isaiah, one finds a graphic depiction of an epoch of peril 'when the blast

---

1 Michael Barry, Johan Lagerfelt and Marie-Odile Terrenoire, 'International Humanitarian Enquiry Commission on Displaced Persons in Afghanistan', *Central Asian Survey*, 5/1 (1986): 65–99, at p. 95.

2 Alissa J. Rubin and Sangar Rahimi, 'Nine Afghan Boys Collecting Firewood Killed by NATO Helicopters', *The New York Times*, 2 March 2011.

3 Alissa J. Rubin, 'Afghan Leader Calls Apology in Boys' Deaths Insufficient', *The New York Times*, 6 March 2011.

4 Thomas Hobbes, *Leviathan* (Cambridge: Cambridge University Press, 1996), p. 89.

of the terrible ones is as a storm against the wall'.[5] To anyone who has lived in a war zone, the aptness of the image will be grimly apparent and, in recent times, few people have been as exposed to such blasts as have the people of Afghanistan. For more than three decades, civilian life has been blighted either by total disaster or by the apprehension – very deep and pervasive – that disaster lies just around the corner. The objective of this chapter is to explore some of the threats that war has posed for these people and to look at how they have contrived to survive in the midst of these threats. It is divided into six sections. The first section notes some of the legal and political ways of addressing civilian casualties in armed conflict. The second outlines the experiences of war and violence that afflicted Afghanistan in the period before 2001. The third seeks to paint a picture of the scale and character of civilian casualties and suffering in the ongoing conflict in Afghanistan and notes some of their complexities. The fourth section identifies some of the political consequences that civilian casualties have created. The fifth section offers some thoughts on how the problem of civilian casualties might be addressed. The final section offers some brief conclusions. The most important is that it is one thing to persuade oneself that the killing of civilians in certain circumstances might be defended under the laws of armed conflict; it is another thing altogether to sell this idea to the population from which the victims are drawn. In some situations, any apology might be simply too late.

Dealing with Civilian Casualties

The lives and safety of civilians can be threatened in diverse ways and these are mirrored in diverse forms of response. One of the classic forms of threat is that posed by interstate war. In the post-1945 era, the Charter of the United Nations has provided the key framework for responding to this threat. It prohibits the threat or use of force unless the Security Council authorizes action under Chapter VII of the UN Charter or such force is used in exercise of the inherent right of individual or collective self-defence recognized in Article 51.[6] To the extent that these provisions act to avert the outbreak of war, civilians undoubtedly benefit from them. They do not, however, provide a perfect solution to the problem of aggression, since in some cases the aggressor might be a permanent member

---

5   Isaiah 25:4, as cited in A.L. Burns, 'Injustice and Evil in the Politics of the Powers', in Ralph Pettman (ed.), *Moral Claims in World Affairs* (Canberra: Australian National University Press, 1979), pp. 115–27, at p. 124.

6   See Ian Brownlie, *International Law and the Use of Force by States* (London: Oxford University Press, 1963); Thomas M. Franck, *Recourse to Force: State Action Against Threats and Armed Attacks* (Cambridge: Cambridge University Press, 2002); Christine Gray, *International Law and the Use of Force* (Oxford: Oxford University Press, 2008); Lindsay Moir, *Reappraising the Resort to Force: International Law, Jus ad Bellum and the War on Terror* (Oxford: Hart Publishing, 2010).

of the Security Council with a right of veto – as was the case when the Soviet Union invaded Afghanistan in December 1979. A second form of threat arises from mass-casualty atrocities. These can occur in the context of interstate war – the activities of the German *Einsatzgruppen* in the USSR after June 1941 and the Holocaust more broadly come to mind. They can also occur, however, in the context of genocide or politicide *within* states, in which membership of a particular political or social group becomes the basis for indiscriminate and large-scale slaughter. In the past, the risks for civilians from such slaughter underpinned doctrines of humanitarian intervention. But for more than a decade, these have been sidelined by the more sophisticated doctrine of the 'Responsibility to Protect' (R2P) – initially articulated in the 2001 report of the International Commission on Intervention and State Sovereignty and now further elaborated as a result of high-level deliberations between states. The doctrine is concerned with mass killings or 'ethnic cleansing', actual or apprehended, and can be disaggregated into responsibilities to prevent, to react and to rebuild.[7]

Where one's focus is punishment for crime that has already been committed, the appropriate response might be through the bodies of law that deal with 'crimes against humanity' and war crimes. These bodies of law reflect the longstanding existence of legal constraints on how war should be waged,[8] although the complexity of the legal landscape should not be underestimated.[9] The notion of crimes against humanity originated with the 1945–46 Nuremberg Trials and typically refers to atrocities that originate in state policy.[10] Article 6(c) of the Charter of the International Military Tribunal defined crimes against humanity as

> murder, extermination, enslavement, deportation, and other inhumane acts committed against any civilian population, before or during the war, or persecutions on political, racial or religious grounds in execution of or in connection with any crime within the jurisdiction of the Tribunal, whether or not in violation of the domestic law of the country where perpetrated.

---

7   See *The Responsibility to Protect: Report of the International Commission on Intervention and State Sovereignty* (Ottawa: International Development Research Centre, 2001); Gareth Evans, *The Responsibility to Protect: Ending Mass Atrocity Crimes Once and For All* (Washington, DC: Brookings Institution Press, 2008); Alex J. Bellamy, *Responsibility to Protect: The Global Effort to End Mass Atrocities* (Cambridge: Polity Press, 2009); Alex J. Bellamy, *Global Politics and the Responsibility to Protect: From Words to Deeds* (New York: Routledge, 2011); Ramesh Thakur, *The Responsibility to Protect: Norms, Laws and the Use of Force in International Politics* (New York: Routledge, 2011).

8   See Frits Kalshoven, *Constraints on the Waging of War* (Geneva: International Committee of the Red Cross, 1991).

9   See Gerry Simpson, *Law, War and Crime: War Crimes Trials and the Reinvention of International Law* (Cambridge: Polity Press, 2007).

10   See Telford Taylor, *The Anatomy of the Nuremberg Trials* (New York: Alfred A. Knopf, 1993); Geoffrey Robertson, *Crimes Against Humanity: The Struggle for Global Justice* (Melbourne: Penguin, 2006).

War crimes, in contrast, need not be mass-casualty offences at all. The most obvious form of war crime is the deliberate slaying of a civilian. Particular protections for civilians are contained in Section I of Part IV of the First 1977 Protocol Additional to the Geneva Conventions of 12 August 1949, and most scholars now accept these provisions also as codifications of customary international law.[11] The protections provided to civilians are not, however, absolute. While deliberate targeting of civilians is prohibited, incidental harm as some other legitimate objective is being pursued ('collateral damage') is permissible in certain circumstances.[12] It is also the case that there are defences that may be legitimately mounted such as mistake of fact, mistake of law, duress, insanity, intoxication or legitimate defence of oneself or others.[13]

The frameworks for responding to threats to civilians that I have discussed so far have been largely Western in origin, although those who initially formulated the responsibility-to-protect doctrine from the outset emphasized its wider pertinence and sought to reassure non-Western audiences that it is not a disguised excuse for renewed colonial domination. The influence on the laws of armed conflict of the *jus in bello* dimension of just-war theory is very obvious. From the point of view of ordinary Afghans, however, there is a different body of principles – namely, those derived from the Islamic faith – that might enjoy stronger claims to legitimacy. The parallels between Christian and Islamic views on the just conduct of war are rather striking. The Koran (2:190) instructs those fighting in the way of God not to 'transgress' (*wala ta t'adu*), which implies boundaries to what kind of actions are deemed legitimate. Hallaq notes that:

> The great majority of jurists espouse the opinion that it is strictly forbidden to kill anyone who cannot fight, or is not trained in the use of weapons, such as women, children, farmers, the handicapped, the elderly, the chronically ill, hermaphrodites, monks and all 'church folk' of the monastic kind.[14]

Alia Brahimi has gone so far as to suggest that 'non-combatant immunity is a staple constituent of the Islamic tradition which is, in its recurring formulations, absolute'.[15] This goes too far; as in the Christian tradition, the prohibition is *not*

---

11   See Jean-Marie Henckaerts and Louise Doswald-Beck, *Customary International Humanitarian Law. Volume I: Rules* (Cambridge: Cambridge University Press, 2005), pp. 3–76.

12   See Judith Gardam, *Necessity, Proportionality and the Use of Force by States* (Cambridge: Cambridge University Press, 2004), pp. 85–137.

13   See Yoram Dinstein, *The Conduct of Hostilities Under the Law of International Armed Conflict* (Cambridge: Cambridge University Press, 2004), pp. 244–9.

14   Wael B. Hallaq, *Shari'a: Theory, Practice, Transformations* (Cambridge: Cambridge University Press, 2009), pp. 328–9.

15   Alia Brahimi, *Jihad and Just War in the War on Terror* (Oxford: Oxford University Press, 2010), p. 188.

absolute[16] and the ethic one sees in play is a limited consequentialism rather than something strictly deontological. What is important to note, however, is that the means of dissemination of these ideas in a country such as Afghanistan differ radically from the ways in which principles of international humanitarian law are disseminated to Western militaries. In Afghanistan, most villagers learn about their religion from mullahs and from elders within a lineage structure. Islam is a way of life,[17] not an elaborate doctrine, and the subtleties that might make deaths of children religiously acceptable in certain circumstances are unlikely to have percolated down from the arcane heights of medieval jurisprudence. It is much more likely that such civilian casualties will fuel the perception that the perpetrators are un-Islamic.

War and Violence in Afghanistan Before 2001

Civilian casualties in war are nothing new to Afghanistan. It has now endured well more than 30 years of serious strife and the cumulative human consequences have been horrendous. Very few families can have been left untouched over this time, whether through direct experience of death or injury or the less direct but nonetheless significant consequences of disability, displacement or loss of social capital. At one level one might think that people are by now inured to suffering, but such a conclusion is profoundly superficial. While Afghan languages are not rich in vocabulary to convey the effects of trauma and depression,[18] they remain major problems, either palpably or just below the surface of social life.

One of the reasons we know so much about civilian suffering during the period before the overthrow of the Taliban regime is that a range of individuals and agencies was indefatigably involved in gathering testimony about atrocities and human rights violations and presenting it in accessible form. In the mid-1980s, the United Nations appointed an Austrian lawyer, Professor Felix Ermacora, as its Special Rapporteur on Human Rights in Afghanistan, and, while for years he was denied access to the country, his reports stand up well despite the passage of time.[19] Asia Watch also commissioned a number of detailed reports – usefully brought

---

16   John Kelsay, *Arguing the Just War in Islam* (Cambridge, Mass.: Harvard University Press, 2007), pp. 107–9.

17   See Thomas J. Barfield, 'An Islamic State is a State Run by Good Muslims: Religion as a Way of Life and Not an Ideology in Afghanistan', in Robert W. Hefner (ed.), *Remaking Muslim Politics: Pluralism, Contestation, Democratization* (Princeton, NJ: Princeton University Press, 2005), pp. 213–39.

18   See Rafiq Waziri, 'Symptomatology of Depressive Illness in Afghanistan', *American Journal of Psychiatry*, 130/2 (1973): 213–17.

19   See *Situation of Human Rights in Afghanistan*, A/41/778 (New York: UN General Assembly, 9 January 1987); *Report on the Situation of Human Rights in Afghanistan*, A/42/667 (New York: UN General Assembly, 23 October 1987); *Report on the Situation of Human Rights in Afghanistan*, A/43/742 (New York: UN General Assembly, 24 October

together in a book by the two main authors, Jeri Laber and Barnett R. Rubin.[20] And bodies such as Amnesty International played important roles in highlighting the persecution of particular individuals. Beyond these circles of analysts concerned with human rights issues was a wider network of engaged individuals. Doctors from French organizations such as Médecins sans Frontières and Médecins du Monde bore witness to what they had seen in the areas of Afghanistan where they worked covertly to support vulnerable communities and one French doctor penned a searing account of his captivity at the hands of the communist regime.[21] Given the exigencies of the Cold War, much of this testimony reached a wide audience. This was much less the case after 1992, but one effect of the relentless scrutiny of these issues was that a new generation of Afghans emerged highly sensitized to the importance of documenting and reporting human rights violations and civilian casualties. This has very much assisted the highlighting of civilian casualties in the years since 2001.

The time of most extensive suffering was undoubtedly the communist period, inaugurated by a Marxist coup in April 1978 and terminated by the collapse of the communist regime in April 1992.[22] For much of this period, Afghanistan was occupied by Soviet forces, which invaded the country in December 1979 and, following change in leadership in Moscow, finally withdrew in February 1989. It was not long before credible evidence surfaced of atrocities carried out by the communist forces and over time this only mounted. Even before the Soviet invasion, the regime had proven itself more than willing to resort to terror. An example from Kabul itself brings this out. On 23 June 1979, there was a revolt in the Hazara quarter of Kabul. Troops fired on the protesters and a gruesome reprisal took place: 300 Hazaras were trucked to a field outside Kabul, where half were buried alive with a bulldozer and the other half drenched with gasoline and set on fire.[23] The Soviet invasion added seriously to the dangers for civilians, since clearing populations on which the Afghan resistance (*Mujahideen*) could rely became a key element of Soviet tactics. One manifestation of this came in the form of huge refugee outflows, in particular to Pakistan and Iran. By 1 January 1990, out of a pre-war population estimated at 13.05 million, an estimated 6.2 million Afghans

---

1988); and *Report on the Situation of Human Rights in Afghanistan*, A/44/669 (New York: UN General Assembly, 30 October 1989).

20   Jeri Laber and Barnett R. Rubin, *'A Nation is Dying': Afghanistan Under the Soviets 1979–87* (Evanston, Ill.: Northwestern University Press, 1988).

21   Philippe Augoyard, *La prison pour délit d'espoir: médecin en Afghanistan* (Paris: Flammarion, 1985).

22   For a more detailed discussion, see William Maley, 'Social Dynamics and the Disutility of Terror: Afghanistan, 1978–1989', in P. Timothy Bushnell, Vladimir Shlapentokh, Christopher K. Vanderpool and Jeyaratnam Sundram (eds), *State Organized Terror: The Case of Violent Internal Repression* (Boulder, Colo.: Westview Press, 1991), pp. 113–31.

23   Michael Barry, 'Répressions et guerre soviétiques', *Les Temps Modernes*, July–August 1980, pp. 171–234, at p. 204.

were living outside the country as refugees.[24] While this might have served the Soviets' tactical interests, it is doubtful whether they benefited strategically, since the refugee camps in Pakistan became venues for the recruitment and training of new *Mujahideen*.[25] But the Soviet desire to clear territory also led to the deaths of vast numbers of civilians. While the course of the conflict varied over time,[26] the most detailed study of mortality in the 1980s concluded that 876,825 Afghans died unnaturally between 1978 and 1987.[27] This represented an average of more than 240 deaths *every day for 10 years straight* or 60 Afghan deaths for each Soviet soldier killed in Afghanistan. Many of these deaths involved violations of Common Article 3 of the 1949 Geneva Conventions and, arguably, provisions relating to armed conflict of an international character as well.[28]

The disintegration of the communist regime in April 1992 in the aftermath of the cessation of aid flows from the Soviet Union led to a new phase of conflict. On the one hand, in many rural areas the situation became far more stable than it had been for years: the UN Special Mission to Afghanistan concluded in a 1994 report that 'most of the country, at least two thirds, was at peace'.[29] This is worth highlighting, since the popular image of Afghanistan at this time was one of near-universal anarchy. On the other hand, since the state as a set of functioning institutions had largely collapsed, a ferocious struggle developed for Kabul as the main remaining symbol of state power. This struggle was itself widely misunderstood and often attributed to Afghanistan's complex and kaleidoscopic social structure. But as one acute observer noted: 'This new war's frequently shifting alliances give the impression of irrationality and chaos, but everything that has happened since 1992 has been the result of a rigorous political logic. The Afghan civil war is not "primitive" or "tribal," but strongly political.'[30] The Pakistan-backed Hezb-e Islami of Gulbuddin Hekmatyar – eager to deny any other *Mujahideen* parties the ability to rule smoothly – rocketed and shelled large parts of the city with

24 William Maley, *The Afghanistan Wars* (Basingstoke: Palgrave Macmillan, 2009), p. 60. For a detailed overview of the experiences of Afghan refugees, see Susanne Schmeidl and William Maley, 'The Case of the Afghan Refugee Population: Finding Durable Solutions in Contested Transitions', in Howard Adelman (ed.), *Protracted Displacement in Asia: No Place to Call Home* (Aldershot: Ashgate, 2008), pp. 131–79.

25 See Fiona Terry, *Condemned to Repeat?: The Paradox of Humanitarian Action* (Ithaca, NY: Cornell University Press, 2002).

26 See Larry P. Goodson, 'Periodicity and Intensity in the Afghan War', *Central Asian Survey*, 17/3 (1998): 471–88.

27 Noor Ahmad Khalidi, 'Afghanistan: Demographic Consequences of War, 1978–1987', *Central Asian Survey*, 10/3 (1991): 101–26.

28 See W. Michael Reisman and James Silk, 'Which Law Applies to the Afghan Conflict?', *American Journal of International Law*, 82/3 (1988): 459–86.

29 *Progress Report of the Special Mission to Afghanistan*, A/49/208, S/1994/766 (New York: United Nations, 1 July 1994), para. 13.

30 Gilles Dorronsoro, 'Afghanistan's Civil War', *Current History*, 84/588 (1995): 37–40, at p. 37.

weapons they had stockpiled during the 1980s for future use; and, in addition, street battles for control of different parts of Kabul occurred between groups such as the Shiite Hezb-e Wahdat, the Ittehad-e Islami of Abdul Rab al-Rasoul Sayyaf, the Shura-i Nazar led by Ahmad Shah Massoud and the Uzbek militia of General Abdul Rashid Dostam.[31] Amnesty International estimated that the total death toll of this period amounted to 25,000 people.[32] While this represented a daily average less than one-tenth of the daily average of unnatural deaths in Afghanistan for the period from 1978 to 1987, the psychological impact was enormous, not least because the civilian losses were concentrated in a relatively small urban area rather than spread across thousands of villages. Furthermore, the street fighting in Kabul on occasion resulted in shocking atrocities – notably, the Afshar massacre of February 1993 in which ethnic Hazaras were killed in large numbers by fighters from Sayyaf's militia.[33]

In September 1996, Kabul was seized by the Pakistan-backed Taliban movement, which had earlier taken over Kandahar (in 1994) and Herat (in 1995). Despairing that Hekmatyar's Hezb-e Islami would be able to occupy and hold territory, Pakistan had sought and found new tools in pursuit of a compliant Afghanistan next door.[34] The Taliban movement was (and is) a complex phenomenon, but it was not squeamish about the use of force against civilians.[35] The rigidly conservative attitudes to gender that its leaders held rapidly attracted international attention and made it a pariah,[36] but for all that women suffered under Taliban rule, ethnic and sectarian minorities were at greatest risk. In August 1998, Taliban forces carried out a massacre in Mazar-e Sharif that the writer Ahmed

31   For more detail, see Maley, *The Afghanistan Wars*, pp. 168–72.

32   *Afghanistan: International Responsibility for Human Rights Disaster*, ASA 11/09/95 (London: Amnesty International, 1995), p. 33.

33   See *Casting Shadows: War Crimes and Crimes Against Humanity: 1978–2001* (Kabul: The Afghanistan Justice Project, 2005), pp. 82–8; and *Blood-Stained Hands: Past Atrocities in Kabul and Afghanistan's Legacy of Impunity* (New York: Human Rights Watch, 2005), pp. 70–100.

34   See Anthony Davis, 'How the Taliban Became a Military Force', in William Maley (ed.), *Fundamentalism Reborn?: Afghanistan and the Taliban* (London: Hurst & Co., 1998), pp. 43–71.

35   See William Maley, 'Human Rights in Afghanistan', in Shahram Akbarzadeh and Benjamin MacQueen (eds), *Islam and Human Rights in Practice: Perspectives Across the Ummah* (New York: Routledge, 2008), pp. 89–107, at pp. 100–103.

36   *The Taliban's War on Women: A Health and Human Rights Crisis in Afghanistan* (Boston: Physicians for Human Rights, 1998); and *Women's Health and Human Rights in Afghanistan: A Population-Based Assessment* (Boston: Physicians for Human Rights, 2001). For a literary depiction of the position of women under the Taliban, see Khaled Hosseini, *A Thousand Splendid Suns* (London: Bloomsbury, 2007).

Rashid described as 'genocidal in its ferocity'.[37] Some of what happened was documented by the UN's Rupert Colville:[38]

> Some were shot on the streets. Many were executed in their own homes, after areas of the town known to be inhabited by their ethnic group had been systematically sealed off and searched. Some were boiled or asphyxiated to death after being left crammed inside sealed metal containers under a hot August sun. In at least one hospital, as many as 30 patients were shot as they lay helplessly in their beds. The bodies of many of the victims were left on the streets or in their houses as a stark warning to the city's remaining inhabitants. Horrified witnesses saw dogs tearing at the corpses, but were instructed over loudspeakers and by radio announcements not to remove or bury them.

A number of other Taliban massacres were documented in some detail – notably at Yakaolang in the Hazarajat region.[39] The tragedy for Afghanistan was that most of these massacres went unnoticed in the wider world. It took the 11 September 2001 terrorist attacks by Osama Bin Laden's al-Qaeda – a terrorist organization that had received shelter from the Taliban – to reclaim the attention of the wider world. The result was the US-led 'Operation Enduring Freedom' of October–December 2001. This overthrew the Taliban regime, but did not bring an end to conflict within the country.

Civilian Casualties in Contemporary Afghanistan

The post-Taliban period falls into roughly two phases where the issue of civilian casualties is concerned, the first being the initial phase of Operation Enduring Freedom, essentially from October to December 2001, and the second being the period of escalation of conflict from roughly 2007. There are no comprehensive data on civilian casualties in the October–December 2001 period; one estimate put the total at 3,767, but many uncertainties surround the figure.[40] The most one can say about this period is that the United States sought to comply strictly with the requirements of international humanitarian law, but questions could be raised

37   Ahmed Rashid, *Taliban: Militant Islam, Oil and Fundamentalism in Central Asia* (New Haven, Conn.: Yale University Press, 2000), p. 73.

38   Rupert Colville, 'One Massacre that Didn't Grab the World's Attention', *International Herald Tribune*, 7 August 1999. For further details, see *Afghanistan: The Massacre in Mazar-i Sharif* (New York: Human Rights Watch, 1998).

39   See *Afghanistan: Massacres in Yakaolang*, ASA 11/008/2001 (London: Amnesty International, 2001).

40   See Robert Cryer, 'The Fine Art of Friendship: *Jus in Bello* in Afghanistan', *Journal of Conflict and Security Law*, 7/1 (2002): 37–83, at p. 48.

about targeting from the air (with bombs twice having struck a compound of the International Committee of the Red Cross) and about the treatment of detainees.

For the period from 2007 onwards, much more detailed information is available, and while the data presented by different organizations vary at the margin, the broad pictures that they paint are similar.[41] In the following remarks, I focus for reasons of space on deaths, but this is not to diminish the significance of the sufferings of the injured, especially in a poor country that is not well placed to cope with disability. Of particular value is the Afghanistan Annual Report on Protection of Civilians in Armed Conflict.[42] The following table, drawn from the most recent issue, sets out basic data on civilian deaths over the past four years.

Table 14.1   Recorded number of civilian deaths in 2007, 2008, 2009 and 2010

	Total	Jan	Feb	Mar	Apr	May	Jun	Jul	Aug	Sep	Oct	Nov	Dec
2007	1523	50	45	104	85	147	253	218	138	155	80	160	88
2008	2118	56	168	122	136	164	172	323	341	162	194	176	104
2009	2412	141	149	129	128	271	236	198	333	336	162	165	164
2010	2777	173	197	198	211	166	322	312	350	207	290	171	180

Source: Afghanistan Annual Report 2010: Protection of Civilians in Armed Conflict, p. 57.

Several points stand out from this basic table. First, the trend of overall casualties has been upwards. The figure for 2010 is 82.3 per cent higher than the figure for 2007. This coincides with anecdotal evidence of a steady deterioration in the security environment over that period. Second, there is a distinctly seasonal pattern to the data. The winter months are safer and the summer months more dangerous, which is what one expects given that the heavy snows that blanket much of Afghanistan in winter act as something of an obstacle to all combatants.

Data are also available from a number of sources on the identity of those responsible for civilian casualties.

---

41   It should also be noted that obtaining comprehensive data on deaths in Afghanistan is very difficult since, in accordance with Islamic practice, the dead are buried quickly and deaths might go unreported, especially if they occur in remote areas at the hands of anti-government elements. It is also the case that not all victims of attack die immediately; some die later of their injuries. Furthermore, anti-personnel landmines (used by the USSR in the 1980s) and cluster munitions (used by the United States in 2001) have the potential to claim innocent civilian lives long after a particular engagement has concluded.

42   The most recent such report is *Afghanistan Annual Report 2010: Protection of Civilians in Armed Conflict* (Kabul: UN Assistance Mission in Afghanistan and Afghanistan Independent Human Rights Commission, March 2011).

Table 14.2   Recorded civilian deaths in 2010 by parties to the conflict and month

	Total	Jan	Feb	Mar	Apr	May	Jun	Jul	Aug	Sep	Oct	Nov	Dec
AGEs	2080	120	98	171	140	117	264	251	272	159	221	147	120
PGFs	440	40	81	11	38	22	35	21	48	41	51	13	39
Other	257	13	18	16	33	27	23	40	30	7	18	11	21

AGEs = Anti-Government Elements
PGFs = Pro-Government Forces

Source: Afghanistan Annual Report 2010: Protection of Civilians in Armed Conflict, p. 57.

These figures suggest 74.9 per cent of deaths were at the hands of anti-government elements (broadly the Taliban, the Hezb-e Islami and the 'Haqqani Network'), while 15.8 per cent were at the hands of pro-government forces and 10.3 per cent at the hands of others. The data collected by a significant Afghan organization, Afghanistan Rights Monitor, differ to some degree. Its most recent report concluded that of a total of 2,421 civilian deaths in 2010, 63 per cent were at the hands of anti-government elements, while 33 per cent were at the hands of pro-government elements and 4 per cent at unknown hands.[43] Nonetheless, both reports are at one in seeing the Taliban and their associates as responsible for the bulk of civilian deaths in Afghanistan.[44] Indeed, this has *consistently* been the case since 2006.[45] These results run counter to the popular perception that foreign forces are responsible for the bulk of civilian casualties, but they are not particularly surprising; Afghanistan Rights Monitor argues that 'Taliban and other AOG [armed opposition group] leaders believe that they have a divine-given right to kill, torture, imprison and violate the rights and freedoms of any Afghan citizen'.[46] The brutality of which these groups are capable is appalling. One recent

43   Afghanistan Rights Monitor, *ARM Annual Report: Civilian Casualties of War January–December 2010* (Kabul: Afghanistan Rights Monitor, February 2011), p. 6.

44   NATO, it should be noted, gives much lower figures for 2010: 1,178 killed by insurgents (85 per cent of the total) and 202 killed by US and Coalition forces (15 per cent of the total). Its figures, however, do not purport to be comprehensive: see Thom Shanker, 'Insurgents Kill Most Civilians, Military Says', *The New York Times*, 10 March 2011.

45   See Rebecca J. Barber, 'The Proportionality Equation: Balancing Military Objectives with Civilian Lives in the Armed Conflict in Afghanistan', *Journal of Conflict and Security Law*, 15/3 (2010): 467–500, at p. 472.

46   *ARM Annual Report*, p. 9. The Taliban has produced a code of conduct for their combatants: see Muhammad Munir, 'The *Layha* for the *Mujahideen*: An Analysis of the Code of Conduct for the Taliban Fighters Under Islamic law', *International Review of the Red Cross*, 93/881 (March 2011): 1–22. This code is at odds, however, with key principles of international humanitarian law, its Islamic credentials are exceedingly suspect and in any case there is little evidence that in practice the anti-government elements feel bound by it.

example was reported by Reuters newsagency. It gives a flavour of what ordinary Afghans in some parts of the country have had to face:[47]

> Afghanistan, June 25 (Reuters) – The bodies of 11 men, their heads cut off and placed next to them, have been found in a violent southern province of Afghanistan, a senior police official said on Friday. A police patrol discovered the bodies on Thursday in the Khas Uruzgan district of Uruzgan province, north of the Taliban stronghold of Kandahar, said police official Mohammad Gulab Wardak. 'This was the work of the Taliban. They beheaded these men because they were ethnic Hazaras and Shi'ite Muslims,' he said.

The Annual Report on Protection of Civilians in Armed Conflict sheds useful light on the specific causes of death. Of the 440 deaths attributable to pro-government forces, 171 (or 39 per cent) resulted from aerial attacks, 80 (or 18 per cent) resulted from searches and raids, 45 (or just more than 10 per cent) occurred in the course of force protection and 144 (33 per cent) had other causes.[48] The figure of 171 for deaths from aerial attacks represented a fall of 43 per cent from the comparable figure of 359 for 2009.[49] This seems to have resulted from a July 2009 Tactical Directive issued by the US Force Commander, General Stanley A. McChrystal, which in turn was updated by General David Petraeus on 1 August 2010, and represented a positive trend: the potential for innocent civilians to come to harm when air strikes are carried out is inevitably high.[50] The deaths at the hands of anti-government elements – 2,080 in total – had quite different causes. Some 904 (or 44 per cent) were caused by improvised explosive devices (IEDs); 462 (or 22 per cent) resulted from executions and assassinations; 237 (or 11 per cent) were caused by suicide attacks; and 477 resulted from other causes.[51] The role of IEDs is especially striking. Disgruntled Afghan villagers have not historically given vent to their grievances by planting bombs along the roadside and a recent report concluded that Afghan insurgents planted a staggering 14,661 IEDs during 2010.[52] This heightens the suspicion that the insurgents in Afghanistan are benefiting from a substantial, sophisticated and militarily professional support operation from circles in Pakistan – the country in which they find sanctuary.[53]

---

47   'Police Find 11 Beheaded Bodies in Afghan South', *Reuters*, 25 June 2010.

48   *Afghanistan Annual Report 2010*, p. 21.

49   *Afghanistan: Annual Report on Protection of Civilians in Armed Conflict, 2009* (Kabul: UNAMA Human Rights, January 2010), p. 17.

50   See *'Troops in Contact': Airstrikes and Civilian Deaths in Afghanistan* (New York: Human Rights Watch, September 2008).

51   *Afghanistan Annual Report 2010*, p. 2.

52   Craig Whitlock, 'Number of U.S. Casualties from Roadside Bombs in Afghanistan Skyrocketed from 2009 to 2010', *The Washington Post*, 25 January 2011.

53   In August 2007, during a visit to Kabul, Pakistani President, Pervez Musharraf, candidly stated that '[t]here is no doubt Afghan militants are supported from Pakistani soil. The problem that you have in your region is because support is provided from our side':

The data assembled in the Annual Report on Protection of Civilians in Armed Conflict point to striking *regional* variations. Some 1,310 deaths (47 per cent of the total) were recorded in the southern region and a further 513 (18 per cent of the total) in the south-east. There were 243 killed in the eastern region (almost 9 per cent). In the north and the north-east, there were 308 killed, or 11 per cent, and in the west there were 168, or 6 per cent.[54] These are entirely what we would expect given the location of conflict more broadly. Provinces in the southern region – Helmand, Kandahar, Nimroz, Uruzgan and Zabul – are the principal theatres of conflict between the different combatant parties. But the data also show striking gender variations. While the Annual Report does not give a breakdown of *deaths* by gender, it does provide a breakdown of *deaths and injuries*. This shows that female deaths and injuries came to 555, of a total of 7,120 – just 7.8 per cent of the total.[55] That more than 90 per cent of civilian casualties are male might in part reflect the impact of the seclusion of women (*purdah*), leaving them less exposed to IEDs and other risks associated with public places, but it might also reflect the specific targeting of males, who might be seen as future combatants whom it would be useful to eliminate. This would accord with evidence from other theatres that highlights the particular dangers faced by men and older boys.[56]

When one compares the level of civilian casualties today with that of the 1980s, it becomes clear that we are talking about two completely different eras. The mortality figure for the earlier period of more than 240 dead a day compares with just less than 8 a day in 2010. Another way of putting it is that daily deaths in 2010 were occurring at 3.3 per cent of the level at which they occurred during the Soviet occupation. At least in terms of this metric, any attempt to see what is occurring now as comparable with what occurred in the 1980s verges on the absurd. (Indeed, in 2007 – the last year for which relevant data are available – the number of deaths in armed conflict, 1,523, was easily exceeded by the number of road accident fatalities: 1,835.)[57] But to this, three important qualifications need to be attached. First, for individuals killed or injured in conflict or for their bereaved or distraught relatives there is little comfort in the claim that they were part of the few rather than part of the many. Second, even if civilian casualties are very low in absolute terms, one can still argue that they might have been indefensible if they arose from a situation in which the importance of the military objective

---

Taimoor Shah and Carlotta Gall, 'Afghan Rebels Find Aid in Pakistan, Musharraf Admits', *The New York Times*, 13 August 2007. See also Matt Waldman, *The Sun in the Sky: The Relationship Between Pakistan's ISI and Afghan Insurgents*, Discussion Paper No. 18, Crisis States Research Centre, London School of Economics and Political Science, June 2010.

54   *Afghanistan Annual Report 2010*, p. xi.

55   Ibid., pp. ii, 58.

56   See R. Charli Carpenter, *'Innocent Women and Children': Gender, Norms and the Protection of Civilians* (Aldershot: Ashgate, 2006).

57   *Global Status Report on Road Safety: Time for Action* (Geneva: World Health Organization, 2009), p. 49.

being pursued was not commensurate with the risks to which civilians were being exposed.[58] Third, depending upon the circumstances, even small numbers of civilian casualties might have dramatic political consequences, which can raise questions as to whether the tactical advantages that might flow from a particular operation actually outweigh the strategic disadvantages or dangers that can flow from civilians losing their lives or limbs as a result.

Political Consequences of Civilian Casualties

The potential political consequences of civilian casualties are complex, but one obvious one is tension between international forces and their formal local partner, Afghan President, Hamed Karzai. On a number of occasions, Karzai has spoken out forcefully when civilians have been killed or injured as a result of military actions. This has often been a source of frustration for the international actors, since President Karzai knows as well as anyone that in war, such casualties will inevitably occur from time to time. Yet his sensitivity on this issue is perfectly understandable. As an Afghan leader, he risks being held responsible for the activities of his allies. But there is a further factor at work here, too. In many respects, the empirical sovereignty of the Karzai administration is low; without the reinforcement provided by foreign forces and revenue from abroad, his government would be unlikely to survive for very long. Under such circumstances, to avoid the charge of simply being a puppet (along the lines of Shah Shuja in the nineteenth century), he has an incentive to make maximum use of his symbolic autonomy in areas where he can, such as the denunciation of actions that result in civilian casualties. This is something with which his backers (and the backers of any Afghan president) simply have to live.

A further political consequence of significance is disaffection in Afghanistan more broadly. Here, the picture is mixed. Survey evidence points more to concern about insecurity in general rather than civilian casualties *per se*; in 2010, when respondents in the Asia Foundation's annual poll were asked what was the most important failing of the central government in the previous two years, 21 per cent referred first to 'insecurity' and only 1 per cent to 'preventing civilian casualties'.[59] And in a broad sense it might be true that many Afghans do not see the problem of civilian casualties as troubling for them in the way that ambient insecurity is. Here, the emphasis that the Taliban has given in their propaganda to civilian casualties[60] might lead to the conclusion that if there is growing popular disaffection for the current dispensation then civilian casualties must have something to do with it.

---

58   See Barber, *passim*.

59   *Afghanistan in 2010: A Survey of the Afghan People* (Kabul: The Asia Foundation, 2010), pp. 206–207.

60   See *Taliban Propaganda: Winning the War of Words?*, Asia Report No. 158, International Crisis Group (Kabul and Brussels, 24 July 2008), pp. 19–20.

Such a conclusion is suspect without further evidence. Many other factors could also account for disaffection: poor governance, corruption, abuse of power, electoral fraud, even proposals to deal with the Taliban. Furthermore, not every civilian victim will win sympathy – for example, when a NATO airstrike near Kunduz on 4 September 2009 killed civilians who were seeking to extract fuel from a broken-down tanker, some Afghans scorned the victims as looters. But that said, if a sense becomes widespread that international forces have outstayed their welcome and that Afghanistan is an occupied country then civilian casualties become an aggravating factor of considerable severity.[61]

In addition, there can be powerful local effects of civilian casualties that add up to a serious political and military problem. In his book *The Accidental Guerrilla*, David Kilcullen has shown how local grievances can underpin insurgent activity.[62] This phenomenon was apparent in the 1980s; the writer Jan Goodwin quoted a young *mujahid*, who remarked: 'I died five years ago when I left Kabul. My soul has gone to heaven; this is just my body.'[63] When people lose family members to air strikes, it is hardly surprising if they join the ranks of the armed opposition. A detailed analysis by the Afghanistan Independent Human Rights Commission pointed to the danger of 'community backlash'.[64] Furthermore, a careful study of statistics on civilian casualties recently pointed to a 'revenge effect': the authors found that 'if the average ISAF [International Security Assistance Force]-caused incident, which resulted in 2 civilian casualties, was eliminated, then in an average-sized district there would be 6 fewer violent incidents between ISAF and insurgents … over the next 6 weeks'. They go on to argue that 'the data are consistent with the claim that civilian casualties are affecting future violence through increased recruitment into insurgent groups after a civilian casualty incident'.[65] Of course, guerrilla activity can occur for reasons other than civilian casualties – as has recently been apparent in northern and north-east Afghanistan[66] – but the danger

---

61   See Najibullah Lafraie, 'Resurgence of the Taliban Insurgency in Afghanistan: How and Why?', *International Politics*, 46/1 (2009): 102–13, at p. 111.

62   David Kilcullen, *The Accidental Guerrilla: Fighting Small Wars in the Midst of a Big One* (New York: Oxford University Press, 2009).

63   Jan Goodwin, *Caught in the Crossfire* (London: Macdonald, 1987), p. 175.

64   *From Hope to Fear: An Afghan Perspective on Operations of Pro-Government Forces in Afghanistan* (Kabul: Afghanistan Independent Human Rights Commission, December 2008), p. 11.

65   Luke N. Condra, Joseph H. Felter, Radha K. Iyengar and Jacob N. Shapiro, *The Effect of Civilian Casualties in Afghanistan and Iraq*, Working Paper 16152, National Bureau of Economic Research (Cambridge, Mass., July 2010), p. 3.

66   See Antonio Giustozzi and Christoph Reuter, *The Insurgents of the Afghan North: The Rise of the Taleban, the Self-Abandonment of the Afghan Government, and the Effects of ISAF's 'Capture and Kill Campaign'*, AAN Thematic Report 04/2011, Afghanistan Analysts Network (Kabul, May 2011). That insurgents can be active for diverse reasons was made clear when a range of Western medical personnel was murdered in August 2010 in Badakhshan, thitherto one of the quieter parts of the country: see William Maley,

that civilian casualties will prove a recruiting bonanza for the enemy should always be borne in mind. One final local factor relates to intelligence gathering. The Afghan population, if its sympathy can be maintained, is a most important source of information as to what is going on, but as one incisive analyst has put it: 'Why would an Afghan villager report on a Taliban presence in his village if he knew that would lead to ISAF operations with the strong possibility that 500 pound bombs could be dropped?'[67]

Finally, civilian casualties can have political effects beyond the immediate arena of operations, as US President Lyndon B. Johnson found to his cost in Vietnam ('Hey, hey, L.B.J./How many kids have you killed today?'). Peace groups will often point to civilian casualties as part of their efforts to de-legitimate involvement in a particular conflict and, on occasion, such advocacy can tap into a dispirited mood within the wider public, especially if conscripted soldiers are being used. That might not be all that likely at present in Afghanistan. The Afghan theatre of operations is far from most Western capitals, civilian casualties often occur in areas remote from where Western correspondents are based and as a result generate little or no footage and the Afghanistan commitment is nowhere near as controversial as was the Vietnamese. It was not a significant issue in the US mid-term congressional elections in 2010 and enjoys broad support in the US Congress, although with the death of Osama Bin Laden that could change if the situation in Afghanistan were to remain stalemated. But while the United States provides one external audience for what is happening in Afghanistan, its allies provide another, and civilian casualties might well undermine the commitment of European NATO states in particular to contribute. The fall of the Dutch Government in 2010 stands as a warning of what could happen elsewhere if images of mayhem and human suffering keep coming out of Afghanistan.[68]

Addressing the Problem of Civilian Casualties

From both moral and political perspectives, the problem of civilian casualties demands urgent attention, but it would be naïve to think that such an intractable problem can be solved by a magic solution. Nonetheless, there are various measures that can be contemplated that might be of assistance.

'Afghanistan in 2010: Continuing Governance Challenges and Faltering Security', *Asian Survey*, 51/1 (January–February 2011): 85–96, at p. 90.

67   Barbara J. Stapleton, 'Security and PRTs', in *State, Security and Economy in Afghanistan: Current Challenges, Possible Solutions*, Liechtenstein Colloquium Report Vol. III, Liechtenstein Institute on Self-Determination, Princeton University (Princeton, NJ, 2008), pp. 29–32, at p. 29.

68   Nicholas Kulish, 'Dutch Pull-Out From War Expected After Government Collapse', *The New York Times*, 22 February 2010.

First, an explicit focus on population protection can assist in giving the problem the salience it deserves. In a counterinsurgency environment, this can make political sense as well. The US *Counterinsurgency Field Manual* recognizes the centrality of such an approach, arguing that the cornerstone of any counterinsurgency effort 'is establishing security for the civilian populace. Without a secure environment, no permanent reforms can be implemented and disorder spread[s].'[69] Yet providing security is more easily preached than achieved. In Afghanistan, where millions of people are scattered through thousands of small villages and settlements, the direct provision of security through permanent force deployment is virtually impossible,[70] especially when the enemy could choose random targets simply to highlight the inability of the state and its backers to provide a safe environment. This has led some writers to preach what might charitably be called a more robust approach. Thus Michael Scheuer has argued:

> Killing in large numbers is not enough to defeat our Muslim foes. With killing must come a Sherman-like razing of infrastructure. Roads and irrigation systems; bridges, power plants, and crops in the field; fertilizer plants and grain mills – all these and more will need to be destroyed to deny the enemy its support base. Land mines, moreover, will be massively reintroduced to deal [with] borders and mountain passes too long, high, or numerous to close with U.S. soldiers. As noted, such actions will yield large civilian casualties, displaced populations, and refugee flows.[71]

This is essentially what the Soviet Union attempted in the 1980s and the consequence, as Marshal Sergei Akhromeev remarked at the November 1986 Politburo meeting that took the decision to withdraw from Afghanistan, was that the USSR 'lost the battle for the Afghan people'.[72]

If direct population protection proves difficult, the next approach to contemplate is investment in better intelligence gathering, so that the enemy can be identified and struck in a more discriminating fashion. Intelligence has been a point of weakness in the Western endeavour.[73] Inadequate investment in language training, rotation of personnel in and out of theatres of operations and a generally

---

69 *The US Army Marine Corps Counterinsurgency Field Manual*, US Army Field Manual No. 3-24, Marine Corps Warfighting Publication No. 3-33.5 (Chicago: University of Chicago Press, 2007), p. 42.

70 See Bing West, *The Wrong War: Grit, Strategy, and the Way Out of Afghanistan* (New York: Random House, 2011), pp. 249–50.

71 Michael Scheuer, *Imperial Hubris: Why the West is Losing the War on Terror* (Washington, DC: Potomac Books, 2004), pp. 241–2.

72 Maley, *The Afghanistan Wars*, p. 110.

73 See Major-General Michael T. Flynn, USA, Captain Matt Pottinger, USMC, and Paul D. Batchelor, DIA, *Fixing Intel: A Blueprint for Making Intelligence Relevant in Afghanistan* (Washington, DC: Center for a New American Security, January 2010).

impenetrable environment all add to the difficulty of intelligence gathering. A particular problem arises from the sense that the United States is on its way out of Afghanistan. Ordinary Afghans can already witness the Taliban murdering those whom they accuse of spying[74] and it would make little sense in such an environment to ally closely with a party that might disengage from the conflict and leave one exposed to retribution. As Hobbes remarked, 'Reputation of power, is Power'[75], and at the moment it is the Taliban who enjoy that advantage.

A third approach – more on display now than in the past – is to admit error freely and promptly when mistakes are made. On a number of occasions, Western forces have been reluctant to admit that civilians have been inappropriately or erroneously targeted and this has added fuel to the fire of local frustration; the killing of civilians near Shindand in Herat in August 2008 provides a prime example.[76] One of General Stanley A. McChrystal's achievements was to move much more expeditiously to concede that things had gone wrong – for example, when innocent travellers, many of them Hazaras, were struck in Daikundi in February 2010.[77]

A fourth approach is to recognize the importance of human rights monitoring as a form of accountability, and here it is particularly important to bolster the work of specialist Afghan organizations such as the Afghanistan Independent Human Rights Commission and Afghanistan Rights Monitor, as well as Afghan bodies with a broader remit such as the Liaison Office and Afghanistan Watch. Such bodies can exploit the detailed local knowledge of Afghan staff as well as their linguistic skills, and investment in such capacities makes a positive contribution to the human rights environment more broadly.

But finally, as long as the Taliban and their associates can operate freely from sanctuaries in Pakistan, which provide security for the leaders of the insurgency, training opportunities for recruits and secret factories where IEDs can be manufactured for dispatch to Afghanistan then the Western endeavour in Afghanistan will be at best a holding operation and the threat of high-level civilian casualties will persist. This wider problem is one that calls for political and diplomatic measures rather than simply the use of military force. It is important, however, to be clear about what political and diplomatic measures are likely to work. At present, much talk has surrounded the idea of negotiations with the Taliban to achieve some kind of 'reconciliation'. There is, of course, no problem with the Afghan Government's seeking to re-engage with disaffected tribal elements, but this is very different from cutting a deal with the Taliban. There is little to suggest that the Taliban is interested in any such deal; the very suggestion of such a deal discourages cooperation with the Afghan Government;

---

74   *Afghanistan Annual Report 2010*, pp. 14–15.

75   Hobbes, *Leviathan*, p. 62.

76   For detailed discussion of this episode, see Barber, pp. 484–90.

77   David S. Cloud, 'Anatomy of an Afghan War Tragedy', *Los Angeles Times*, 10 April 2011.

many Afghans are appalled by the prospect of the Taliban's returning in any form; the gender and human rights achievements of the past decade would most likely be lost; a deal with the Taliban might be no more meaningful than the 1973 Paris Accords on Vietnam; and the ultimate result is more likely to be renewed civil war.[78] A much more promising approach for Washington and its allies would be to seize the opportunity created by the discovery of Osama Bin Laden in Pakistan to press Islamabad to arrest and hand over the Taliban's Quetta Shura, as well as the top leaders of the Hezb-e Islami and the Haqqani network. This is well within Pakistan's capacity and it would do more than any other single move to address the issue of civilian casualties in Afghanistan, for, as Thomas J. Barfield puts it: 'If Pakistan ever reversed its policy of support, as it did to Mullah Omar in 2001, the insurgency in Afghanistan would be dealt a fatal blow.'[79]

Conclusion

All that said, it is important to reiterate that the problem of civilian casualties in war is one for which there is no easy solution. Deontological and consequentialist ethics come into conflict with each other. As long as war is in certain circumstances a legitimate instrument of policy and human agents remain capable of acting in error then the problem of civilian casualties will remain. The moment that the British decided in September 1939 to honour Prime Minister Chamberlain's commitment to Poland, civilian casualties became inevitable. The same was true when Stalin responded to the German invasion of the USSR on 22 June 1941 and when President Roosevelt responded to the Japanese bombing of Pearl Harbor on 7 December 1941. Those who on deontological grounds would see civilian casualties as unacceptable even as collateral to legitimate military action will be challenged by consequentialists to factor into their calculus the harm to civilians that a triumphant tyranny can afflict. This is pertinent in a conflict such as the Afghan one, where even now, the bulk of civilian casualties result from the actions of the Taliban insurgents and those insurgents themselves have a gruesome and grisly record of past atrocities committed against vulnerable and innocent civilians. Coverage of civilian casualties in Afghanistan remains severely skewed. Accidental harm caused by Western forces receives much more coverage than the deliberate and brutal targeting of Afghan civilians by the Taliban, the Haqqani network and the Hezb-e Islami, who seek to deny their opponents the ability to rule peacefully.

---

78   See Ashley J. Tellis, *Reconciling with the Taliban? Toward an Alternative Grand Strategy in Afghanistan* (Washington, DC: Carnegie Endowment for International Peace, 2009).

79   Thomas J. Barfield, *Afghanistan: A Cultural and Political History* (Princeton, NJ: Princeton University Press, 2010), p. 328.

But that said, it is important to recognize that for all the sentimentality about war that one can find in both literature and popular culture, even a just war can be a profoundly dehumanizing activity. The legal and institutional steps that can be taken to minimize the impact of war on civilians are not necessarily equal to the task of addressing this deep moral and psychological problem. Two dreadful recent cases from Afghanistan bear this out all too starkly. On 1 May 2011, a twelve-year-old suicide bomber detonated an explosives vest in Paktika, killing four civilians and injuring twelve.[80] The kind of mentality that sanctions the use of innocent children as bombers is by no means new, but it still almost defies description.[81] And on 15 January 2010, a totally innocent Afghan civilian, a fifteen-year-old boy named Gulmuddin, was reportedly murdered in Kandahar province in a 'thrill killing' by soldiers from Bravo Company, 2nd Battalion, 1st Infantry Regiment. This triggered what one report called a 'months long shooting spree against Afghan civilians' by soldiers 'who had a fondness for hashish and alcohol'.[82] The killers took numerous photographs, which, according to another report, 'portray a front-line culture among U.S. troops in which killing Afghan civilians is less a reason for concern than a cause for celebration'.[83] While the details of the case remain under investigation, there is already abundant evidence in the public domain that points to sociopathic dehumanization of the very people whom the foreign forces were deployed to protect and a frightening collapse in any capacity for empathy. The parallels with the mind-set that led to the My Lai massacre in Vietnam are striking, and when a culture of this kind takes root in a military unit, it creates a situation that is exceedingly dangerous not only for civilians, but for the wider mission that honest and decent soldiers are seeking to discharge. As the United States celebrates the elimination by its military forces of Osama Bin Laden, it needs to be sure not to lose sight of the darker side of its military as well.

---

80   'Taliban Renews Offensive in Afghanistan', *The New York Times*, 1 May 2011.

81   A famous literary exploration of the cynical use of a child as a suicide bomber can be found in Saki's short story 'The Easter Egg': see Hector Hugh Munro, *The Collected Short Stories of Saki* (Ware: Wordsworth Classics, 1993), pp. 133–6.

82   Craig Whitlock, 'Members of Stryker Combat Brigade in Afghanistan Accused of Killing Civilians for Sport', *The Washington Post*, 18 September 2010.

83   'The Kill Team', *Rolling Stone*, 27 March 2011.

Chapter 15

The Protection of Civilians During the Israeli–Hamas Conflict: The Goldstone Report

Richard D. Rosen

Introduction

The protection of non-combatants, especially civilians, is the *raison d'être* of international humanitarian law.[1] The law rests upon the twin principles of distinction and proportionality – that is, only combatants and military objects may be attacked[2] and even then not if the resulting harm to civilians is excessive to the military advantage to be gained.[3]

Fulfilment of these principles depends to a large measure upon adherence to the law of war by both sides to a conflict; the law is based upon reciprocal responsibilities of the conventional belligerents.[4] For example, to ensure that an attacker can distinguish combatants from civilians, belligerents differentiate their soldiers from the civilian population[5] by having them wear fixed, distinctive signs

---

1 See, for example, Michael Ignatieff, *The Warrior's Honour: Ethnic War and the Modern Conscience* (Toronto: Penguin, 1998), p. 119; *Legality of the Threat or Use of Nuclear Weapons*, International Court of Justice Advisory Opinion, 1996 ICJ 226, 257 (8 July); Nils Melzer, *Interpretive Guidance on the Notion of Direct Participation in Hostilities Under International Humanitarian Law* (Geneva: ICRC, May 2009), p. 4.

2 See generally, *Protocol Additional to the Geneva Conventions of August 12, 1949, and Relating to the Protection of Victims of International Armed Conflicts (Protocol I)*, Opened for signature 12 December 1977, 1125 UNTS 3, Arts 48 and 51(4), http://www. icrc.org/ihl.nsf (hereinafter 'Additional Protocol I'). The term 'attacker' does not mean 'aggressor'. A nation may attack an adversary as a defensive measure (Art. 49.1).

3 See generally, ibid., Art. 57.2(b).

4 See W. Hays Parks, 'Part IX of the ICRC "Direct Participation in Hostilities" Study: No Mandate, No Expertise, and Legally Incorrect', *New York University Journal of International Law and Politics*, 42 (2010): 769, 772; Amachai Cohen, *Proportionality in Modern Asymmetrical Wars* (Jerusalem Center for Public Affairs, 2010), p. 5, http://www. jcpa.org/text/proportionality.pdf; Dr Barry A. Feinstein, 'Proportionality and War Crimes in Gaza Under the Law of Armed Conflict', *Rutgers Law Record*, 36 (2009): 224, 232.

5 Yoram Dinstein, *The Conduct of Hostilities Under the Law of International Armed Conflict* 2nd Edition, (Cambridge and New York: Cambridge University Press, 2010), p. 83.

recognizable at a distance (that is, uniforms) and by carrying their arms openly at all times.[6] And because the presence of civilians near a military objective does not render the objective immune from attack,[7] conventional belligerents avoid locating military objectives or conducting their military operations within or near the civilian populations so as to avoid placing the civilians in danger of attack.[8]

Today, however, wars are rarely fought between symmetrical, conventional belligerents; instead, conflicts are asymmetrical – generally between technologically advanced armies and military forces that are not.[9] To compensate for their inability to confront modern armies directly on the battlefield, less advanced forces, particularly insurgents and terrorists, often discard attempts to distinguish themselves from the civilian population and conduct their military operations from civilian population centres.[10] Many depend upon their adversaries' adherence to international humanitarian norms, believing the presence of civilians will force their enemies to either restrict the employment of technologically advanced weapons or avoid targeting the groups altogether.[11]

Civilians not only afford protection to insurgent and terrorist groups; the presence of civilians also serves the groups' greater strategic political objectives.[12] If the insurgent or terrorist groups are attacked, any resulting civilian casualties are dutifully reported by the media and usually condemned by non-governmental organizations (NGOs) and often the United Nations.[13] Thus, insurgents win when

---

6   See *Geneva Convention Relative to the Treatment of Prisoners of War, August 12, 1949*, 6 UST 3316, TIAS 3364, 75 UNTS 135, Art. 4a(1–2) [hereafter 'GPW'].

7   Additional Protocol I, Art. 51.7.

8   Ibid., Art. 58.

9   Joint Chiefs of Staff, *Joint Publication 3-0, Joint Operations xi*, I-6 (16 September 2006, with Change No. 2, 22 March 2010). See generally, Laurie R. Blank and Amos Guirora, 'Teaching an Old Dog New Tricks: Operationalizing the Law of Armed Conflict in New Warfare, *Harvard National Security Journal*, 1 (2010): 45–7.

10   Michael N. Schmitt, 'Asymmetrical Warfare and International Humanitarian Law', *Air Force Law Review*, 62 (2008): 1, 14, 18; Blank and Guirora, pp. 47–8, 53; Daphne Richemond, 'Transnational Terrorist Organizations and the Use of Force', *Catholic University Law Review*, 56 (2007): 1001, 1026.

11   Emanuel Gross, 'Use of Civilians as Human Shields: What Legal and Moral Restrictions Should Pertain to a War Waged by a Democratic State Against Terrorism?', *Emory International Law Review*, 16 (2002): 445, 447; Schmitt, 'Asymmetrical Warfare', pp. 14–15, 18.

12   Gross, 'Use of Civilians as Human Shields', p. 456; Schmitt, 'Asymmetrical Warfare', pp. 14–15, 18.

13   See, for example, W. Chadwick Austin and Antony Barone Kolenc, 'Who's Afraid of the Big Bad Wolf? The International Criminal Court as a Weapon of Asymmetric Warfare', *Vanderbilt Journal of International Law*, 39 (2006): 291, 305–6; Alan Baker, 'Legal and Tactical Dilemmas Inherent in Fighting Terror: Experience of the Israeli Army in Jenin and Bethlehem April–May 2002', in Richard B. Jaques (ed.), *Issues in International Law and Military Operations* (Newport, RI: Naval War College, 2006), Vol. 80, p. 273; Gross, 'Use of Civilians as Human Shields', pp. 447, 467; Michael Y. Kieval, 'Be Reasonable!

an adversary refrains from attack in fear of causing civilian casualties and wins if they are attacked and civilian casualties occur. Given the strategic and tactical advantages insurgents and terrorists obtain from non-compliance with the law of war, they have absolutely no reason *not* to place civilians at risk.[14]

The armed conflict between Israel and Hamas in the Gaza Strip in December 2008 and January 2009 is emblematic of asymmetrical warfare in which one side employs civilians and civilian casualties to achieve tactical and strategic objectives with predictably devastating effects on the civilian population. The conflict embodied the problems modern armies face when dealing with sophisticated insurgent or terrorist groups who embed themselves in and fight from civilian population centres without distinguishing themselves from civilians around them.

To investigate possible human rights violations during the conflict, the UN Human Rights Council established a fact-finding mission headed by South African jurist Richard Goldstone.[15] The mission had a unique opportunity to provide an impartial assessment of asymmetrical conflicts and how modern armed forces might successfully comply with international humanitarian law while at the same time achieving military objectives.[16] It could have produced a document that addressed the imbalance in compliance with the law of war, where one side to the conflict perceives no duty to adhere to any legal restraints.

Instead, the mission delivered a nearly 500-page report that, in large part, contained an anti-Israel polemic dealing with a variety of Palestinian grievances

---

Thoughts on the Effectiveness of State Criticism in Enforcing International Law', *Michigan Journal of International Law*, 26 (2005): 869, 897–8; Jeremy Rabkin, 'The Fantasy World of International Law: The Criticism of Israel Has Been Disproportionate', *Weekly Standard*, 21 August 2006, http://weeklystandard.com/Content/Public/Articles/000/000/012/580uttca.asp; Jefferson D. Reynolds, 'Collateral Damage on the 21st Century Battlefield: Enemy Exploitation of the Law of Armed Conflict, and the Struggle for the Moral High Ground', *Air Force Law Review*, 56 (2005): 1, 35.

14   See A.P.V. Rogers, *Law on the Battlefield*, 2nd ed. (Huntington, NY: Juris Publishing, 2004), p. 128; Charles J. Dunlap Jr, 'A Virtuous Warrior in a Savage World', *US Air Force Academy Journal of Legal Studies*, 8 (1997–98): 71, 73; Jeremy Rabkin, 'The Politics of the Geneva Conventions: Disturbing Background to the ICC Debate', *Virginia Journal of International Law*, 44 (2003): 155, 169.

15   *The Grave Violations of Human Rights in the Occupied Palestinian Territory, Particularly Due to the Recent Israeli Military Attacks Against the Occupied Gaza Strip*, UN Human Rights Council Res. S-9/1, A/HRC/S-1/L.1 (12 January 2009), para. 14, http://www2.ohchr.org/english/bodies/hrcouncil/specialsession/9/docs/A-HRC-S-91-L1.doc (hereinafter 'HRC Resolution 9/1').

16   See, for example, Moshe Halbertal, 'The Goldstone Illusion', *The New Republic*, 6 November 2009, http://www.tnr.com/article/world/the-goldstone-illusion; David Landau, 'The Gaza Report's Wasted Opportunity', *The New York Times*, 20 September 2009, http://www.nytimes.com/2009/09/20/opinion/20landau.html

against Israel,[17] but consciously failed to deal with the central issues surrounding Palestinian civilian casualties during the hostilities: what was Hamas's tactical and strategic doctrine, how was it actually employed and did the Israel Defence Force (IDF) respond in a manner consistent with the principles of distinction and proportionality given the facts known to commanders at the time.[18] The mission was unwilling or unable to undertake the rigorous analysis necessary to determine whether – given the nature of the battlefield – war crimes had in fact been committed.[19] Nevertheless, while avoiding an inquiry into Hamas's tactics during the fighting in Gaza, the mission concluded that Israel intentionally attacked civilians during the conflict, seeking to produce terror and suffering.

Background

In August 2005, Israel withdrew its military forces and civilian settlers from the Gaza Strip.[20] Among other objectives, Israel hoped that disengagement from Gaza would lead to better security and reduce friction with the Palestinian population.[21] In January 2006, Hamas won Palestinian Legislative Council elections and in June 2007 violently seized control of the Gaza Strip from the Palestinian Authority.[22] As the *Goldstone Report* notes, after Hamas took control of the Gaza Strip,

17   UN Human Rights Council, *Fact-Finding Mission on the Gaza Conflict, Human Rights in Palestine and Other Occupied Arab Territories*, A/HRC/12/48 (15 September 2009) (hereinafter *Goldstone Report*). For example, the report deals with such subjects as the treatment of Palestinians on the West Bank (paras 1373–440); the detention of Palestinians in Israeli prisons (paras 1441–502); restrictions on Palestinian movement (paras 1508–34); Israeli settlements (paras 1538–41); and repression of dissent in Israel proper (paras 1692–772). While the Human Rights Council's mandate was sufficiently broad to cover these matters (HRC Resolution S-9/1, para. 14), the mission's primary responsibility was to deal with the Gaza conflict. See Trevor Norwitz, 'An Open Letter to Richard Goldstone', *Commentary*, 19 October 2009, p. 8, http://www.commentarymagazine.com/viewarticle.cfm/an-open-letter-to-richard-goldstone-15284

18   Intelligence and Terrorism Information Center, *Hamas and the Terrorist Threat from the Gaza Strip* (March 2010), p. 132, http://www.terrorism-info.org.il/malam_multimedia/English/engn/pdf/g_report_e1.pdf See also Norwitz, p. 5; Cohen, p. 27.

19   Intelligence and Terrorism Information Center, p. x; Richard Landes, 'Goldstone's Gaza Report Part One: A Failure of Intelligence', *Middle East Review of International Affairs*, December 2009, p. 2, http://www.gloria-center.org/meria/2009/12/landes1.html; Chris Jenks & Geoffrey Corn, 'Siren Song: The Implications of the Goldstone Report on International Criminal Law', *Berkeley J. Int'l L. Publicist*, Winter 2011. http://bjil.typepad.com/publicist/2011/03/publicist07-jenks-corn.html

20   Elisha Efrat, *The West Bank and Gaza Strip* (UK: Taylor & Francis Ltd, 2006), pp. 183–95.

21   *Disengagement Plan of Prime Minister Ariel Sharon*, 16 April 2004, http://www.knesset.gov.il/process/docs/DisengageSharon_eng.htm

22   *Goldstone Report*, para. 190.

Israel declared Gaza 'hostile territory' and followed the declaration with 'severe reductions in the transfers of goods and supplies of electricity to the Strip'.[23]

Surprisingly, the mission neither provided context for Israel's declaration and subsequent blockade nor discussed the nature of Hamas or its abject refusal to recognize Israel or the peace process. By its charter, Hamas seeks the complete destruction of Israel by violent means[24] and the extermination of the Jews;[25] it absolutely rejects any peaceful settlement with Israel.[26] Hamas is considered a terrorist organization not only by Israel, but by other nations as well.[27]

Even before Hamas's seizure of Gaza, Hamas militants crossed into Israel and killed two Israeli soldiers and kidnapped a third: Corporal Gilad Shalit.[28] And within only two weeks of coming to power, Hamas joined other armed groups and fired thousands of rockets into Israel.[29] In June 2008, Egypt brokered a six-month

23   Ibid., para. 192. See Israel Ministry of Foreign Affairs, *Security Cabinet Declares Gaza Hostile Territory*, 17 September 2007, http://www.mfa.gov.il/MFA/Government/Communiques/2007/Security+Cabinet+declares+Gaza+hostile+territory+19-Sep-2007.htm

24   *Covenant of the Islamic Resistance Movement – Hamas* (New Haven, Conn.: Yale Law School Avalon Project, 18 August 1988), Art. 11, http://avalon.law.yale.edu/20th_century/hamas.asp See also Anthony H. Cordesman, *The 'Gaza War': A Strategic Analysis* (Center for Strategic and International Studies, 2009), p. 6, http://csis.org/files/media/csis/pubs/090202_gaza_war.pdf

25   Hamas Covenant, Art. 7.

26   Ibid., Art. 13.

27   See, for example, Office of the Coordinator for Counterterrorism, *Foreign Terrorist Organizations* (Washington, DC: US Department of State, 19 January 2010), http://www.state.gov/s/ct/rls/other/des/123085.htm; Department of the Attorney-General, *Listing of Terrorist Organizations* (Canberra: Commonwealth of Australia), http://www.ag.gov.au/agd/www/nationalsecurity.nsf/AllDocs/95FB057CA3DECF30CA256FAB00 1F7FBD?OpenDocument (listing Hamas's Izz al-Din Al-Qassam Brigades as a terrorist group and renewed listing in September 2009); Canadian Ministry of Public Safety web site (reviewed 20 November 2008), http://www.publicsafety.gc.ca/prg/ns/le/cle-eng.aspx; European Union, Council Decision 2005/930/EC (21 December 2005), http://eur-lex.europa.eu/LexUriServ/site/en/oj/2005/l_340/l_34020051223en00640066.pdf; Home Office, *Proscribed Terrorist Groups* (London: Government of the United Kingdom), http://www.homeoffice.gov.uk/publications/counter-terrorism/proscribed-terror-groups/proscribed-groups?view=Binary (listing Hamas's Izz al-Din Al-Qassam Brigades).

28   Thomas Omestad, 'The Flames of War, and Small Hopes for Peace', *US News & World Report*, 24 July 2006, pp. 12–14, http://www.usnews.com/usnews/news/articles/060716/24week.htm

29   See, for example, Nathan Shachar, *The Gaza Strip* (Sussex: Sussex Academic Press, 2010), p. 177; Ed Blanche, 'Behold, the Humble Qassem', *Middle East*, April 2008, p. 18; 'The Gaza Strip: Are the Palestinians' Weapons Getting More Lethal?', *Economist*, 13 October 2007, p. 50; David Eshel, 'Military Confrontation with Hamas is Unavoidable', *Military Technologies*, 31 (2007): 5.

ceasefire between Israel and Hamas.[30] On 4 November 2008, Israeli ground and air forces attacked Hamas militants to destroy a 250-m tunnel being built under the Israel–Gaza border to enable Hamas to abduct Israelis.[31] Hamas, in turn, fired dozens of rockets into Israel.[32]

The ceasefire was never fully restored, as Hamas continued to fire rockets and mortars into Israel[33] – deliberately targeting its southern cities[34] – while Israel attempted to stop the rockets and mortars by striking at militants[35] and periodically closing its border with Gaza.[36] Israeli officials expressed the desire to extend the six-month ceasefire; however, Hamas refused.[37] The ceasefire expired

---

30   Intelligence and Terrorism Information Center, *The Six Months of the Lull Arrangement* (December 2008), p. 2, http://www.terrorism-info.org.il/malam_multimedia/English/eng_n/pdf/hamas_e017.pdf See also Rory McCarthy, 'Israel and Hamas Agree Ceasefire as Strikes Kill Six Palestinian Fighters', *Guardian*, 18 June 2008, http://www.guardian.co.uk/world/2008/jun/18/israelandthepalestinians.egypt

31   Intelligence and Terrorism Information Center, *The Six Months of the Lull*, p. 9; James Hider, 'Back in the Line of Fire: Rocket War Resumes After Raid on "Kidnap Plot" Tunnel', *The Times*, 6 November 2008, p. 44 (2008 WLNR 21173188).

32   Nidal al-Mughrabi, 'Israel–Hamas Violence Disrupts Gaza Truce', *Reuters*, 5 November 2008, http://reuters.com/articlePrint?articleId=USTRE4A37B520081105; Diaa Hadid, 'Israel Launches First Airstrike on Gaza Since June', *Charleston Gazette & Daily Mail*, 5 November 2008, p. 15A (2008 WLNR 21144545); Ethan Bronner and Taghreed El-Khodary, 'Hamas Rockets Hit Israel, Sending 18 to Hospital', *The New York Times*, 15 November 2008, p. A7 (2008 WLNR 21812926).

33   Intelligence and Terrorism Information Center, *The Six Months of the Lull*, pp. 9–10; Isabel Kirshner and Taghreed El-Khodary, 'Airstrike Kills Four Palestinian Militants', *Pittsburgh Post-Gazette*, 11 November 2008, p. A4 (2008 WLNR 21928051); Ethan Bronner and Taghreed El-Khodary, 'Rocket Barrage into Israel Heightens Gaza Tensions', *Globe & Mail*, 15 November 2008, p. A4 (2008 WLNR 21816760).

34   Ministry of Foreign Affairs, *Violations of Calm: Rockets Strike Sderot, Ashkelon, Western Negev* (Jerusalem: State of Israel, 18 December 2008), http://www.mfa.gov.il/MFA/Terrorism-+Obstacle+to+Peace/Hamas+war+against+Israel/Rockets_strike_Sderot_Ashkelon_western_Negev_16-Nov-2008.htm?DisplayMode=print; Diaa Hadid, 'Israeli Airstrikes Imperil Gaza Truce with Hamas', *Seattle Times*, 6 November 2008, p. A11 (2008 WLNR 21280555); Reuters, 'Gaza: Rocket Fire and Israeli Strike Disrupt Ceasefire', *The New York Times*, 6 November 2008, p. A19 (2008 WLNR 21173891); Diaa Hadid, 'Rocket Attacks Escalate Gaza Violence', *Deseret Morning News*, 15 November 2008 (2008 WLNR 21837697).

35   Intelligence and Terrorism Information Center, *The Six Months of the Lull*, p. 9.

36   'Israel Closes Gaza Crossings', *Aljazeera.net*, 18 November 2008 (2008 WLNR 22000226).

37   *Goldstone Report*, para. 262; Yaakov Kaatz, Khaled Abu Tomeh and Herb Keinon, 'Hamas Divided Over Continuing Ceasefire', *Jerusalem Post*, 15 December 2008, p. 1 (2008 WLNR 24598446); Yaakov Kaatz, 'Why Israel Prefers the Cease-Fire in Gaza', *Jerusalem Post*, 15 December 2008, p. 2 (2008 WLNR 24598450); Taghreed El-Khodary and Isabel Kershner, 'Hamas, Showing Split, May Extend Israel Truce', *The New York Times*, 15 December 2008, p. A10 (2008 WLNR 23990603).

on 19 December 2008[38] and Hamas responded by firing more rockets into Israel, including at Israeli cities.[39] Facing increasing domestic pressure from the incessant attacks,[40] Israel issued warnings of imminent military action.[41] Hamas ignored the warnings and, on 27 December 2008, Israel launched 'Operation Cast Lead'.[42]

Operation Cast Lead and the Fact-finding Mission

Operation 'Cast Lead' began with an air campaign against Hamas targets in the Gaza Strip.[43] A week later, on 3 January 2009, the IDF commenced ground operations,[44]

---

38   Richard Boudreaux, 'Hamas Formally Ends Gaza Cease-Fire with Israel', *Los Angeles Times*, 19 December 2008, p. 15 (2008 WLNR 24369458); 'Hamas Refuses to Renew Gaza Truce', *Evening Standard*, 19 December 2008, p. 28 (2008 WLNR 24401760).

39   Yaakov Kaatz, Khaled Abu Tomeh and Herb Keinon, 'Gazans Fire Dozens of Rockets at Negev Towns as "Truce" Ends', *Jerusalem Post*, 21 December 2008, p. 1 (2008 WLNR 25000385); 'Gaza Rockets Hit Southern Israel', *Aljazeera.net*, 21 December 2008 (2008 WLNR 24485745); Ben Lynfield, 'Livni and Netanyahu Vow to Oust Hamas After Gaza Rocket Strikes', *Independent*, 22 December 2008 (2008 WLNR 24502385); 'Israel Hit by Rocket Fire from Gaza', *Aljazeera.net*, 24 December 2008 (2008 WLNR 24663434); Matt Brown, 'Hamas Unleashes Artillery Barrage on Israel', *Australian Broadcasting Corporation*, 25 December 2008 (2008 WLNR 24691971); 'Peace in Bethlehem as Hamas Fires on Israel', *The Australian*, 26 December 2008 (2008 WLNR 24726004); Isabel Kirshner and Taghreed El-Khodary, 'Gaza Rocket Fire Intensifies', *Pittsburgh Post-Gazette*, 25 December 2008, p. A4 (2008 WLNR 24695964); Herb Keinon and Yaakov Kaatz, 'IDF Poised for Limited Gaza Operation', *Jerusalem Post*, 26 December 2008, p. 1 (2008 WLNR 25046531).

40   Patrick Martin, 'Israelis Question Reasons for Restraint', *Globe & Mail*, 22 December 2008, p. A11 (2008 WLNR 24514418); Khaled Abu Toameh, 'Hamas Mocks Israel's Nonresponse to Rocket Attacks', *Jerusalem Post*, 25 December 2008, p. 2 (2008 WLNR 25046493); Reuters, 'Israel Issues an Appeal to Palestinians in Gaza', *The New York Times*, 26 December 2008, p. A15 (2008 WLNR 24747964).

41   Orly Halpern, 'Israel Vows Attack if Rockets from Gaza Don't Stop', *Globe & Mail*, 26 December 2008, p. A1 (2008 WLNR 24747079); Ashraf Khalil, 'Israel Warns of Gaza Action', *Chicago Tribune*, 26 December 2008, p. 18 (2008 WLNR 24751030).

42   Yaakov Katz, '225 Killed as Israel Rains Fire on Hamas in Bid to End Kassams', *Jerusalem Post*, 28 December 2008, p. 1 (2008 WLNR 25052442); Todd Venzia, 'Hell Fire Rains on Gaza', *New York Post*, 28 December 2008, p. 4 (2008 WLNR 25008702).

43   Matt M. Matthews, 'Hard Lessons Learned: A Comparison of the 2006 Hezbollah–Israeli War and Operation CAST LEAD', in *Back to Basics: A Study of the Second Lebanon War and Operation Cast Lead* (Fort Leavenworth, Kan.: Combat Studies Institute, May 2009), p. 27, http://www.cgsc.edu/carl/download/csipubs/farquhar.pdf

44   Ministry of Foreign Affairs, *Operation Cast Lead Expanded* (Jerusalem: State of Israel, 3 January 2009), http://www.mfa.gov.il/MFA/Government/Communiques/2009/Second_stage_Operation_Cast_Lead_begins_3-Jan-2009.htm

which lasted until 18 January, when a ceasefire was declared.[45] According to Israel, Operation Cast Lead had two objectives: 1) to stop the bombardment of Israeli civilians by destroying Hamas's mortar and rocket-launching apparatus and infrastructure; and 2) to reduce the ability of Hamas and other terrorist organizations in Gaza to perpetrate future attacks against the civilian population in Israel.[46]

By a resolution adopted on 12 January 2009, the UN Human Rights Council

> [d]ispatch[ed] an urgent, independent international fact-finding mission, to be appointed by the President of the Council, to investigate all violations of international human rights law and international humanitarian law *by the occupying Power, Israel,* against the Palestinian people throughout the Occupied Palestinian Territory, particularly in the occupied Gaza Strip, due to the current aggression, and calls upon Israel not to obstruct the process of investigation and to fully cooperate with the mission.[47]

By the same resolution, before the appointment of the fact-finding mission to determine whether war crimes had occurred, the council condemned Israel for its 'massive violation of human rights' of Palestinian civilians.[48] Even prior to the ceasefire, the UN Special Rapporteur for the Palestinian Territories accused Israel of committing war crimes during its Gaza campaign.[49] On 9 April 2009, the council president appointed Justice Richard J. Goldstone to lead the fact-finding mission, expanding the mission to include all 'international human rights and humanitarian law violations related to the recent conflict in the Gaza Strip'.[50] The Mission conducted field visits and interviews, including publicly broadcast hearings in Gaza and Geneva,[51] and in September 2009, the Mission issued its findings and conclusions.

---

45   Isabel Kirshner and Michael Slackman, 'Cease-Fire Holding as Israelis Pull out of Gaza', *International Herald Tribune*, 20 January 2009, p. 5 (2009 WLNR 1106907).

46   Ministry of Foreign Affairs, *Gaza Facts – The Israeli Perspective* (Jerusalem: State of Israel), http://www.mfa.gov.il/GazaFacts

47   HRC Resolution 9/1, para. 19 (emphasis added).

48   Ibid., para. 1.

49   UN High Commissioner for Human Rights, *Statement of Special Rapporteur for the Palestinian Territories Occupied Since 1967 for Presentation to the Special Session of the Human Rights Council on the Situation in the Gaza Strip*, 9 January 2009, pp. 9–11, http://www.unhchr.ch/huricane/huricane.nsf/view01/14B004C3AE39004BC12575390059 9B5D?opendocument

50   UN Human Rights Council, 'Richard J. Goldstone Appointed to Lead Human-Rights Council Fact-Finding Mission on Gaza Conflict', Press Release, 9 April 2009, http://www.ohchr.org/EN/NewsEvents/Pages/DisplayNews.aspx?NewsID=8469&LangID=E

51   *Goldstone Report* paras 5, 7, 141; Statement by Richard Goldstone on behalf of the Members of the United Nations Fact Finding Mission on the Gaza Conflict before the Human Rights Council, Sep. 29, 2011, http://www2.ohchr.org/english/bodies/hrcouncil/specialsession/9/factfindingmission.htm

Based upon the number of civilian casualties,[52] statements by current and former Israeli officials about Israeli military objectives in Gaza and other conflicts[53] and Israel's advanced targeting technology and proficiency[54] the mission found (without considering the conditions the IDF actually confronted on the ground) that the IDF's mission was to kill civilians and destroy their property[55] and that Israel committed grave violations of the law of war.[56]

What the Mission Did Not Address: The Operational Environment

The Mission's Approach and Findings

Any determination of whether the IDF violated international humanitarian law must take into account the combat environment Israeli soldiers actually faced on the ground. Civilian casualties by themselves do not violate the law of armed conflict.[57] While attacks may not be directed at civilians,[58] their presence does not immunize a legitimate military objective from attack, provided the attacker does not cause disproportionate collateral damage to the civilian population.[59] Article

---

52   Ibid., para. 360–362. The ratio of combatant-to-civilian deaths upon which the mission relied has been significantly undermined by admissions of the Hamas leadership that it suffered a much higher number of combatant casualties than previously reported. See, for example, 'Hamas Confirms Losses in Cast Lead for the First Time', *Jerusalem Post*, 1 November 2010, http://www.jpost.com/MiddleEast/Article.aspx?id=193521

53   *Goldstone Report*, paras 1179, 1192–219.

54   Ibid., paras 576–8, 1185–91.

55   Ibid., paras 1213–16; UN Human Rights Council, *Fact-Finding Mission on the Gaza Conflict, Conclusions and Recommendations, Human Rights in Palestine and Other Occupied Arab Territories*, A/HRC/12/48 (24 September 2009), paras 1877, 1881–95 (hereinafter *Goldstone Conclusions*). See also Abraham Bell, *A Critique of the Goldstone Report and its Treatment of International Humanitarian Law*, p. 6, http://ssrn.com/abstract=1581533 On 1 April 2011, Justice Goldstone seemingly retreated from the mission's conclusion that Israel intentionally targeted civilians during combat operations in Gaza. Richard Goldstone, 'Reconsidering the Goldstone Report on Israel and War Crimes', *Washington Post*, 1 April 2011), http://www.washingtonpost.com/opinions/reconsidering-the-goldstone-report-on-israel-and-war-crimes/2011/04/01/AFg111JC_story.html   Other mission members, however, have refused to reconsider the mission's conclusions. See Hina Jilani, Christine Chinkin and Desmond Travers, 'Goldstone Report; Statement Issued by Members of UN Mission on Gaza War', *Guardian.co.uk*, 14 April 2011, http://www.guardian.co.uk/commentisfree/2011/apr/14/goldstone-report-statement-un-gaza

56   *Goldstone Report*, para. 46; *Goldstone Conclusions*, para. 1935.

57   Dinstein, p. 123, 136.

58   Protocol I, Article 51.2.

59   Amnon Rubinstein & Yaniv Roznai, 'Human Shields in Modern Asymmetrical Conflicts: The Need for a Proportionate Proportionality, *Stanford Law & Policy Review*, 22 (2011): 93, 100.

58 of Protocol I, which the mission 'curiously' never mentions, requires defending combatants to take precautions to protect civilians under their control from the dangers resulting from military operations.[60] Thus, the mission should have asked not only whether the IDF violated the law of armed conflict in its attacks in Gaza, but also whether Hamas 'observed the limits IHL places on what fighters can do to defend themselves', including protection of its civilian population.[61]

Moreover, any assessment of whether the IDF behaved unlawfully must be made through the eyes of a 'reasonable commander' acting under the facts *known at the time of the attack*,[62] and not through information developed after-the-fact.[63] Ultimately, 'the kind and degree of force can be regarded as necessary in an attack against a particular military target involves a complex assessment based on a wide variety of ... circumstances.'[64]

Justice Goldstone admitted that the mission never undertook this type of thorough inquiry, discrediting the mission's principal finding—that Israel intentionally targeted Gaza's civilian population.[65] On 16 October 2009, British Colonel Richard Kemp, the former commander of British forces in Afghanistan, testified before the UN Human Rights Council:

> [B]ased upon my knowledge and experience, I can say this: During Operation Cast Lead, the Israeli Defence Forces did more to safeguard the rights of civilians in a combat zone than any other army in the history of warfare. [Israel] did so while facing an enemy that deliberately positioned its military capability behind the human shield of the civilian population ...
>
> [O]f course innocent civilians were killed. War is chaos and full of mistakes ... But mistakes are not war crimes ... [More] than anything, the civilian casualties

---

60   Laurie R. Blank, 'Finding Facts But Missing the Law: The Goldstone Report, Gaza and Lawfare, *Case Western Reserve Journal of International Law*, 43 (2010): 279, 301.

61   Samuel Estreicher, 'Privileging Asymmetric Warfare? Part I: Defender Duties under International Humanitarian Law,' *Chicago Journal of International Law*, 11 (2011): 425, 435; see also Peter Berkowitz, 'The Goldstone Report and International Law', *Policy Review*, 162 (1 August 2010), Hoover Institute, Stanford University, http://www.hoover.org/publications/policy-review/article/43281

62   Theo Boutruche, 'Credible Fact-Finding and Allegations of International Humanitarian Law Violations: Challenges in Theory and Practice, *Journal of Conflict & Security Law*, 16 (2011): 105, 126.

63   Dinstein, p. 139; Michael A. Newton, 'Illustrating Illegitimate Lawfare,' *Case Western Reserve Journal International Law*, 43 (2010): 255, 275–6.

64   Melzer, p. 80. See also *Prosecutor v Galic*, No. IT-98-29-T (3 December 2002), para. 58.

65   See Bell, p. 6.

were a consequence of Hamas' way of fighting. Hamas deliberately tried to sacrifice their own civilians.[66]

When asked about Colonel Kemp's testimony, Justice Goldstone replied:

> I would also mention that there was no reliance on Col. Kemp mainly because in our Report we did not deal with the issues he raised regarding the problems of conducting military operations in civilian areas and second-guessing decisions made by soldiers and their commanding officers 'in the fog of war'. We avoided having to do so in the incidents we decided to investigate.[67]

More disturbingly, the mission did publish conclusions about the character of Israel's military operations in the incidents it did investigate without seriously considering the operational environment in which the incidents occurred.[68] In this regard, the mission's report about the combat operations of Palestinian military groups during Operation Cast Lead is truly surreal.

First, the mission describes the 'Gaza authorities' as a seemingly disembodied entity with no connection to Hamas or its military arm, the Al-Qassam Brigades, or to any other Palestinian armed organization.[69] The mission generally took the

---

66   Statement of Colonel Richard Kemp, UN Human Rights Council, 12th Special Session, Geneva, 16 October 2009, http://www.unwatch.org/site/apps/nlnet/content2.aspx?c=bdKKISNqEmG&b=1313923&ct=7536409

67   Email from Judge Richard Goldstone to Maurice Ostroff, International Coalition of Hasbara Volunteers, 21 September 2009, 22:34:29, http://maurice-ostroff.tripod.com/id233.html See also Alan Dershowitz, *The Case Against the Goldstone Report*, Public Law & Legal Theory Working Papers Series, Paper No. 10-26, 2010, Harvard Law School, p. 23, http://ssrn.com/abstract=1542897

68   *Goldstone Conclusions*, paras 1880–95; High Commissioner for Human Rights, *UN Fact Finding Mission Finds Strong Evidence of War Crimes and Crimes Against Humanity Committed During the Gaza Conflict; Calls for End to Impunity*, UN Human Rights Council, 15 September 2009, http://www.ohchr.org/EN/NewsEvents/Pages/DisplayNews.aspx?NewsID=91&LangID=E ('The report underlines that in most of the incidents investigated by it, and described in the report, loss of life and destruction caused by Israeli forces during the military operation was a *result of disrespect for the fundamental principle of "distinction" in international humanitarian law that requires military forces to distinguish between military targets and civilians and civilian objects at all times*') (emphasis added).

69   *Goldstone Report*: 'The Mission also addressed questions regarding the tactics used by Palestinian armed groups to the Gaza authorities. They responded that they had nothing to do, directly or indirectly, with al-Qassam Brigades or other armed groups and had no knowledge of their tactics' (para. 441). 'In response to questions by the Mission ... the Gaza authorities stated that they had "nothing to do, directly or indirectly, with al-Qassam or other resistance factions"' (para. 1635).

'Gaza authorities' at their word in denying any connection to the ongoing military conflict.[70]

Second, the mission neither interviewed members of the 'Palestinian armed groups' nor had any direct contact with Palestinian combatants involved in the conflict.[71] Instead, the mission relied principally upon the public testimony of Gaza residents, who were accompanied by Hamas officials and who were reluctant to speak openly, particularly about Hamas's misdeeds.[72] Incredibly, the mission did not ask the witnesses 'whether Palestinian fighters were in the area of the incidents about which they were testifying'.[73]

Third, the mission received considerable information about Palestinian combatants conducting offensive and defensive operations in civilian population centres and while dressed in civilian clothing;[74] however, the mission took no steps

---

70   Ibid., paras 441, 1635. Why the mission would accept at all the assertion that the Gaza authorities and Hamas's military wing – the Al Qassam Brigades – were unrelated is difficult to comprehend; they are essentially one and the same. See Penny L. Mellies, 'Hamas and Hezbollah: A Comparison of Tactics', in *Back to Basics: A Study of the Second Lebanon War and Operation Cast Lead* (Fort Leavenworth, Kan.: Combat Studies Institute, May 2009), p. 47. See also Intelligence and Terrorism Information Center, *Hamas and the Terrorist Threat*, pp. 4–8, 24–6; Khaled Hroub, *Hamas: A Beginner's Guide* (London and Ann Arbor, Mich.: Pluto Press, 2006), p. 121.

71   *Goldstone Report*, para. 441: 'To gather first-hand information on the matter, the Mission requested a meeting with representatives of armed groups. However, the groups were not agreeable to such a meeting. The Mission, consequently, had little option but to rely upon indirect sources to a greater extent than for other parts of its investigation.' See also para. 1636.

72   Ibid., paras 440, 455; Dr Hanan Chehata, 'Exclusive MEMO Interview with Colonel Desmond Travers – Co-Author of the UN's Goldstone Report', *Middle East Monitor*, 2 February 2010, p. 7, http://www.middleeastmonitor.org.uk/articles/62-europe/625-qgaza-is-the-only-gulag-in-the-western-hemisphere-maintained-by-democracies-closed-off-from-food-water-airq-says-colonel-desmond-travers-co-author-of-the-goldstone-report-in-an-exclusive-memo-interview

73   Joshua Muravchik, 'Goldstone: An Exegesis', *World Affairs*, May–June 2010, http://www.worldaffairsjournal.org/articles/2010-MayJune/full-Muravchik-Traub-MJ-2010.html Based on Justice Goldstone's remarks at the public hearings in Gaza, the hearings' purpose was not to determine the appropriateness of Israel's conduct in the context of the conditions it confronted on the ground; rather, their aim was 'primarily to allow the face of human suffering to be seen and to let the voices of victims be heard'. Statements of Richard Goldstone before the UN Fact-Finding Mission on the Gaza Conflict, 28 June 2009, Unofficial Transcript, p. 6, http://www2.ohchr.org/english/bodies/hrcouncil/specialsession/9/FactFindingMission.htm; ibid., 29 June 2009, pp. 29–30.

74   For example, the mission had information about: 1) Palestinian combatants firing at Israeli soldiers from the vicinity of a UN school (*Goldstone Report*, para. 446); 2) Palestinian combatants firing rockets from residential areas and near schools (paras 448–50, 452–3); 3) Palestinian combatants firing at Israelis from and operating in residential areas (paras 455–7, 460); and 4) Palestinian combatants dressed in civilian clothes (paras 479–80).

to corroborate the reports[75] and discounted them,[76] minimized their impact on the IDF's ability to distinguish military targets from civilians and their property[77] or applied improper legal standards in measuring Israel's response.[78]

Fourth, the mission made no effort to study Hamas's combat doctrine or the means by which it was employed.[79] The mission evidently could not spare resources to review open-source materials that would have laid out in detail how Hamas intended to fight Israel.[80]

Hamas's Military Operations

In developing its defensive and offensive doctrine, Hamas took its cue from Hezbollah, which had achieved a measure of success against the Israeli military in its 2006 war.[81] Hamas's approach is not surprising given that both Hezbollah and

---

75   The mission did not ask witnesses who testified about the presence of Palestinian combatants in the vicinity of the incidents about which they were testifying. See Footnote 76. And, with few exceptions, the mission did not investigate the use of mosques for weapons storage (*Goldstone Report*, paras 464–5, 486) or the use of hospitals for military purposes (paras 467–8).

76   See, for example, ibid., paras 456–588: dismissing claims of a Palestinian militant group that it engaged in such tactics as 'seizing houses as military positions for the purpose of staging ambushes against IDF forces' and 'employing explosive charges of various types (IEDs, penetrating, bounding, anti-personnel etc.) in the vicinity of residences and detonating them', 'boobytrapping houses … and detonating the charges' and 'conducting fighting and sniper fire at IDF forces operating in the built-up areas'. Although the mission stated that it did not investigate Israeli claims of Hamas's use of hospitals for military purposes and asserted that it could not make findings about the allegations (para. 469). It in fact concluded that it could not find evidence that Gaza officials used hospital facilities to shield military activities (para. 486).

77   Intelligence and Terrorism Information Center, *Hamas and the Terrorist Threat*, pp. 119–20.

78   Laurie R. Blank, *The Application of IHL in the Goldstone Report: A Critical Commentary*, Emory University Public Law & Legal Theory Research Paper Series, Paper No. 10–96 (2009), pp. 15, 17, 24, http://ssrn.com/abstract=1596214

79   See Footnotes 66–68 and accompanying text.

80   See, for example, Cordesman, *The 'Gaza War'*; Combined Studies Institute, *Back to Basics: A Study of the Second Lebanon War and Operation Cast Lead* (Fort Leavenworth, Kan.: Combined Studies Institute, May 2009), http://www.cgsc.edu/carl/download/csipubs/farquhar.pdf; Intelligence and Terrorism Information Center, *Hamas's Military Buildup in the Gaza Strip* (Intelligence and Terrorism Information Center, 8 April 2007; updated April 2008), http://www.terrorism-info.org.il/malam_multimedia/English/eng_n/pdf/hamas_080408.pdf

81   Matthews, 'Hard Lessons Learned', p. 25.

Hamas receive funding, weapons and training from Iran, which is reflected in their military strategy and tactics.[82]

After Israel's military withdrawal from southern Lebanon in 2000, Hezbollah filled the resulting vacuum.[83] Unfettered by an Israeli military presence and supported financially and materially by Iran,[84] Hezbollah built an extensive military infrastructure, using civilian population centres for military depots and fighting positions. During the 2006 conflict, it used this infrastructure to great effect, particularly in the villages of southern Lebanon such as Maroun al-Ras and Bint Jebeil.[85] Throughout the conflict, Hezbollah used the civilian population to screen its military operations and to provide a level of security for its forces.[86]

Hamas intended to copy Hezbollah's success.[87] After Israel's disengagement from Gaza in 2005 and Hamas's violent takeover of the Strip in 2007, Hamas began to embed its military infrastructure into populated areas, using mosques, hospitals, schools and residences for storage facilities, command and communication centres and fighting positions.[88] It planned to fight and hide among the civilian population[89] – a tactic at the centre of asymmetrical conflicts in urban environments.[90] Early in 2008, a senior Hamas leader acknowledged that the employment of human shields was integral to Hamas's strategy in a conflict with Israel:

---

82   Intelligence and Terrorism Information Center, *Hamas's Military Buildup*, p. 5; Yoram Cohen and Jeffrey White, *Hamas in Combat: The Military Performance of the Palestinian Islamic Resistance Movement*, Policy Focus No. 97, Washington Institute for Near East Policy (October 2009), p. ix; Bruce P. Schwartz and Christopher C. Donaldson, 'Protecting the Playground: Options for Confronting the Iranian Regime', *Brooklyn Journal of International Law*, 35 (2010): 395, 396; Keith A. Petty, 'Veiled Impunity: Iran's Use of Non-State Armed Groups', *Denver Journal of International Law and Policy*, 36 (2008): 191, 203–5.

83   See Matt M. Matthews, *We Were Caught Unprepared: The 2006 Hezbollah–Israeli War 16*, Long Paper Series, Occasional Paper No. 26 (US Army Combined Arms Center, 2008), http://carl.army.mil/download/csipubs/matthewsOP26.pdf

84   Petty, pp. 194–203.

85   Anthony H. Cordesman, *Lessons of the 2006 Israeli–Hezbollah War* (Washington, DC: Center for Strategic and International Studies, 2007), pp. 80–84; Matthews, *We Were Caught Unprepared*, pp. 43–50; Dr Reuven Erlich, *Hezbollah's Use of Lebanese Civilians as Human Shields* (Intelligence and Terrorism Information Center, November 2006), pp. 28, 32, 39, 48–51, http://www.ajcongress.org/site/DocServer/Part1.pdf?docID=861

86   Cordesman, *Israeli–Hezbollah War*, pp. 41–4.

87   Cohen and White, p. 9.

88   Ibid., p. x; Intelligence and Terrorism Information Center, *Hamas and the Terrorist Threat*, p. 110. See also Bruce Maddy-Weitzman, 'The Israel–Hamas War: A Preliminary Assessment', *RUSI Journal*, February 2009, pp. 24, 25.

89   Cohen and White, pp. 9–10; Matthews, 'Hard Lessons Learned', p. 25.

90   See, for example, Department of the Army, *Field Manual 3-06.11, Combined Operations in Urban Terrain* (28 February 2002), pp. 1–3b(2), 1–5f, http://www.globalsecurity.org/military/library/policy/army/fm/3-06-11/ch1.htm#par3;

[The enemies of Allah] do not know that the Palestinian people has developed its [methods] of death and death-seeking. For the Palestinian people, death has become an industry, at which women excel, and so do all the people living on this land. The elderly excel at this, and so do the *mujahideen* and the children. This is why they have formed human shields of the women, the children, the elderly, and the *mujahideen*, in order to challenge the Zionist bombing machine. It is as if they were saying to the Zionist enemy: 'We desire death like you desire life.'[91]

Any resulting civilian casualties caused by Israeli attacks, no matter how discriminate and proportional, became part of Hamas's strategic narrative of Israel's disproportionate response and war crimes.[92]

During the Gaza conflict, Hamas and other Palestinian military groups fought from civilian areas while dressed as civilians,[93] making it difficult for Israeli forces to identify them. They fired rockets from residential neighbourhoods and engaged Israeli forces from or near houses, hospitals, mosques, schools and UN compounds.[94] Seeking protection from Israeli attacks, Hamas established its major

---

91   'Speech by Hamas MP Fathi Hammad', *Al-Aqsa Television*, 29 February 2008, http://www.peacewithrealism.org/headline/admit.htm The mission mentioned the speech (*Goldstone Report*, para. 477), but discarded it as irrelevant (para. 478).

92   Cohen and White, pp. 14–15; Lieutenant Colonel Michael D. Snyder, 'Information Strategies Against a Hybrid Threat: What Recent Experiences of Israel Versus Hezbollah/Hamas Tell the US Army', in *Back to Basics: A Study of the Second Lebanon War and Operation Cast Lead* (Fort Leavenworth, Kan.: Combined Studies Institute, May 2009), pp. 106, 130; Cohen, p. 4; Dershowitz, p. 26.

93   Steven Erlanger, 'A Gaza War Full of Traps and Trickery', *The New York Times*, 11 January 2009, http://www.nytimes.com/2009/01/11/world/middleeast/11hamas.html; Landes, p. 8; Intelligence and Terrorism Information Center, *Hamas and the Terrorist Threat*, pp. 196–20, 213–15.

94   See Footnote 77. See also Amnesty International, *Israel/Gaza Operation: 22 Days of Death & Destruction* (London, July 2009), 4.2.1; Cordesman, *The 'Gaza War'*, pp. 43–7, 49, 51–2, 54–5; Yaakov Katz, 'Gazans Tell Israeli Investigators of Hamas Abuses', *Jerusalem Post*, 1 February 2009, http://www.jpost.com/Home/Article.aspx?id=131380; Ulrike Putz, 'Gaza in Ruins: "Who Has Won Here?"', *Spiegel Online*, 23 January 2009, http://www.spiegel.de/international/world/0,1518,603203,00.html;   Ethan   Bronner, 'Parsing Gains of Gaza War', *The New York Times*, 19 January 2009, http://www.nytimes.com/2009/01/19/world/middleeast/19assess.html; Yoav Stern, 'Gaza Reporter Caught on Tape Confirming Hamas Fired Rockets Near TV Station', *Haaretz.com*, 20 January 2009, http://www.haaretz.com/hasen/spages/1057129.html; Dominic Lawson, 'No, We Are Not All Hamas Now', *Sunday Times*, 11 January 2009, http://www.timesonline.co.uk/tol/comment/columnists/dominic_lawson/article5489436.ece; 'IDF Unveils Hamas Map Seized in Gaza', *Jerusalem Post*, 8 January 2009, http://www.jpost.com/Home/Article.aspx?id=128484; Yaakov Katz, 'Shelled UN Building Used by Hamas', *Jerusalem Post*, 15 January 2009, http://www.jpost.com/Home/Article.aspx?id=129393; Abraham Cooper and Harold Brackman, 'The Threat of the Human Shield Strategy Hamas Uses Extends Beyond Gaza', Opinion, *US News & World Report*, 9 January 2009, http://www.usnews.

command post at Gaza's main hospital,[95] stored weapons and ammunition in civilian buildings[96] and used civilians to shield combatants from attack.[97] In short:

> Hamas used the urban terrain to its advantage in terms of providing cover and operational and tactical shielding. It placed fighters and weapons caches inside schools, mosques, and other public buildings in addition to homes. In preparation, Hamas booby-trapped houses and buildings, placed IEDs in homes, and used its tunnel network to move and resupply, albeit not as effectively as Hezbollah. Hamas used Gaza's main hospital as a command center and defensive fighting position.[98]

Hamas intentionally added to the normal 'fog of war'; the conditions created by its tactics necessarily made it much more difficult for the Israelis to distinguish military targets from civilians and civilian objects.[99] Israel took steps to minimize

---

com/articles/opinion/2009/01/09/the-threat-of-the-human-shield-strategy-hamas-uses-extends-beyond-israel-gaza.html; Craig Whitlock and Reyham Abdel Kareem, 'Gaza Clan Finds One Haven After Another Ravaged in Attacks', *Washington Post*, 16 January 2009, http://www.washingtonpost.com/wp-dyn/content/article/2009/01/15/AR2009011503832. html; Rod Norland, 'Hamas and its Discontents', *Newsweek*, 20 January 2009, http://www. newsweek.com/2009/01/19/hamas-and-its-discontents.html; Sebastian Rotella, 'Conflict in Gaza: Hamas' Weapon of Choice', *Los Angeles Times*, 15 January 2009 (2009 WLNR 775471); Andy Soltis, 'Hamas in "Human Shield" Atrocity – Uses School as Mortar Lair Where Children Die', *New York Post*, 7 January 2009 (2009 WLNR 313151).

95   Amos Harel, 'Sources: Hamas Leaders Hiding in Basement of Israel-Built Hospital in Gaza', *Haaretz.com*, 22 February 2009, http://www.haaretz.com/hasen/spages/1054569. html; Intelligence and Terrorism Information Center, *Hamas and the Terrorist Threat*, pp. 164, 166–7; Norwitz, pp. 2–3. Oddly, the mission did not investigate this matter (*Goldstone Report*, para. 468), even though the misuse of such a protected facility arguably constitutes perfidy (Additional Protocol I, Art. 37). See Blank, *The Application of IHL in the Goldstone Report: A Critical Commentary*, pp. 19–21; Feinstein, p. 236; The Judge Advocate General's School, US Army, *Operational Law Handbook* (2009), p. 24.

96   Steve Erlanger, 'Weighing Crimes and Ethics in the Fog of Urban Warfare', *The New York Times*, 16 January 2009, http://www.nytimes.com/2009/01/17/world/ middleeast/17israel.html; Intelligence and Terrorism Information Center, *Hamas and the Terrorist Threat*, pp. 145–62, 165, 172–7, 179–94, 202–11.

97   Dore Gold, 'The Dangerous Bias of the United Nations Goldstone Report', Opinion, *US News & World Report*, 10 March 2010 (2010 WLNR 6217934); Intelligence and Terrorism Information Center, *Hamas and the Terrorist Threat*, p. 141.

98   Mellies, p. 69. See also *Gaza Operation Investigations: Second Update* (Jerusalem: State of Israel, 19 July 2010), p. 146, http://www.mfa.gov.il/NR/rdonlyres/1483B296-7439-4217-933C-653CD19CE859/0/GazaUpdateJuly2010.pdf (hereinafter *Gaza Operation Investigations*).

99   According to the Government of Israel: 'The Gaza Operation presented complex military challenges in protecting civilians from the hazards of battle. Urban warfare and the cynical choice made by Hamas to imbed itself in civilian urban areas and to use civilian

civilian casualties – not all of them successful.[100] For example, it gave warnings of impending attacks,[101] it chose (in some cases) weapon systems likely to cause the least collateral harm,[102] and it avoided targets where the resulting collateral damage would be too great;[103] however, 'many Hamas targets were so deeply embedded in densely populated areas and located so close to civilian buildings that it was impossible to avoid collateral damage'.[104]

International Humanitarian Law Considerations: The 'Big' Picture

If the mission did not find supporting evidence of Hamas's doctrine and tactics, it was because it did not look.[105] The mission correctly recognized that Hamas and other Palestinian armed groups were bound by international humanitarian law,[106] but on those occasions when the mission acknowledged that Palestinian combatants fought from civilian areas or wore civilian clothing, it diminished the significance of such tactics by questioning whether the armed groups had done so intentionally or for the purpose of shielding themselves from attack. What is one to make of such findings? That Hamas and other Palestinian combatants accidentally found themselves in civilian areas? That, as Professor Moshe Halbertal has wondered, Palestinian militants did 'not wear their uniforms because they were inconveniently at the laundry'?[107]

How Hamas planned and conducted its combat operations during the conflict *is* exactly the issue the mission should have examined. Civilian casualties, while

---

structures as shields contributed to the great challenges for Israeli air and ground forces' (*Gaza Operation Investigations*, p. 146). See also Dershowitz, p. 21; Landes, p. 4.

100   Erlanger, 'Weighing Crimes and Ethics'.

101   'Interview, Colonel Richard Kemp, Former Commander of British Forces in Afghanistan', *BBC News*, 18 January 2009, http://www.youtube.com/watch?v=WssrKJ3Iqcw See also Cordesman, *The 'Gaza War'*, p. 17.

102   *Gaza Operation Investigations*, p. 85; Cordesman, *The 'Gaza War'*, p. 17. Professor Cordesman noted that 'the use of lighter weapons sometimes had to be mixed with the use of the equivalent of larger bombs in order to strike successfully at larger, hardened and sheltered targets'.

103   Statement of Colonel Richard Kemp.

104   Cordesman, *The 'Gaza War'*, pp. 17–18.

105   See Footnotes 18–19, 66–8, 71–83, and accompanying text. See also Bell, p. 8.

106   *Goldstone Report*, para. 304. See *Prosecutor v Sam Hinga Norman*, Case No. SCSL-2004-14-AR72(E), Decision on Preliminary Motion Based on Lack of Jurisdiction (Child Recruitment) (31 May 2004), p. 22.

107   Halbertal, p. 2. International humanitarian law does not explicitly require that combatants wear uniforms *per se*, only that they wear a distinctive sign recognizable at a distance. GPW Article 4. Nevertheless, combatants are generally expected to wear uniforms, Dinstein, p. 44, and Hamas has uniforms, which it displays during ceremonies, but apparently not during combat operations. See, for example, photograph at http://zioneocon.blogspot.com/hamas%20parade%20gaza%20053004.jpg

always a tragedy, are not always a war crime,[108] particularly when a belligerent intentionally places itself in the civilian population.[109] Thus, the mission needed to give context to the Israeli military campaign.[110] What did the IDF commanders and soldiers on the ground know? What threats were they confronting? Where were Hamas and other Palestinian combatants situated? Did they distinguish themselves from the civilian population? Where were Hamas's command and control centres and its storage facilities? If Israeli soldiers deliberately targeted civilians, they must be punished,[111] but bare assertions of the unlawful targeting of civilians do not warrant indictments against the IDF or the Government of Israel.

More fundamentally, the mission should have addressed how a military committed to compliance with the law of war is supposed to deal with an insurgent or terrorist group that implants itself into a civilian population either to deter an attack or to reap the strategic 'benefits' of the inevitable civilian casualties that result from an attack.[112] While recognizing (at least to some extent) that Hamas and other militant groups used civilian areas for their combat operations,[113] the mission erroneously placed the onus of avoiding civilian casualties entirely on Israel.[114]

Conclusion

An international legal regime that rewards belligerents who deliberately place civilians at risk is untenable. States can be expected neither to permit their citizens to be placed in jeopardy from insurgent or terrorist attacks nor to endure

---

108   *Prosecutor v Kordic & Cerkez*, IT-95-14/2-A (Appellate Chamber, 17 December 2004), p. 52; W. Hays Parks, 'Air War and the Law of War', *Air Force Law Review*, 32 (1990): 1, 177; Judith Gail Gardam, 'Proportionality and Force in International Law', *American Journal of International Law*, 87 (1993): 391, 398.

109   See Johan D. van der Vyver, 'Legal Ramifications of the War in Gaza', *Florida Journal of International Law*, 21 (2009): 403, 430–31.

110   See Samuel Vincent Jones, 'Has Conduct Confirmed the Moral Inadequacy of International Humanitarian Law? Examining the Confluence Between Contract Theory and the Scope of Civilian Immunity During Armed Conflict', *Duke Journal of Comparative and International Law*, 16 (2006): 249, 277.

111   Landes, p. 4.

112   Ibid., p. 2. See generally, Michael N. Schmitt, 'The Principle of Proportionality in 21st Century Warfare', *Yale Human Rights and Development Law Journal*, 2 (1999): 143, 169; Jonathan Keiler, 'The End of Proportionality', *Parameters* (Spring 2009), pp. 53, 58.

113   See Footnote 71 and accompanying text.

114   An editorial written by Justice Goldstone after release of the report is instructive: 'Israel is correct that identifying combatants in a heavily populated area is difficult, and that Hamas fighters at times mixed and mingled with civilians. *But that reality did not lift Israel's obligation to take all feasible measures to minimize harm to civilians.*' Richard Goldstone, 'Justice in Gaza', *The New York Times*, 17 September 2009, http://www.nytimes.com/2009/09/17/opinion/17goldstone.html (emphasis added).

severe combat losses because insurgent or terrorist forces discard international law and base their strategy on their opponent's adherence to the law.[115] All the fulminations of the UN Human Rights Council, NGOs and the media will not alter a state's obligation to protect its citizens or minimize its combat losses – nor should they. And by countenancing or ignoring the operational doctrine embraced by insurgent and terrorist groups to use civilians as tools in their military operations, these groups become 'enablers', tacitly encouraging such tactics as employed by Hamas in Gaza. The consequence will inevitably be higher civilian casualties in future conflicts.[116]

---

115 See Newton, p. 277.

116 Kenneth Anderson, 'A Public Call for International Attention to Legal Obligations of Defending Forces as well as Attacking Forces to Protect Civilians in Armed Conflicts', *Crimes of War Project*, 19 March 2003, http://www.crimesofwar.org/special/Iraq/news-iraq3.html

Chapter 16

An Assessment of the Gaza Report's Contribution to the Development of International Humanitarian Law

Susan Breau

A major focus of attention by the international community in late 2008 and early 2009 were the military operations carried out by Israel in the Gaza Strip.[1] 'Operation Cast Lead' was launched in response to the increasing incidents of rocket fire by Hamas into Israel and continued from 27 December 2008 until 18 January 2009. The Israeli military operations began with a week-long air attack (27 December – 3 January 2009) followed by a ground offensive (3–18 January 2009). The Israeli Navy was also deployed in part to shell the Gaza coast during the operations.[2] During this short period, the UN Security Council met several times to consider the situation in Gaza.[3] In particular, the Israeli strike on three schools run by the UN Relief and Works Agency for Palestine Refugees in the Near East (UNRWA) – each of which had during the hostilities been used as a civilian shelter – was heavily criticized by members of the Security Council.[4] Nevertheless, the resolution resulting from such deliberations was not as critical and took an even approach by calling on all parties to protect civilians.[5]

The distinctive development in international law occurred after the ending of hostilities and took place on the initiation of the Human Rights Council. On 3 April 2009, the UN Fact-Finding Mission on the Gaza Conflict was established by the council with the mandate

> to investigate all violations of international human rights law and international humanitarian law that might have been committed at any time in the context of

---

1 The other armed conflicts ongoing at the time were Afghanistan, Iraq and the Russia/Georgia conflict.

2 *Report of the United Nations Fact-Finding Mission on the Gaza Conflict*, UN Doc. A/HRC/12/48, 25 September 2009, para. 29.

3 Security Council Meeting 6072, 21 January 2009.

4 UN Doc. S/PV. 6061, took place on 6 and 7 January 2009.

5 UN Doc. S/Res/1860 (2009), 8 January 2009.

the military operations that were conducted in Gaza during the period from 27 December 2008 and 18 January 2009, whether before, during or after.[6]

The mission investigated 36 incidents and issued recommendations on a variety of matters including accountability for serious violations of international humanitarian law and human rights law.[7] Although some of the methods and conclusions might be criticized, the *Report of the United Nations Fact-Finding Mission on the Gaza Conflict*[8] provides a unique opportunity for the international humanitarian law community to review an extensive assessment of compliance (or lack thereof) with the rules and customs governing the conduct of an armed conflict, particularly with respect to the protection of civilians.

Notwithstanding this view of the report, it has to be acknowledged that the report attracted a storm of criticism within Israel and the United States. The US House of Representatives passed a resolution opposing unequivocally any endorsement or further consideration of the *Gaza Report*.[9] The focus of this chapter is to examine specifically some of the conclusions made with respect to allegations of violations of international humanitarian law and to address the various criticisms of the report including those made in the chapter in this book by Professor Rosen. Furthermore, as this article was just about to be published, Justice Richard Goldstone, the chair of the mission, in an 'op-ed' piece for the *Washington Post* seemed to back down from some of the recommendations of the mission. This development will also be addressed within this chapter.[10]

This chapter will first address allegations of bias; second, assess the criticisms concerning the methodology of the report; third, assess the legal framework employed; and last, review the report's consideration of the various violations of international humanitarian law by the parties of the conflict. Although there is also extensive discussion of violations of international human rights law for the purposes of this analysis, the focus is on international humanitarian law's treaty and customary provisions that protect civilian populations. There are also major debates with respect to the applicability of international criminal law and the jurisdiction of the International Criminal Court raised by the report, which are also thoroughly discussed elsewhere and not raised in this contribution although

---

6   UN Doc. A/HRC/S-9/L.1, 12 January 2009, and Human Rights Council, Press Release, 3 April 2009. This body is hereinafter referred to as 'the mission'.

7   Ibid., para. 1764.

8   For the purposes of this chapter, the report hereinafter will be referenced as the *Gaza Report*.

9   H. Res. 867, 3 November 2009.

10   R. Goldstone, 'Reconsidering the Goldstone Report on Israel and War Crimes', *The Washington Post*, 1 April 2011, http://www.washingtonpost.com/opinions/reconsidering-the-goldstone-report-on-israel-and-war-crimes/2011/04/01/AFg111JC_story.html

it is evident that international criminal justice is essential in the protection of civilians.[11]

Allegations of Bias

In this review of the various recommendations and conclusions of the report, it is first necessary to address the allegations of bias on the part of the committee as this type of charge could invalidate the whole process. The committee was led by Justice Richard Goldstone, former judge of the Constitutional Court of South Africa and former Prosecutor of the International Criminal Tribunals for the former Yugoslavia and Rwanda. The other three members of the mission were Professor Christine Chinkin, Professor of International Law at the London School of Economics and Political Science, Hina Jilani, Advocate of the Supreme Court of Pakistan and former Special Rapporteur of the UN Secretary-General on the situation of human rights defenders, and Colonel Desmond Travers, a former officer in Ireland's Defence Forces and member of the Board of Directors of the Institute for International Criminal Investigations.[12] Although some might question the composition of the panel as including those who are biased against Israel, it cannot be disputed that all members were experienced international lawyers.[13]

The particular allegation of bias was directed towards Christine Chinkin, who had signed a letter on the Gaza conflict that was critical of Israel before being selected to the committee. In this letter, Chinkin and a group of prominent academics and practitioners argued that Israel's justification of self-defence in the bombardment of Israel had no merit and that it constituted a war crime.[14] The letter, however, also equally condemned the firing of rockets by Hamas into Israel and suicide bombings and stated that they were also war crimes. The letter indicated that Israel had a right to protect its civilian population from such attacks. Therefore, it could perhaps be argued that Chinkin has an equal bias against Israel and Hamas.

The Oxford Dictionary of Law, under natural justice, discusses the rules against bias, which are defined as a departure from the standard of even-handed justice required of those who occupy judicial office that no human may be a judge in their own cause.[15] Applying that rigorous standard in *R.V. Bow Street*

---

11   See, for example, Y. Ronen, 'ICC Jurisdiction Over Acts Committed in the Gaza Strip', *Journal of International Criminal Justice*, 8 (2010): 3; and D. Benoliel and R. Perry, 'Israel, Palestine and the ICC', *Michigan Journal of International Law*, 32 (2010): 73.

12   Human Rights Council, Press Release, 3 April 2009.

13   The Israelis accused the panel of bias against Israel. See, for example, the Israeli web site http://www.haaretz.com/news/goldstone-punish-commanders-who-broke-laws-in-gaza-1.7706

14   Letter in *Sunday Times*, 11 January 2009.

15   *Oxford Dictionary of Law*, 6th edn (Oxford University Press, 2006), p. 351.

Metropolitan Stipendiary Magistrate, ex-parte Pinochet Ugarte (No. 2), Judge Browne-Wilkinson stated of Lord Hoffmann's role as a member of Amnesty International: 'If the absolute impartiality of the judiciary is to be maintained, there must be a rule which automatically disqualifies a judge who is involved, whether personally or as a Director of a company in promoting the same causes in the same organization as is party to the suit.'[16]

Even though it could be argued that Chinkin was not holding a judicial office, the nature of this inquiry arguably was similar to a judicial inquiry. What is described as bias in the case law is not, however, as broad as to encompass the situation of a person signing a letter of protest. There is no allegation that Chinkin had any membership whatsoever in any organization with an interest in Gaza or Israel or indeed a humanitarian law or aid organization.

An expert meeting was conducted at Chatham House in 2009, which conducted an assessment of the *Gaza Report*, and one of the topics under review was this allegation of bias.[17] This meeting of experts in the field expressed their 'complete confidence in the personal integrity of Professor Chinkin ... and that her participation would have had no detrimental impact on the impartiality of the Mission's conclusions'. This has to be the correct conclusion in that one letter of protest did not constitute a previous investigation and could not constitute a disqualification given the even tenor of the letter and the lack of specificity as to the allegations of violations of humanitarian law.

There was a further allegation of bias within the resolution of the House of Representatives: that the mandate for the fact-finding mission 'pre-judged the outcome of its investigation, by one-sidedly mandating' investigation of the violations of international human rights law and international humanitarian law by 'Israel, against the Palestinian people ... due to the current aggression'. What this resolution fails to consider is the amending of the mandate on 3 April 2009 by the President of the Human Rights Council, which stated:

> [T]o investigate all violations of international human rights law and international humanitarian law that might have been committed at any time in the context of the military operations that were conducted in Gaza during the period from 27 December 2008 and 18 January 2009, whether before, during or after.[18]

The question remains as to whether a press release and statement by the President of the Human Rights Council could cure the flawed mandate in the resolution.

---

16   *R v Bow Street Metropolitan Stipendiary Magistrate, ex parte Pinochet Ugarte (No. 2)* (House of Lords) [1999] All ER 577 at 588; and see K. Malleson, 'Judicial Bias and Disqualification after Pinochet No. 2', *Modern Law Review*, 63 (2000): 119.

17   *Report of an Expert Meeting which Assessed Procedural Criticisms Made of the UN Fact-Finding Mission on the Gaza Conflict (The Goldstone Report)*, Chatham House, 27 November 2009.

18   UN Human Rights Council, Press Release, 3 April 2009.

This was also addressed by the expert panel at Chatham House, which labelled the resolution as 'aggressively biased against Israel'.[19] This was contrary to the original resolution of the General Assembly considering these sorts of missions that declared that '[f]act-finding should be comprehensive, objective, impartial and timely'.[20] The expert committee and this writer argued, however, that the way the mission was conducted was the important question and there is no doubt that the mission considered violations of the rules of international humanitarian and human rights law on both sides of the conflict and thus responded to the amended mandate.[21] This was later confirmed by Goldstone, who indicated that he insisted on changing the original mandate, which 'skewed against Israel'.[22]

A final criticism related to bias levelled by the panel that met in London was the style and presentation of the report. The Chatham House group argued that the criticisms in the report of Hamas were tentative, while the language addressed to Israel was 'stronger and more condemnatory'. The group suggested that if the conclusions had been presented as *prima-facie* findings rather than conclusions, the report would have been stronger. It was also suggested that the titles of some of the incidents disclosed bias, such as 'Deliberate Attacks on the Gaza Police'.[23] This criticism might have some merit, however, the carefully considered facts, following the extensive methodology employed (as discussed below), showed that the violations of international humanitarian law by the Israelis during this operation were grievous indeed and merited the titles used and the condemnatory language. It is correct, however, that the violation of the rule of distinction between civilians and military objectives occasioned by Hamas firing missiles into Israel deserved equally strong language.

Methodology

One of the other major criticisms of the report was that the methodology employed in the preparation of the report was one-sided due to the lack of participation of Israel. Yet it must be seen that the method of gathering evidence employed was comprehensive and robust and included:

> (a) the review of reports from different sources; (b) interviews with victims, witnesses and other persons having relevant information; (c) site visits to specific locations in Gaza where incidents had occurred; (d) the analysis of video and photographic images, including satellite imagery; (e) the review of medical reports about injuries to victims; (f) the forensic analysis of weapons

---

19   *Report of an Expert Meeting*, p. 4.
20   UN Doc. GA Res. 46/59, 9 December 1991, para. 3.
21   *Report of an Expert Meeting*, p. 5.
22   Goldstone.
23   *Report of an Expert Meeting*, pp. 13 and 14.

and ammunition remnants collected at incident sites; (g) meetings with a variety of interlocutors; (h) invitations to provide information relating to the Mission's investigation requirements; (i) the wide circulation of a public call for written submissions; (j) public hearings in Gaza and in Geneva.[24]

Israel's decision not to cooperate with the mission was regrettable in that facts that might otherwise have resulted in supplementary and/or different assessments were simply unavailable to it.[25] The Israeli Government did not provide answers to questions directed to it by the mission.[26] As Goldstone indicated, the lack of cooperation meant that the mission was not able to corroborate how many of Gaza's people killed were civilians and how many were combatants.[27] Nevertheless, it can be argued that the lack of cooperation was not fatal to the methodology. The drafters of the report had access to a number of documents amongst the 300 reports they reviewed setting out the Israeli position.[28]

There are certainly precedents in law for proceeding without the presence or cooperation of one of the parties. The Statute of the International Court of Justice specifically provides for that eventuality. Article 53 of the statute states:

1. Whenever one of the parties does not appear before the Court, or fails to defend its case, the other party may call upon the Court to decide in favour of its claim.
2. The Court must, before doing so, satisfy itself, not only that it has jurisdiction in accordance with Articles 36 and 37, but also that the claim is well founded in fact and law.

They proceeded on that basis in the *Corfu Channel* case and the *Nicaragua Judgment* phase (after the United States refused to participate in the hearing after the jurisdiction phase). It is not an ideal result but certainly has become accepted practice when ruling on matters that affect state responsibility for violent activity.

Given the constraints the mission was working under, the report contains a remarkable degree of specificity regarding the 36 incidents that were investigated and importantly evaluates extensive Israeli information and justification for every incident.

---

24 *Gaza Report*, para. 18. And in para. 19 the report indicated that the mission conducted 188 individual interviews. It reviewed more than 300 reports, submissions and other documentation researched of its own motion, received in reply to its call for submissions and notes verbales or provided during meetings or otherwise, amounting to more than 10,000 pages, more than 30 videos and 1,200 photographs.

25 Ibid., para. 20.

26 Ibid., para. 26.

27 Goldstone.

28 *Gaza Report*, para. 19.

There were other criticisms directed at the *Gaza Report* concerning the methodology employed. First, the expert panel convening in London discussed the hearing of evidence in public in Gaza; this was also criticized by the US House of Representatives.[29] The issue was the potential intimidation of witnesses who would be reluctant to speak about the conduct of Hamas. The expert committee stated that 'more information would have been obtained by taking evidence in confidence and teasing out the information rather than trying to do so in a public forum'. [30] Yet these public hearings formed only a small part of the activities of the mission and on the whole information was gathered outside these hearings.[31] The mission justified the conduct of the hearings as the aim was giving voice to those who had direct experiences and expertise that related to the mandate of the mission.[32] There is another important justification advanced by the expert meeting and this is that this type of testimony would be similar to a truth and reconciliation mission. That cannot be accurate given the refusal of Israel to participate. A more apt justification would be that this bolstered the credibility of the mission in Gaza by giving public attention to their investigations.

The next criticism was that of the pre-selection and pre-screening of witnesses who were not asked questions concerning the conduct of the Hamas forces. This was addressed in paragraphs 164–7 of the *Gaza Report*. The witnesses were selected on the basis that they had firsthand experience or information or specialized knowledge of the issues under investigation. The mission also contacted community representatives, local authorities, members of non-governmental organizations and experts. Therefore, it cannot be argued that the witnesses were those who could not be asked questions regarding the conduct of Hamas and the conclusions of the report of violations of international humanitarian law by Hamas do not support that contention. One difficulty was the access to witnesses because of restrictions imposed by Israel on freedom of movement. The mission took the factor of intimidation into account. The report stated: 'Taking into account the demeanour of witnesses, the plausibility of their accounts and the consistency of these accounts with the circumstances observed by it and with other testimonies, the Mission was able to determine the credibility and reliability of those people it heard.'[33]

This seems to be the standard way in which any quasi-judicial body or indeed court may assess the credibility of its witnesses and partly addresses the issue of pre-selection and pre-screening of witnesses. It is certainly the case that it would have been better for the mission to have had access to all the witnesses, which would have necessitated cooperation by Israel.

---

29   *Report of an Expert Meeting*, p. 6; and see H. Res. 867, 3 November 2009.
30   Ibid., p. 7.
31   Ibid., p. 8; and the *Gaza Report* in total.
32   *Gaza Report*, para. 167.
33   Ibid., para. 170.

The Legal Framework

There is a criticism that can be levelled against the report with respect to one specific aspect of the legal framework employed. First, however, the general legal regime employed was entirely appropriate. The report stated that the legal framework applicable to situations of occupation included provisions in the Hague Regulations (especially Articles 42–56), the Fourth Geneva Convention (especially Articles 47–78) and those provisions of Additional Protocol I that had been incorporated into customary international law. The drafters observed that the development of the legal framework represented attempts by the international community to better protect human beings from the effects of war while giving due account to military necessity.[34] The mission found that at all times relevant to the mandate of the mission, Israel exercised effective control over the Gaza Strip and that, as a result, the provisions of the Fourth Geneva Convention applied.[35] The report declared that the ultimate authority over the Occupied Palestinian Territory still rested with Israel even though Israel had transferred to the Palestinian Authority a series of functions within certain designated zones. In so concluding, the mission cited the Advisory Opinion of the International Court of Justice (ICJ) on the *Legal Consequences of the Construction of a Wall in the Occupied Palestinian Territory* that the transfer of powers and responsibilities by Israel under various agreements with the Palestine Liberation Organization (PLO) had 'done nothing' to alter the character of Israel as an occupying power.[36] This was an extremely important and accurate finding as it engages Israel in the obligations to comply with the Fourth Geneva Convention and a number of other obligations under customary humanitarian law.

The problem area of application of international law was that the analysis contained in the *Gaza Report* failed to characterize the armed conflict that occurred in the Gaza Strip as international or non-international (internal) conflict. The mission rightly maintained that developments in the past two decades, through the jurisprudence of international tribunals, particularly the International Criminal Tribunal for the former Yugoslavia, had led to the conclusion that the substantive rules applicable to international and non-international armed conflict were converging. This is also supported by the influential International Committee of the Red Cross publication on Customary Humanitarian Law which argues that the vast majority of customary humanitarian rules are identical in both types of conflict.[37]

---

34   Ibid., para. 273.

35   Ibid., para. 276.

36   Ibid., para. 279; and *Legal Consequences of the Construction of a Wall in the Occupied Palestinian Territory*, Advisory Opinion of 9 July 2004, ICJ Reports 2004, paras 76–8.

37   Jean-Marie Henckaerts and Louise Doswald-Beck, *Customary International Humanitarian Law: Volume I. The Rules* (Cambridge: Cambridge University Press, 2005).

The report recognized, however, that certain differences still existed particularly in relation to the regime of enforcement established by treaty law, particularly the system of 'grave breaches' contained in the Geneva Convention, which is applicable only in international armed conflict.[38] While the mission did not render an opinion on the characterization of the Gaza conflict, it indicated that the military hostilities took place between the Israeli armed forces and the military wing of Hamas and other Palestinian factions.[39] Citing the Israeli Supreme Court's opinion that the confrontation between Israeli armed forces and 'terrorist organizations' active in the Occupied Palestinian Territories was an international armed conflict,[40] the report then recalled the statement made by the Government of Israel that the classification of the armed conflict in question might not be too important, as 'many similar norms govern both types of conflict'. There is an equally compelling argument that can be made that the conflict is a non-international armed conflict taking place within the occupation by Israel of the Palestinian territories between the armed forces of Israel and armed Palestinian groups.[41]

In keeping with not classifying the conflict the report also noted that the rules contained in Common Article 3 (applicable to non-international armed conflict) represented the 'baseline rules applicable to all conflicts' and that the rules in Article 75 of Additional Protocol I (applicable in international armed conflict), which reflect customary international law, 'define a series of fundamental guarantees and protections' that are recognized under human rights law.[42] The report cited with approval the ruling of the Appeals Chamber of the International Criminal Tribunal in the *Tadić* case that 'what is inhumane, and consequently proscribed, in international wars, cannot but be inhumane and inadmissible in civil strife' and argued that this ruling related not only to the protection of civilians but also to the methods and means of warfare.[43] This is clearly the case in assessing the violations of international humanitarian law during the conduct of the conflict, but it is not as plain for assessing the consequences of the breaches of the laws and customs of armed conflict.

---

38   *Gaza Report*, para. 281.

39   Ibid., para. 282.

40   *The Public Committee Against Torture in Israel v The Government of Israel (Targeted Killings case)*, HCJ 796/02.

41   G. Blum, 'Re-Envisaging the International Law of Internal Armed Conflict: A Reply to Sandesh Sivakumaran', (2011) 22 *EJIL* 265.

42   Israeli Ministry of Foreign Affairs, *The Operation in Gaza: Factual and Legal Aspects*, July 2009, http://www.mfa.gov.il/MFA/Terrorism-+Obstacle+to+Peace/Terroris m+and+Islamic+Fundamentalism-/Operation_in_Gaza-Factual_and_Legal_Aspects.htm; *Gaza Report*, paras 282 and 283.

43   *Prosecutor v Tadić*, Case No. IT-94-1-AR72, Decision on the defence motion for interlocutory appeal on jurisdiction of 2 October 1995, para. 119. See also para. 96 ff.

A determination on the classification of the conflict is critical as the grave-breaches regime is inapplicable to non-international armed conflict.[44] The section of the report on international criminal law therefore becomes quite problematic as both the grave-breaches provisions in Article 147 of the Fourth Geneva Convention and war crimes are discussed by reference to Articles 8(2)(a)(grave breaches) and 8(2)(b) (other serious violations of the laws and customs applicable in international armed conflict) of the Statute of the International Criminal Court. It is not definitively set out which regime applies to this conflict and there is no discussion of the separate provisions for non-international armed conflict in the Rome Statute.[45] One difficulty with the lack of clarification is that throughout the report the findings of violations with respect to the investigated incidents are categorized as 'grave breaches' as defined in Article 147 of the Fourth Geneva Convention.[46] Even if the classification issue was not resolved, there should have been a discussion of the criminal consequences that would arise in a non-international armed conflict. As stated above, these findings are in keeping with Israel's categorization of the conflict in Gaza as an international armed conflict and thus a system of grave breaches would be applicable.[47] The report, in assessing the various humanitarian law violations against the law applicable to international armed conflict, is accepting the Israeli position.

The next issue of significance is the discussion of the applicability of international human rights obligations in armed conflict. The mission relied on the International Court of Justice's Advisory Opinion on the *Legality of the Threat or Use of Nuclear Weapons* case that in the context of armed conflict, international humanitarian law is *lex specialis* in relation to human rights law.[48] The report thus concludes that 'human rights law would continue to apply as long as it is not modified or set aside by IHL [international humanitarian law]' and, furthermore, that 'the general rule of human rights law does not lose its effectiveness and will remain in the background to inform the application and interpretation of the relevant humanitarian law rule'.[49] This is a correct statement of the relationship between the two branches of law but the major focus of much of the report is in the *lex specialis* of international humanitarian law known as the *jus in bello*.

---

44 For discussion of this issue, see L. Moir, 'Grave Breaches and Internal Armed Conflict', *Journal of International Criminal Justice*, 7 (2009): 763.

45 *Gaza Report*, paras 288–92; and *Rome Statute of the International Criminal Court, July 17, 1998*, 2187 UNTS 3, Art. 8(2)(c), (d) and (e).

46 *Gaza Report* – see, for example, para. 390.

47 For discussion of this issue, see George Bisharat, Timothy Crawley, Sara Elturk, Carey James, Rose Mishaan, Akila Radhakrishnan and Anna Sanders, 'Israel's Invasion of Gaza in International Law', *Denver Journal of International Law and Policy*, 38 (2009): 41, at pp. 51–6.

48 *Gaza Report*, para. 296; and *Legality of the Threat or Use of Nuclear Weapons (Advisory Opinion)*, 8 July 1996, ICJ Reports 1996, p. 226, para. 25.

49 *Gaza Report*, para. 296.

Another substantial criticism of the report in the Resolution of the US House of Representatives was the lack of consideration in the report of Israel's argument of self-defence. Once again, it is necessary to view the mandate of the committee. The committee was not to consider the '*jus ad bellum*' issues but rather to consider the violations that took place within the conflict regardless of its legality. This specific criticism falls into a common trap of confusing the two branches of international law. Israel may not invoke self-defence to justify violations of the laws and customs of war as these rules apply regardless of who is at fault in instituting the conflict. Self-defence in a particular conflict may be used to defend against deprivation of the right to life but that is assumed in the basic exception to the absolute right to life that exists in armed conflict. In an armed conflict, it is accepted that civilian casualties will occur and the test then is whether those civilian casualties are necessary and proportionate to the direct military advantage.[50] The expert panel convened at Chatham House also supported this position.[51]

Consideration of Various Violations of International Humanitarian Law

A preliminary objection that could be advanced with respect to the discussion of the various incidents is the contention that the incidents selected seemed to be chosen for political effect. The expert meeting in London cited the example that the Goldstone mission failed to investigate allegations that the Shifa Hospital in Gaza had been used as a command centre for Hamas fighters.[52] The reason given by the mission was that it had a short time in which to conclude its investigations, but a more appropriate response might have been that lack of access to Israeli intelligence hampered any in-depth discussion of the issue of human shields and the use of protected objects as locations of military activity. Notwithstanding this criticism, there was extensive analysis of three major humanitarian law issues: blockades, targeting and weaponry. The report details significant and flagrant violations of international humanitarian law, particularly in the area of targeting, that could not be explained by operational constraints or the 'fog of war'.

Blockades

The first extensive consideration of a violation of international humanitarian law involved a discussion of the Israeli 'blockade' of the Gaza Strip. The finding of

---

50   Although the test for proportionality is set out in Additional Protocol 1 of 1977 to the Geneva Convention, which Israel is not a party to, it is argued to be part of customary international law. See Jean-Marie Henckaerts and Louise Doswald-Beck, *Customary International Humanitarian Law: Volume I. The Rules* (Cambridge: Cambridge University Press, 2005).

51   *Report of the Expert Panel*, p. 5.

52   Ibid., p. 10.

the mission was that the closure of the border crossing – subjecting the civilian population to extreme hardship and deprivation inconsistent with their protected status – resulted in increased dependence on foreign aid, increased unemployment and economic hardship inconsistent with their protected status. The committee concluded that:

> Israel continues to be duty-bound under the Fourth Geneva Convention and to the full extent of the means available to it to ensure the supply of foodstuff, medical and hospital items and others to meet the humanitarian needs of the population of the Gaza Strip without qualification. Furthermore, the Mission notes the information it received regarding the lack of compliance by the Government of Israel even with the minimum levels set by the Israeli Court, and in this regard observes that the Government retains wide discretion about the timing and manner of delivering fuel and electricity supplies to the Gaza Strip, and that this discretion appears to have been exercised capriciously and arbitrarily.[53]

First, it has to be noted that blockades are lawful within an international armed conflict. According to the *San Remo Manual of International Law Applicable to Armed Conflicts at Sea*, a naval or maritime blockage consists of 'the blocking of the approach to the enemy coast, or a part of it, for the purpose of preventing ingress and egress of vessels or aircraft of all States'.[54] Second, there are important limitations on the right to impose a blockade. A blockade is prohibited if its sole purpose is 'starving the civilian population or denying it other objects essential for its survival' and if 'the damage to the civilian population is, or maybe expected to be, excessive in relation to the concrete and direct military advantage anticipated from the blockade'.[55]

Another legal issue that arises in the context of an international armed conflict is how the obligations of an occupying power under the Fourth Geneva Convention relate to blockades. Article 59 of the Fourth Geneva Convention mandates that if whole or part of a population is inadequately supplied then the occupying power must agree to a relief scheme, in particular providing foodstuffs, medical supplies and clothing. This applies, as well, in a situation of legal blockade. The *San Remo Manual* states:

> If the civilian population of the blockaded territory is inadequately provided with food and other objects essential for its survival, the blockading party must provide for free passage of such foodstuffs and other essential supplies subject to:

---

53   *Gaza Report*, para. 326.

54   Louise Doswald-Beck (ed.), *San Remo Manual on International Law Applicable to Armed Conflicts at Sea* (Cambridge: Cambridge University Press, 1995).

55   Ibid., s. 102.

a) the right to prescribe the technical arrangements, including search, under which such passage is permitted, and

b) the condition that the distribution of such supplies shall be made under the local supervision of the Protecting Power or a humanitarian organization which offers guarantees of impartiality, such as the International Committee of the Red Cross.[56]

It could be argued, however, that this conflict is most probably a non-international armed conflict and there is little state practice or discussion on whether blockades may be imposed in a non-international armed conflict.[57] These two issues – applicability of blockade in situations of occupation and non-international armed conflict – require further study and analysis. The conclusion of the report that Israel violated the obligation of an occupier to provide food and objects necessary for survival is surely a correct one.

Targeting

The substantial contribution of the report to the development of international humanitarian law was the discussion of the military attacks during the conflict. The significance of the analysis was the application of the specialised law of targeting to the various incidents. This specific facet of humanitarian law receives most of its treaty elucidation within Additional Protocol I of 1977 to the Geneva Conventions – a treaty to which Israel is not a party. In spite of this fact, the report applies customary humanitarian law to several incidents and thus brings clarity to the law of targeting even to those powers not party to the Additional Protocols.

The context of the targeting decisions by the Israelis was a reliance on the Dahiya doctrine coined by the Israelis in operations in Southern Lebanon in 2006, which endorsed the use of 'disproportionate force and the causing of great damage and destruction to civilian property and infrastructure, and suffering to the civilian population'.[58] The mission concluded that this was the strategy put into place in Operation Cast Lead.[59] Falk, in his assessment of the report, concludes that this strategy 'comes close to raising the issue as to whether waging a one-sided war against an essentially defenceless population can even be reconciled with international humanitarian law or the customary international law of war'.[60] The Dahiya doctrine clearly conflicts with the primary obligations in international

---

56   Ibid., s. 103.

57   For further discussion on this complex issue, see Katherine Iliopoulos, *The Legality of Israel's Blockage of Gaza* (Washington, DC: Crimes of War Project), http://www.crimesofwar.org/onnews/news-gaza9.html

58   R. Falk, 'The Goldstone Report: Ordinary Text, Extraordinary Event', *Global Governance*, 16 (2010): 173, at p. 177; and *Gaza Report*, paras 1191–4.

59   *Gaza Report*, para. 1195.

60   Falk, p. 178.

humanitarian law of distinguishing between civilians and combatants and as far as possible sparing civilians.

The report discusses several attacks and this chapter can discuss only a few of these. The incidents chosen represent vital issues in humanitarian law. The first is the issue of distinction between civilian and military objects and civilians and combatants. The second is the prohibition against targeting specially protected objects. The third is the issue of dual-use targets. The fourth is the necessity to use precautions to spare civilian casualties in an attack. Finally, there is discussion of proportionality, which involves the difficult concept of military advantage.

Combatant Status and Distinction between Civilian Objects and Military Objectives

The report identified the failure to distinguish between civilian objects and military objectives, as exemplified by the attacks on Gaza's government buildings, prisons and police stations. The mission concluded that the strikes on the government buildings and prison amounted to a clear violation of international humanitarian law given the 'absence of evidence or, indeed, any allegation from the Israeli Government and armed forces that the Legislative Council building, the Ministry of Justice or the Gaza main prison "made an effective contribution to military action"'. As a result, the mission found that '[o]n the information available to it … the attacks on these buildings constituted deliberate attacks on civilian objects in violation of the rule of customary international humanitarian law whereby attacks must be strictly limited to military objectives'. The mission concluded that, in its view, 'these facts further indicate [to] the Mission of [sic] the grave breach of extensive destruction of property, not justified by military necessity'.[61]

Another related operation canvassed in depth was the attack on Gaza policemen on 27 December 2008. The legal issue in this attack was whether the Gaza police were combatants and thus could be lawfully attacked, as Israel had argued the police were Hamas fighters. The mission found that there was insufficient information to conclude that the Gaza police as a whole had been incorporated into the armed forces of the Gaza authorities.[62] The mission report found that the policemen killed could not be considered to have been combatants by virtue of their membership in the police nor did they take direct part in hostilities. Therefore, they did not lose their civilian immunity.[63] They also considered whether an allegation of members of Palestinian armed groups being among the police could justify the attacks.[64]

---

61   *Gaza Report*, paras 389–90.

62   Ibid., para. 433.

63   Ibid., paras 433–4; and *Protocol Additional to the Geneva Conventions of 12 August 1949, and Relating to the Protection of Victims of International Armed Conflicts (Protocol I) 1977*, 1125 UNTS, Art. 51(3), which the ICRC argues is part of customary international law. See Henckaerts and Doswald-Beck.

64   *Gaza Report*, para. 435.

The consideration of proportionality began with the definition of proportionality in Additional Protocol I, which prohibits launching attacks 'which may be expected to cause incidental loss of civilian life, injury to civilians, damage to civilian objects, or a combination thereof, which would be excessive in relation to the concrete and direct military advantage anticipated'.[65] The report accepted that there might have been individual members of the Gaza police who were at the same time members of Palestinian armed groups and thus combatants, but that did not deprive the whole police force of its status as a civilian law-enforcement agency.

The issue of civilian status is an ongoing debate in international humanitarian law, particularly with the release earlier in 2009 of the International Committee of the Red Cross (ICRC) *Guidance on Direct Participation in Hostilities*.[66] Although some of the ICRC conclusions are controversial, the basic notion that in order to lose civilian status one must be a member of an organized armed group or army is not. Second, a civilian, if not a member of an organized armed group, loses immunity only if they participate in armed activities.[67] The careful analysis performed with respect to determining the status of the government, police and prison employees and facilities is a credit to the authors of the report and the conclusion that these targets are civilian persons and objects is well supported.

Importantly and fairly, the mission considered the targeting by Hamas of the missiles fired towards Israel. The mission determined that the rockets and the mortars fired by the Palestinian armed groups were incapable of being directed towards specific military objectives having been fired into areas where civilian populations were based. The mission concluded that these attacks constituted 'indiscriminate attacks upon the civilian population of southern Israel'. Furthermore, as there was no intended military target, they constituted a deliberate attack against a civilian population and could amount to a crime against humanity and could constitute war crimes. The other possible criminal charge was the war crime of attempting to spread terror amongst a civilian population.[68] It was also found by the mission that Hamas had expressed an intention to target civilians in reprisal for civilian fatalities in Gaza, which was also contrary to international humanitarian law.[69]

Specially Protected Objects

The mission considered attacks on hospitals – specially protected objects within the Geneva Convention. Article 18 of the Fourth Geneva Convention provides that civilian hospitals may in no circumstances be the object of attack but shall at all

---

65   Additional Protocol I, Art. 57(2)(a)(iii), once again argued to be part of customary international law as accepted by the Israelis.

66   Nils Melzer, *Interpretive Guidance on the Notion of Direct Participation in Hostilities*, (Geneva: ICRC, 2009), www.icrc.org

67   Ibid., p. 16.

68   *Gaza Report*, para. 108.

69   Ibid., para. 109.

times be respected and protected by the parties to the conflict. Article 19 provides that the protection to which civilian hospitals are entitled shall cease 'only after due warning has been given, naming, in all appropriate cases, a reasonable time limit and after such warning has remained unheeded'.[70] Considering the attack on Al-Quds hospital on 15 January 2009, when it was hit by a high-explosive shell and by white phosphorous shells, the commission stated that '[e]ven in the unlikely event that there was any armed group present on hospital premises, there is no suggestion even by the Israeli authorities that a warning was given to the hospital of an intention to strike it'.[71] The mission found that Israeli armed forces violated Articles 18 and 19. The mission next considered the attacks on al-Wafa hospital on 5 and 16 January 2009. The mission made the same finding, but added customary international law as reflected in Additional Protocol I, Articles 57 (2) (b) and (c).[72]

One criticism that could be levelled at the mission was the failure to consider the case of the al-Shifa hospital where the Government of Israel alleged that Hamas used two units and a ground-floor wing as a military base. The mission failed to investigate these allegations, which might have given more balance to the report, although there were no civilian deaths or injuries associated with an attack on this hospital. As the London group proposed, it could have been investigated for the use of human shields.[73] Notwithstanding this important omission, the analyses of the hospitals as specially protected objects were impressive in the detailed consideration of whether they could have been used for military purposes and thus lose their protection. The mission found that the Palestinian armed groups were active in the vicinity of the hospitals and the UN shelters but not within the facilities themselves. They did fairly criticize these fighters for exposing civilians to danger.[74]

Dual-use Targets

An interesting finding by the mission was the assertion that international humanitarian law recognizes a category of civilian objects that may nonetheless be targeted in the course of armed conflict to the extent that they have a 'dual use'. Examples given in the report of objects that serve both civilian and military purposes are civilian infrastructure such as telecommunications, power-generating stations or bridges – '*in so far as they are used by the military in addition to civilian use*'.[75] The issue of whether dual-use targets may be attacked in the first

---

70   *Geneva Convention IV Relative to the Protection of Civilian Persons in Time of War, August 12, 1949*, 75 UNTS 287.
71   *Gaza Report*, para. 624.
72   Ibid., para. 650.
73   Ibid., para. 466; and *Report of the Expert Panel*, p. 10.
74   *Gaza Report*, paras 36 and 40.
75   Ibid., para. 386.

place is not resolved, although the United States and Israel maintain the position that they may be attacked.[76] It has to be noted that nowhere in the treaties or customs that constitute international humanitarian law is the term 'dual-use' to be found; rather it was a term coined by the military.[77] What is interesting about the report is that it accepts the Israeli position on this issue and conducts the analysis of targeting in that perspective. Each target is assessed as to whether it had a military purpose. This adds to the perception of fairness of the report, although the military community does not accept dual-use targets universally.[78]

This assessment was conducted in light of the provision in Additional Protocol I, Article 52(2), on civilian objectives, which states:

> Attacks shall be limited strictly to military objectives. In so far as objects are concerned, military objectives are limited to those objects which by their nature, location, purpose or use make an effective contribution to military action and whose total or partial destruction, capture or neutralization, in the circumstances ruling at the time, offers a definite military advantage.[79]

The mission investigated several incidents involving the destruction of industrial infrastructure, food production, water installations, sewage treatment plants and housing to see whether these were indeed dual-use targets.[80] For example, at the beginning of the operation, the el-Bader flour mill was hit by a series of strikes. The mission concluded that its destruction had no military justification and argued that this was a grave breach within the Fourth Geneva Convention, as its destruction was to deny sustenance to the civilian population.[81] The mission also found that there was a 'deliberate and systematic policy on the part of the Israeli armed forces to target industrial sites and water installations'.[82] The general conclusion was that it could not be argued that the targets were dual-use targets and the campaign was to deny the basics of sustaining life to the civilian community. Once again this was a well-reasoned conclusion based on clear evidence.

---

76 For an excellent discussion on this issue, see A. Boivin, *The Legal Regime with Respect to Targeting, Military Objectives in the Context of Contemporary Warfare*, Research Paper No. 2 (Geneva: University Centre for International Humanitarian Law, 2006), http://www.adh-geneva.ch/docs/publications/collection-research-projects/CTR_objectif_militaire.pdf

77 Ibid., p. 23.

78 See, for example, W. Clark, *Waging Modern War* (New York: Public Affairs, 2001), in which, as Supreme Allied Commander Europe, he criticised other governments being unwilling to agree to certain dual-use targets in the campaign concerning Kosovo.

79 Additional Protocol I.

80 *Gaza Report*, para. 50.

81 Ibid.

82 Ibid., para. 54.

Precautions

There were two aspects to consideration of the obligation to take feasible precautions to protect civilian persons and objects. The first was the Palestinian launching of rockets from civilian areas and the second was the obligation to warn civilian populations they were launching attacks in their areas.

With respect to the first aspect, the mission found that the Palestinian armed groups did not at all times adequately distinguish themselves from the civilian population but that there was no evidence that they directed civilians to areas from which they were launching attacks or forced them to remain in the area.[83] Nevertheless, they were criticized for launching attacks near civilian sites such as mosques and hospitals.[84]

The mission acknowledged the significant efforts made by Israel to issue warnings through telephone calls, leaflets and radio broadcasts. There were factors, however, that undermined the effectiveness of this such as the lack of specificity of many prerecorded messages and leaflets. Also Israeli officials were criticized for advising civilians to move to the city centres when those locations were subject to intense attack during the air phase of operations. Further, the practice of dropping lighter explosives on roofs (called roof-knocking) was not effective as a warning and constituted an attack.[85]

Once again, the assessment of precautions was comprehensive and could be used by future military commanders in considering the effectiveness of warnings to be given to civilian populations. One of the major issues highlighted was the timing of warnings in many incidents. The Israelis did not allow civilians enough time to vacate the areas under attack, as the warnings were proximate to the attack. In one case, the destruction of Abu Askar's house took place seven minutes after he received the warning telephone call.[86]

Proportionality and Military Advantage

The general rule with respect to proportionality and military advantage in targeting is reflected in Article 57 (1)(a)(iii), which states:

> a) those who plan or decide upon an attack shall:
> (iii) refrain from deciding to launch any attack which may be expected to cause incidental loss of civilian life, injury to civilians, damage to civilian objects, or a combination thereof, which would be excessive in relation to the concrete and direct military advantage anticipated.

---

83   Ibid., para. 35.
84   Ibid.
85   Ibid., paras 36–7.
86   Ibid., para. 501.

This provision can be seen to represent customary international law.[87] This is one of the most difficult concepts to grasp in international humanitarian law and the report is impressive in its sophisticated understanding of this customary rule. Early in the report, the mission acknowledged that 'proportionality decisions, weighing the military advantage to be gained against the risk of killing civilians, will present very genuine dilemmas in certain cases'.[88] The attack on the police stations discussed above is one in which the mission considered the rules concerning proportionality in great depth. The report found that the deliberate killing of 99 members of the police at police headquarters and three police stations during the first minutes of the military operation constituted an attack that failed to strike an acceptable balance between the direct military advantage anticipated and the loss of civilian life and thus was disproportionate and a violation of customary international humanitarian law.[89]

The next main incident that attracted an extensive analysis of proportionality was the shelling in al-Fakhura Street by the Israelis on 6 January 2009 when at least four mortar bombs fired by Israeli armed forces exploded near the al-Fakhura junction in the al-Fakhura area of the Jabaliyah Camp in northern Gaza.[90] Importantly, this was very near a school that was being used as a shelter by the United Nations. The four shells killed at least 35 people and injured another 40, as the street was busy due to the nearness of the shelter holding more than 1,300 people.[91] The mission accepted the Israeli view that there was some firing of mortars by Hamas from the area.[92] The issue, however, was to assess the military advantage of removing the threat coming from these mortars against the possibility of killing numerous civilians in the UN shelter. The mission in this case did not consider this to be one of the difficult proportionality calculations discussed earlier. The report criticized the choice of mortars in response as being incapable of distinguishing between civilians and combatants, as they are area weapons exploding on impact.[93] The report concluded:

> Whatever the truth, the Mission is of the view that the deployment of at least four mortar shells to attempt to kill a small number of specified individuals in a setting where large numbers of civilians were going about their daily business and 1,368 people were sheltering nearby cannot meet the test of what a reasonable commander would have determined to be an acceptable loss of civilian life for the military advantage sought.[94]

---

87   Henckaerts and Doswald-Beck, Rule 14.
88   *Gaza Report*, para. 42.
89   Ibid., paras 434 and 435.
90   Ibid., para. 651.
91   Ibid., paras 652–64.
92   Ibid., para. 673.
93   Ibid., see paras 692–701 for the complete legal assessment.
94   Ibid., para. 701.

Although this conclusion might have been obvious, it is the careful and deliberate way in which the humanitarian law of military advantage and proportionality was analyzed that is a real contribution to the field.

It seems evident that the conclusion that there was a deliberate policy of the Israeli Army to target civilians and civilian objects is made out in the report, given the scope and depth of analysis of the various and numerous attacks. The evidence supported the conclusion that Israeli forces committed war crimes by deliberately targeting civilians.

Weaponry

The report also considered the law of weaponry particularly in the discussion of the use of white phosphorous and other controversial weapons in the conflict. The report found that there were frequent incidents of the use of ordnance containing white phosphorous at or near civilian targets[95] and concluded:

> While accepting that white phosphorous is not at this stage proscribed under international law, the Mission considers that the repeated misuse of the substance by the Israeli armed forces during this operation calls into question the wisdom of allowing its continued use without some further degree of control. The Mission understands the need to use obscurants and illuminants for various reasons during military operations and especially in screening troops from observation or enemy fire. There are, however, other screening and illuminating means which are free from the toxicities, volatilities and hazards that are inherent in the chemical white phosphorous. The use of white phosphorous in any form in and around areas dedicated to the health and safety of civilians has been shown to carry very substantial risks. The Mission therefore believes that serious consideration should be given to banning the use of white phosphorous in built-up areas.[96]

Although one might wish that the use of white phosphorous in an armed conflict was unlawful, the mission was entirely accurate in the assessment of the specialized and difficult area of weapons law. This report will, however, provide support to those who seek to abolish weaponry that causes unnecessary suffering or that is inherently dangerous to the civilian population, even if the civilians are not specifically targeted.

Another weapon considered was flechettes. The report defined flechettes as 4 cm-long metal darts used as anti-personnel weapons that penetrate straight through human bone and can cause serious, often fatal, injuries.[97] The particular context

---

95   See, for example, the consideration of the use of white phosphorous in attacks on hospitals. Ibid., paras 629, 648, 649 and 650.

96   Ibid., para. 897.

97   Ibid., para. 876.

was an attack with these weapons at a condolence tent, killing five mourners. The mission found that flechettes were area weapons incapable of distinguishing between objects after detonation.[98] The mission conceded that the Israeli High Court rejected the argument that flechette munitions were by their nature indiscriminate and stated that subject to the general requirements of the rules of armed conflict their use was legal.[99] In this case, however, the mission found that their use in these circumstances violated the principles of proportionality and precautions. In this case, the mission had no information that there was any sort of military target nearby and that the attack was unjustified and unnecessary and was designed to kill and maim the victims directly. In this case, the mission found a grave breach pursuant to Article 147 of the Fourth Geneva Convention.[100] Once again, the analysis is carefully conducted and conclusions with respect to the weaponry involved and the nature of the attack are entirely justified.

The mission also considered DIME weapons containing a tungsten alloy. These weapons consist of a carbon-fibre casing filled with an explosive powder of heavy metal including the tungsten alloy. Upon impact, the casing disintegrates into extremely small fibres and causes very severe wounds, which might need amputation. Furthermore, expert evidence to the mission alleged that the tungsten alloy can be highly carcinogenic and is so small that it cannot be extracted from the body. The mission asked for further medical investigation concerning the use of this weapon. The weapon did have a feature of 'focused lethality', which could be seen as advancing compliance with the principle of distinction, but using these weapons in built-up areas such as Gaza could particularly impact on the right to health of survivors.[101]

Although the mission accepted that the use of white phosphorous, flechettes and heavy metals such as the tungsten alloy was not unlawful, in its recommendations it asked the General Assembly to promote an urgent discussion, drawing on the expertise of the ICRC, on their future legality. They also recommended that the Government of Israel undertake a moratorium on their use 'in light of the human suffering and damage they have caused in the Gaza strip'.[102] This analysis is particularly helpful as the use of this weaponry in built-up areas is problematic and at the very least their use could be limited to the battlefield. It was one of those rare occasions when it was possible to conduct an expert assessment on the use of particular weapons. This is a truly impressive discussion of the law of weaponry – a complex and specialized area of international humanitarian law.

---

98   Ibid., paras 45 and 48.

99   Ibid., para. 871; and *Physicians for Human Rights et al. v Israel et al.*, HCJ 8990/02, Judgement, 27 April 2003.

100   *Gaza Report*, paras 876–81; see also paras 898–901 for discussion of the physical effects of flechettes.

101   Ibid., paras 902–6.

102   Ibid., para. 1768.

292 *Protecting Civilians During Violent Conflict*

Conclusion

The UN Human Rights Council report on the conflict in Gaza is the type of comprehensive assessment of the compliance with the rules and customs of war that will influence analysis of future conflicts. The thorough discussion of all of the alleged violations of these rules, particularly with respect to blockades, targeting and weaponry, is remarkable, particularly in the detailed recounting of the evidence that supported the finding of violations. Furthermore, this report is unique in bringing together the range of treaty and customary obligations that applies in a situation of armed conflict.

The mission ended its extensive investigation by issuing a series of concrete recommendations to the parties in the conflict and the international community. Notwithstanding the unsurprising lack of response by the Security Council, there has been a significant reaction to the report within the General Assembly that remains seized of this issue. There have also been criminal investigations launched in Israel concerning violations of international humanitarian law by Israeli forces although these actions have been criticized.[103] Goldstone, however, in his op-ed contribution to the *Washington Post*, expressed confidence in the Israeli investigation of the killing of the 29 members of the al-Simouni family in their home, even though 'the length of the investigation is frustrating'.[104] He also complimented Israel for the adoption of new Israel Defence Forces procedures for protecting civilians in urban warfare. One might query, however, whether this new policy would have been promulgated had the *Gaza Report* not been published. Goldstone also rightly condemned Hamas for continuing to target civilians in Israel and for its failure to launch investigations into its own behaviour.[105]

For the international humanitarian lawyer, however, discussions of the principles of distinction, military necessity and the rule of proportionality within both the report and the international academic community in response will result in further elaboration of these cardinal rules. The report cannot be said to exist without its flaws. The London group, however, arrived at the correct conclusion that the report 'was very far from being invalidated by the criticisms. The Report raised extremely serious issues which had to be addressed.'[106] Goldstone in his op-ed piece suggests that with Israeli cooperation and hindsight the report might well have been different, but, even as it is, it remains a substantial and important analysis of the laws that are applicable in an armed conflict.[107] There is no question that the report should be taken seriously by anyone who is concerned with the protection of civilians in armed conflict.

---

103   See http://www.pchrgaza.org/files/2010/israeli-inve.-%20english.pdf
104   Goldstone.
105   Ibid.
106   *Report of an Expert Meeting*, p. 14.
107   Goldstone.

References

Abresch, William, 'A Human Rights Law of Internal Armed Conflict: The European Court of Human Rights in Chechnya', *European Journal of International Law*, 16 (2005).

Afghanistan Independent Human Rights Commission, *From Hope to Fear: An Afghan Perspective on Operations of Pro-Government Forces in Afghanistan* (Kabul: Afghanistan Independent Human Rights Commission, December 2008).

Afghanistan Rights Monitor (ARM), *ARM Annual Report: Civilian Casualties of War January–December 2010* (Kabul: Afghanistan Rights Monitor, February 2011).

Afghanistan Rights Monitor (ARM), *ARM Mid-Year Report. Civilian Casualties of Conflict. January–June 2010* (Kabul: Afghanistan Rights Monitor, 2010), arm.org.af/file.php?id=2

Agence France-Presse, 'Sri Lanka in Talks with UN Over War Crimes: Report', *Agence France-Presse*, 6 March 2011.

Al-Aqsa Television, 'Speech by Hamas MP Fathi Hammad', *Al-Aqsa Television*, 29 February 2008, http://www.peacewithrealism.org/headline/admit.htm

Aljazeera.net, 'Gaza Rockets Hit Southern Israel', *Aljazeera.net*, 21 December 2008 (2008 WLNR 24485745).

Aljazeera.net, 'Israel Closes Gaza Crossings', *Aljazeera.net*, 18 November 2008 (2008 WLNR 22000226).

Aljazeera.net, 'Israel Hit by Rocket Fire from Gaza', *Aljazeera.net*, 24 December 2008 (2008 WLNR 24663434).

al-Mughrabi, Nidal, 'Israel–Hamas Violence Disrupts Gaza Truce', *Reuters*, 5 November 2008, http://reuters.com/articlePrint?articleId=USTRE4A3 7B520081105

Alston, P., *Study on Targeted Killings: Addendum to the Report of the Special Rapporteur on Extrajudicial, Summary or Arbitrary Executions* (A/HRC/12/24/ Add.6).

Amnesty International, Afghanistan: *International Responsibility for Human Rights Disaster*, ASA 11/09/95 (London: Amnesty International, 1995).

Amnesty International, *Afghanistan: Massacres in Yakaolang*, ASA 11/008/2001 (London: Amnesty International, 2001).

Amnesty International, *Amnesty International's Concerns About Taser Use: Statement to the US Justice Department Inquiry into Deaths in Custody* (London, 1 October 2007), http://www.amnesty.org/en/library/info/AMR51/ 151/2007/en

Amnesty International, *Israel/Gaza Operation: 22 Days of Death & Destruction* (London, July 2009).

Anderson, Kenneth, 'A Public Call for International Attention to Legal Obligations of Defending Forces as well as Attacking Forces to Protect Civilians in Armed Conflicts', *Crimes of War Project*, 19 March 2003, http://www.crimesofwar.org/special/Iraq/news-iraq3.html

Anscombe, Elizabeth, 'War and Murder', in Walter Stein (ed.), *Nuclear Weapons: A Catholic Response* (London: Merlin, 1961).

Arendt, Hannah, *Eichmann in Jerusalem: A Report on the Banality of Evil* (New York: Viking Press, 1963).

Aristotle, *The Nicomachean Ethics*, trans. David Ross (London: Oxford University Press, 1963).

Arnold, Roberta and Noëlle Quénivet (eds), *International Humanitarian Law and Human Rights Law: Towards a New Merger in International Law* (Leiden/Boston: Brill/Martinus Nijhoff, 2008).

Asia-Pacific Centre for the Responsibility to Protect, *Protecting Civilians in Uncivil Wars*, Working Paper No. 1 (University of Queensland, August 2009).

Augoyard, Philippe, *La prison pour délit d'espoir: médecin en Afghanistan* (Paris: Flammarion, 1985).

Avalon Project, *Covenant of the Islamic Resistance Movement – Hamas* (New Haven, Conn.: Yale Law School, 18 August 1988), http://avalon.law.yale.edu/20th_century/hamas.asp

Bagnall, Randall, 'The Threat Assessment Process (TAP): The Evolution of Escalation of Force', *The Army Lawyer* (April 2008).

Baker, Alan, 'Legal and Tactical Dilemmas Inherent in Fighting Terror: Experience of the Israeli Army in Jenin and Bethlehem April–May 2002', in Richard B. Jaques (ed.), *Issues in International Law and Military Operations* (Newport, RI: Naval War College, 2006), Vol. 80.

Barber, Rebecca J., 'The Proportionality Equation: Balancing Military Objectives with Civilian Lives in the Armed Conflict in Afghanistan', *Journal of Conflict and Security Law*, 15/3 (2010).

Barfield, Thomas J., 'An Islamic State is a State Run by Good Muslims: Religion as a Way of Life and Not an Ideology in Afghanistan', in Robert W. Hefner (ed.), *Remaking Muslim Politics: Pluralism, Contestation, Democratization* (Princeton, NJ: Princeton University Press, 2005).

Barfield, Thomas J., *Afghanistan: A Cultural and Political History* (Princeton, NJ: Princeton University Press, 2010).

Barry, Michael, 'Répressions et guerre soviétiques', *Les Temps Modernes*, July–August 1980.

Barry, Michael, Johan Lagerfelt and Marie-Odile Terrenoire, 'International Humanitarian Enquiry Commission on Displaced Persons in Afghanistan', *Central Asian Survey*, 5/1 (1986).

Bartone, Paul T., 'Preventing Prisoner Abuse: Leadership Lessons of Abu Ghraib', *Ethics and Behaviour*, 20/2 (2010).

Barutciski, Michael, 'Opinion: A Critical View on UNHCR's Mandate Dilemmas', *International Journal of Refugee Law*, 14 (2002).

Baxter, Richard R., 'So-Called "Unprivileged Belligerency": Spies, Guerrillas, and Saboteurs', *British Year Book of International Law*, 28 (1951).

BBC News, 'CIA "Killed al-Qaeda Suspects" in Yemen', *BBC News*, 5 November 2002, http://news.bbc.co.uk/1/hi/2402479.stm

BBC News, 'Embassy Strike "A Mistake"', *BBC News*, 8 May 1999, http://news. bbc.co.uk/1/hi/world/europe/338557.stm

BBC News, 'Interview, Colonel Richard Kemp, Former Commander of British Forces in Afghanistan', *BBC News*, 18 January 2009, http://www.youtube. com/watch?v=WssrKJ3Iqcw

BBC News, 'Iran Unveils First Bomber Drone', *BBC News*, 22 August 2010, http://www.bbc.co.uk/news/world-middle-east-11052023

BBC News, 'Srebrenica Report Blames UN', *BBC News*, 16 November 1999, http://news.bbc.co.uk/2/hi/europe/521825.stm

BBC News, 'State of the Union Address', *BBC News*, 28 January 2010, http:// news.bbc.co.uk/1/hi/8484451.stm

Bell, Abraham, *A Critique of the Goldstone Report and its Treatment of International Humanitarian Law*, San Diego Legal Studies Paper No. 10-019, http://ssrn.com/abstract=1581533

Bellamy, Alex J., 'Supreme Emergencies and the Protection of Non-Combatants in War', *International Affairs*, 80 (2004).

Bellamy, Alex J., *Global Politics and the Responsibility to Protect: From Words to Deeds* (New York: Routledge, 2011).

Bellamy, Alex J., *Responsibility to Protect: The Global Effort to End Mass Atrocities* (Cambridge: Polity Press, 2009).

Benoliel, D. and R. Perry, 'Israel, Palestine and the ICC', *Michigan Journal of International Law*, 32 (2010).

Bentham, Jeremy, *An Introduction to the Principles of Morals and Legislation* (1781).

Benvenisti, Eyal, *The International Law of Occupation* (Princeton, NJ: Princeton University Press, 1993).

Beran, Matthew L., 'The Proportionality Test Revisited: How Counterinsurgency Changes "Military Advantage"', *The Army Lawyer* (August 2010).

Berkowitz, Peter, 'The Goldstone Report and International Law', *Policy Review*, 162 (1 August 2010), Hoover Institute, Stanford University, http://www. hoover.org/publications/policy-review/article/43281

Best, Geoffrey, 'The Restraint of War in Historical and Philosophical Perspective', in *Humanitarian Law of Armed Conflict – Challenges Ahead, Essays in Honour of Frits Kalshoven* (Dordrecht: M. Nijhoff, 1991).

Bilefsky, Dan and Mark Landler, 'Military Action Against Qaddafi is Backed by U.N.', *The New York Times*, 18 March 2011.

Birnbacher, D., 'Philosophical Foundations of Responsibility', in Ann E. Auhagen and Hans-Werner Bierhoff (eds), *Responsibility: The Many Faces of a Social Phenomenon* (London/New York: Routledge, 2001).

Bisharat, George, Timothy Crawley, Sara Elturk, Carey James, Rose Mishaan, Akila Radhakrishnan and Anna Sanders, 'Israel's Invasion of Gaza in International Law', *Denver Journal of International Law and Policy*, 38 (2009).

Blanche, Ed, 'Behold, the Humble Qassem', *Middle East*, April 2008.

Blank, Laurie R. and Amos Guirora, 'Teaching an Old Dog New Tricks: Operationalizing the Law of Armed Conflict in New Warfare', *Harvard National Security Journal*, 1 (2010).

Blank, Laurie R., *The Application of IHL in the Goldstone Report: A Critical Commentary*, Emory University Public Law & Legal Theory Research Paper Series, Paper No. 10-96 (2009), http://ssrn.com/abstract=1596214

Boal, Mark, 'The Kill Team', *Rolling Stone*, 27 March 2011, http://www.rollingstone.com/kill-team

Boivin, A., *The Legal Regime with Respect to Targeting, Military Objectives in the Context of Contemporary Warfare*, Research Paper No. 2 (Geneva: University Centre for International Humanitarian Law, 2006), http://www.adh-geneva.ch/docs/publications/collection-research-projects/CTR_objectif_militaire.pdf

Bok, Derek C., 'Can Ethics Be Taught?', *Change*, 8/9 (October 1976).

Boothby, B., '"And for Such Time As": The Time Dimension to Direct Participation in Hostilities', *Journal of International Law and Politics*, 42/3 (2010).

Bothe, Michael, Karl Joseph Partsch and Waldemar A. Solf (eds), *New Rules for Victims of Armed Conflicts* (The Hague: Martinus Nijhoff, 1982).

Boudreaux, Richard, 'Hamas Formally Ends Gaza Cease-Fire with Israel', *Los Angeles Times*, 19 December 2008 (2008 WLNR 24369458).

Bovens, M., *The Quest for Responsibility: Accountability and Citizenship in Complex Organisations* (Cambridge: Cambridge University Press, 1998).

Brahimi, Alia, *Jihad and Just War in the War on Terror* (Oxford: Oxford University Press, 2010).

Brandt, Richard, 'Utilitarianism and the Laws of War', in M. Cohen, T. Nagel and T. Scanlon (eds), *War and Moral Responsibility* (Princeton, NJ: Princeton University Press, 1974).

Brandt, Richard, *Morality, Utility, and Rights* (Cambridge: Cambridge University Press, 1992).

Brett, Rachel and Eve Lester, 'Refugee Law and International Humanitarian Law: Parallels, Lessons and Looking Ahead', *International Review of the Red Cross*, 83 (2001).

Bronner, Ethan and Taghreed El-Khodary, 'Hamas Rockets Hit Israel, Sending 18 to Hospital', *The New York Times*, 15 November 2008 (2008 WLNR 21812926).

Bronner, Ethan and Taghreed El-Khodary, 'Rocket Barrage into Israel Heightens Gaza Tensions', *Globe & Mail*, 15 November 2008 (2008 WLNR 21816760).

Bronner, Ethan, 'Parsing Gains of Gaza War', *The New York Times*, 19 January 2009, http://www.nytimes.com/2009/01/19/world/middleeast/19assess.html

Brown, Kenneth L., '"Supreme Emergency": A Critique of Michael Walzer's Moral Justification for Allied Obliteration Bombing in World War II', *Manchester College Bulletin of the Peace Studies Institute*, 13 (1983).

Brown, Matt, 'Hamas Unleashes Artillery Barrage on Israel', *Australian Broadcasting Corporation*, 25 December 2008 (2008 WLNR 24691971).

Brownlie, Ian, *International Law and the Use of Force by States* (London: Oxford University Press, 1963).

Burns, A.L., 'Injustice and Evil in the Politics of the Powers', in Ralph Pettman (ed.), *Moral Claims in World Affairs* (Canberra: Australian National University Press, 1979).

Canadian Security Intelligence Service, 'Conflicts Between and Within States', *Perspectives*, Report # 2000/06 (Canadian Security Intelligence Service Publication, 2000), http://www.csis-scrs.gc.ca/eng/miscdocs/200006e.html.2000

Carens, Joseph H., 'A reply to Meilaender: Reconsidering Open Borders', *International Migration Review*, 33/4 (1999).

Carpenter, R. Charli, *'Innocent Women and Children': Gender, Norms and the Protection of Civilians* (Aldershot: Ashgate, 2006).

Cassimatis, Anthony E., 'International Humanitarian Law, International Human Rights Law, and Fragmentation of International Law', *International and Comparative Law Quarterly*, 56 (2007).

Castles, Stephen and Mark J. Miller, *The Age of Migration: International Population Movements in the Modern World*, 3rd edn (New York: The Guilford Press, 2003).

Chadwick Austin, W. and Antony Barone Kolenc, 'Who's Afraid of the Big Bad Wolf? The International Criminal Court as a Weapon of Asymmetric Warfare', *Vanderbilt Journal of International Law*, 39 (2006).

Chairman of the Joint Chiefs of Staff (US), *Standing Rules of Engagement for US Forces*, CJCS Instruction CJCSI 3121.01A (15 January 2000), Enclosure A, http://www.fas.org/man/dod-101/dod/docs/cjcs_sroe.pdf

Chehata, Dr Hanan, 'Exclusive MEMO Interview with Colonel Desmond Travers – Co-Author of the UN's Goldstone Report', *Middle East Monitor*, 2 February 2010, http://www.middleeastmonitor.org.uk/articles/62-europe/625-qgaza-is-the-only-gulag-in-the-western-hemisphere-maintained-by-democracies-closed-off-from-food-water-airq-says-colonel-desmond-travers-co-author-of-the-goldstone-report-in-an-exclusive-memo-interview

Clark, W., *Waging Modern War* (New York: Public Affairs, 2001).

Cloud, David S., 'Anatomy of an Afghan War Tragedy', *Los Angeles Times*, 10 April 2011.

Coady, C.A.J., 'Terrorism, Morality, and Supreme Emergency', *Ethics*, 114 (2003–04), p. 784.

Coady, C.A.J., *Morality and Political Violence* (Cambridge: Cambridge University Press, 2008).

Cobbledick, Bruce, 'Innovation Aims to Reduce Collateral Damage in Afghanistan', 7 July 2010, http://www.army.mil/-news/2010/07/07/41913-innovation-aims-to-reduce-collateral-damage-in-afghanistan/

Cohen, Amachai, *Proportionality in Modern Asymmetrical Wars* (Jerusalem Center for Public Affairs, 2010), http://www.jcpa.org/text/proportionality.pdf

Cohen, Yoram and Jeffrey White, *Hamas in Combat: The Military Performance of the Palestinian Islamic Resistance Movement*, Policy Focus No. 97, Washington Institute for Near East Policy (October 2009).

Cole, Alan, Philip Drew, Rob McLaughlin and Dennis Mandsager, *Rules of Engagement Handbook* (San Remo: International Institute of Humanitarian Law, 2009), http://www.iihl.org/iihl/Documents/Sanremo%20ROE%20 Handbook%20(English).pdf

Cole, Darrell, 'Death Before Dishonor or Dishonor Before Death? Christian Just War, Terrorism, and Supreme Emergency', *Notre Dame Journal of Law, Ethics and Public Policy*, 16 (2002).

Colville, Rupert, 'One Massacre that Didn't Grab the World's Attention', *International Herald Tribune*, 7 August 1999.

Combined Studies Institute, *Back to Basics: A Study of the Second Lebanon War and Operation Cast Lead* (Fort Leavenworth, Kan.: Combined Studies Institute, May 2009), http://www.cgsc.edu/carl/download/csipubs/farquhar. pdf

Commission on Human Security, *Human Security Now, Final Report of the Commission on Human Security* (New York, 1 May 2003).

Commonwealth of Australia, *Criminal Code Act 1995* (Cwlth), s. 10.4 (http:// www.comlaw.gov.au/ComLaw/Legislation/ActCompilation1.nsf/current/byt itle/2EF9353C62DC16D9CA2578010007D95E?OpenDocument&mostrece nt=1).

Condra, Luke N., Joseph H. Felter, Radha K. Iyengar and Jacob N. Shapiro, *The Effect of Civilian Casualties in Afghanistan and Iraq*, Working Paper 16152, National Bureau of Economic Research (Cambridge, Mass., July 2010).

Cook, Martin L., 'Michael Walzer's Concept of "Supreme Emergency"', *Journal of Military Ethics*, 6 (2007).

Cooper, Abraham and Harold Brackman, 'The Threat of the Human Shield Strategy Hamas Uses Extends Beyond Gaza', Opinion, *US News & World Report*, 9 January 2009, http://www.usnews.com/articles/opinion/2009/01/09/the-threat-of-the-human-shield-strategy-hamas-uses-extends-beyond-israel-gaza.html

Cordesman, Anthony H., *Lessons of the 2006 Israeli–Hezbollah War* (Washington, DC: Center for Strategic and International Studies, 2007).

Cordesman, Anthony H., *The 'Gaza War': A Strategic Analysis* (Center for Strategic and International Studies, 2009), http://csis.org/files/media/csis/ pubs/090202_gaza_war.pdf

Corlett, Angelo, *Terrorism: A Philosophical Analysis* (Dordrecht: Kluwer, 2003).

Couch, Dick, *A Tactical Ethic: Moral Conduct in the Insurgent Battlespace* (Annapolis, MD: Naval Institute Press, 2010).

Crime and Misconduct Commission, *OC Spray: Oleoresin Capsicum (OC) Spray Use by Queensland Police* (Brisbane: Government of Queensland, 2005).

Cryer, Robert 'The Fine Art of Friendship: *Jus in Bello* in Afghanistan', *Journal of Conflict and Security Law*, 7/1 (2002).

Cullen, Anthony, *The Concept of Non-International Armed Conflict in International Humanitarian Law* (Cambridge: Cambridge University Press, 2010).

Curnow, Jane and Jacqueline Joudo Larsen, *Deaths in Custody in Australia: National Deaths in Custody Program 2007* (Canberra: Australian Institute of Criminology, 2009).

Daccord, Yves, Director-General of the ICRC, Statement, UN Security Council, New York, 22 November 2010, http://www.icrc.org/eng/resources/documents/statement/protection-civilian-statement-2010-11-22.htm

Davis, Anthony, 'How the Taliban Became a Military Force', in William Maley (ed.), *Fundamentalism Reborn?: Afghanistan and the Taliban* (London: Hurst & Co., 1998).

de Chazournes, Laurence Boisson and Luigi Condorelli, 'Common Article 1 of the Geneva Conventions Revisited: Protecting Collective Interests', *International Review of the Red Cross*, 82 (2000).

de Wijze, Stephen, 'Dirty Hands: Doing Wrong to do Right', in Igor Primoratz (ed.), *Politics and Morality* (Basingstoke and New York: Palgrave Macmillan, 2007).

Dennis, Michael J., 'Application of Human Rights Treaties Extraterritorially in Times of Armed Conflict and Military Occupation', *American Journal of International Law*, 99 (2005).

Department of the Army, *Field Manual 3-06.11, Combined Operations in Urban Terrain* (28 February 2002), http://www.globalsecurity.org/military/library/policy/army/fm/3-06-11/ch1.htm#par3

Department of the Army, *Pamphlet 27-9, Military Judges' Benchbook* (September 2002).

Department of the Attorney-General, *Listing of Terrorist Organizations* (Canberra: Commonwealth of Australia), http://www.ag.gov.au/agd/www/nationalsecurity.nsf/AllDocs/95FB057CA3DECF30CA256FAB001F7FBD?OpenDocument

Department of the Navy, *The Commander's Handbook on the Law of Naval Operations* (NWP 1-14M) (2007).

Dershowitz, Alan, *The Case Against the Goldstone Report*, Public Law & Legal Theory Working Papers Series, Paper No. 10-26, 2010, Harvard Law School, http://ssrn.com/abstract=1542897

Dictionary of Military and Associated Terms (12 April 2001, as amended through 30 September 2010), JP 1-02, http://www.dtic.mil/doctrine/new_pubs/jp1_02.pdf

Dilanian, Ken, 'CIA Drones May Be Avoiding Pakistan Civilians', *The Sacramento Bee*, 7 March 2011, http://www.sacbee.com/2011/02/21/3419750/cia-drones-may-be-avoiding-pakistan.html

Dinstein, Yoram, 'Targeting: Discussion', in Andru E. Wall (ed.), *Legal and Ethical Lessons of NATO's Kosovo Campaign, International Law Studies*, 78 (2002).

Dinstein, Yoram, *The Conduct of Hostilities Under the Law of International Armed Conflict* (Cambridge: Cambridge University Press, 2004).

Dinstein, Yoram, *The Conduct of Hostilities Under the Law of International Armed Conflict*, 2nd edn (Cambridge: Cambridge University Press, 2010).

Dinstein, Yoram, *The International Law of Belligerent Occupation* (Cambridge: Cambridge University Press, 2009).

Dodd, Mark, 'Allies Target Volatile Province', *The Australian*, 23 February 2010.

Dörmann, Knut, 'Applicability of Additional Protocols to Computer Network Attack', Paper delivered at the International Expert Conference on Computer Network Attacks and the Applicability of International Humanitarian Law, Stockholm, 17–19 November 2004, //www.icrc.org/web/eng/siteeng0.nsf/htmlall/68lg92?opendocument

Dörmann, Knut, 'The Legal Situation of "Unlawful/Unprivileged Combatants"', *International Review of the Red Cross*, 849 (2003).

Dorronsoro, Gilles, 'Afghanistan's Civil War', *Current History*, 84/588 (1995).

Doswald-Beck, Louise (ed.), *San Remo Manual on International Law Applicable to Armed Conflicts at Sea* (Cambridge: Cambridge University Press, 1995).

Doswald-Beck, Louise, 'The Value of the 1977 Geneva Protocols for the Protection of Civilians', in M. Meyer (ed.), *Armed Conflict and the New Law* (London, 1989).

Dowley, Anthony and Matt Schultz, 'OC Spray Man Dies in Police Van on Way to Dandenong Police Station', *Herald Sun*, 22 December 2009.

Downes, Alexander, *Targeting Civilians in War* (Ithaca, NY: Cornell University Press, 2008).

Drumin, W.A., 'Sabotage: Chaos Unleashed and the Impossibility of Utopia', in D. Baggett and W. A. Drumin, *Hitchcock and Philosophy: Dial M for Metaphysics* (Chicago: Open Court, 2007).

Dunant, Henry, *A Memory of Solferino* (Geneva: ICRC, 1986 [1939]).

Dunlap, Charles J. jr, 'A Virtuous Warrior in a Savage World', *US Air Force Academy Journal of Legal Studies*, 8 (1997–98).

Dury, Ian, 'Mission Aborted on Orders of SAS', *HMForces.co.uk*, 22 March 2011, http://www.hmforces.co.uk/news/articles/6375-mission-aborted-on-orders-of-sas

Economist, 'The Gaza Strip: Are the Palestinians' Weapons Getting More Lethal?', *Economist*, 13 October 2007.

Edwards, Alice, 'Human Security and the Rights of Refugees: Transcending Territorial and Disciplinary Borders', *Michigan Journal of International Law*, 30 (2009).

Edwards, Alice, 'Refugee Status Determination in Africa', *African Journal of International and Comparative Law*, 14 (2008).

Efrat, Elisha, *The West Bank and Gaza Strip* (UK: Taylor & Francis Ltd, 2006).

El-Khodary, Taghreed and Isabel Kershner, 'Hamas, Showing Split, May Extend Israel Truce', *The New York Times*, 15 December 2008 (2008 WLNR 23990603).

Elliot, J., 'Gen McChrystal: We've Shot "an amazing number of people" Who Were Not Threats', *Sholtis*, 2 April 2010.

Erlanger, Steve, 'Weighing Crimes and Ethics in the Fog of Urban Warfare', *The New York Times*, 16 January 2009, http://www.nytimes.com/2009/01/17/world/middleeast/17israel.html

Erlanger, Steven, 'A Gaza War Full of Traps and Trickery', *The New York Times*, 11 January 2009, http://www.nytimes.com/2009/01/11/world/middleeast/11hamas.html

Erlich, Dr Reuven, *Hezbollah's Use of Lebanese Civilians as Human Shields* (Intelligence and Terrorism Information Center, November 2006), http://www.ajcongress.org/site/DocServer/Part1.pdf?docID=861

Eshel, David, 'Military Confrontation with Hamas is Unavoidable', *Military Technologies*, 31 (2007).

European Council, *Council Directive 2004/83/EC of 29 April 2004 on Minimum Standards for the Qualification and Status of the Third Country Nationals or Stateless Persons as Refugees or as Persons Who Otherwise need International Protection and the Content of the Protection Granted*, OJ L 304, 30 September 2004.

European Union, *Council Decision* 2005/930/EC (21 December 2005), http://eur-lex.europa.eu/LexUriServ/site/en/oj/2005/l_340/l_34020051223en00640066.pdf

Evans, Gareth, *The Responsibility to Protect: Ending Mass Atrocity Crimes Once and For All* (Washington, DC: Brookings Institution Press, 2008).

Evening Standard, 'Hamas Refuses to Renew Gaza Truce', *Evening Standard*, 19 December 2008 (2008 WLNR 24401760).

Falk, R., 'The Goldstone Report: Ordinary Text, Extraordinary Event', *Global Governance*, 16 (2010).

Federation of Community Legal Centres, *Taser Trap: Is Victoria Falling for It?* (Melbourne), http://www.communitylaw.org.au/cb_pages/taser_trap_.php

Feinstein, Dr Barry A., 'Proportionality and War Crimes in Gaza Under the Law of Armed Conflict', *Rutgers Law Record*, 36 (2009).

Fenrick, William J., 'Law Applicable to Targeting and Proportionality After Operation Allied Force', *Yearbook of International Humanitarian Law*, 3 (2000).

Fidler, D., 'Non-Lethal Weapons and International Law: Three Perspectives on the Future', *Medicine, Conflict and Survival*, 17 (2001).

Fidler, D., 'The Meaning of Moscow: "Non-Lethal" Weapons and International Law in the Early 21st Century', *International Review of the Red Cross*, 87/859 (2005).

Finkel, David, *The Good Soldiers* (Melbourne: Scribe, 2009).

Fleck, Dieter (ed.), *The Handbook of International Humanitarian Law*, 2nd edn (New York: Oxford University Press, 2008).

Fleck, Dieter, 'The Law of Non-International Armed Conflicts', in Dieter Fleck (ed.), *The Handbook of International Humanitarian Law*, 2nd edn (New York: Oxford University Press, 2008).

flightglobal.com, 'USMC Moves Closer to Deciding on Unmanned Resupply for Afghanistan', *flightglobal.com*, 17 February 2010, http://www.flightglobal.com/articles/2010/02/17/338476/usmc-moves-closer-to-deciding-on-unmanned-resupply-for.html

Flynn, Major-General Michael T., USA, Captain Matt Pottinger, USMC, and Paul D. Batchelor, DIA, *Fixing Intel: A Blueprint for Making Intelligence Relevant in Afghanistan* (Washington, DC: Center for a New American Security, January 2010).

Focarelli, Carlo, 'Common Article 1 of the 1949 Geneva Conventions: A Soap Bubble?', *European Journal of International Law*, 21 (2010).

Foster, Michelle, *International Refugee Law and Socio-Economic Rights: Refuge From Deprivation* (Cambridge: Cambridge University Press, 2007).

Franck, Thomas M., *Recourse to Force: State Action Against Threats and Armed Attacks* (Cambridge: Cambridge University Press, 2002).

Gabriel, Richard A., *To Serve With Honor: A Treatise on Military Ethics and the Way of the Soldier* (Westport, Conn.: Greenwood Press, 1982).

Gardam, Judith Gail, 'Proportionality and Force in International Law', *American Journal of International Law*, 87 (1993).

Gardam, Judith, *Necessity, Proportionality and the Use of Force by States* (Cambridge: Cambridge University Press, 2004).

Gasser, Hans-Peter, 'Protection of the Civilian Population', in Dieter Fleck (ed.), *The Handbook of International Humanitarian Law*, 2nd edn (New York: Oxford University Press, 2008).

Giustozzi, Antonio and Christoph Reuter, *The Insurgents of the Afghan North: The Rise of the Taleban, the Self-Abandonment of the Afghan Government, and the Effects of ISAF's 'Capture and Kill Campaign'*, AAN Thematic Report 04/2011, Afghanistan Analysts Network (Kabul, May 2011).

Gladwell, Malcolm, *Blink: The Power of Thinking Without Thinking* (New York: Little, Brown and Company, 2005).

Gold, Dore, 'The Dangerous Bias of the United Nations Goldstone Report', Opinion, *US News & World Report*, 10 March 2010 (2010 WLNR 6217934).

Goldstone, Judge Richard, Email to Maurice Ostroff, International Coalition of Hasbara Volunteers, 21 September 2009, 22:34:29, http://maurice-ostroff.tripod.com/id233.html

Goldstone, R., 'Reconsidering the Goldstone Report on Israel and War Crimes', *The Washington Post*, 1 April 2011, http://www.washingtonpost.com/opinions/reconsidering-the-goldstone-report-on-israel-and-war-crimes/2011/04/01/AFg111JC_story.html

Goldstone, Richard, 'Justice in Gaza', *The New York Times*, 17 September 2009, http://www.nytimes.com/2009/09/17/opinion/17goldstone.html

Goldstone, Richard, Statements before the UN Fact-Finding Mission on the Gaza Conflict, 28 June 2009, Unofficial Transcript, http://www2.ohchr.org/english/bodies/hrcouncil/specialsession/9/FactFindingMission.htm

Goodson, Larry P., 'Periodicity and Intensity in the Afghan War', *Central Asian Survey*, 17/3 (1998).

Goodwin, Jan, *Caught in the Crossfire* (London: Macdonald, 1987).

Goodwin-Gill, Guy S., *Challenges to the Protection of Refugees and Stateless Persons – Compliance with International Law* (London: Blackstone Chambers, March 2009), http://www.blackstonechambers.com/news/publications/protection_refugees.html

Gourevitch, Philip, *We Wish to Inform You That Tomorrow We Will Be Killed with Our Families: Stories From Rwanda* (New York: Farrar, Straus and Giroux, 1998).

Government of Canada, *Canadian Military Doctrine (2009)*, CFJP 01, http://dsp-psd.pwgsc.gc.ca/collection_2010/forces/D2-252-2009-eng.pdf

Gray, Christine, *International Law and the Use of Force* (Oxford: Oxford University Press, 2008).

Gray, J. Glenn, *The Warriors: Reflections on Men in Battle* (New York: Harper & Row, 1970 [1959]).

Grayling, A.C., *Among the Dead Cities* (London: Bloomsbury, 2006).

Greenspan, Morris, *The Modern Law of Land Warfare* (Berkeley and Los Angeles: University of California Press, 1959).

Greenwood, Christopher, 'Scope of Application of Humanitarian Law', in Dieter Fleck (ed.), *The Handbook of International Humanitarian Law*, 2nd edn (New York: Oxford University Press, 2008).

Gross, Emanuel, 'Use of Civilians as Human Shields: What Legal and Moral Restrictions Should Pertain to a War Waged by a Democratic State Against Terrorism?', *Emory International Law Review*, 16 (2002).

Gross, Michael L., 'The Second Lebanon War: The Question of Proportionality and the Prospect of Non-Lethal Warfare', *Journal of Military Ethics*, 7 (2008).

Gross, Michael, *Moral Dilemmas of Modern War: Torture, Assassination and Blackmail in an Age of Asymmetric Conflict* (Cambridge: Cambridge University Press, 2010).

Grossman, Dave, *On Killing: The Psychological Cost of Learning to Kill in War and Society* (Boston: Little Brown, 1996).

Grotius, Hugo, *The Law of War and Peace in Three Books* (1625) [*De Jure Belli ac Pacis Libris Tres*].

Grunawalt, Richard J., 'The JCS Standing Rules of Engagement: A Judge Advocate's Primer', *Air Force Law Review*, 42 (1997).

Hadid, Diaa, 'Israel Launches First Airstrike on Gaza Since June', *Charleston Gazette & Daily Mail*, 5 November 2008 (2008 WLNR 21144545).

Hadid, Diaa, 'Israeli Airstrikes Imperil Gaza Truce with Hamas', *Seattle Times*, 6 November 2008 (2008 WLNR 21280555).

Hadid, Diaa, 'Rocket Attacks Escalate Gaza Violence', *Deseret Morning News*, 15 November 2008 (2008 WLNR 21837697).

Halbertal, Moshe, 'The Goldstone Illusion', *The New Republic*, 6 November 2009, http://www.tnr.com/article/world/the-goldstone-illusion

Hallaq, Wael B., *Sharī'a: Theory, Practice, Transformations* (Cambridge: Cambridge University Press, 2009).

Halpern, Orly, 'Israel Vows Attack if Rockets from Gaza Don't Stop', *Globe & Mail*, 26 December 2008 (2008 WLNR 24747079).

Hampson, Françoise J., 'The Relationship Between International Humanitarian Law and Human Rights Law from the Perspective of a Human Rights Treaty Body', *International Review of the Red Cross*, 90 (2008).

Happold, Matthew, 'Bankovic v Belgium and the Territorial Scope of the European Convention on Human Rights', *Human Rights Law Review*, 3 (2003).

Harel, Amos, 'Sources: Hamas Leaders Hiding in Basement of Israel-Built Hospital in Gaza', *Haaretz.com*, 22 February 2009, http://www.haaretz.com/hasen/spages/1054569.html

Harris Rimmer, Susan, 'Refugees, Internally Displaced Persons and the "Responsibility to Protect"', *New Issues in Refugee Research*, Research Paper No. 185 (Geneva: UNHCR, March 2010).

Hathaway, James C., 'New Directions to Avoid Hard Problems: The Distortion of the Palliative Role of Refugee Protection', *Journal of Refugee Studies* (1995).

Hathaway, James C., *The Law of Refugee Status* (Toronto: Butterworths, 1991).

Hatzfeld, Jean, *Machete Season: The Killers in Rwanda Speak* (New York: Farrar, Straus & Giroux, 2005/Picador, 2006).

Haviland, Charles, 'Sri Lankan War Inquiry Commission Opens Amid Criticism', *BBC News*, Sri Lanka, 11 August 2010, http://www.bbc.co.uk/news/world-south-asia-10934663

Hays Parks, W., 'Air War and the Law of War', *Air Force Law Review*, 32 (1990).

Hays Parks, W., 'Part IX of the ICRC "Direct Participation in Hostilities" Study: No Mandate, No Expertise, and Legally Incorrect', *New York University Journal of International Law and Politics*, 42 (2010).

Hegel, G.W.F., *Philosophy of Right*, trans. T.M. Knox (Oxford: Oxford University Press, 1965).

Henckaerts, Jean-Marie and Louise Doswald-Beck, *Customary International Humanitarian Law: Volume I. The Rules* (Cambridge: Cambridge University Press, 2005).

Hider, James, 'Back in the Line of Fire: Rocket War Resumes After Raid on "Kidnap Plot" Tunnel', *The Times*, 6 November 2008 (2008 WLNR 21173188).

Hobbes, Thomas, *Leviathan* (Cambridge: Cambridge University Press, 1996).

Hogg, Russell, 'Executive Proscription of Terrorist Organisations in Australia: Exploring the Shifting Border Between Crime and Politics', in Miriam

Gani and Penelope Mathew (eds), *Fresh Perspectives on the War on Terror* (Canberra: ANU E Press, 2008).

Home Office, *Proscribed Terrorist Groups* (London: Government of the United Kingdom), http://www.homeoffice.gov.uk/publications/counter-terrorism/ proscribed-terror-groups/proscribed-groups?view=Binary

Honig, Jan Willem and Norbert Both, *Srebrenica: Record of a War Crime* (Harmondsworth: Penguin Books, 1996).

Hooker, Brad, *Ideal Code, Real World* (Oxford: Oxford University Press, 2000).

Hosseini, Khaled, *A Thousand Splendid Suns* (London: Bloomsbury, 2007).

Houben, Marc, 'Making Waves and Building Bridges: Dutch Experiences in the Arabian Sea', *RUSI Defence Systems* (June 2007), http://www.rusi.org/ downloads/assets/Houben,_Making_Waves_and_Building_Bridges.pdf

Howard, Michael, George J. Andreopoulos and Mark R. Shulman (eds), *The Laws of War: Constraints on Warfare in the Western World* (New Haven, Conn.: Yale University Press, 1997).

Hroub, Khaled, *Hamas: A Beginner's Guide* (London and Ann Arbor, Mich.: Pluto Press, 2006).

Human Rights Council, Press Release, 3 April 2009.

Human Rights Watch, *'Troops in Contact': Airstrikes and Civilian Deaths in Afghanistan* (New York: Human Rights Watch, September 2008).

Human Rights Watch, *Afghanistan: The Massacre in Mazar-i Sharif* (New York: Human Rights Watch, 1998).

Human Rights Watch, *Blood-Stained Hands: Past Atrocities in Kabul and Afghanistan's Legacy of Impunity* (New York: Human Rights Watch, 2005).

Human Rights Watch, *Sri Lanka: Protests Against UN Echo Anti-Justice Campaign* (New York: Human Rights Watch, 11 July 2010), http://www.hrw.org/en/ news/2010/07/11/sri-lanka-protests-against-un-echo-anti-justice-campaign

Humphries, John G., 'Operations Law and the Rules of Engagement in Operations Desert Shield and Desert Storm', *Airpower Journal* (Fall 1992), http://www. airpower.maxwell.af.mil/airchronicles/apj/apj92/fall92/hump.htm

Hyndman, Jennifer, 'Preventive, Palliative, or Punitive? Safe Spaces in Bosnia-Herzegovina, Somalia and Sri Lanka', *Journal of Refugee Studies*, 16 (2003).

Ignatieff, Michael, 'To Fight But Not to Die', *The World Today*, February 2000, p. 21.

Ignatieff, Michael, *The Warrior's Honour: Ethnic War and the Modern Conscience* (London: Chatto & Windus, 1998).

Ikle, Fred, *Every War Must End* (New York: Columbia University Press, 1991).

Iliopoulos, Katherine, *The Legality of Israel's Blockage of Gaza* (Washington, DC: Crimes of War Project), http://www.crimesofwar.org/onnews/news-gaza9.html

Intelligence and Terrorism Information Center, *Hamas and the Terrorist Threat from the Gaza Strip* (March 2010), http://www.terrorism-info.org.il/malam_ multimedia/English/engn/pdf/g_report_e1.pdf

Intelligence and Terrorism Information Center, *Hamas's Military Buildup in the Gaza Strip* (Intelligence and Terrorism Information Center, 8 April 2007;

updated April 2008), http://www.terrorism-info.org.il/malam_multimedia/
English/eng_n/pdf/hamas_080408.pdf

Intelligence and Terrorism Information Center, *The Six Months of the Lull Arrangement* (December 2008), http://www.terrorism-info.org.il/malam_ multimedia/English/eng_n/pdf/hamas_e017.pdf

Inter-American Commission on Human Rights, *Report on Terrorism and Human Rights*, OEA/Ser. L/-V/II.116 Doc. 5 Rev. 1 Corr., 22 October 2002.

International Commission on Intervention and State Sovereignty, *The Responsibility to Protect: Report of the International Commission on Intervention and State Sovereignty* (Ottawa: International Development Research Centre, 2001).

International Committee of the Red Cross, *Professional Standards for Protection Work* (Geneva, 2009).

International Committee of the Red Cross, *Under the Protection of the Palm: Wars of Dignity in the Pacific* (Geneva: ICRC, 2009).

International Court of Justice (ICJ), *Legal Consequences of the Construction of a Wall in the Occupied Palestinian Territory*, Advisory Opinion of 9 July 2004, ICJ Reports 2004.

International Court of Justice (ICJ), *Legality of the Threat or Use of Nuclear Weapons*, Advisory Opinion, 8 July 1996, ICJ Reports 1996.

International Court of Justice, *Statute of the International Court of Justice*, 26 June 1945, 59 Stat. 1055, 33 UNTS 993.

International Criminal Court, *Rome Statute of the International Criminal Court*, July 17, 1998, 2187.

International Crisis Group, 'War Crimes in Sri Lanka', *Asia Report*, 191 (17 May 2010), http://www.crisisgroup.org/~/media/Files/asia/south-asia/sri-lanka/191%20War%20Crimes%20in%20Sri%20Lanka.ashx

International Crisis Group, *Taliban Propaganda: Winning the War of Words?*, Asia Report No. 158, International Crisis Group (Kabul and Brussels, 24 July 2008).

Israel Law Review, 40 (2007): 310–660.

Israel Ministry of Foreign Affairs, *Security Cabinet Declares Gaza Hostile Territory*, 17 September 2007, http://www.mfa.gov.il/MFA/Government/ Communiques/2007/Security+Cabinet+declares+Gaza+hostile+territory+19-Sep-2007.htm

Israeli Ministry of Foreign Affairs, *The Operation in Gaza: Factual and Legal Aspects*, July 2009, http://www.mfa.gov.il/MFA/Terrorism-+Obstacle+to+Peace/Terrorism+and+Islamic+Fundamentalism-/Operation_ in_Gaza-Factual_and_Legal_Aspects.htm

Jerusalem Post, 'Hamas Confirms Losses in Cast Lead for the First Time', *Jerusalem Post*, 1 November 2010, http://www.jpost.com/MiddleEast/Article. aspx?id=193521

Jerusalem Post, 'IDF Unveils Hamas Map Seized in Gaza', *Jerusalem Post*, 8 January 2009, http://www.jpost.com/Home/Article.aspx?id=128484

Jilani, Hina, Christine Chinkin and Desmond Travers, 'Goldstone Report; Statement Issued by Members of UN Mission on Gaza War', *Guardian*.

co.uk, 14 April 2011, http://www.guardian.co.uk/commentisfree/2011/apr/14/goldstone-report-statement-un-gaza

Joint Chiefs of Staff, *Joint Publication 3-0, Joint Operations xi, 1-6* (16 September 2006, with Change No. 2, 22 March 2010).

Jones, Samuel Vincent, 'Has Conduct Confirmed the Moral Inadequacy of International Humanitarian Law? Examining the Confluence Between Contract Theory and the Scope of Civilian Immunity During Armed Conflict', *Duke Journal of Comparative and International Law*, 16 (2006).

Journal of Conflict & Security Law, 'Symposium: The Relationship Between International Humanitarian Law and International Human Rights Law', *Journal of Conflict & Security Law*, 14/3 (2010).

Journal of Military Ethics, 'Special Issue: Ethics and Emerging Military Technologies', *Journal of Military Ethics*, 9/4 (2010).

Judge Advocate General's School, *US Army, Operational Law Handbook* (2010), http://www.loc.gov/rr/frd/Military_Law/pdf/operational-law-handbook_2010.pdf

Junger, Sebastian, *War* (London: Fourth Estate, 2010).

Junod, Sylvie, 'Additional Protocol II: History and Scope', *American University Law Review*, 33 (1983).

Kaatz, Yaakov, 'Why Israel Prefers the Cease-Fire in Gaza', *Jerusalem Post*, 15 December 2008 (2008 WLNR 24598450).

Kaatz, Yaakov, Khaled Abu Tomeh and Herb Keinon, 'Gazans Fire Dozens of Rockets at Negev Towns as "Truce" Ends', *Jerusalem Post*, 21 December 2008 (2008 WLNR 25000385).

Kaatz, Yaakov, Khaled Abu Tomeh and Herb Keinon, 'Hamas Divided Over Continuing Ceasefire', *Jerusalem Post*, 15 December 2008 (2008 WLNR 24598446).

Kalshoven, Frits and Liesbeth Zegveld, *Constraints on the Waging of War*, 3rd edn (Geneva: ICRC, 2001).

Kalshoven, Frits, 'The Undertaking to Respect and Ensure Respect in All Circumstances: From Tiny Seed to Ripening Fruit', *Yearbook of International Humanitarian Law*, 2 (1999).

Kalshoven, Frits, *Constraints on the Waging of War* (Geneva: International Committee of the Red Cross, 1991).

Kant, Immanuel, *Grounding for the Metaphysics of Morals*, 3rd edn (Indianapolis, Ind.: Hackett Publishing, 1993).

Karlsen, Elibritt, *Bills Digest*, No. 79 (2010–11), Migration Amendment (Complementary Protection) Bill 2011.

Karpinski, Janis L., 'Ethical Behaviour and Ethical Challenges in the Complex Security Environment', in Daniel Lagacé-Roy and Bernd Horn (eds), *The War on Terror – Ethical Considerations: Proceedings from the 7th Canadian Conference on Ethical Leadership. Volume 2* (Kingston, On.: Canadian Defence Academy Press, 2008).

Kasher, Asa, 'Problems in Military Ethics of Fighting Terrorism', in Daniel Lagacé-Roy and Bernd Horn (eds), *The War on Terror – Ethical Considerations: Proceedings from the 7th Canadian Conference on Ethical Leadership. Volume 1* (Kingston, On.: Canadian Defence Academy Press, 2008).

Katz, Yaakov, '225 Killed as Israel Rains Fire on Hamas in Bid to End Kassams', *Jerusalem Post*, 28 December 2008 (2008 WLNR 25052442).

Katz, Yaakov, 'Gazans Tell Israeli Investigators of Hamas Abuses', *Jerusalem Post*, 1 February 2009, http://www.jpost.com/Home/Article.aspx?id=131380

Katz, Yaakov, 'Shelled UN Building Used by Hamas', *Jerusalem Post*, 15 January 2009, http://www.jpost.com/Home/Article.aspx?id=129393

Kaufman, Frederik, 'Just War Theory and Killing the Innocent', in Michael W. Bough, John W. Lango and Harry van der Linden (eds), *Rethinking the Just War Tradition* (New York: State University of New York Press, 2007).

Kaus, Mickey, 'What *Black Hawk Down* Leaves Out', *Slate*, 21 January 2002, http://www.slate.com/id/2060941/

Keegan, John, *The Face of Battle* (London: Folio, 2007 [1976]).

Kegan, Robert, *In Over Our Heads: The Mental Demands of Modern Life* (Harvard, Mass.: Harvard University Press, 1994).

Keiler, Jonathan, 'The End of Proportionality', *Parameters* (Spring 2009).

Keinon, Herb and Yaakov Kaatz, 'IDF Poised for Limited Gaza Operation', *Jerusalem Post*, 26 December 2008 (2008 WLNR 25046531).

Kellenberger, Jacob, *Strengthening Legal Protection for Victims of Armed Conflicts* (Geneva: ICRC, 21 September 2010), http://www.icrc.org/web/eng/siteeng0.nsf/html/ihl-development-statement-210910

Kelly, Michael J., *Restoring and Maintaining Order in Complex Peace Operations: The Search for a Legal Framework* (The Hague: Kluwer Law International, 1999).

Kelsay, John, *Arguing the Just War in Islam* (Cambridge, Mass.: Harvard University Press, 2007).

Kemp, Colonel Richard, UN Human Rights Council, Statement to 12th Special Session, Geneva, 16 October 2009, http://www.unwatch.org/site/apps/nlnet/content2.aspx?c=bdKKISNqEmG&b=1313923&ct=7536409

Khalidi, Noor Ahmad, 'Afghanistan: Demographic Consequences of War, 1978–1987', *Central Asian Survey*, 10/3 (1991).

Khalil, Ashraf, 'Israel Warns of Gaza Action', *Chicago Tribune*, 26 December 2008 (2008 WLNR 24751030).

Kieval, Michael Y., 'Be Reasonable! Thoughts on the Effectiveness of State Criticism in Enforcing International Law', *Michigan Journal of International Law*, 26 (2005).

Kilcullen, David, *The Accidental Guerrilla: Fighting Small Wars in the Midst of a Big One* (New York: Oxford University Press, 2009).

Kirshner, Isabel and Michael Slackman, 'Cease-Fire Holding as Israelis Pull out of Gaza', *International Herald Tribune*, 20 January 2009 (2009 WLNR 1106907).

Kirshner, Isabel and Taghreed El-Khodary, 'Airstrike Kills Four Palestinian Militants', *Pittsburgh Post-Gazette*, 11 November 2008 (2008 WLNR 21928051).

Kirshner, Isabel and Taghreed El-Khodary, 'Gaza Rocket Fire Intensifies', *Pittsburgh Post-Gazette*, 25 December 2008 (2008 WLNR 24695964).

Klappe, Ben F., 'International Peace Operations', in Dieter Fleck (ed.), *The Handbook of International Humanitarian Law*, 2nd edn (Oxford: Oxford University Press, 2008).

Knickerbocker, Brad, 'The Fuzzy Ethics of Nonlethal Weapons', *Christian Science Monitor*, 14 February 2003.

Kohlberg, Lawrence, *The Psychology of Moral Development: The Nature and Validity of Moral Stages* (San Francisco: Harper & Row, 1984).

Koplow, David A., *Non-Lethal Weapons: The Law and Policy of Revolutionary Technologies for the Military and Law Enforcement* (Cambridge: Cambridge University Press, 2006).

Kritzman-Amir, Tally and Yonatan Berman, 'Responsibility Sharing and the Rights of Refugees: The Case of Israel', *George Washington International Law Review*, 41 (2011).

Kulish, Nicholas, 'Dutch Pull-Out From War Expected After Government Collapse', *The New York Times*, 22 February 2010.

Laber, Jeri and Barnett R. Rubin, *'A Nation is Dying': Afghanistan Under the Soviets 1979–87* (Evanston, Ill.: Northwestern University Press, 1988).

Lafraie, Najibullah, 'Resurgence of the Taliban Insurgency in Afghanistan: How and Why?', *International Politics*, 46/1 (2009).

Lamb, Christina, 'McChrystal's Publicity Blitzkrieg', *The Australian*, 15 February 2010.

Lambert, Helene and Theo Farrell, 'The Changing Character of Armed Conflict and the Implications for Refugee Protection Jurisprudence', *International Journal of Refugee Law*, 22 (2010).

Lammers, Stephen E., 'Area Bombing in World War II: The Argument of Michael Walzer', *Journal of Religious Ethics*, 11 (1983).

Landau, David, 'The Gaza Report's Wasted Opportunity', *The New York Times*, 20 September 2009, http://www.nytimes.com/2009/09/20/opinion/20landau.html

Landes, Richard, 'Goldstone's Gaza Report Part One: A Failure of Intelligence', *Middle East Review of International Affairs*, December 2009, http://www.gloria-center.org/meria/2009/12/landes1.html

Landgren, K., 'Safety Zones and International Protection: A Dark Grey Area', *International Journal of Refugee Law*, 7 (1995).

Lawson, Dominic, 'No, We Are Not All Hamas Now', *Sunday Times*, 11 January 2009, http://www.timesonline.co.uk/tol/comment/columnists/dominic_lawson/article5489436.ece

Lawson, Rick, 'Life After Bankovic: On the Extraterritorial Application of the European Convention on Human Rights', in F. Coomans and M.T. Kamminga (eds), *Extraterritorial Application of Human Rights Treaties* (Antwerp: Intersentia, 2004).

LeVine, Susan, Principal Deputy, Strategy and Policy, Department of Defense Joint Non-Lethal Weapons Directorate, Panel Discussion, 2010 McCain Conference of Service Academies, Annapolis, Md.

Lorenz, F.M., 'Forging Rules of Engagement: Lessons Learned in Operation United Shield', *Military Review* (November–December 1995).

Lynfield, Ben, 'Livni and Netanyahu Vow to Oust Hamas After Gaza Rocket Strikes', *Independent*, 22 December 2008 (2008 WLNR 24502385).

Macintyre, Ben, 'All Quiet on the Afghan–Iraqi Fiction Front', *The Times*, 10 August 2010.

Maddy-Weitzman, Bruce, 'The Israel–Hamas War: A Preliminary Assessment', *RUSI Journal*, February 2009.

Maley, Paul, 'Successful Asylum Claims Plummet', *The Australian*, 21 July 2010.

Maley, William, 'Afghanistan in 2010: Continuing Governance Challenges and Faltering Security', *Asian Survey*, 51/1 (January–February 2011).

Maley, William, 'Human Rights in Afghanistan', in Shahram Akbarzadeh and Benjamin MacQueen (eds), *Islam and Human Rights in Practice: Perspectives Across the Ummah* (New York: Routledge, 2008).

Maley, William, 'Social Dynamics and the Disutility of Terror: Afghanistan, 1978–1989', in P. Timothy Bushnell, Vladimir Shlapentokh, Christopher K. Vanderpool and Jeyaratnam Sundram (eds), *State Organized Terror: The Case of Violent Internal Repression* (Boulder, Colo.: Westview Press, 1991).

Maley, William, *The Afghanistan Wars* (Basingstoke: Palgrave Macmillan, 2009).

Malleson, K., 'Judicial Bias and Disqualification after Pinochet No. 2', *Modern Law Review*, 63 (2000).

Mardell, Alison, 'Unmanned Aerial Vehicles – The Legal Perspective', *Air Power UAVs: The Wider Context* (Northolt, UK: Ministry of Defence, 2009).

Martin, Patrick, 'Israelis Question Reasons for Restraint', *Globe & Mail*, 22 December 2008 (2008 WLNR 24514418).

Martins, Mark S., 'Rules of Engagement for Land Forces: A Matter of Training, Not Lawyering', *Military Law Review*, 143 (1994).

Massing, Michael, 'Trial and Error', [Sunday Book Review], *The New York Times*, 17 October 2004.

Mathew, Penelope, 'Resolution 1373 – A Call to Pre-Empt Asylum Seekers? (Or "Osama the Asylum Seeker")', in Jane McAdam (ed.), *Forced Migration, Human Rights and Security* (Portland, Ore.: Hart Publishing, 2008).

Mathew, Penelope, 'The Myth of Border Control', *The Drum Unleashed* (Sydney: Australian Broadcasting Corporation), (http://www.abc.net.au/unleashed/stories/s2736660.htm).

Matthews, Matt M., 'Hard Lessons Learned: A Comparison of the 2006 Hezbollah–Israeli War and Operation CAST LEAD', in *Back to Basics: A Study of the Second Lebanon War and Operation Cast Lead* (Fort Leavenworth, Kan.:

Combat Studies Institute, May 2009), http://www.cgsc.edu/carl/download/csipubs/farquhar.pdf

Matthews, Matt M., *We Were Caught Unprepared: The 2006 Hezbollah–Israeli War 16*, Long Paper Series, Occasional Paper No. 26 (US Army Combined Arms Center, 2008), http://carl.army.mil/download/csipubs/matthewsOP26.pdf

Mayer, C., 'Nonlethal Weapons and Noncombatant Immunity: Is it Permissible to Target Noncombatants?', *Journal of Miltiary Ethics*, 6/3 (2007).

Mayer, Jane, 'The Risks of a Remote-Controlled War', *National Public Radio*, 21 October 2009.

McAdam, Jane, 'Individual Risk, Armed Conflict and the Standard of Proof in Complementary Protection Claims: The European Union and Canada Compared', in James C. Simeon (ed.), *Critical Issues in International Refugee Law* (Cambridge: Cambridge University Press, 2010).

McCarthy, Rory, 'Israel and Hamas Agree Ceasefire as Strikes Kill Six Palestinian Fighters', *Guardian*, 18 June 2008, http://www.guardian.co.uk/world/2008/jun/18/israelandthepalestinians.egypt

McDougal, Myres S. and Florentino P. Feliciano, *Law and Minimum World Public Order* (New Haven, Conn.: Yale University Press, 1961).

McGoldrick, Dominic, 'Human Rights and Humanitarian Law in the UK Courts', *Israel Law Review*, 40 (2007).

McIntyre, Alison, 'Doing Away With Double Effect', *Ethics*, 111/2 (2001).

Mellies, Penny L., 'Hamas and Hezbollah: A Comparison of Tactics', in *Back to Basics: A Study of the Second Lebanon War and Operation Cast Lead* (Fort Leavenworth, Kan.: Combat Studies Institute, May 2009).

Melzer, Nils, *Interpretive Guidance on the Notion of Direct Participation in Hostilities* (Geneva: ICRC, 2009), www.icrc.org

Mental Health Advisory Team IV, *Operation Iraqi Freedom 05-07: Final Report*, 17 November 2006, http://www.armymedicine.army.mil/reports/mhat/mhat_iv/MHAT_IV_Report_17NOV06.pdf

Michigan Guidelines on Nexus to a Convention Ground, http://www.refugeecaselaw.org/documents/Nexus.pdf

Michigan Journal of International Law, 'Michigan Guidelines on the Right to Work', *Michigan Journal of International Law*, 31 (2010): 289–91.

Milanović, Marco, 'From Compromise to Principle: Clarifying the Concept of State Jurisdiction in Human Rights Treaties', *Human Rights Law Review*, 8 (2008).

Ministry of Foreign Affairs, *Gaza Facts – The Israeli Perspective* (Jerusalem: State of Israel), http://www.mfa.gov.il/GazaFacts

Ministry of Foreign Affairs, *Operation Cast Lead Expanded* (Jerusalem: State of Israel, 3 January 2009), http://www.mfa.gov.il/MFA/Government/Communiques/2009/Second_stage_Operation_Cast_Lead_begins_3-Jan-2009.htm

Ministry of Foreign Affairs, *Violations of Calm: Rockets Strike Sderot, Ashkelon, Western Negev* (Jerusalem: State of Israel, 18 December 2008), http://www.mfa.

gov.il/MFA/Terrorism-+Obstacle+to+Peace/Hamas+war+against+Israel/Rockets_
strike_Sderot_Ashkelon_western_Negev_16-Nov-2008.htm?DisplayMode=print

Moir, L., 'Grave Breaches and Internal Armed Conflict', *Journal of International Criminal Justice*, 7 (2009).

Moir, Lindsay, *Reappraising the Resort to Force: International Law, Jus ad Bellum and the War on Terror* (Oxford: Hart Publishing, 2010).

Moir, Lindsay, *The Law of Internal Armed Conflict* (Cambridge: Cambridge University Press, 2002).

Morgenthau, Hans, *Politics Among Nations: The Struggle for Power and Peace*, 2nd edn (New York: Alfred Knopf, 1954).

Morton, Adam, *On Evil* (London: Routledge, 2004).

MSNBC, 'U.S. Confirms Incursion into Pakistan', *MSNBC*, 3 September 2008, http://www.msnbc.msn.com/id/26522492/ns/world_news-south_and_central_asia/

Munir, Muhammad, 'The Layha for the Mujahideen: An Analysis of the Code of Conduct for the Taliban Fighters Under Islamic law', *International Review of the Red Cross*, 93/881 (March 2011).

Münkler, H., *Die neuen Krige* (Hamburg: Rowohlt, 2003).

Munro, Hector Hugh, *The Collected Short Stories of Saki* (Ware: Wordsworth Classics, 1993).

Muravchik, Joshua, 'Goldstone: An Exegesis', *World Affairs*, May–June 2010, http://www.worldaffairsjournal.org/articles/2010-MayJune/full-Muravchik-Traub-MJ-2010.html

Nagel, Thomas, *The View From Nowhere* (Oxford: Oxford University Press, 1986).

Nasu, Hitoshi, 'Status of Rebels in Non-International Armed Conflict', in Jahid Hossain Bhuiyan, Louise Doswald-Beck and Azizur Rahman Chowdhury (eds), *International Humanitarian Law – An Anthology* (Dehli: LexisNexis, 2009).

Nasu, Hitoshi, *International Law on Peacekeeping: A Study of Article 40 of the UN Charter* (The Hague: Martinus Nijhoff, 2009).

Nathanson, Stephen, 'Are Preventive Wars Always Wrong?', in Deen Chatterjee (ed.), *Gathering Threats: The Ethics of Preventive War* (Cambridge, Cambridge University Press, forthcoming).

Nathanson, Stephen, 'Patriotism, War, and the Limits of Permissible Partiality', *Journal of Ethics*, 13/4 (2009).

Nathanson, Stephen, 'Terrorism, Supreme Emergency, and Noncombatant Immunity: A Critique of Michael Walzer's Ethics of War', *Iyyun: The Jerusalem Philosophical Quarterly*, 55 (2006).

Nathanson, Stephen, *Terrorism and the Ethics of War* (Cambridge: Cambridge University Press, 2010).

Neighbour, Sally, 'Half of Sri Lankan Arrivals Have Ties to Tigers', *The Australian*, 14 July 2010, http://www.theaustralian.com.au/news/nation/half-of-sri-lankan-arrivals-have-ties-to-tigers/story-e6frg6nf-1225891388934

Norland, Rod, 'Hamas and its Discontents', *Newsweek*, 20 January 2009, http://www.newsweek.com/2009/01/19/hamas-and-its-discontents.html

North Atlantic Treaty Organization (NATO), *COMISAF Tactical Directive*, 6 July 2009, http://www.nato.int/isaf/docu/official_texts/Tactical_Directive_090706.pdf

Norwitz, Trevor, 'An Open Letter to Richard Goldstone', *Commentary*, 19 October 2009, http://www.commentarymagazine.com/viewarticle.cfm/an-open-letter-to-richard-goldstone-15284

NSW Ombudsman, *The Use of Taser Weapons by New South Wales Police Force* (Sydney: Government of New South Wales, 2008).

O'Connell, D.P., *The Influence of Law on Seapower* (Annapolis, Md: Naval Institute Press, 1975).

O'Regan, Greg, Letter to the Editor, *The Canberra Times*, 17 July 2010, http://www.canberratimes.com.au/news/opinion/letters/general/letters-to-the-editor/1888087.aspx?storypage=0#

Office of Police Integrity, *Review of the Use of Force By and Against Victorian Police* (Melbourne: Government of Victoria, 2009).

Office of the Coordinator for Counterterrorism, *Foreign Terrorist Organizations* (Washington, DC: US Department of State, 19 January 2010), http://www.state.gov/s/ct/rls/other/des/123085.htm

Okoth-Obbo, George, 'Thirty Years On: A Legal Review of the 1969 Refugee Convention Governing the Specific Aspects of Refugee Problems in Africa', *Refugee Survey Quarterly*, 20/1 (2001).

Omestad, Thomas, 'The Flames of War, and Small Hopes for Peace', *US News & World Report*, 24 July 2006, http://www.usnews.com/usnews/news/articles/060716/24week.htm

Opotow, Susan, 'Moral Exclusion and Injustice: An Introduction', *Journal of Social Issues*, 46/1 (Spring 1990).

Orakhelashvili, Alexander, 'The Interaction Between Human Rights and Humanitarian Law: Fragmentation, Conflict, Parallelism, or Convergence?', *European Journal of International Law*, 19 (2008).

Orend, Brian, 'Is there a Supreme Emergency Exemption?', in Mark Evans (ed.), *Just War Theory: A Reappraisal* (Edinburgh: Edinburgh University Press, 2005).

Orend, Brian, *Michael Walzer on War and Justice* (Montreal: McGill–Queen's University Press, 2001).

Orford, Anne, *International Authority and the Responsibility to Protect* (Cambridge: Cambridge University Press, 2011).

Oswald, Bruce, Helen Durham and Adrian Bates, *Documents on the Law of United Nations Peace Operations* (Oxford: Oxford University Press, 2010).

Oxfam, *NGOs and the Prevention of Mass Atrocity Crimes* (London, 23–24 November 2009), http://responsibilitytoprotect.org/Oxfam%20R2P%20workshop%20outcome%20doc%20March%202010-2.pdf

Oxford Dictionary of Law, 6th edn (Oxford University Press, 2006).

Parke Hughes, Thomas, *American Genesis: A Century of Invention and Technological Enthusiasm 1870–1970* (Chicago: University of Chicago Press, 2004).

Parnell, Sean and Rory Callinan, 'Soldiers' Despair Confronts Defence', *The Weekend Australian*, 10–11 July 2010.

Pavković, Aleksandar, 'Towards Liberation: Terrorism from a Liberation Ideology Perspective', in Tony Coady and Michael O'Keefe (eds), *Terrorism and Justice* (Melbourne: Melbourne University Press, 2002).

Petrović, Dražen, 'Ethnic Cleansing – An Attempt at Methodology', *European Journal of International Law*, 5 (1994): 351.

Petty, Keith A., 'Veiled Impunity: Iran's Use of Non-State Armed Groups', *Denver Journal of International Law and Policy*, 36 (2008).

Phillipson, Coleman, *The International Law and Custom of Ancient Greece and Rome. Volume II* (London: Macmillan, 1911).

Physicians for Human Rights, *The Taliban's War on Women: A Health and Human Rights Crisis in Afghanistan* (Boston: Physicians for Human Rights, 1998).

Physicians for Human Rights, *Women's Health and Human Rights in Afghanistan: A Population-Based Assessment* (Boston: Physicians for Human Rights, 2001).

Pictet, Jean, *The Geneva Conventions of 12 August 1949: Commentary IV* (Geneva: ICRC, 1958).

Primoratz, Igor (ed.), *Civilian Immunity in War* (Oxford: Oxford University Press, 2007).

Primoratz, Igor, 'Can the Bombing Be Morally Justified?', in Igor Primoratz (ed.), *Terror From the Sky: The Bombing of German Cities in World War II* (Oxford and New York: Berghahn Books, 2010).

Primoratz, Igor, 'Civilian Immunity, Supreme Emergency, and Moral Disaster', *The Journal of Ethics*, 15 (2011).

Program on Humanitarian Policy and Conflict Research, *Manual on International Law Applicable to Air and Missile Warfare* (Harvard University, 2009).

Putz, Ulrike, 'Gaza in Ruins: "Who Has Won Here?"', *Spiegel Online*, 23 January 2009, http://www.spiegel.de/international/world/0,1518,603203,00.html

Quéguiner, J.-F., 'Precautions Under the Law Governing the Conduct of Hostilities', *International Review of the Red Cross*, 88 (2006).

Quinn, Warren, 'Actions, Intentions, and Consequences: The Doctrine of Double Effect', *Philosophy and Public Affairs*, 18/4 (1989).

Rabkin, Jeremy, 'The Fantasy World of International Law: The Criticism of Israel Has Been Disproportionate', *Weekly Standard*, 21 August 2006, http://weeklystandard.com/Content/Public/Articles/000/000/012/580uttca.asp

Rabkin, Jeremy, 'The Politics of the Geneva Conventions: Disturbing Background to the ICC Debate', *Virginia Journal of International Law*, 44 (2003).

Ramesh Thakur, *The Responsibility to Protect: Norms, Laws and the Use of Force in International Politics* (New York: Routledge, 2011).

Rashid, Ahmed, *Taliban: Militant Islam, Oil and Fundamentalism in Central Asia* (New Haven, Conn.: Yale University Press, 2000).

Reisman, W. Michael and James Silk, 'Which Law Applies to the Afghan Conflict?', *American Journal of International Law*, 82/3 (1988).

Report of an Expert Meeting which Assessed Procedural Criticisms Made of the UN Fact-Finding Mission on the Gaza Conflict (The Goldstone Report), Chatham House, 27 November 2009.

Report of the Secretary-General Pursuant to General Assembly Resolution 53/35: The Fall of Srebrenica, UN Doc. A/54/549 (15 November 1999), http://www.un.org/peace/srebrenica.pdf

Report of the Somalia Commission of Inquiry, http://www.forces.gc.ca/somalia/vol2/v2c22e.htm

Report of the United Nations Fact-Finding Mission on the Gaza Conflict, UN Doc. A/HRC/12/48, 25 September 2009.

Report on the Situation of Human Rights in Afghanistan, A/41/778 (New York: UN General Assembly, 9 January 1987).

Report on the Situation of Human Rights in Afghanistan, A/42/667 (New York: UN General Assembly, 23 October 1987).

Report on the Situation of Human Rights in Afghanistan, A/43/742 (New York: UN General Assembly, 24 October 1988).

Report on the Situation of Human Rights in Afghanistan, A/44/669 (New York: UN General Assembly, 30 October 1989).

Reuters, 'Gaza: Rocket Fire and Israeli Strike Disrupt Ceasefire', *The New York Times*, 6 November 2008 (2008 WLNR 21173891).

Reuters, 'Israel Issues an Appeal to Palestinians in Gaza', *The New York Times*, 26 December 2008 (2008 WLNR 24747964).

Reuters, 'Karzai Says Air Strike Kills 40 in Afghanistan', *Reuters*, 5 November 2008, http://www.reuters.com/article/2008/11/05/us-afghan-violence-idUSTRE4A44EW20081105

Reuters, 'Libya Engulfed in Civil War as Casualties Rise: ICRC', *Reuters*, 10 March 2011, http://www.reuters.com/article/2011/03/10/us-tripoli-cross-idUSTRE72927N20110310

Reuters, 'Police Find 11 Beheaded Bodies in Afghan South', *Reuters*, 25 June 2010.

Reynolds, Jefferson D., 'Collateral Damage on the 21st Century Battlefield: Enemy Exploitation of the Law of Armed Conflict, and the Struggle for the Moral High Ground', *Air Force Law Review*, 56 (2005).

Richemond, Daphne, 'Transnational Terrorist Organizations and the Use of Force', *Catholic University Law Review*, 56 (2007).

Richter, Paul, 'U.N. Security Council Authorizes Action Against Moammar Kadafi', *Los Angeles Times*, 18 March 2011, http://articles.latimes.com/2011/mar/18/world/la-fg-un-libya-20110318

Rikhof, Joseph, 'War Criminals Not Welcome: How Common Law Countries Approach the Phenomenon of International Crimes in the Immigration and Refugee Context', *International Journal of Refugee Law*, 21 (2009).

Roach, J. Ashley, 'Rules of Engagement', *Naval War College Review* (January–February 1983).

Roberts, Adam and Richard Guelff, *Documents on the Laws of War*, 3rd edn (Oxford: Oxford University Press, 2000).

Roberts, Adam, 'Transformative Military Occupation: Applying the Laws of War and Human Rights', *American Journal of International Law*, 100 (2006).

Robertson, Geoffrey, *Crimes Against Humanity: The Struggle for Global Justice* (Melbourne: Penguin, 2006).

Robinson, P., 'Introduction: Ethics Education for Irregular Warfare', in Don Carrick, James Connelly and Paul Robinson (eds), *Ethics Education for Irregular Warfare* (Surrey: Ashgate, 2009).

Rogers, A.P.V., 'The Principle of Proportionality', in Howard Hensel (ed.), *The Legitimate Use of Military Force* (Aldershot: Ashgate, 2008).

Rogers, A.P.V., 'Zero-Casualty Warfare', *International Review of the Red Cross*, 837 (2000), http://www.icrc.org/eng/resources/documents/misc/57jqcu.htm

Rogers, A.P.V., *Law on the Battlefield*, 2nd edn (Huntington, NY: Juris Publishing, 2004).

Ronen, Y., 'ICC Jurisdiction Over Acts Committed in the Gaza Strip', *Journal of International Criminal Justice*, 8 (2010).

Ross, W.D., *The Right and the Good*, ed. Philip Stratton-Lake (Oxford: Oxford University Press, 2002).

Rotella, Sebastian, 'Conflict in Gaza: Hamas' Weapon of Choice', *Los Angeles Times*, 15 January 2009 (2009 WLNR 775471).

Rowe, Peter, 'The Rules of Engagement in Occupied Territory: Should They be Published?', *Melbourne Journal of International Law*, 8/2 (2007).

Rowe, Peter, *The Impact of Human Rights Law on Armed Forces* (Cambridge: Cambridge University Press, 2006).

Rubenstein, Kim, 'Rethinking Nationality in International Humanitarian Law', in Ustinia Dolgopol and Judith Gardam (eds), *The Challenge of Conflict: International Law Responds* (Leiden: Martinus Nijhoff, 2006).

Rubin, Alissa J. and Sangar Rahimi, 'Nine Afghan Boys Collecting Firewood Killed by NATO Helicopters', *The New York Times*, 2 March 2011.

Rubin, Alissa J., 'Afghan Leader Calls Apology in Boys' Deaths Insufficient', *The New York Times*, 6 March 2011.

Rüth, A. and M. Trilsch, 'International Decisions: Banković v. Belgium (Admissibility)', *American Journal of International Law*, 97 (2003).

Samet, Elizabeth D., *Soldier's Heart: Reading Literature Through Peace and War at West Point* (New York: Farrar, Strauss and Giroux, 2007).

San Remo Manual on the Law of Non-International Armed Conflict with Commentary (2006).

Sandoz, Yves, Christophe Swinarski and Bruno Zimmerman (eds), *Commentary on the Additional Protocols of 8 June 1977 to the Geneva Conventions of 12 August 1949* (Geneva: ICRC, 1987).

Sassòli, Marco, 'Legislation and Maintenance of Public Order and Civil Life by Occupying Powers', *European Journal of International Law*, 16 (2005).

Sassòli, Marco, 'The Status of Persons Held in Guantánamo Under International Humanitarian Law', *Journal of International Criminal Justice*, 2 (2004).

Scanlon, T.M., *Moral Dimensions: Permissibility, Meaning, Blame* (Cambridge, Mass.: Harvard University Press, 2008).

Scheuer, Michael, *Imperial Hubris: Why the West is Losing the War on Terror* (Washington, DC: Potomac Books, 2004).

Schmeidl, Susanne and William Maley, 'The Case of the Afghan Refugee Population: Finding Durable Solutions in Contested Transitions', in Howard Adelman (ed.), *Protracted Displacement in Asia: No Place to Call Home* (Aldershot: Ashgate, 2008).

Schmidt, M., 'Deconstructing Direct Participation in Hostilities: The Constitutive Elements', *Journal of International Law and Politics*, 42/3 (2010).

Schmitt, Michael N., 'Asymmetrical Warfare and International Humanitarian Law', *Air Force Law Review*, 62 (2008).

Schmitt, Michael N., 'The Interpretive Guidance on the Notion of Direct Participation in Hostilities: A Critical Analysis', *Harvard National Security Journal*, 1 (2010).

Schmitt, Michael N., 'The Principle of Proportionality in 21st Century Warfare', *Yale Human Rights and Development Law Journal*, 2 (1999).

Schwartz, Bruce P. and Christopher C. Donaldson, 'Protecting the Playground: Options for Confronting the Iranian Regime', *Brooklyn Journal of International Law*, 35 (2010).

Shachar, Nathan, *The Gaza Strip* (Sussex: Sussex Academic Press, 2010).

Shah, Taimoor and Carlotta Gall, 'Afghan Rebels Find Aid in Pakistan, Musharraf Admits', *The New York Times*, 13 August 2007.

Shanker, Thom, 'Insurgents Kill Most Civilians, Military Says', *The New York Times*, 10 March 2011.

Shoyele, Olugbenga, 'Armed Conflicts and Canadian Refugee Law and Policy', *International Journal of Refugee Law*, 16 (2004).

Shraga, Daphna, 'The Secretary-General's Bulletin on the Observance by United Nations Forces of International Humanitarian Law – A Decade Later', *Israel Yearbook on Human Rights*, 39 (2009).

Shue, Henry, 'Liberalism: The Impossibility of Justifying Weapons of Mass Destruction', in Sohail Hashmi and Steven Lee (eds), *Ethics and Weapons of Mass Destruction* (Cambridge: Cambridge University Press, 2004).

Simms, Andrew, 'A Magnificent Man and His Flying Machines', *Soldier Magazine* (October 2010).

Simpson, Gerry, *Law, War and Crime: War Crimes Trials and the Reinvention of International Law* (Cambridge: Polity Press, 2007).

Singer, P.W., 'The Ethics of Killer Applications: Why is it So Hard to Talk About Morality When it Comes to New Military Technology?', *Journal of Military Ethics*, 9/4 (2010).

Singer, P.W., *Wired for War: The Robotics Revolution and Conflict in the 21st Century* (New York: Penguin, 2010).

Singer, Peter, *Practical Ethics* (Cambridge: Cambridge University Press, 1979).

Sinnott-Armstrong, Walter, *Moral Dilemmas* (Oxford: Basil Blackwell, 1988).

Skerker, Michael, 'Just War Criteria and the New Face of War: Human Shields, Manufactured Martyrs, and Little Boys with Stones', *Journal of Military Ethics*, 3/1 (2004).

Slim, Hugo, *Killing Civilians: Method, Madness, and Morality in War* (New York: Columbia University Press, 2008).

Smart, J.J.C., 'Extreme and Restricted Utilitarianism', in *Essays Metaphysical and Moral* (Oxford: Basil Blackwell, 1987).

Smith, Adam, *The Theory of Moral Sentiments*, eds D.D. Raphael and A.L. Macfie (Oxford: Oxford University Press, 1976 [1759]).

Smith, Rupert, *The Utility of Force: The Art of War in the Modern World* (London: Allen Lane, 2005).

Snyder, Lieutenant Colonel Michael D., 'Information Strategies Against a Hybrid Threat: What Recent Experiences of Israel Versus Hezbollah/Hamas Tell the US Army', in *Back to Basics: A Study of the Second Lebanon War and Operation Cast Lead* (Fort Leavenworth, Kan.: Combined Studies Institute, May 2009).

Solis, Gary D., *Law of Armed Conflict* (Cambridge: Cambridge University Press, 2010).

Soltis, Andy, 'Hamas in "Human Shield" Atrocity – Uses School as Mortar Lair Where Children Die', *New York Post*, 7 January 2009 (2009 WLNR 313151).

Sparrow, Jeff, *Killing: Misadventures in Violence* (Carlton, Vic.: Melbourne University Press, 2009).

Sparrow, Robert, '"Hands Up Who Wants to Die": Primoratz on Responsibility and Civilian Immunity in Wartime', *Ethical Theory and Practice*, 8 (2005).

Spencer, Emily and Daniel Lagacé-Roy (eds), *Ethical Decision-Making in the New Security Environment. Proceedings from the Canadian Conference on Ethical Leadership. Volume 2* (Kingston, On.: Canadian Defence Academy Press, 2008).

Stahn, C., 'Responsibility to Protect: Political Rhetoric or Emerging Legal Norm?', *American Journal of International Law*, 101 (2007).

Stapleton, Barbara J., 'Security and PRTs', in *State, Security and Economy in Afghanistan: Current Challenges, Possible Solutions, Liechtenstein Colloquium Report Vol. III*, Liechtenstein Institute on Self-Determination, Princeton University (Princeton, NJ, 2008).

State of Israel, *Disengagement Plan of Prime Minister Ariel Sharon*, 16 April 2004, http://www.knesset.gov.il/process/docs/DisengageSharon_eng.htm

State of Israel, *Gaza Operation Investigations: Second Update* (Jerusalem: State of Israel, 19 July 2010), http://www.mfa.gov.il/NR/rdonlyres/1483B296-7439-4217-933C-653CD19CE859/0/GazaUpdateJuly2010.pdf

Statman, Daniel, 'Moral Tragedies, Supreme Emergencies and National-Defense', *Journal of Applied Philosophy*, 23 (2006).

Statman, Daniel, 'Supreme Emergencies Revisited', *Ethics*, 117 (2006–07).

Stavridis, James, 'Let Us Dare', *Australian Defence Force Journal*, 181 (2010).

Steinhoff, U., 'Torture: The Case for Dirty Harry and Against Alan Dershowitz', *Journal of Applied Philosophy*, 23 (2006).

Stephens, Dale, 'Rules of Engagement and the Concept of Unit Self Defence', *Naval Law Review*, 45 (1998).

Stern, Yoav, 'Gaza Reporter Caught on Tape Confirming Hamas Fired Rockets Near TV Station', *Haaretz.com*, 20 January 2009, http://www.haaretz.com/hasen/spages/1057129.html

Stockdale, James B., *A Vietnam Experience: Ten Years of Reflection* (Stanford, Calif.: Hoover Institution Press, 1984).

Storey, Hugo and Rebecca Wallace, 'War and Peace in Refugee Law Jurisprudence', *American Journal of International Law*, 95 (2001).

Strawser, B.J., 'Moral Predators: The Duty to Employ Uninhabited Aerial Vehicles', *Journal of Military Ethics*, 9/4 (2010).

Swiss Federal Institute of Technology, *Are ISAF's Tenuous Supply Lines Sustainable?* (Zurich, 2 March 2011), http://www.isn.ethz.ch/isn/Current-Affairs/ISN-Insights/Detail?lng=en&id=127187&contextid734=127187&contextid735=127186&tabid=127186

Szurek, Sandra, 'La responsabilité de protéger, nature de l'obligation et responsabilité internationale', in Société Française pour le Droit International (ed.), *La responsabilité de protéger – colloque de Nanterre* (Paris: Editions Pedone, 2008).

Taylor, Telford, *The Anatomy of the Nuremberg Trials* (New York: Alfred A. Knopf, 1993).

Tellis, Ashley J., *Reconciling with the Taliban? Toward an Alternative Grand Strategy in Afghanistan* (Washington, DC: Carnegie Endowment for International Peace, 2009).

Terry, Fiona, *Condemned to Repeat?: The Paradox of Humanitarian Action* (Ithaca, NY: Cornell University Press, 2002).

The Afghanistan Justice Project, *Casting Shadows: War Crimes and Crimes Against Humanity: 1978–2001* (Kabul: The Afghanistan Justice Project, 2005).

The Asia Foundation, *Afghanistan in 2010: A Survey of the Afghan People* (Kabul: The Asia Foundation, 2010).

The Australian, 'Peace in Bethlehem as Hamas Fires on Israel', *The Australian*, 26 December 2008 (2008 WLNR 24726004).

The New York Times, 'Statement From the New York City Police Department', *The New York Times*, 25 September 2008.

The New York Times, 'Taliban Renews Offensive in Afghanistan', *The New York Times*, 1 May 2011.

The Responsibility to Protect: Report of the International Commission on Intervention and State Sovereignty (Ottawa: International Development Research Centre, 2001).

The Telegraph, 'One in Three Killed by US Drones in Pakistan is a Civilian, Report Claims', *The Telegraph*, 4 March 2010, http://www.telegraph.co.uk/news/worldnews/asia/pakistan/7361630/One-in-three-killed-by-US-drones-in-Pakistan-is-a-civilian-report-claims.html

The US Army Marine Corps Counterinsurgency Field Manual, US Army Field Manual No. 3-24, Marine Corps Warfighting Publication No. 3-33.5 (Chicago: University of Chicago Press, 2007).

Thienel, Tobias, 'The ECHR in Iraq: The Judgment of the House of Lords in R (Al-Skeini) v. Secretary of State for Defence', *Journal of International Criminal Justice*, 6 (2008).

Tick, Edward, *War and the Soul: Healing Our Nation's Veterans from Post-Traumatic Stress Disorder* (Wheaton, Ill.: Quest Books, 2005).

Toameh, Khaled Abu, 'Hamas Mocks Israel's Nonresponse to Rocket Attacks', *Jerusalem Post*, 25 December 2008, p. 2 (2008 WLNR 25046493).

Toner, Christopher, 'Just War and the Supreme Emergency Exemption', *Philosophical Quarterly*, 55 (2005).

Tripodi, Paolo, 'Understanding Atrocities', in D. Whetham (ed.), *Ethics, Law and Military Operations* (Basingstoke: Palgrave, 2010).

Tuccille, Jerome, 'Texas Cop Tasers Great-Grandmother', *Examiner*, 2 June 2009, http://www.examiner.com/civil-liberties-in-national/texas-cop-tasers-great-grandmother

Tucker-Lowe, *Does the Advent of Uninhabited Systems Fundamentally Affect the Ethical Landscape of Contemporary Conflict?*, Defence Research Paper (Unpublished Defence Studies MA Dissertation, King's College, London, July 2010).

UK Ministry of Defence, *British Defence Doctrine*, 3rd edn (London: August 2008), JDP 0-01, http://www.mod.uk/NR/rdonlyres/CE5E85F2-DEEB-4694-B8DE-4148A4AEDF91/0/20100114jdp0_01_bddUDCDCIMAPPS.pdf

UK Ministry of Defence, *The Joint Service Manual of the Law of Armed Conflict* (London, 2004).

UN Assistance Mission in Afghanistan (UNAMA), *Afghanistan: Annual Report on Protection of Civilians in Armed Conflict 2009* (Kabul, 2010).

UN Assistance Mission in Afghanistan and Afghanistan Independent Human Rights Commission, *Afghanistan Annual Report 2010: Protection of Civilians in Armed Conflict* (Kabul: UN Assistance Mission in Afghanistan and Afghanistan Independent Human Rights Commission, March 2011).

UN High Commissioner for Human Rights, *Statement of Special Rapporteur for the Palestinian Territories Occupied Since 1967 for Presentation to the Special Session of the Human Rights Council on the Situation in the Gaza Strip*, 9 January 2009, http://www.unhchr.ch/huricane/huricane.nsf/view01/14B004C3AE39004BC125753900599B5D?opendocument

UN High Commissioner for Human Rights, *UN Fact Finding Mission Finds Strong Evidence of War Crimes and Crimes Against Humanity Committed During the Gaza Conflict; Calls for End to Impunity*, UN Human Rights Council, 15 September 2009, http://www.ohchr.org/EN/NewsEvents/Pages/DisplayNews.aspx?NewsID=91&LangID=E

UN High Commissioner for Refugees (UNHCR), *Country Operations Profile – Afghanistan* (Geneva: UNHCR, 2011), http://www.unhcr.org/cgi-bin/texis/vtx/page?page=49e486eb6

UN High Commissioner for Refugees (UNHCR), *Country Operations Profile – Iran* (Geneva: UNHCR, 2011), http://www.unhcr.org/cgi-bin/texis/vtx/page?page=49e486f96

UN High Commissioner for Refugees (UNHCR), *Eligibility Guidelines for Assessing International Protection Needs of Asylum-Seekers from Sri Lanka*, HRC/EG/SLK/10/03, 5 July 2010.

UN High Commissioner for Refugees (UNHCR), *Guidelines on International Protection: Application of the Exclusion Clauses: Article 1F of the 1951 Convention Relating to the Status of Refugees*, UN Doc. HCR/GIP/03/05 (4 September 2003).

UN High Commissioner for Refugees (UNHCR), *Handbook on Procedures and Criteria for Determining Refugee Status Under the 1951 Convention and the 1967 Protocol Relating to the Status of Refugees*, 2nd edn (Geneva: UNHCR, 1992).

UN High Commissioner for Refugees (UNHCR), *Position on Claims for Refugee Status Under the 1951 Convention Relating to the Status of Refugees Based on a Fear of Persecution Due to An Individual's Membership of a Family or Clan Engaged in a Blood Feud* (Geneva: UNHCR, 17 March 2006), http://www.unhcr.no/Pdf/Position_countryinfo_papers_06/Membership_clan_family_blood_feud.pdf

UN High Commissioner for Refugees (UNHCR), *Refugee Protection and International Migration in the Americas: Trends, Protection Challenges and Responses, Background Document* (Geneva: UNHCR, December 2009).

UN Human Rights Council, 'Richard J. Goldstone Appointed to Lead Human-Rights Council Fact-Finding Mission on Gaza Conflict', Press Release, 9 April 2009, http://www.ohchr.org/EN/NewsEvents/Pages/DisplayNews.aspx?NewsID=8469&LangID=E

UN Human Rights Council, *Fact-Finding Mission on the Gaza Conflict, Human Rights in Palestine and Other Occupied Arab Territories*, A/HRC/12/48 (15 September 2009).

UN Human Rights Council, *Fact-Finding Mission on the Gaza Conflict, Conclusions and Recommendations, Human Rights in Palestine and Other Occupied Arab Territories*, A/HRC/12/48 (24 September 2009).

UN Human Rights Council, *The Grave Violations of Human Rights in the Occupied Palestinian Territory, Particularly Due to the Recent Israeli Military Attacks Against the Occupied Gaza Strip*, UN Human Rights Council Res. S-9/1, A/HRC/S-1/L.1 (12 January 2009), http://www2.ohchr.org/english/bodies/hrcouncil/specialsession/9/docs/A-HRC-S-91-L1.doc

UN Security Council, Resolution 1373 (2001).

UN Security Council, Statement SC/10089, 22 November 2010.

UN Security Council, *The Situation in Libya*, Resolution 1973 (2011), http://www.un.org/News/Press/docs/2011/sc10200.doc.htm#Resolution

UN Special Mission to Afghanistan, *Progress Report of the Special Mission to Afghanistan*, A/49/208, S/1994/766 (New York: United Nations, 1 July 1994).

Uniacke, Suzanne, *Permissible Killing: The Self-Defense Justification of Homicide* (Cambridge: Cambridge University Press, 1994).

United Nations, *2005 World Summit Outcome*, UNGA Res. A/Res/60/1, 24 October 2005.

United Nations, *General Comment No. 31 on Article 2 of the Covenant: The Nature of the General Legal Obligation Imposed on States Parties to the Covenant*, UN Doc. CCPR/C/74/CRP.4/Rev.6 (21 April 2004).

United Nations, *Implementing the Responsibility to Protect*, Report of the Secretary General, UN Doc. A/63/677 (2009).

United Nations, *Report of the Secretary-General's Panel of Experts on Accountability in Sri Lanka*, Publicly released on 25 April 2011, http://www.un.org/News/dh/infocus/Sri_Lanka/POE_Report_Full.pdf

US Army Judge Advocate General's School, *Law of War Documentary Supplement* (2010).

US Department of Defense Joint Non-Lethal Weapons Directorate, *Non-Lethal Weapons for Today's Operations: DoD Non-Lethal Weapons Program Annual Report 2010 & DOD Non-Lethal Weapons and Capabilities 2011* (Washington, DC, 2011), https://www.jnlwp.usmc.mil/public_affairs/annual_report.asp

US Department of Defense, *Dictionary of Military and Associated Terms* (http://www.dtic.mil/doctrine/dod_dictionary/)

US Navy, *Annotated Supplement to the Commanders Handbook on the Law of Naval Operations*, http://www.usnwc.edu/Research---Gaming/International-Law/RightsideLinks/Studies-Series/documents/Naval-War-College-vol-73.aspx

US War Department, *Instructions for the Government of Armies of the United States in the Field*, General Order No. 100 [Leiber Code].

USAF TJAG, *Air Force Operations and the Law*, 2nd edn (2009), http://www.afjag.af.mil/shared/media/document/AFD-100510-059.pdf

van Baarda, T. and F. van Iersel, 'The Uneasy Relationship Between Conscience and Military Law: The Brahimi Report's Unresolved Dilemma', *International Peacekeeping*, 9/3 (2002).

van der Vyver, Johan D., 'Legal Ramifications of the War in Gaza', *Florida Journal of International Law*, 21 (2009).

Venzia, Todd, 'Hell Fire Rains on Gaza', *New York Post*, 28 December 2008 (2008 WLNR 25008702).

Vité, Sylvain, 'Typology of Armed Conflicts in International Humanitarian Law: Legal Concepts and Actual Situations', *International Review of the Red Cross*, 91 (2009).

Waldman, Matt, *The Sun in the Sky: The Relationship Between Pakistan's ISI and Afghan Insurgents*, Discussion Paper No. 18, Crisis States Research Centre, London School of Economics and Political Science, June 2010.

Walker, Richard J., 'Quarter and Jus in Bello: Meeting the Challenge of Ethical Uncertainty Within the Asymmetrical Battlespace', in Daniel Lagacé-Roy and Bernd Horn (eds), *The War on Terror – Ethical Considerations: Proceedings from the 7th Canadian Conference on Ethical Leadership. Volume 1* (Kingston, On.: Canadian Defence Academy Press).

Walzer, Michael, 'Emergency Ethics', in Michael Walzer, *Arguing About War* (New Haven, Conn., and London: Yale University Press, 2004).

Walzer, Michael, 'Political Action: The Problem of Dirty Hands', *Philosophy and Public Affairs*, 2 (1972–73).

Walzer, Michael, 'Terrorism: A Critique of Excuses', in Michael Walzer, *Arguing About War* (New Haven, Conn., and London: Yale University Press, 2004).

Walzer, Michael, *Arguing About War* (New Haven, Conn., and London: Yale University Press, 2004).

Walzer, Michael, *Just and Unjust Wars* (New York: Basic Books, 1977).

Walzer, Michael, *Just and Unjust Wars: A Moral Argument with Historical Illustrations*, 3rd edn (New York: Basic Books, 2000).

Watkin, Kenneth, 'Opportunity Lost: Organized Armed Groups and the ICRC "Direct Participation in Hostilities" Interpretive Guidance', *New York University Journal of International Law and Politics*, 42/3 (2010).

Waziri, Rafiq, 'Symptomatology of Depressive Illness in Afghanistan', *American Journal of Psychiatry*, 130/2 (1973).

Wedgwood, Ralph, 'Scanlon on Double Effect', *Philosophy and Phenomenological Research* (forthcoming, 2011).

West, Bing, *The Wrong War: Grit, Strategy, and the Way Out of Afghanistan* (New York: Random House, 2011).

Whetham, David (ed.), *Ethics, Law, and Military Operations* (Basingstoke: Palgrave, 2010).

Whetham, David, 'Ethics, Law and Conflict', in David Whetham (ed.), *Ethics, Law and Military Operations* (Basingstoke: Palgrave, 2010).

Whetham, David, 'The Just War Tradition: A Pragmatic Compromise', in David Whetham (ed.), *Ethics, Law and Military Operations* (Basingstoke: Palgrave, 2010).

Whitlock, Craig and Reyham Abdel Kareem, 'Gaza Clan Finds One Haven After Another Ravaged in Attacks', *Washington Post*, 16 January 2009, http://www.washingtonpost.com/wp-dyn/content/article/2009/01/15/AR2009011503832.html

Whitlock, Craig, 'Members of Stryker Combat Brigade in Afghanistan Accused of Killing Civilians for Sport', *The Washington Post*, 18 September 2010.

Whitlock, Craig, 'Number of U.S. Casualties from Roadside Bombs in Afghanistan Skyrocketed from 2009 to 2010', *The Washington Post*, 25 January 2011.

Wilde, Ralph, 'Triggering State Obligations Extraterritorially: The Spatial Test in Certain Human Rights Treaties', *Israel Law Review*, 40 (2007).

Wills, Siobhán, *Protecting Civilians: The Obligations of Peacekeepers* (Oxford: Oxford University Press, 2009).

Wilson, Peter, 'A Combat Classic', *The Australian Literary Review*, 2 June 2010.

World Health Organization, *Global Status Report on Road Safety: Time for Action* (Geneva: World Health Organization, 2009).

Yoder, John Howard, *When War is Unjust: Being Honest in Just-War Thinking*, 2nd edn (Eugene, Ore.: Wipf and Stock Publishers, 2001).

Zegveld, Liesbeth, 'The Inter-American Commission on Human Rights and International Humanitarian Law: A Comment on the Tablada Case', *International Review of the Red Cross*, 38 (1998).

Zimbardo, Phillip G., *The Lucifer Effect: Understanding How Good People Turn Evil* (New York: Random House, 2007).

International Conventions

1967 Protocol Relating to the Status of Refugees, January 31, 1966, 606 UNTS 267.

Amended Protocol on Prohibitions or Restrictions on the Use of Mines, Booby Traps and Other Devices, May 3, 1996, S. Treaty Doc. No. 105-1 (1997).

Cartagena Declaration on Refugees, Colloquium on the International Protection of Refugees in Central America, Mexico and Panama, November 22, 1984, Annual Report of the Inter-American Commission on Human Rights, OAS Doc. OEA/Ser.L/V/II.66/doc.10 (1984–85), Rev. 1.

Convention Against Torture and Other Cruel, Inhuman or Degrading Treatment or Punishment, 1465 UNTS 113.

Convention Governing the Specific Aspects of Refugee Problems in Africa, September 10, 1969, 1001 UNTS 45.

Convention on Prohibitions or Restrictions on the Use of Certain Conventional Weapons Which May Be Deemed to Be Excessively Injurious or to Have Indiscriminate Effects.

Convention on the Prevention and Punishment of the Crime of Genocide (1948).

Convention on the Prohibition of the Development, Production, Stockpiling and Use of Chemical Weapons and on their Destruction (1993).

Convention on the Rights of the Child, 1577 UNTS 3.

Convention Relating to the Status of Refugees, July 28, 1951, 189 UNTS 137.

Convention Respecting the Laws and Customs of War on Land, October 18, 1907, 36 Stat. 2277, 207 Consol. TS 277.

Declaration Renouncing the Use, in Time of War, of Explosive Projectiles Under 400 Grammes Weight pmbl., 29 November 1868, 18 Martens Nouveau Recueil (Ser. 1) 474.

European Convention for the Protection of Human Rights and Fundamental Freedoms, ETS 005.

Geneva Convention for the Amelioration of the Condition of the Wounded and Sick in Armed Forces in the Field of August 12, 1949, 75 UNTS 31 (entered into force 21 October 1950).

Geneva Convention for the Amelioration of the Condition of Wounded, Sick and Shipwrecked Members of Armed Forces at Sea of August 12, 1949, 75 UNTS 85 (entered into force 21 October 1950).

Geneva Convention Relative to the Protection of Civilian Persons in Time of War of August 12, 1949, 75 UNTS 287 (entered into force 21 October 1950).

International Convention for the Protection of All Persons from Enforced Disappearance, A/RES/61/177.

International Convention for the Protection of All Persons from Enforced Disappearances, E/CN.4/2002/71.

International Covenant on Civil and Political Rights, 999 UNTS 171.

International Covenant on Economic, Social and Cultural Rights, 993 UNTS 360.

Protocol Additional to the Geneva Conventions of 12 August 1949, and Relating to the Protection of Victims of International Armed Conflicts, June 8, 1977 (Protocol I), 1125 UNTS 3.

Protocol Additional to the Geneva Conventions of 12 August 1949, and Relating to the Protection of Victims of Non-International Armed Conflicts (Protocol II), 1125 UNTS 609 (entered into force 7 December 1978).

Protocol on Prohibitions or Restrictions on the Use of Incendiary Weapons (Protocol III), October 10, 1980, S. Treaty Doc. No. 105-1 (1997), 1342 UNTS 171.

Regulations Respecting the Laws and Customs of War on Land, Annex to the 1907 Convention (IV) Respecting the Laws and Customs of War on Land, (1910) 9 UKTS Cd 5030 (entered into force 26 January 1910).

Use of Force for Canadian Forces Operations (August 2008), CFJP 5.1.

Legal Proceedings

Ali v Canada (FC) [1999] FCJ No. 63.

Amnesty International Canada and British Columbia Civil Liberties Association v Chief of the Defence Staff for the Canadian Forces, Minister of National Defence and Attorney General of Canada [2009] 4 FCR 149 (Federal Court of Appeal) (per Desjardins JA with whom Richard CJ and Noël JA agreed).

Armed Activities on the Territory of the Congo (Democratic Republic of the Congo v Uganda), 2005 ICJ 168 (19 December).

Banković v Belgium and others (2001) 11 BHRC 435; (2007) 44 EHRR SE5.

Case Concerning Armed Activities on the Territory of the Congo (Democratic Republic of the Congo v Uganda) [2005] ICJ Rep 116.

Case of NA v The United Kingdom (Application No. 25904/07), 17 July 2008.

Cases Concerning Deportation Orders, Israeli Supreme Court Judgment of 10 April 1988, (1990) 29(1) ILM 139, 177–79.

Coard et al. v United States, Inter-American Commission on Human Rights, Report No. 109/99, Case 10.951 (1999).

D v United Kingdom, ECHR Appl. No. 30240/96 (2007).

Demiray v Turkey (ECHR) Application No. 27308/95, Judgment of 21 November 2000.

Elgafaji v Staatssecretaris van Justitie, C-465/07 (European Court of Justice, 17 February 2009).

Eritrea/Ethiopia Claims Commission, Partial Award, Central Front (28 April 2004); *Partial Award, Western Front* (19 December 2005).

German Federal Administrative Court, Judgment of the Tenth Division of 27 April 2010, BverwG 10 C 4.09.

GS (Article 15(c): indiscriminate violence) Afghanistan CG, [2009] UK AIT 00044, 19 October 2009.

HM and Others (Article 15(c)) Iraq CG, [2010] UKUT 331.

Ilascu v Moldova and Russia (ECHR) (Grand Chamber) (2005) 40 EHRR 46.

International Criminal Tribunal for Rwanda (ICTR), *Bagilishema*, Judgement (2001).

Issa v Turkey (ECHR) (2004) 41 EHRR 567, 589.

Juan Carlos Abella v Argentina (Inter-American Commission of Human Rights), Case 11.137, 18 November 1997, http://www.cidh.org/annualrep/97eng/argentina11137.htm#_ftn17

Knezevic v Attorney-General 367 F.3d 1206; 2004 US App. LEXIS 10162.

Law and Military Operations in East Timor (UNTAET) Feb 2000 – May 2002 (Australian Defence Force Military Law Centre/Asia Pacific Centre for Military Law, 2003).

Law and Military Operations in East Timor (UNTAET) Feb 2000 – May 2002, Annexure X (ROE for the Military Component of UNTAET, 28 April 2000, MPS/3633).

Loizidou v Turkey (ECHR) (1997) 23 EHRR 513, 531.

Mamatkulov & Askarov v Turkey, Nos 46827/99 and 46951/99, 2005-I.

Mengstu v Holder, 560 F3d 1055; 2009 US App. LEXIS 6988; and *S---P--- v INS*, 1996 BIA LEXIS 25.

Minister for Immigration and Multicultural Affairs v Hussein Mohamed Haji Ibrahim (2000) 204 CLR 1.

N v United Kingdom, ECHR Appl. No. 26565/05 (27 May 2008).

Nuremberg Tribunal. *1 Trial of the Major War Criminals Before the International Military Tribunal* 254 (1947).

Ocalan v Turkey 2005-IV; 41 EHRR 985 [166 GC].

Physicians for Human Rights et al. v Israel et al., HCJ 8990/02, Judgement, 27 April 2003.

Physicians for Human Rights v Commander of the Israeli Defense Forces in the Gaza Strip, HCJ 4764/04 (2004) (Supreme Court of Israel).

Prosecutor v Akayesu (ICTR) (Trial Chamber), ICTR-96-4-T, Judgment of 2 September 1998.

Prosecutor v Blaškić (ICTY) (Trial Chamber), Case No. IT-95-14-T, Judgment of 3 March 2000.

Prosecutor v Delalić (ICTY) (Trial Chamber), Case No. IT-96-21-T, Judgment of 16 November 1998.

Prosecutor v Galic, No. IT-98-29-T (3 December 2002).

Prosecutor v Haradinaj (ICTY) (Trial Chamber), Case No. IT-04-84-T, Judgment of 3 April 2008.

Prosecutor v Kordic & Cerkez, IT-95-14/2-A (Appellate Chamber, 17 December 2004).

Prosecutor v Kupreškić (ICTY), Case No. IT-95-16-T, Judgment of 14 January 2000, para. 521.

Prosecutor v Sam Hinga Norman, Case No. SCSL-2004-14-AR72(E), Decision on Preliminary Motion Based on Lack of Jurisdiction (Child Recruitment) (31 May 2004).

Prosecutor v Tadić (ICTY) (Appeals Chamber), Case No. IT-94-1-A, Judgment of 15 July 1999.

Prosecutor v Tadić (Jurisdiction) (Appeals Chamber) (1997), 105 ILR 453, 488.

Prosecutor v Tadić, Case No. IT-94-1-AR72, Decision on the defence motion for interlocutory appeal on jurisdiction of 2 October 1995.

QD (Iraq) and AH (Iraq) v Secretary of State for the Home Department [2009] EWCA Civ. 620.

R (Al-Skeini and others) v Secretary of State for Defence [2007] QB 140 (Court of Appeal).

R (Al-Skeini and others) v Secretary of State for Defence [2008] 1 AC 153 (House of Lords).

R v Bow Street Metropolitan Stipendiary Magistrate, ex parte Pinochet Ugarte (No. 2) (House of Lords) [1999] All ER 577.

R v Brocklebank (1996) 134 DLR (4th) 377 (Court Martial Appeal Court of Canada).

R v Clegg [1995] WLR 80.

R v Special Adjudicator, ex parte Ullah [2004] 2 AC.

Refugee Appeal No. 71462/99.

Regina v Secretary of State for the Home Department (Appellant), ex parte Adam (FC)(Respondent); *Regina v Secretary of State for the Home Department (Appellant), ex parte Limbuela (FC)(Respondent)*; *Regina v Secretary of State for the Home Department (Appellant), ex parte Tesema (FC)(Respondent)* (conjoined appeals), [2005] UKHL 66.

Regina v Secretary of State for the Home Department, ex parte Adan [1999] 1 AC 293.

Soering v United Kingdom, ECHR 7 July 1989, Series A, No. 161.

SOFA, see Coalition Provisional Authority (CPA) Order No. 17 (Iraq), s. 2 (http://
    www.iraqcoalition.org/regulations/20040627_CPAORD_17_Status_of_
    Coalition__Rev__with_Annex_A.pdf).
Special Court for Sierra Leone (SCSL), *Fofana and Kondewa*, Judgement (2007).
*The Public Committee Against Torture in Israel v The Government of Israel
    (Targeted Killings case)*, HCJ 796/02.

Web Sites

ArmyofDude:http://armyofdude.blogspot.com/2009/06/most-entertaining-movie-
    review-ever.html
http://www.abc.net.au/news/stories/2011/04/30/3204403.htm
http://www.abc.net.au/news/stories/2011/05/01/3204737.htm
http://www.youtube.com/watch?v=cNpT-lZLC4A
Canadian Ministry of Public Safety: http://www.publicsafety.gc.ca/prg/ns/le/cle-
    eng.aspx
CBS News: http://www.cbsnews.com/video/watch/?id=6461150n
CNN.com: http://articles.cnn.com/2004-11-14/us/children.tasers_1_taser-
    international-police-car-officers?_s=PM:US
pchrgaza.org: http://www.pchrgaza.org/files/2010/israeli-inve.-%20english.pdf
US Department of Defense Joint Non-Lethal Weapons Directorate: https://www.
    jnlwp.usmc.mil/ads.asp

Index